D0667041

# The Allure of Order

# THE ALLURE OF ORDER

*High Hopes, Dashed Expectations,*
*and the Troubled Quest to Remake*
*American Schooling*

JAL MEHTA

OXFORD
UNIVERSITY PRESS

# OXFORD
UNIVERSITY PRESS

Oxford University Press is a department of the University of Oxford.
It furthers the University's objective of excellence in research, scholarship,
and education by publishing worldwide.

Oxford   New York
Auckland   Cape Town   Dar es Salaam   Hong Kong   Karachi
Kuala Lumpur   Madrid   Melbourne   Mexico City   Nairobi
New Delhi   Shanghai   Taipei   Toronto

With offices in
Argentina   Austria   Brazil   Chile   Czech Republic   France   Greece
Guatemala   Hungary   Italy   Japan   Poland   Portugal   Singapore
South Korea   Switzerland   Thailand   Turkey   Ukraine   Vietnam

Oxford is a registered trademark of Oxford University Press
in the UK and certain other countries.

Published in the United States of America by
Oxford University Press
198 Madison Avenue, New York, NY 10016

Library of Congress Cataloging-in-Publication Data
Mehta, Jal.
The allure of order: high hopes, dashed expectations, and the troubled quest to remake
American schooling / Jal Mehta.
pages cm. — (Studies in postwar American political development)
ISBN 978-0-19-994206-0 (hardback)
1. Public schools—United States.   2. Educational change—United States.
3. Education and state—United States.   I. Title.
LA217.2.M436 2013
371.010973—dc23
2012046809

ISBN 978-0-19-994206-0

1 3 5 7 9 8 6 4 2
Printed in the United States of America
on acid-free paper

*To my parents, Cheryl, and Alex*

# Contents

# The Allure of Order: Rationalizing Schools from the Progressives to the Present

IN LATE 2001, three months after the September 11 attacks, the No Child Left Behind Act (NCLB) passed both House and Senate with strong bipartisan majorities and was signed by a Republican president. Promising to use the power of the state to ensure that all children were proficient in reading and math by 2014, proponents heralded the act as the greatest piece of federal education legislation since the creation of the original Elementary and Secondary Education Act in 1965. By requiring the states to set high standards, pairing them with assessments that measured whether students were achieving those standards, and holding schools accountable if students failed to do so, NCLB, in the eyes of its sponsors, would close achievement gaps and make America's schools the envy of the world.

A decade later, the bloom is off the rose. While almost everyone today continues to share the aim of leaving no child behind, the act itself has come in for criticism from many quarters, to the point that Bush's former Education Secretary Margaret Spellings declared that NCLB is now a "toxic brand" in American politics.[1] Careful studies of the implementation of NCLB have shown that it has done what less bullish observers might have predicted from the outset. It has increased the focus on the education of poor and minority students, but it has not provided schools with needed tools to create higher quality schooling for these students. There has been improvement in some national test scores (e.g., 4th and 8th grade math), while others have remained largely unchanged (e.g., 4th and 8th grade reading). Even accounting for the progress in math, there is no sign that the reforms have had a significant impact in closing achievement gaps or in improving America's mediocre international educational standing. Particularly in the most troubled schools, there has been rampant teaching to the test and some outright cheating. In-depth studies have shown that some schools now devote a large part of their year to test prep; Atlanta and DC public schools have both contended with widespread cheating scandals. There are substantial concerns that simplistic testing is crowding out richer forms of learning. While reasonable people continue to disagree about the legacy and future of No Child Left Behind, there is broad agreement that it has not stimulated the kind of widespread improvement that we want and need for our schools.

This outcome might have been surprising if it were the first time policymakers tried to use standards, tests, and accountability to remake schooling from above. But NCLB was actually the third such movement. In the Progressive Era, newly empowered superintendents sought to use methods of rational administration, including early standards, tests, and accountability measures, to make schools more efficient and effective. In the 1960s and 1970s, newly empowered state departments of education sought to use state standards, assessments, and accountability to clarify goals and improve school performance. Not once, not twice, but three different times, school reformers have hit upon the same idea for how to remake American schools. The surprise is less that results have not met expectations than that we have repeatedly placed a high degree of faith in reforms promising to rationalize schools from above. After all, how many other policies were cochampioned by George W. Bush and Edward Kennedy?

This is a book about these repeated efforts to "order" schools from above. It seeks to answer a series of questions about these movements. Perhaps the most important question is the most basic: Why have American reformers repeatedly invested such high hopes in these instruments of control despite their track record of mixed results at best? What assumptions about human nature, individual psychology, organizational sociology, teachers, and students underlie these repeated efforts to "rationalize" schooling? Politically, why have the recent movements triumphed despite the resistance of the strongest interest group in the arena, the teachers unions? Why do these movements draw support from both liberals and conservatives? In the most recent movement, why did a Republican president push for the most powerful version of this vision and in so doing buck the traditions of his own party and create the greatest expansion of the federal role in education in the country's history? What have been the consequences of these rationalizing movements, not just for test scores, but for the teaching profession, for educational and social justice, and for the shape of the educational enterprise as a whole? And finally, if not rationalization of schools, then what? Is there an alternative that is more likely to yield the results that we seek?

## How Schooling Was Rationalized over the Course
## of the 20th Century

In the pages that follow, I tell the story of how schooling was rationalized over the course of the 20th century. The story starts in the Progressive Era (1890–1920), when an educational crisis was identified by a group of muckraking journalists, who used the power of the press to expose what they saw as a corrupt, nepotistic, and highly inefficient patchwork of schooling. This crisis was seized upon by a group of "administrative progressives"; using the newly ascendant ideas of Taylorism, they sought to develop a system of efficient, rationally governed schools. At the top of this pyramid was a group of city superintendents, who utilized rudimentary tests and cost accounting procedures to compare teachers and schools in an effort to hold practitioners accountable and derive the most bang for their buck. Then, as now, teachers charged that such movements were wrongly applying the logic of industry to schools and argued that education had a deeper "bottom line" than could be measured through actuarial techniques. Ultimately, however, they were overwhelmed by the administrative progressives, who were able to tap into political allies from both parties as well as the legitimacy bestowed by industry. Using scientific management techniques, they transformed a set of one-room schoolhouses into the bureaucratic "one best system" of city administration that still persists today. Universities were a major supporter of this effort, as newly formed departments and schools of education, seeking to establish their scientific bona fides, embraced scientific management in the training of (primarily male) superintendents and distanced themselves from the pedagogical training of the (primarily female) teaching force.

If the Progressive Era created the organizational imprint for the rationalization of schooling, a now almost forgotten standards movement in the 1960s and 1970s reenergized the desire for scientific management of schools, this time at the state rather than the district level. The key document in framing the crisis this time was the Coleman Report, which highlighted the ways in which educational inputs did not translate into educational outputs and thus motivated legislators to see schooling as a production function that needed to be made more efficient. Although overshadowed by more spectacular conflicts over desegregation, community control, and open schooling, the movement in the late 1960s and early 1970s generated more than 70 state laws seeking to create educational accountability and hundreds of articles, pamphlets, and books about how to create more efficient and accountable educational systems. The supporting logic this time came not only from industry but also from the US Defense Department, whose pioneering quantitative techniques were transposed to education. Teachers and other educators again decried what they saw as a mindless regimen of quantification; they argued, much as they do today, that it was unfair to hold them responsible for outcomes that were created at least partially outside the schools. While this movement was only partially successful because it was unable to generate broad and deep political momentum, it did set the stage for what followed. By creating state assessments and the template for state standards-based reform, the movement forged a bridge between the district-level rationalization of the Progressive Era and the state and federal rationalization at the end of the century.

Developments in the 1960s and 1970s brought schools under fire, but the driving force behind the modern standards and accountability movement was the linking of educational to economic concerns in the 1980s. The impetus this time was the famous *A Nation at Risk* report, which framed the educational problem in dire economic terms and launched an avalanche of state-level efforts at reform. Again, these reforms were popular on both the political left and right: the left saw in standards a way to create greater uniformity across the school system; the right saw in accountability a way to impose greater pressure on an unresponsive public bureaucracy. With education cast as an economic development issue, state legislators and governors became involved in an arena that had previously been left primarily to local schools and school boards. The convergence of the states around standards in turn enabled federal legislation in an arena where the federal government had historically lacked legitimacy: it allowed federal law to piggyback on an already established state consensus. First Bill Clinton and then George W. Bush—both former governors with state records on education—pushed for legislation that would make standards and accountability a requirement of federal aid. The culmination of this effort was No Child Left Behind, which required states to hold schools accountable for meeting standards and to impose an escalating series of consequences on schools that failed to do so. What began at the turn of the 20th century as a movement from highly variable one-room schoolhouses to a district-level "one best system" had by century's end become a national effort to use the power of the federal government to create uniformity across the nation's public schools.

This is a story of both cycles and trends. The three reform movements share certain features of organizational rationalization. In the name of efficiency, all three sought to reduce variation among schools in favor of greater centralized standardization and control, hallmarks of the rationalizing process. In each of these cases power shifted upwards, away from teachers and schools and toward central administrators. Similar conceptions of motivation drove the three sets of reformers, each using some version of standards and testing to incentivize teachers to do their bidding. Each of the movements prized quantitative data and elevated a scientific vision of data-driven improvement over a more humanistic view of educational purposes. Across the decades, the essence of the rationalizing vision has remained remarkably unchanged.

At the same time, these cycles of policy reform have overlain an evolving set of institutional, political, and social trends. One such trend is the move away from locally controlled schooling. Progressive Era reforms transformed a set of one-room schoolhouses into the "one best system," shifting power from the teacher and the school to the superintendent who ran the district. The 1960s reforms, building on this organization at the local level, asked schools and districts to become accountable to their states. The most recent reforms have further expanded the role of the states and built federal reforms on top of these state efforts.

## *The Allure of Order*

Across this history, we see some recurring themes, to be discussed in more depth in the pages to come. The first is the outsized faith that Americans have placed in the tools of scientific management as a mechanism for improving schools. Reliance on the techniques of American industry, an unshakable faith in science, and a belief in the ability to remake ourselves by remaking our schools have created a potent combination. Each of these movements has been justified on the grounds that it would bring objective data to a "soft" and undisciplined field and standardization to a highly variable social landscape. Each was bolstered by attaching its claims to higher status fields, particularly business, but also the Defense Department, and leading management ideas from the academy and industry. Despite the fact that both experience and research has told us that teaching is not like factory work, that it requires skill and discretion as opposed to the following of rules and procedures, we continue to be attracted to the idea that if we can only get the right outcome targets in place, we will be able to "order" the whole system for the better. Scientific management also seems to promise that the answer can be found without confronting difficult questions of distributive justice; we persist in the illusion that science combined with policy can fix our problems without requiring any difficult choices or tradeoffs.

The second recurring theme is the inability of the educational profession to take control of its sphere, creating a long-standing susceptibility to these external movements for reform. Unlike law, medicine, or higher education, teaching was institutionalized as a "semiprofession": it lacks lengthy training, a distinctive knowledge base, an ability to exclude unqualified practitioners, and standards of practice that govern its daily work. Moreover, since teaching was institutionalized in the Progressive Era within a bureaucratically administered hierarchy, teachers did not possess the kind of guild power seen in stronger professions. Instead, teachers sat at the bottom of implementation chains; their primary responsibility was to implement the ideas created by others. The great expansion of teacher unionization in the 1960s succeeded in giving teachers more political influence and higher pay, but it also further institutionalized teachers as labor rather than as professionals ready to control their own sphere. The weakness of the field has left it highly susceptible to external logics, particularly to business ideas that promise to improve the educational bottom line.

The third recurring theme is the double-edged nature of movements to impose scientific rationality on schooling. As Weber famously noted, rationalization creates order out of chaos, but it does so at the cost of creating an "iron cage" that often emphasizes the measurable to the exclusion of the meaningful. Both sides of this equation are important; there are legitimate reasons why policymakers seek to rationalize schools: they are trying to decrease the variation that protects privilege and perpetuates inequality. But at the same time, trying to do this by specifying simple and easily measured outcomes and raising the stakes for achieving those outcomes tends to produce education focused more on preparing students for tests than on developing genuine learning.* The details may be education specific, but the double-edged nature of the process is pure Weberian rationalization.

The pages that follow suggest that this combination has produced an alluring but ultimately failing brew. By comparative standards, America has a weak welfare state, a decentralized education system, a segregated and unequal social geography, an underprofessionalized educational field, and very high expectations for its schools. Within this context, "crises" of schooling are inevitable; critics need only point out the very real variation in outcomes or the gaps between what schools are producing and what we wish them to achieve. Policymakers, in turn, quite reasonably seek to act but act

---

* This is *not* to say that schools, particularly high poverty schools, stimulated genuine learning before external tests and accountability. Most clearly did not. What I am suggesting here is that the tools of standards, tests, and accountability have limited power to generate sustained improvement. I suggest in the pages that follow an alternative route that is much more likely to yield the high-quality academic outcomes we seek.

within constraints imposed by a fairly conservative political economy. They want to improve schools, but they cannot (or perceive they cannot) integrate students by race or income level or provide significantly stronger social supports. Within this context, a logic of scientific rationalization is an attractive solution. Backed by science and drawing on the logic of industry, it promises to impose efficiency across an unruly educational landscape—centralizing a decentralized system, holding educators accountable, and protecting taxpayer money. Unfortunately, standards and accountability are a weak technology to produce the outcomes policymakers seek. Improving teaching and learning requires the development of skill and expertise; simply increasing expectations does little to bring about results. Teachers, meanwhile, perceiving policymakers to be remote from the realities of their schools, are highly resistant to efforts to control them from afar. Realizing this, policymakers seek to increase the pressure and tighten a loosely coupled system, a response that only increases distrust. A downward spiral between policymakers and frontline practitioners is the result. Particularly where students are most unable to reach the targets, teaching to the test becomes the norm, and a reform initially advanced in the name of improving educational quality can drive practice toward the most anti-intellectual and least academic of ends.

## Beyond Rationalization: Learning from the Past and Finding a Better Way Forward

It is incumbent upon us to learn from this history and not repeat the mistakes of the past. While most educational reforms today are at the level of program or policy, this analysis suggests that the problem is more fundamental. One of the advantages of historical analysis is that it allows one to step back and expose to scrutiny the whole range of structures and assumptions that govern current debate. To overstate only slightly, one might say that the overarching lesson of this book is that *the entire educational sector was put together backwards*. The people we draw into teaching are less than our most talented; we give them short or nonexistent training and equip them with little relevant knowledge; we send many of them to schools afflicted by high levels of poverty and segregation; and when they don't deliver the results we seek, we increase external pressure and accountability, hoping that we can do on the back end what we failed to create on the front end.

This largely historical analysis dovetails with an emerging body of international research on the countries that are far ahead of us on respected international assessments, particularly the Programme for International Student

Assessment (PISA). Countries (or national subdivisions) that lead the PISA, including Singapore, Shanghai, Canada, Finland, South Korea, and Japan, very broadly share a model one could see as the inverse of ours: they draw teachers from among their most talented people, prepare them extensively and with close attention to practice, put them in schools buffered from some of the effects of poverty by social welfare supports, and give them time while in school to collaborate to develop and improve their skills.[2] In some cases, as in Finland, such practices largely obviate the need for testing and external accountability, because selection and preparation on the front end makes extensive monitoring on the back end unnecessary. While the United States remains the world leader in assessments and accountability, Finland and Shanghai are the leaders in student performance, and they get there in an entirely different way.

This way of cutting the problem differs from much of the polarized thinking that currently governs the American school debate. On the one side are Michelle Rhee and Joel Klein, who insist that the system is broken, that we need to infuse new providers and create greater levels of external testing and accountability. On the other side is Diane Ravitch, who argues that testing has corrupted the schools and that if only we could throw out the tests and return to the neighborhood schools of yesteryear, everything would be all right. The argument here is that both are partially right but also partially wrong: Rhee and Klein are right to have faith in some of the new providers (many of whom are embracing the international lessons in terms of selecting talent and carefully preparing them for practice), and they are also right that the culture of bureaucratic districts tends to produce a compliance mentality that we need to escape. But they are too comfortable with simplistic external assessments and too focused on developing increasingly intricate test-based teacher evaluation systems. Conversely, Ravitch is right about the corrosive effects of testing but is not honest enough about the failings of the current and past systems and the real changes that would be needed to generate improvement at scale.

A third position is needed, one grounded in avoiding the mistakes of the past and drawing on the best exemplars abroad as well as the best providers here. This position would be the inverse of our current approach of providing little up front and demanding heavy accountability on the back end. We would instead begin by building a more relevant knowledge base, anchored in practice, one that would underpin efforts to create consistently high-quality teaching. We would then develop a human capital pipeline, which would allow us to select from among our best, train them extensively, and then give them opportunities to grow once in the classroom. Having developed a corps of knowledgeable teachers that we were confident would meet professional standards, we would then be able to increase the level of autonomy of schools, which could be freed of bureaucratic regulations and empowered to create the kind of thoughtful and intentional communities that both students and teachers deserve. The role of the higher levels of the system would be to support and enable this work on the ground rather than seek to control it from above.

In the final chapter I sketch how this would work in more detail, but whether we take this new path depends less on the technicalities of implementation and more on our values and our overall approach to our educational future. Will we see the limits of scientific management and understand that good education is not susceptible to simple rationalization and instead can be created only by skilled teachers and administrators who engage their students with a mixture of intelligence, empathy, and substantive and pedagogical knowledge? Will we come to see "data" less as a cudgel to be used on its unwilling subjects and more as an empowering tool for analyzing and shaping one's environment? Will we recognize that education is inherently a question of politics and justice and that logics of efficiency will never replace the hard political choices that will be needed to give a better education to our most disadvantaged citizens? Will teachers move away from industrial-style bargaining, take responsibility for school outcomes, and become the professionals that some have hoped they might become? Will we continue to see teachers as people who need to be controlled from above, or will we accord them the respect and control over their practice given to more established professionals? And finally, will we be content to see schooling solely as an instrumental mechanism for improving our economic future, or will we abandon our romance with rationalization and come to see education as the deep, engaging, and freeing activity that schooling at its best can be?

## 2

# *The Cultural Struggle for Control over Schooling: The Power of Ideas and the Weakness of the Educational Field*

HOW CAN WE best understand the repeated efforts to rationalize schools across the 20th century? Traditional approaches to explaining political phenomena—interest groups, institutions, partisan theories, and rational choice—are limited in their ability to explain this recurring impulse. Instead, a complementary set of cultural lenses—ideas, professions, fields, logics, moral power, and institutional vantage points—can shed more light on these repeated movements. Together, these perspectives also offer a different way of thinking about the nature of social and political contestation, one that is deeply cultural in its ontology and that integrates ideas, interests, and institutions, links the social and the political, and explains both continuity and change.

## *What Happened: Cycles and Trends of Rationalizing Schooling*

### Cycles: Three Efforts to Rationalize Schooling

In one sense, movements to "rationalize" schools have cycled across the 20th century. As will be discussed in more detail in the chapters to come, at three different times reformers have embraced the rationalization of schools. In the Progressive Era, a group of reformers, comprising mostly businessmen, city elites, and university professors, sought to shift power from large, local ward boards, which they viewed as parochial and unprofessional, to smaller boards controlled by professional elites. They made the superintendent the equivalent of the CEO of the school system and directed him to use the latest in scientific methods and modern management techniques to measure outcomes and to ensure that resources were being used efficiently to produce the greatest possible bang for the buck. The newly emerging science of testing was widely employed to ensure that teachers and schools were meeting standards and to sort students into appropriate tracks, with the aim of "efficiently" matching students with the curriculum appropriate to their ability.

In the late 1960s and early 1970s, a second accountability movement sought to take hold of American schooling. Seeking to realize both a civil rights agenda of improving the quality of schooling and to satisfy more conservative concerns about the efficient spending of public dollars, state after state passed laws designed to inject greater accountability into the school system. Frequently overlooked by educational historians in favor of more prominent movements around desegregation and open schooling, this template, which developed largely under the radar in the late 1960s and early 1970s, prefigured the modern accountability movement.

The current initiative is in fact the third such movement of the century. Sweeping the states in the 1990s before becoming part of federal law in the 1994 and 2001 reauthorizations of the Elementary and Secondary Education Act (the 2001 reauthorization became known as No Child Left Behind), this reform movement has been the most comprehensive national attempt to introduce school accountability. As we will see, many of the objections to NCLB—that there was too much testing; that testing narrowed the curriculum; that the law unfairly held schools accountable for events outside their control—almost exactly duplicate criticisms of accountability movements earlier in the century.

## Trends: The Institutional Transformation of American Education and the Rise of Accountability Politics

At the same time, the most recent movement has facilitated a powerful institutional transformation of American education. Perhaps American education's defining aspect has been its emphasis on local control of schooling; in only one generation, the state and federal role in schooling has grown dramatically. If the "cycles" story is about repetition of a vision over and over, there is also a "trends" story about the major shift in the governance of education from local to state to federal.

Remarkably, this change has largely happened over only 20 years, between roughly 1980 and 2001. While the share of state funding (as opposed to local funding) of education increased gradually over the 20th century's course, up until the mid-1980s the states had not exercised their authority to define the goals of schooling or to direct schools' inner workings. This changed in the 1980s and 1990s, as the standards movement spread across the states; state after state began to use standards, assessments, and accountability as the linked technology for improvement from afar. Beginning in a few states, notably Maryland, Kentucky, Texas, and California, standards-based reform spread across the nation in the 1990s: 49 states had adopted some version of standards before the 2001 federal requirement under No Child Left Behind.

Meanwhile, this movement by the states enabled a major shift in the federal role. The federal government had provided funds to high poverty schools through Title I since the passage of the ESEA (1965), but it had not become centrally involved in the day-to-day organization of public schooling—in fact, it was unthinkable that it would. The passage of the 1994 Elementary and Secondary Education Act and then its reauthorization, No Child Left Behind, fundamentally changed the federal role, to the point that its reach now extends over the entire public school landscape. The fact that more recent efforts, like Race to the Top, passed with little resistance to their potential infringement on states' rights shows how widely this shift has been legitimized.

A particularly surprising aspect of this shift is that it was championed by a Republican president, George W. Bush. In 1980, Ronald Reagan promised on the campaign trail to try to eliminate the Department of Education; only two decades later, President Bush presided over the largest expansion of the federal educational role in the nation's history. In so doing, he repudiated his party's long-standing position on states' rights and its skepticism of federal authority. Understanding how a Republican president came to preside over this institutional transformation is one of the tasks of the chapters ahead.

Finally, it is worth noting that if one trend concerns shifts in education over time, there is also an important trend in the rise of "accountability politics" across a range of sectors and professional fields. Politicians, doctors, lawyers, and police officers, among many others, are now constantly being held accountable for what they have and have not accomplished. Scarcely a day passes without a story on television or in the newspaper of someone pledging to hold someone else accountable for something. As later chapters show in more detail, while some degree of democratic accountability is built into any system of public governance, the degree and extent of holding one another accountable has increased greatly over the past four decades. This more general rise in accountability politics is important to understand and explain, as the increasing emphasis on educational accountability is driven by some of these larger forces.

## Puzzles of Rationalizing Schools and Limits of Existing Approaches: Interest Groups, Partisan Explanations, Rational Choice, and Historical Institutionalism

Accountability movements pose a number of problems for the leading theories in political science and political sociology. While the debate between competing approaches on education policy is not as fully developed as the debate about the welfare state, the leading explanations can be grouped under four headings: interest groups, partisan explanations, rational choice, and historical institutionalism.

Interest group perspectives do not by themselves explain the repeated impulse toward school accountability. As is shown in more detail in the chapters to come, in looking across the three cases, one finds an almost bewildering array of actors who have championed the reforms: "good government" reformers and schools of education in the Progressive Era; state departments of education, state legislators, and taxpayer groups in the 1960s and 1970s; and presidents, governors, state and federal legislators, foundations, business groups, and civil rights groups in the most recent round of reforms. Business groups, which might be the most natural suspect given the character of the reforms, have played a secondary role to governors in the contemporary reforms and were not a central factor in the 1960s reforms.[1] Schools of education, key supporters of the Progressive Era reforms, have frequently been critics of the most recent accountability movement. In short, while various power brokers have been involved in each of the reforms, no group has repeatedly championed school accountability efforts.

The recent move to school accountability is particularly difficult to understand from an interest group perspective because of the failure of the teachers unions to thwart reform. Unions are frequently seen as the most powerful actor in education politics: one study in the 1990s suggested that in 43 of 50 states they were the most powerful group.[2] The NEA has consistently opposed the accountability movement. The national AFT has shown greater support for standards and accountability, due in large part to the leadership of Albert Shanker, but local AFT affiliates have not been as supportive. Teachers often view state standards and accountability for performance as a thinly veiled attack on the quality of their profession,[3] and more progressive educators perceive a wrongheaded attempt to impose standardization on a largely creative process. Any interest group explanation has to explain why accountability triumphed (even among Democrats) despite objections from teachers and their union representatives.

Partisan theory also falls short. Movements for school accountability do not reflect clear partisan patterns. David Tyack and Larry Cuban note that, in contrast to other countries, in the United States "at any one time Democratic and Republican parties have not differed very much in their views of education even if they had quite different policies in other domains."[4] This bipartisan pattern applies similarly to accountability policies: in each era members of both parties have been supportive of the reforms, if not always for the same reasons. In the Progressive Era, members of both parties pushed for control of schools by centralized professional administrators. In both the 1960s–1970s period and the present, liberals have supported accountability as a way to improve schooling for high poverty students, while conservatives have embraced its ability to monitor the efficient spending of public dollars.[5] In part because of this bipartisan support, accountability and standards have flourished regardless of which party was in power, most recently in the championing of standards first by President Bill Clinton and then by George W. Bush. In each era, the key question is not which party advocated the reforms but how politicians of both parties came to see accountability as the promised path to school improvement. The question of why the parties supported what they did is particularly intriguing in the case of No Child Left Behind: a Republican president championed a set of reforms that greatly expanded the federal role and contradicted the long-standing ideological preferences of his party.

A third potential explanation draws on the "rational choice" tradition, particularly the median voter theorem. Patrick McGuinn, although not a rational choice theorist himself, argues that with respect to the most recent movement, strategic imperatives have led both parties increasingly to emphasize education reform. In his balanced and carefully documented account of federal education reform over the past 40 years, McGuinn argues that as education rose on the agenda in recent years, first state and later federal politicians were compelled to offer plans for education reform in order to win voters to their cause. Education, as an apple-pie issue, is attractive to both parties. For Democrats it is critical to their electoral coalition, and for Republicans it provides an opportunity to "issue trespass" and win over Democratic voters. McGuinn notes that Bush's move in 2000 to embrace education reform was prefigured by internal Republican polling after the 1996 election showing that the GOP's traditional position of abolishing the Department of Education was becoming unpopular with voters. By adopting a message of "compassionate conservatism" and emphasizing his support for education reform, candidate Bush effectively neutralized the Democrats' advantage on education and successfully presented himself as a bipartisan reformer. Rational choice theory, thus, can explain why Republicans embraced educational reform and why politicians of both parties have bucked interest groups from the left and right to propose centrist reforms that they hope will score points with voters.

The problem with the rational choice approach is less that it is wrong than that it is incomplete. As Paul Pierson has emphasized, rational choice theories are among the modes of explanation in political science that employ a short time horizon, consequently minimizing potentially more important longer-term causes.[6] The rational choice approach assumes as given many of the most interesting features of education politics that need to be explained. These features include: Why is education now a salient issue for states and the federal government when that was not the case in the past? What has primed the public to see the problem in terms that make standards and accountability the logical solution? What makes it seem appropriate to assert that the problem of education can be solved by holding teachers accountable when similar approaches have largely been rebuffed in higher education and medicine? Why has the same mode of reform repeatedly been so attractive? In sum, while rational choice approaches can explain the strategic behavior of political actors in pursuing education reform, they do not address how the context for these strategic actions was created.

Because rational choice theories focus on a short time horizon, historical institutionalism is often the preferred approach for those whose questions focus on change over longer periods.[7] Historical institutionalism, as its name suggests, emphasizes both history and institutions. History provides opportunities for change, but earlier decisions represent branching points, or critical junctures, that limit later choices through a process known as path dependence.[8] One key institution is the state and its bureaucracy, which is not simply a processor of interest group demands but an active agent in constructing and implementing policy. Another key institution—with "institution" here understood as the rules that govern political interaction—is the American system of separated powers, multiple veto points, and federalism. In contrast to the more centralized political bodies of some other countries, America's more fragmented system makes it much harder to pass universal social policies. As applied to the educational question, historical institutionalism can explain why it has been so difficult to move the American educational system, since divided powers limit the federal government's ability to mandate change.

But while historical institutionalism can explain the baseline from which the recent changes depart—decentralized federalism had long inhibited

national action on schools—its long-standing emphasis on path dependence forecloses the institutional changes that are so remarkable about the
case under study. In partial answer to this objection, an important book by
Paul Manna has argued that while historical institutionalism has traditionally
focused on how America's system of federalism impedes major policy development, in the case of education multiple venues provided opportunities for
"borrowing," with state and federal developments feeding off one another. Of
course, this argument begs a further question: Given that American education had embraced local control of schooling since its inception and that the
arrangements of federalism had always permitted borrowing between levels
of government, what prompted increased state and federal involvement over
the past 20 years? As is often true of historical institutionalist approaches,
the mechanism for change is not specified. Further, because historical institutionalism does not specifically attend to the content of the reforms, it is also
not well suited to explaining why there has been a repeated impulse to reform
schools using the same policy levers of school rationalization and control.

To sum up, a number of questions are not easily answered by existing
approaches:

- What explains the repeated cycles of school rationalization movements in
  spite of the fact that no single group has advocated the reforms across the
  cases?
- Why did standards and accountability triumph in recent years despite the
  opposition of the strongest interest group in the field?
- Why was the long tradition of local control of education sacrificed in
  favor of greater state and federal control?
- Why did the Republican Party move from its position of seeking to
  abolish the Department of Education in 1980 to leading the greatest
  expansion of federal control in the nation's history in 2001?
- Why has school accountability repeatedly created strange bedfellows,
  bringing together the left and the right?
- Why have teachers repeatedly been unable to resist movements for
  external accountability?

## *A Cultural Approach: The Power of Ideas and the Weakness of the Educational Field*

The limits of these approaches suggest a need for new thinking. The argument
that follows builds upon two literatures—one in political science and one

in sociology—to develop a theory both about how to understand repeated cycles of school rationalization and, more generally, how to think about the cultural dimensions of social and political contestation. From the political scientists, the argument seeks to extend the thinking on the role of ideas in the policy process, suggesting that dominant problem definitions or paradigms have political as well as cognitive consequences. When a particularly potent idea or problem definition crystallizes, it has the power to entirely recast a policy domain, to shape what is seen as desirable and who participates in the subsequent debate. New problem definitions can attract new actors, change the interests of existing actors, and delimit the arguments and credibility of actors whose views are out of step with the prevailing ideas. In some cases, new ideas can even provoke or enable institutional transformation, because new views of the problem can stimulate or enable new levels of government to take on issues that were previously outside their jurisdiction. Ideas are particularly well suited to explaining change (or in this case multiple episodes of change). Different views of a problem are constantly circulating, and when one achieves master status, it can rapidly spark a series of interrelated developments, leading to significant change in a relatively short period of time. In sum, ideas can complement interests and institutions by explaining why actors take the positions they do and how institutions shift; ideas are also well suited to explaining the substantive direction of a policy debate and why particular policies are selected.

From the sociologists, the argument builds on the literature about fields and professions. Pierre Bourdieu has conceptualized society as a series of fields, with each seeking to develop and extend its logic into other fields. Similarly, Andrew Abbott's work has seen professions as competing with one another for jurisdictional control. The present study, building on those traditions and seeking to link them more directly to politics, suggests that the way in which a field institutionalizes directly affects its social, cultural, and political power and thus the degree of respect it garners from other actors. If the power of ideas helps to explain bursts of activity in educational reform, the failed professionalization of teaching explains the continuity in the nature of the reforms proposed and the recurring inability of educators to resist those reforms.

These two perspectives are interrelated and mutually reinforcing. The literature on the politics of ideas is about the consequences of how the *problem space* is shaped and defined, whereas the literature on professions and fields is about which *actors* are seen as culturally powerful and legitimate. But, as we will see, these two arenas are linked: how a problem is defined deeply shapes who is seen as a legitimate advocate; at the same time, credible advocates can define public issues in ways consistent with their views. Taken together, the two perspectives can help us understand continuity and change, the political and the social, and the ways the cultural can complement the structural in explaining recurring episodes of school rationalization.

## The Power of Ideas: How Paradigms Shape Politics

There is now a substantial and growing literature on the role of ideas in politics. Over the past 20 years, scholars have invoked paradigms, road maps, worldviews, or simply ideas as ways to explain actors' commitments to their chosen ends.[9] In areas as diverse as human rights policy, airline and trucking deregulation, and industrial policy and the welfare state, research suggests that ideas provide important templates that guide policy action.[10] Responding to earlier materialist contentions that ideas are largely epiphenomenal, much of this work, seeking to contrast interest-based and ideational approaches, has shown that ideas were important in creating policy even when interest groups were arrayed against their triumph.[11] Such work has had considerable impact in the field, and even those who were at one time skeptical about the causal role of ideas have begun to incorporate this strand into their work.[12]

Over time, idea-centered scholarship has moved from a largely defensive posture of seeing *whether* ideas matter to a much richer exploration of *how* ideas matter.[13] Scholars such as John Kingdon, Frank Baumgartner and Bryan Jones, Peter Hall, Shari Berman, Mark Blyth, Daniel Beland, and Brian Steensland have offered increasingly complex accounts of the different kinds of ideas that exist and the different mechanisms by which they can affect political outcomes.[14] Since those working in history, intellectual history, and the history of science have long incorporated notions of culture and ideas into their analyses, the focus on the how has allowed social scientists to contribute on the ground on which they have the most to offer: specifying the underlying theoretical mechanisms and processes that are important in explaining recurring patterns and outcomes in political life.

In this work, I explore the salience of one particular kind of idea: a "problem definition," or "policy paradigm." A problem definition is a particular way of understanding a complex reality. For example, homelessness can be seen as the product of a housing shortage, high unemployment, or a lack of individual gumption. Problem definitions resist efforts to separate the normative and the empirical, as they generally evoke both normative and empirical descriptions in ways that are mutually reinforcing.[15] The way a problem is framed has significant implications for the types of policy solutions that will seem desirable, and hence much of the political argument is fought at the level of problem definition. During the conflict stage, "problem definition" is the appropriate term; when one definition has triumphed and assumes the status of a master narrative, it can be called a "policy paradigm," following Kuhn's view of paradigms as dominant views that preclude significant dissent. Problem definitions and policy paradigms sit at an intermediate level in the hierarchy of ideas: they are not as specific as particular policy solutions (e.g., vouchers, charters) nor are they as general as broader public philosophies or ideologies (e.g., the government is the problem). While they intersect with these other levels of ideas, for the purpose of understanding the evolution of a substantive domain, the problem definition or policy paradigm is the critical unit of analysis.

In Chapter Five, I take up the question of how policy paradigms are chosen or set, but here I focus on the consequences of these powerful paradigms. Much existing scholarship on paradigms has situated them within a policy learning tradition, where the argument, following Kuhn, concerns how accumulated anomalies can lead to nonincremental changes when one paradigm replaces another.[16] Building on Hugh Heclo's early observation that policymakers "puzzle" as well as "power," this research is essentially *cognitive* in its focus, seeing changes in the worldviews of key players as the primary mechanism through which paradigms have their effect. Here I argue that paradigms can also play a powerful *political* role. As new ways of seeing problems take hold, these ideas can reshape the landscape in three essential ways.

The first consequence of a new paradigm is that it *changes the nature of the debate*. A dominant problem definition serves to bound the potential possibilities of what can be advocated, thus acquiring a powerful agenda-setting function. Policy entrepreneurs who offer solutions that are consistent with the broader agenda are elevated, while those whose solutions do not fit the master narrative are marginalized. In this way, not only does the new problem definition provide a template for its proponents; it also can constrain the positions its opponents take.

A second effect of a new problem definition is that it *changes the constellation of actors*. When new problem definitions come to the fore, new actors become involved, and new cleavages are created.[17] New paradigms can motivate the formation of new groups, which in turn can have a significant effect on subsequent debate. Precisely because these new groups accept the dominant conception of the problem, they are welcomed by the broader political environment and can play a critical role in shaping policy alternatives. New problem definitions can also create opportunities for policy entrepreneurs and experts as existing groups seek guidance on how to position themselves in a new environment.

Third, a new problem definition can also *create an opportunity for major institutional change*. Which actors are motivated and legitimated to act in an area is dependent in part upon how the area is defined. As we will see, when education became more heavily defined as an economic issue, state and federal actors who had previously viewed education as largely a local function were motivated and enabled to act because the issue was now regarded as falling within their jurisdiction. While institutional theories tend to emphasize stability, idea-oriented theories can provide an account of major shifts in institutional responsibility.

Cross-cutting these dimensions of change are differences in the modes of action they can provoke (see Table 2.1). There have been fierce debates in the literature between those in the rational choice tradition, who see ideas as resources that are used by actors, and those of a more sociological bent, who

### Table 2.1 How paradigms shape politics

|  | Changes to debate | Changes to actors | Changes to institutions |
|---|---|---|---|
| Constitutive (interpretive) | Changes the way an issue is conceived and discussed | Reshapes the identities of existing actors and creates new actors whose views are consistent with the paradigm | Creates interest in issue at new institutional levels |
| Strategic (incentives) | Creates opportunities for those whose views are consistent with the new paradigm | Provides rhetorical resources and increases standing of aligned actors | Creates opportunities for institutional actors at new levels to claim an issue |
| Regulative (intersubjective) | Delimits possibilities to ones consistent with the paradigm | Limits rhetorical resources and diminishes standing of unaligned actors | Makes it harder for critics to resist institutional change |

think that ideas play a more foundational role in shaping goals and identities. Arguing for a more inclusive position, I suggest that ideas can play both of those roles, which we might think of as the strategic and the constitutive ones, as well as a third, less frequently discussed alternative, the regulative role of ideas.

Perhaps the most powerful impact of a new paradigm is *constitutive*—it affects how people interpret or understand the world. Newspapers, legislative debates, and other forums where issues are debated and decided take up issues different from those they did before because they are now working within the new paradigm. Existing actors' identities are reshaped as the new problem definition changes the way people think about an issue; people who would have put their efforts in one direction are now moving in another because they see the world in a different way. New actors and groups are also created; as a new problem becomes central, new people are drawn to taking on the issue. Institutionally, actors at levels of the system that have not previously seen the problem as their concern become interested in it if it now seems more akin to others within their purview. The research stance here is what Weber calls *Verstehen*—understanding how people interpret the world is critical.

At the same time, a new paradigm can also create change by provoking *strategic* actions. When a new way of defining a problem becomes central, actors can promote their existing positions by linking them to the new paradigm. Whereas the constitutive view emphasizes the way in which new paradigms reshape actors' interests and identities, the strategic view stresses the way in which new problem definitions create opportunities for intentional actors with unchanged goals to pursue them by using the rhetorical resources the new problem definition affords. In terms of institutional change, a new problem definition also can create an opportunity for those at a particular level of government to pursue an issue that was previously off-limits. The questions here are less about how a paradigm changes people's understandings and more about how it changes their incentives and strategic calculations.[18]

Finally, drawing on Durkheim, ideas can also serve a *regulative* function. Once ideas become accepted collective properties or social facts, they constrain the positions that those who oppose the dominant idea can take. In terms of the debate itself, paradigms limit the range of positions that are possible. In terms of actors, opponents may not believe in the dominant idea, but its existence still has a powerful effect on what they can advocate or how they choose to position themselves. In terms of institutional change, the power of a new problem definition can also disadvantage those seeking to resist such change: if a new way of seeing a problem makes it natural for a different level of government to take up an issue, those who want to keep it within its current institutional context are largely on the defensive. If the constitutive mode is about how ideas affect actors' *interpretive* understandings, and the strategic mode is about how ideas change actors' *incentives*, the regulative mode is about how the *intersubjective context* itself can have an important impact in shaping the debate and the political landscape that surrounds it.

One consequence of this view is that it avoids contrasting idea-centered explanations with interest group or institutional explanations and instead shows how ideas can be integrated with these other modes of explanation. As Colin Hay has forthrightly pointed out, those who believe in ideas cannot contrast "interest groups" with "ideas," as their underlying ontological assumptions are that interests are interpretively constructed and that institutions embody ideas.[19] The integrated view has a dual benefit: it does not deny the importance of an obviously critical factor like the distribution of interest group power or the nature of institutional structure but also specifies the particular contributions that ideas can make.

This view of how paradigms shape politics departs from several influential accounts of the policy process. Compared with John Kingdon's account, in which policy entrepreneurs link three streams—problems, solutions, and politics—to make new policy, the view offered here focuses on how the boundaries of possibility in an arena are shaped over an extended period. Kingdon's view can explain episodes of policymaking but overlooks the essential continuities in policy direction over longer periods of time. Kingdon also takes the strategic view of actors described above: he does not investigate constitutive questions about how they come to take the positions that they do. He also does not address institutional change. Thus the "paradigm shapes politics" perspective offered here can complement Kingdon's theory by examining how the prevailing ideational context shapes the nature of the debate, the positions of the actors, and the institutions which take up the issue.

Frank Baumgartner and Bryan Jones consider the longer time frame emphasized here, in their case suggesting the ways in which changing policy images can destabilize policy monopolies, lead to shifting venues for issues, and thus ultimately create policy change. There are some clear similarities between that account and this one. However, this account offers a more specific and varied set of mechanisms through which changing problem definitions can reshape politics. Baumgartner and Jones do not discuss the strategic, constitutive, and regulative role of ideas, nor do they talk about how new ideas can reshape actors' interests and create new actors, delimit the possible arguments of critics, and provoke institutional change.

In sum, once crystallized, a new paradigm not only delimits policy options to conform to that paradigm but restructures the political landscape around an issue, raises the agenda status of the issue, and changes the players involved, their standing to speak, and the venue in which the issue is debated. In recent years, scholars in American political development have seized on E. E. Schattschneider's observation that "policies create politics."[20] Scholars of paradigm change should recognize that "paradigms create politics" as well.

## *The Weakness of the Educational Field*

By incorporating the role of ideas, political scientists can address some of the limitations of interest group and institutional accounts. But ideas, particularly policy ideas, are not the only contributions that culture can make to political life. Culture is also essential to the nature of group conflict—the ways in which the standing that groups have in debate is in part a function of how they are viewed by others. Particularly for an issue like schooling, in which everyone is at least putatively "in it for the good of the children," the struggle over who can claim power is in large part a struggle over whose views are taken as legitimate and worthy of respect. In this struggle, the failure of education to crystallize as a stronger profession has proven to be a substantial liability, one which has permitted other fields to take control of schooling.

### The Failure of Education to Crystallize as a Profession

As the chapters to come will show in more detail, K–12 education in the United States was organized as a bureaucratic hierarchy rather than a full-fledged profession. Beginning in the Progressive Era, one-room schoolhouses were transformed into a "one best system," in which superintendent CEOs were expected to exercise administrative control over schools and teachers. In subsequent years, this hierarchy has grown, as states and, most recently, the federal government have taken increasing responsibility for schooling, but the organizational principle has remained the same: administrative authority flows downward through an increasingly layered hierarchical structure. In practice, as scholars have observed, this system is loosely coupled; teachers are frequently able to ignore top-down mandates, given the difficulty of monitoring their work from afar. But while the mechanisms of administrative control have not always been effective, the chosen form was consequential. In such a hierarchical bureaucracy, teachers possessed little collective power to shape the conditions of their work; policymakers frequently used standards, tests, and other instruments to more tightly couple the system; and teachers were often resistant to what they perceived as ill-informed mandates from above.

Another way the field might have been organized—as a full-fledged profession—was the road not taken. Stronger fields, like medicine, law, and higher education, are organized, not as bureaucracies under the thumb of the state, but as self-regulated professions in which members take responsibility for organizing the work in the field. Specifically, stronger professions possess three characteristics that are absent from or not fully realized in education: 1) a well-developed knowledge base that practitioners are required to possess; 2) social closure: the profession defines who can become a certified practitioner and licenses providers of training to assure that entering members meet initial standards of quality; 3) common norms and standards of practice that assure that practitioners meet the standards of the field (hospital rounds in medicine and peer review in higher education are two examples of such mechanisms).

Teaching, like nursing, social work, and other highly feminized fields, does not fully possess any of these characteristics. Preparation for teaching takes much less time than training for other professions, and by teachers' reports, it is often of little use in guiding the actual practice of teaching. In part due to skepticism about traditional preparation programs, alternative certification programs have grown dramatically in recent years, with the result that many teachers are, by design, entering the classroom with little formal training at all.[21] Emergency credentialing allows many teachers to stand before children before receiving a full teaching license. And teacher licensing exams, in comparison with licensing exams in medicine, law, and other fields, require much less field-specific knowledge and are much easier to pass. Once in the field, teachers are not guided by established standards of practice, and norms of teacher individualism and autonomy preclude efforts to collectively develop appropriate ways to handle recurring issues in teaching. In all of these respects, teaching is highly underprofessionalized in comparison with more powerful fields.

The substantive consequences of this underprofessionalization for the provision of quality schooling cannot be underestimated. As Dan Lortie astutely chronicled more than 30 years ago, the combination of weak, ineffective teacher preparation programs, the absence of a shared technical core of knowledge, and the lack of ongoing mechanisms for assuring consistent practice generates the pattern we see: widely divergent levels of skill from one teacher to the next.[22] Lacking the professionalizing mechanisms that produce doctors, lawyers, professors, engineers, and professionals in other fields, teaching is much more dependent upon what each individual is able to master, with experience as the main source of knowledge. In addition, teaching has developed a defensive professionalism of individual autonomy in response to what teachers perceive as ill-informed demands from above, a stance which reinforces the pattern of each practitioner needing to discover teaching anew.

Critics of varying stripes have offered a number of reasons why it has been or would be difficult to professionalize teaching along the lines of other fields. One early set of criticisms flatly asserted that there was just not much knowledge within teaching and thus that organizing around expertise was a wrong-headed approach.[23] A second, more nuanced argument suggested that there is significant knowledge involved in teaching, but that it is not the kind that is amenable to nomothetic, or generalizable, theories. In this view, teachers are like bricoleurs, seeking on the fly to discover materials, examples, and units that will work with their students; the idea of a more general knowledge base is flawed.[24] A third view has suggested that it is the external circumstances around teaching that make it hard to develop a profession: working with an involuntary clientele (students required to come to school) in an environment with highly ambiguous goals (schools are supposed to meet academic, civic, and social purposes) and in a field seeking to develop not only students' minds but also their characters. This situation makes it much more difficult to develop the bounded professional expertise that characterizes other fields.[25]

At the same time, there are reasons to think that some of these objections could be met in ways that would allow teaching to develop a more professional identity, albeit one that is not exactly like that of other fields and is adapted to the particular circumstances of school teaching. The old idea that there isn't much knowledge in teaching has been refuted through careful examination of what good teachers do. Researchers suggest that skilled teachers possess three kinds of knowledge: substantive knowledge about their subjects, pedagogical knowledge about how to teach, and pedagogical content knowledge about how students think in particular subjects and how to represent in multiple ways ideas in a particular domain.[26] Teachers make literally hundreds of decisions or moves in a given class, and very skilled teachers, like skilled experts in other domains, know how to put together these complex repertoires in ways that move learning forward.[27] Research on expertise suggests that it consists in large part of the ability to recognize patterns quickly and to draw upon a wide repertoire of strategies to respond to the patterns one perceives. Good teachers, like experts in other domains, have these abilities.[28] It is hard to argue today that teaching isn't highly skilled work, especially as its goals shift toward helping students master increasingly open-ended and high-level content.

What sort of knowledge would support good teaching? This is a more complicated question. Most professions rely on both an academic or theoretical knowledge base, which describes the underlying social system in which they work, and a more practical knowledge base that is problem focused and describes how to handle particular situations. It may be the case that the balance of the two in teaching is more skewed toward the second kind, practical knowledge, than it is to underlying theoretical knowledge, given that there is quite a distance from understanding how people learn or how children develop to knowing how to teach a lesson to 25 students at different levels of skill and motivation. The problem is that education as a field has failed both to develop more practical knowledge stemming from the field and to draw on its theoretical knowledge to create applied knowledge that would be useful for the field.

Let us treat these two parts in turn. First, the field has failed to develop a stock of widely shared, usable, practical knowledge. As Lortie points out, "Nor do we find [in education] an equivalent to the centuries of codified experience encountered in law, engineering, medicine, divinity, architecture and accountancy; no way has been found to record and crystallize teaching for the benefit of beginners. Law students have their precedents; and engineers have exemplars dating back to ancient Rome; physicians recall Galen and centuries of empirical treatments, and clergymen can pore over thousands of published sermons and exegeses.... But what meaningful record exists of the millions of teaching transactions that have occurred since the City on the Hill?"[29] David Cohen similarly faults the field for not developing what he calls the social infrastructure—terminology, materials, how-to guides for the work, training—that exists in other fields.[30] For historical reasons (to be further explored in the chapters that follow), teaching failed to develop the practical knowledge base and infrastructure that would have strengthened its claim to professional knowledge and control over its work.

Second, the way in which the theoretical research developed was remarkably disconnected from questions that matter to practice. As Chapter Three will describe in more detail, university schools of education deliberately sought to distance themselves from applied questions in order to increase their status by imitating their arts and science peers. In particular, questions about pedagogy were shunned as potential contaminants because of teaching's association with low-level, women's work; instead, universities focused on developing administrative methods potentially of use to the predominantly male group of administrators. The result has been an ongoing divide between questions pursued in the university and questions that might matter for teachers in the field. Furthermore, we have not seen the creation of a body of high-quality applied research that builds on basic research but might lend itself to more immediate use by practitioners. Thus the relationship between university research and field practice is particularly troubled in education, with the consequence that the profession as a whole has struggled to develop the kind of usable knowledge that supports professional practice in other fields.[31]

Finally, there is the question of whether the external circumstances that surround teaching make it difficult to assert professional expertise. The short answer is yes; it is easier to do skilled work of any kind if the goals are clear, if the clients are committed, and if the work is bounded to the domain of the profession (i.e., the divorce lawyer wants to know about your plans for your property, whereas the therapist wants to know about your plans for your love life). Education, particularly American education, suffers on all three fronts: the goals are often ill defined and conflicted, the clients don't necessarily want to be there, and teachers are expected not only to instruct academically but also to take on a wide variety of roles related to helping young people turn into successful adults.

However, it is also possible to see these challenges as a *consequence* as much as a cause of underprofessionalization. In other words, if education had developed a more professional core, it might have been able to shape external circumstances to make professionally skilled work more achievable. Specifically, the profession might have had a larger role in developing a set of achievable and long-standing goals. Countries with strong education ministries controlled by the profession do exactly that (set long-term goals that change only gradually), in contrast to the American pattern of rapid, political lurching from one goal to another. With respect to involuntary clients, the profession might have developed more sophisticated ways of engendering commitment from students and also delimited what it is reasonable to ask of the profession in the absence of that commitment. Finally, like other fields with potentially much broader mandates—imagine if doctors were responsible not just for treating patients but for all the factors that affect public health or if lawyers were responsible not just for representing clients but for developing social justice in society—a stronger teaching profession might have been able to more forcefully assert that teachers should be responsible for academic instruction, while the very worthwhile broader goals of human improvement for young people should be much more widely shared across a variety of social institutions.

## The Politics of the Professions

Professions do not exist in a vacuum. They contend with other actors for power, authority, and the ability to control "their" work. If, following Elliott

Krause, we imagine a triangle with states, markets, and professions at the corners, a critical question is how power is distributed among them.[32]

In this contentious world, professions are not simply *granted* authority or deference; they have to fight for it. The traditional relationship is one in which the state grants the profession exclusive license over its work, with the idea that the profession can produce expert work more efficiently and consistently than can open markets or state hierarchies. There can also be alliances between the contending parties: states can choose to organize state-run services largely through a profession (as in the National Health Service in Britain), professions can work within markets (as in old-style fee-for-service medicine), and states and markets can combine (as in the contracting out or privatization of government services).[33] Of course, partnership arrangements do not necessarily imply equal standing between the parties: often at stake in these mixed arrangements is who controls what aspects of the work and by what standard the work will be judged.[34]

In this context, the failure of education to professionalize its *internal* operations has had significant *external* consequences for its ability to advocate for itself politically.[35] While existing scholarship by Linda McNeil and others has emphasized the way in which invasive testing and scripted teaching deprofessionalizes teachers' work, here I argue that the relationship can also run in the opposite direction.[36] As will be discussed in more detail in pages to come, in the absence of a respected knowledge base, clear standards for how to do the work, extensive training of new practitioners, and consistency in outcomes, education has left itself exceedingly vulnerable to external movements that seek to shape and control schooling and teachers' work. In a nutshell: *failed professionalization breeds external rationalization.*

Part of the challenge for educational professionalism in the United States is that education has always been an owned subsidiary of the state. More than 90 percent of students attend public schools. Consequently, the state is the primary financier of the profession, and lay bodies such as school boards, districts, states, and the federal government assume ultimate authority over it. Unlike American medicine, which initially crystallized as a private fee-for-service profession, teaching has always been under the thumb of the state. The result is that the fields have evolved in different ways. In education, the power of the state has been used to increasingly expand access to schooling, but the absence of a professional core has meant that this access is to a highly variable level of professional work. In American medicine, by contrast, the developed nature of the profession has assured more consistent quality across doctors' work, but the strength of the profession has frequently been a barrier to state efforts to increase access, curb costs, and equalize the relationship between patients and doctors.[37]

Thus the point, from the perspective of the public interest, is not that more professionalization is always good; it is that professions can reliably produce particular kinds of expertise. The challenge is how to balance the virtues of professionalization with the benefits brought by the state and the market. Particularly over the past 40 years, professions have increasingly been on the retreat, as the seemingly contradictory combination of expanding state ambitions (e.g., in health care, education, and other social services) and expanding skepticism of both state and professional competence has wrought a politics of retrenchment and accountability in which claims of professional authority are under ever-increasing scrutiny. In this context, a number of professions have seen their authority diminish, but education, as a semiprofessional field, has been particularly hard hit, because it does not have a respected internal professional core that it can use to defend itself. Chapter Six compares K–12 and higher education in some detail, illustrating the ways in which the more developed professionalization of American higher education has enabled it (thus far) to rebuff the external accountability movements that have penetrated primary and secondary education.

## The Fight among Fields: Interpenetrating Logics and Institutional Vantage Points

Professions contend not only with states and markets; they also contend with other fields whose logics seek to invade and colonize them. Pierre Bourdieu has described society as made up of a series of intersecting fields—different spheres of life, which possess different "currencies" and compete with one another for legitimacy and authority.[38] Universities and capitalists, for example, compete constantly over whether academic or financial capital should be valorized in politics and other spheres. Relatedly, Andrew Abbott has argued that professions are defined by the reach of their jurisdictional control; literally, their power lies in the degree to which they are able to defend their boundaries from competitors trying to claim cultural jurisdiction over their work.[39]

Particularly of interest for the educational case is the possibility of the *interpenetration of logics* from one sphere into another.[40] Most of the writing on the professions, following Abbott, has focused on the issue of jurisdictional competition, which centers on whether the work of a profession is being raided by others who want to do the same job. But the educational case raises the possibility of interpenetration, whereby a logic that character-izes one sphere (i.e., a business logic of organizational rationality) becomes increasingly prevalent within another sphere (i.e., the educational sphere). In contrast to jurisdictional competition, the prospect is not that the practitio-ners in the field will suddenly be replaced en masse by outsiders.[41] What is at stake is subtler but no less significant: that the standards of the field and the activities within the field will gradually be transformed into a metric for-eign to its internal standards of practice.[42] A full accounting of educational accountability needs to assess it in terms of not only whether it produces bet-ter test scores but also whether its fundamental logic is consistent with the highest aspirations of the educational field.[*]

The question of interpenetrating logics raises a set of dilemmas for mem-bers of the weaker field. At least three options are possible: to *resist* the exter-nal logic, on the grounds that it undermines central aspects of the field; to be *co-opted* by the logic, which will increase one's status with external actors but will diminish one's standing with many of those internal to the field; or to *transform* the logic, in a way that draws what is useful from the external logic but changes it to make it true to the highest internal standards of the field. As we will see, educators have followed all three of these roads at different points in the 20th century and have been riven by internal debates over which choice best embodies the greatest hopes for the field.

Viewing the fight over schooling as a conflict among fields also draws attention to how where actors "sit" affects what they "see" about the issue. Consultants, for example, often visit their client organizations briefly before dispensing advice; they are more likely to see things in terms of roles and posi-tions, whereas longtime employees may be more likely to see people and per-sonalities. Particularly relevant in this case is the state, which in recent years has been seen less as a mediator of interest group pressures and more as an actor in its own right.[43] Viewing the state as one field among others helps us to understand the distinctive attributes of its worldview: it largely "sees" things from afar, in terms of their measurable attributes—in particular, how much output is achieved for each unit of input. Policymakers are, by definition, responsible for many schools and sit at a considerable distance from them.

---

* This is a more specific case of Michael Walzer's "spheres of justice" notion: namely, that dif-ferent domains are governed by different standards, and justice is violated when standards from one domain are used in another. For instance, elections are supposed to be settled by the demo-cratic principle of voting; thus, buying votes violates the principle that governs the electoral domain. See Michael Walzer, *Spheres of Justice: A Defense of Pluralism and Equality* (New York: Basic Books, 1983).

Teachers and principals are responsible for a single school and sit inside it. The result is that the two groups have different ways of seeing. Policymakers see general properties of schools, things that can be counted and measured from afar. School people see the particulars; they may know little to nothing about the school landscape as a whole, but they know much, including much that is not easily measured, about the schools in which they sit.[44]

This conflict is a more specific manifestation of a general phenomenon discussed by James Scott in *Seeing Like a State*.[45] Scott's masterful book explores the limits in how state bureaucracies "see" as they seek to make legible a varied social landscape. Scott canvasses a series of examples, ranging from a Soviet Five-Year Plan for food production to German forests where trees were planted in lines, to illustrate the folly of acting on the basis of only what is visible from afar. In his examples, decontextualized knowledge is privileged over more local, contextual, and particular knowledge, often with disastrous results. Forests, for example, grow best in a mixed ecosystem; seeking to impose the rational order of an industrial grid onto them deprives them of what they literally need to survive. More recent research on "commensuration"—the process of turning social qualities into measurable quantities—reaches similar conclusions.[46]

The usefulness of this research when it comes to K–12 schooling is its demonstration that fights over policy are due not only to differences in interests or values but also to the different institutional vantage points at which the contesting actors sit. Quantification serves the interests of the people from afar much more than those of the people up close because it allows legislators to assign schools to categories and hold them accountable from afar on the basis of easily legible information. While most analyses of recent changes have viewed school reform primarily in terms of what might be called the "horizontal politics" of education—specifically, that a centrist coalition triumphed over the objections of left and right—the core cleavages in contemporary education reflect, rather, a "vertical politics" governed more by institutional position than by ideology.[47] In this new politics, whether one sits on the right or left of the aisle is less important than whether one spends one's days in the schoolhouse or the statehouse.[48]

## Intersections: *The Virtues of a Cultural Ontology and the Importance of Moral Power*

The two perspectives developed above are highly interrelated. The discussion of paradigms focuses on the nature of the *problem space* in which issues are debated: which issues are seen to be important, how they are framed, and what the consequences of those choices are. The discussion of professions and fields examines the nature of the *actors*: who they are, what they see, and how credible they are as advocates for their positions. Missing from these accounts, when considered separately, are the ways in which they reinforce one another. *How* a problem or issue is defined has a considerable impact on *who* is seen as a relevant or credible advocate; conversely, the most credible advocates can shape public issues in ways that reinforce their own importance and centrality.

For example, if the problem of schooling is that schools are not as efficient as for-profits, business leaders become emboldened; if the problem is that students' creativity is not being tapped, then artists and teachers are empowered. Similar points could be made in other domains; a recent study of terrorism expertise, for example, finds that as the issue shifted from the more technical question of "insurgency" to the more charged label of "terrorism," new experts who were more comfortable speaking in moral terms became increasingly empowered.[49] How the problem is defined affects which actors are seen as relevant, and which actors are seen as relevant affects how the problem is defined.

Underlying this perspective is a shared ontology that emphasizes *cultural and moral power*. Much of the older sociological literature on culture and power has tended to treat the two as if they were opposed concepts: culture is about shared norms that hold society together; power is about the competing interests that pull it apart. Similarly, morality and power are often taken to be opposites, with morality grounded in altruism and a commitment to the common good and power located in self-interest. The contention here is that rather than being an oxymoron, a central dimension of power is rooted in cultural and moral standing. In other words, if power is the ability to shape events and the action of other actors, one's ability to do that is largely rooted in how one is perceived, culturally and morally, by others in one's milieu.

Cultural power is the more familiar of the two concepts. Bourdieu's writing about the struggle among fields implicitly adopts this perspective: unlike older sociological notions of society as an undifferentiated whole, social life is viewed as a series of spheres that compete with one another for supremacy. The case of the professions, described above, is a specific version of the general idea that actors' external standing is affected in part by their internal competence and overall reputation. Similarly, Daniel Carpenter's work on the importance of organizational reputations suggests the ways in which an actor's ability to be seen as efficacious in pursuit of its ends—technically competent, procedurally transparent, and ethically defensible—affects the ways in which it is treated by other actors. While we frequently think of power in terms of money, votes, or other material resources, it is worthwhile to remember that less tangible factors, including the external perception of credibility and competence, are also critical determinants of power. This credibility can come from characteristics of individual actors or can flow from the standing of the broader field of which the actor is a part. In turn, as Bourdieu points out, "The imposition of a definition of the world is in itself an act of mobilization which tends to confirm or transform power relations."[50] In other words, actors' power flows in part from their cultural standing, and they deploy that power in large part by rhetorically defining situations in ways that are consistent with their worldview.

A related idea that is less well developed in the literature is what Christopher Winship and I call *moral power*. As we have argued elsewhere, moral power is the ability to convince others that one is trustworthy and seeks to advance the common good.[51] Actors that are perceived as well intentioned by others are granted greater degrees of trust, deference, and leadership than those seen as self-interested. Martin Luther King exercised moral power through his appeal to universal principles and his practice of nonviolent resistance; similarly, parents can develop moral power with their children by living up to the principles they espouse. Perhaps the easiest way to accrue moral power is actually to behave morally; of course, it is also possible to be perceived as morally upstanding by external audiences by keeping one's less savory motives and actions out of sight. Scandal is an ever-present threat to moral power: John Edwards's political success, which rested largely on his moral arguments about the injustice of inequality and poverty, was undermined by revelations of his mistress, illegitimate child, and attempted cover-up. In eliminating his ability to make moral claims, they presumably ended his political career. In addition to the cultural power actors accrue from competence and credibility, actors' strength also rests on their ability to be seen as well intentioned and seeking to support the public good.

Later chapters will explore in more detail how the way in which teachers have responded since the 1960s to their weak professionalization has undermined their moral power and further limited their influence in public debate. Beginning in the 1960s, teachers, responding to their low pay, status and respect, organized themselves to bargain collectively. This tack brought about increases in pay and considerable political clout for the teachers unions, whose relentless focus on bread-and-butter issues yielded significant gains for their members. But at the same time, by moving towards an industrial

bargaining model (a union), as opposed to a professional association, teachers defined themselves as labor in a labor-management dispute, as opposed
to professionals who controlled their practice. The emphasis on wages and
job protection has weakened their public claims to speak on educational
issues and undermined their position in the eyes of legislators and the public.
Groups that are far less traditionally powerful than they, in terms of members
and money, have been able to trump them in political debate because of their
greater moral power.

In sum, a world of ideas, professions, fields, logics, institutional vantage
points, and cultural and moral power helps us see dimensions of the political and social world largely missing from more traditional political science
accounts of interests and institutions. Connecting to and building upon the
work of Bourdieu, Carpenter, and Abbott, this work portrays a world of contestation and struggle—but one in which the primary medium of competition is the ability to define the world as one sees it and one's primary asset
is the ability to convince others of one's competence, credibility, and moral
standing. Such a view integrates the political and the social: the nature of the
prevailing problem definition shapes which actors are seen as relevant, while
powerful actors exert their strength largely by shaping the problem space in
favorable directions.

## Putting the Pieces Together: A Theory of Rationalizing Schools

So why does our society repeatedly try to rationalize, or "order," schools from
above? A look across a century of such movements suggests that their cycli-
cal nature is a product of two factors: certain stable features of the American
school system that make it amenable to rationalization and a more dynamic
intermittent process that has sparked each reform cycle.

Three features of the American school system make it particularly susceptible to movements for external accountability. The first is the contrast
between the high hopes invested in our schools and our low ability to realize these hopes. In a country with a weak welfare state, high levels of child
poverty, and increasingly unequal social geography, it is not surprising that
schools have frequently been unable to live up to the utopian expectations
placed upon them. Second, as David Cohen and Susan Moffitt have recently
emphasized, the fragmented nature of American federalism makes it difficult
for centralized authorities to provide the supports and infrastructure needed
to consistently produce high-quality schooling.[52] State and local control over

education also creates wide variation in the level of performance across units of schooling. This inequality in turn provides grist for the mill of reformers, who seize upon it as a rallying cry for greater standardization. Third, as discussed in more detail above, the institutionalization of teaching as a semiprofession has left it unable to develop the standards of high-quality practice needed to create greater consistency of outcomes or to defend itself politically.

Within this long-standing context, each of the reform movements has followed a remarkably similar four-part pattern.

The first step is that a group of analysts *identifies a crisis of quality*. The medium through which this crisis is identified varies, but the effect is the same. In the Progressive Era, the bell was sounded by muckraking journalists; in the 1960s, the spark was the largest-ever quantitative survey of schools, the Coleman Report; and from the 1980s to the present, the precipitating document has been the famous report *A Nation at Risk*. Each of these documents framed the problem as one of schools underperforming expectations and failing to turn "inputs" into high-quality "outputs." As suggested above, the creation of such a master narrative or paradigm around the problems of schooling structures subsequent debate.

Second, with the problem so defined, *a logic from a higher-status field is proposed to address the crisis*: Taylorism in the Progressive Era, systems analysis from the Defense Department in the 1960s, and business management strategies from the 1980s to the present. These logics benefit from both their perceived fit with the nature of the defined problem and their association with higher-status epistemic communities. Specifically, each time a logic of external target setting, assessment, and accountability promised a way to rationalize an unruly school system. Perhaps not surprisingly, the ideas frequently originated in business, with business logic applied to the educational field.

Third, *the definition of the problem stimulates political action, and elites seeking to move the system back the new logic as a way to remedy the problem*. The identity of the elites has varied over the reform periods, but in each case the lead actors have embraced the newly created definition of the problem and have seized upon a logic of efficiency as the way to address it. Critics of these proposals are stymied in part because their underlying assumptions are not consistent with the governing paradigm.

Fourth, in each case, *a highly feminized teaching profession seeks unsuccessfully to resist*. From the early 20th century to the present, teachers and their representatives have decried these rationalizing movements as unfairly targeting schools for the problems of society and have deplored the obsession with testing as subordinating the educational to the measurable. But the fact that teaching was organized as a weak, highly feminized semiprofession has meant that teachers have been largely unable to resist movements for external accountability. Despite the different time periods and institutional contexts—first city, then state, then federal—the essence of this four-part pattern was constant in efforts to rationalize schools across the 20th century.

This analysis addresses many of the questions posed above. While there is no single *actor* that is repeatedly responsible for reforms, a similar *logic* comes to the fore time and time again. This technocratic logic appeals to a wide variety of external actors for different reasons. Liberals see it as a way to generate a greater equalization of school resources across a highly decentralized landscape. Conservatives see it as a way to assure that public dollars are being spent efficiently and to motivate a recalcitrant sector to reform. Civil rights actors, courts, and would-be system planners see it as a way to take control of a huge and unwieldy system and focus it on results. The cleavages of rationalizing movements are less left versus right than top versus bottom or outsiders versus insiders. The commensurating logic of measurement-driven change unites those who are outside the schools, seeking to create change within them, against teachers who are being held to account.

It can also explain why teachers and, in more recent years, teachers unions have been unable to resist external accountability. Teachers are repeatedly isolated as one of the few actors opposed to the reforms; therefore their repeated pleas against the standardization of learning or the scapegoating of schools are seen as self-interested pleading. The context of crisis and the very real failings of the status quo undermine efforts to defend existing arrangements. Teaching, as a weakly organized profession, possesses neither the means to improve its own quality nor the political strength or credibility to respond to external actors. In the most recent movement, the material and political power of teachers unions has been undermined by their inability to speak credibly to issues of school reform. The strongest interest groups have been unable to stop a rolling tide of accountability.

This approach also explains the recent institutional transformation of American education. As education became seen as an issue of economic development, powerful state actors, such as governors and business groups, became newly interested in education reform. The economic hook also legitimated their involvement. As standards spread across the states, that development, in turn, enabled the federal government to build on the state efforts and create federal reform, culminating in No Child Left Behind. The fact that two governors (Bill Clinton and George W. Bush) became president enabled this movement, as both had significant records on education in their respective states. The crisis provoked by *A Nation at Risk* stimulated states to work en masse in an area that had previously been left largely to districts; in turn, the congruence among the state efforts around standards enabled an unprecedented expansion of the federal role.

Finally, this view can explain the continuity of these movements as well as their intermittent nature. Since the field institutionalized as a hierarchically administered bureaucracy, with teachers at the bottom of an implementation chain, rather than as a fully developed profession, the problem has repeatedly been seen as a loosely coupled system in need of tightening and greater rationalization from above. This structural fact explains the persistence of efforts to order schools across the 20th century. At the same time, structural realities do not provoke action. Three different invocations of crisis brought new external actors to the table and sparked each of the episodes of reform. The later movements built on the earlier ones, and each round of rationalization paved the road for the next, culminating in a remarkably ambitious effort to use the power of the federal government to "order" all of the nation's public schools through No Child Left Behind.

## *New Lenses, New Questions*

Not only can a culturally centered view explain existing puzzles about the nature of school accountability; it also allows us to explore a different set of questions, questions that are less visible from more traditional perspectives. Existing approaches are particularly good at answering some of the traditional questions about politics, famously summarized by Harold Lasswell as "who gets what when and how." These questions are still important in the cultural approach developed here, but the emphasis on ideas, fields, and professions opens up a wider range of queries to be explored.

One set of questions concerns the relationship between education accountability movements and accountability movements in other fields. If the traditional perspective can explain why there have been cycles of school rationalization across the 20th century, what explains the rise of accountability movements in a variety of other fields (medicine, higher education, etc.) over the past four decades? And why have educators been comparatively less able to resist external accountability movements than practitioners in other fields? As we will see, a lens from the sociology of professions helps us to explore these puzzles.

A second set of questions relates to the deeper assumptions embedded in efforts to rationalize schools. The emphasis on ideas allows us to explore the intellectual and cultural underpinnings of school accountability movements. What are the assumptions of these movements about individual psychology, organizational sociology, and human nature? Why, at least in more recent years, have such efforts combined such an optimistic or even utopian vision of what is possible for students with such a pessimistic, behaviorist view of how teachers need to be incentivized and motivated? Through an examination of the competing logics that characterize school reform, we will begin to explore these questions.

A third set of questions addresses the consequences of rationalizing schools. While such discussions are usually limited to student test scores, school accountability movements also have implications for the teaching profession, for educational justice, and for the educational field as a whole. What have been the consequences of these movements for the teaching profession across the 20th century? In each of these episodes, how have the profession and its leadership sought both to exert greater jurisdictional control and to improve its practice? In terms of justice, how should we understand school accountability—is it using a safe technocratic logic to retreat from broader notions of equity, or is it, as its proponents claim, the civil rights legislation of our generation? And finally, what are the consequences of rationalization for education as a whole? What purposes are elevated or diminished, and what educational values are supported or betrayed in the rush to rationalize schools? All of these questions will be examined using the range of lenses described above.

## Looking Back, Looking Forward

School accountability movements have always been as much a declaration of our faith in the value of a certain vision of organizational rationality as they have been evidence-based reform interventions. The impulse to use rationality and state power to impose order and create social improvement is very much a Progressive Era inclination, and the school system created in the Progressive Era provided the template upon which later movements built. We start our story there.

## 3

# Taking Control from Above: The Rationalization of Schooling in the Progressive Era

THE PROGRESSIVE ERA saw a massive rationalization of American school-ing; its imprint stretches into the present day. Drawing on the ideas of (then) modern management techniques, a heterogeneous group of elites trans-formed a localized and highly varied system of schooling into what David Tyack famously called "the one best system."[1] This movement both created the form and structure of the school system that would profoundly shape later events and, as the benefit of hindsight makes evident, was driven by much the same underlying vision and set of forces that recurred in subsequent efforts to rationalize schools.

What motivated the Progressive Era transformation of schooling was the image of a rationally organized system of production. Whether in the public or private sector, the hallmarks of this approach are distinct organizational categories of work, clear delineation of roles and responsibilities, specializa-tion of labor, and hierarchical control of workers by more powerful superiors. In the case of the school system, this meant a shift from one-room school-houses of age-mixed groups, with instruction and assessment largely decided by the teacher, to larger schools, with grades sorted by age, Carnegie units to measure student progress, and teachers' work structured and assessed by their administrative superiors. In the larger context, one might say that this is just the story of the shift from preindustrial to industrial society, from small-scale institutions in which social connections and individual discretion were para-mount to larger social organizations with systems, roles, and rules.

But there are different versions of modernity, and the American school system was decisively shaped by a particularly rationalistic, scientific, and hier-archical approach to social organization.[2] As we will see, the Progressive Era reformers were enthralled by the emerging power of scientific and business techniques that, they were convinced, would make schooling more efficient and effective. In particular, the brand of management techniques they embraced sought to shift power upwards from frontline workers (teachers) to administrative superiors, who would set goals, prescribe desired strategies, and use an early form of assessment to hold teachers accountable for their performance. In this form, which draws heavily on the factory model, expertise and hence power reside at the top rather than on the front line, work is prescribed from above, and teachers are motivated by external incentives set by their superiors rather than by internal motivations to do quality work. These assumptions were consistent with the broader Taylorist management theories ascendant at the time; they also fit a gendered division of labor in which power was placed in a largely male administrative corps to oversee a largely female teaching force.

Bypassed in this move to factory-style rationalization was an alternative form of social organization advocated by John Dewey, one that would be taken up by those who sought to professionalize teaching later in the century. In this vision, teachers are knowledge producers rather than implementers of knowledge created by others; administrators support the work of teachers rather than seek to monitor and control them; and teachers' intrinsic motivation, not external measures and incentives, is the key to producing consistent quality practice across thousands of classrooms.

The triumph of the former vision over the latter has had powerful and enduring consequences. It has linked a structure of schooling—hierarchical bureaucracy—with an accompanying cultural assumption: that the way to improve schooling is to get those on the ground to do what central administrators decree. In this view, loose coupling is the problem, and tighter implementation the solution. Unfortunately, subsequent history suggests that this implementation logic is a highly limited strategy for improving schools, because teaching is complex work that is difficult to rationalize from afar.[3] District (and, later, state and federal) administrators are too distant from schools to direct their improvement effectively, teachers are resistant to dicta from above, and the result is reciprocal mistrust between teachers and policymakers, with little of the sought-after improvement in teacher practice. But while subsequent chapters will show that this approach to reform does not work as well as its proponents have hoped, it has held enduring appeal, in part because it is consistent with the hierarchical organization of schooling established in the Progressive Era.

How did we get this system in the first place? The cultural lenses developed in the previous chapter are helpful here: the desire to rationalize the system was fundamentally shaped by the desire to respond to a dominant definition of the problem—variability of performance and amateur political control—to which technocratic rationalization was the antidote. The high regard for business and its methods bolstered the claims of those who would apply its logics to schools; politically, the definition of the problem rallied a range of elites to its cause and weakened the power of teachers and other critics who opposed rationalization. Perhaps most troublingly, education schools, which might have been a counterforce fighting for the professionalization of teaching, were instead central proponents of administrative rationalization, choosing to associate themselves with the training of mostly male leaders in administrative methods and distancing themselves from women and the low-status study of pedagogy.

Readers familiar with the scholarship in this area will recognize my debts to existing historical accounts of education in the Progressive period, particularly the seminal work of David Tyack and Raymond Callahan. My aim in this chapter is to draw on these classics in the service of a broader thesis about the century-long rationalization of American schooling, a perspective not available to these scholars writing in the 1960s and early 1970s. The theoretical tools on which I draw have also been developed subsequent to their writing. What was not apparent then but is clear now is that the Progressive Era rationalization was eerily similar to later rationalization efforts, both in the forces that drove it and in the language in which it was discussed, and created the form of a bureaucratically administered school system, a form that fundamentally shaped subsequent efforts at reform.

## *An Early Movement for Efficiency*

The movement toward administrative centralization of schooling that took place between 1890 and 1930 bears a remarkable number of parallels to similar accountability efforts today. Led by an elite composed of "good government" reformers, foundations, business elites, university presidents, and professors of education, the movement had considerable success in creating the system of organized schooling that still prevails.

There is debate among historians over whether the desire to rationalize schools was motivated by a genuine belief in the rationality of science and progress or was the backlash of an elite seeking to retain power over a rapidly growing immigrant population.[4] In either case, it is clear that the "administrative progressives" sought to wrest control away from a ward-based system of local politics, which seemed to them resistant to developing models of scientific management and efficiency.[5] The reformers sought to concentrate administrative power in the superintendent, a figure who should resemble the chief executive officer of a business, and oversight power in a small, ostensibly nonpolitical school board, largely composed of themselves or men of a similar class background. In these aims they were quite successful, as the average size of school boards in large cities was reduced from an average of 21.5 in 1893 to 10.2 in 1914 to a median of 7 by 1923. Both case studies and larger-scale investigations suggest that school boards after centralization were largely composed of business and professional men.[6]

Administrative progressives also exercised their influence through an ever greater use of the school survey, a device by which outside experts were asked to make brief site visits and evaluate school districts or even entire state school systems. Between 1911 and 1930, nearly 200 cities and states were surveyed by experts from the major schools of education; chief experts who appeared time and again included Ellwood P. Cubberley of Stanford, George Strayer of Teachers College, and John Franklin Bobbitt of the University of Chicago.[7] David Tyack and Elisabeth Hansot report that "when a member of the Portland Chamber of Commerce wrote to seven educators across the nation for nominations of people to do a survey of city schools, they nominated each other with astonishing regularity."[8]

Reigning models for increasing productivity in industrial settings heavily influenced the changes that the reformers proposed. The Taylor system of industrial management hit the public eye in 1910, with a promise to increase efficiency, raise profits, and eliminate waste through a careful accounting of the costs and productivity of the various components of the production process. Perhaps the most famous manifestation of the efficiency movement was in the time-and-motion studies, which sought to capture in minute detail the differences between more and less effective workers and to use these findings to boost productivity. In the years between 1910 and the Great Depression, when the status of business was at perhaps an all-time high, the scientific efficiency models were spread widely through popular newspapers and magazines and were applied to everything from farms to families to churches.[9]

Applied to the school system, scientific management meant an increased focus on cost accounting, empowering superintendents to use their discretion to increase the productivity of teachers and the system as a whole and using measurement and testing to compare, improve, and standardize practice across districts. One prominent strand of accountability, then as now, is its focus on financial *accounting*. This took the familiar form of demands for improved record keeping, but it also took more novel forms, such as the system proposed by the Newton, Massachusetts, superintendent Frank Spaulding and Chicago's Professor Bobbitt to calculate the costs that school districts were spending per subject per hour. Spaulding claimed, for example, that he didn't know whether music was more valuable than Greek but he knew that Greek cost more than music and was therefore a far less efficient use of resources.[10] Bobbitt conducted a survey of 25 high schools in seven states and used the data to specify the range of costs appropriate for a given subject; he excoriated the schools that fell above that range and hence wasted valuable taxpayer money. Bobbitt drew out the comparisons to industry in a more prescriptive section of his report:

> Practical men, before buying wheat, or cotton, or railroad stocks, examine into market conditions and pay something in the neighborhood of current market prices. These figures appear to indicate that the same practical school board members, when they are investing the people's money in a supposedly necessary community commodity, are, certain of them, paying prices in excess of current market prices as represented by the standards of practice in those cities that lie within the "zone of safety." It probably is sufficiently extravagant to pay even the price of $90 for its Latin, when the median city is getting it done for $71.[11]

It was a short step from financial accounting to arguing (exactly as is argued today) that schools needed to be held accountable for the results they produced. Calvin Kendall, commissioner of education in New Jersey at the time, reflected this spirit of the age when he told the National Education Association in 1912 that the motivation behind school surveys was to answer the following two questions: "What return is the community getting from its investment in the schools? How can the investment be made to yield greater returns?"[12]

The answer, as laid out by Bobbitt, was to create a system that was, at the time, an adaptation of the Taylor system and would look much like what we call standards-based reform—set standards, set up systems of measurement to evaluate progress towards those standards (testing), and then evaluate performance and use rewards and punishment to spur improvement (accountability). The first stage, according to Bobbitt, was for standards to be set externally to the school itself. Standards would serve both as a goal against which success could be measured and as a way of motivating schools to higher levels of performance. A second stage was measuring whether the students had achieved the standards. This could be accomplished through testing (standardized mathematics tests and handwriting scales were particularly popular standardized tests in use at the time) or simply through accurate accounting, such as counting the number of mathematical calculations that an eighth grader could complete in a minute with a given level of accuracy. According to Bobbitt, with goals clarified and a system of measurement in place, the teacher can know "whether she is a good teacher, a medium teacher or a poor teacher," and supervisors would have "incontestable evidence against the weak teacher who cannot or refuses to improve."

Data, in turn, would provide all the benefits that are claimed for it today. Teachers would know which students were failing; principals would know when teachers were inefficient and how their schools compared to other schools; and superintendents, the CEOs of the system, could look at the data distribution of schools and see which teachers and principals were succeeding and failing. On the basis of these data, superintendents and principals could make the necessary changes to improve the system, either by changing personnel or by adopting the practices that comparative analysis indicated were most effective.

The recommendations of Bobbitt and Edward Cubberley, a Stanford education professor who was another prominent advocate of reform at the time, were widely adopted, particularly in the large cities. National Education Association meetings, the primary gathering point for educators at the time, were increasingly full of discussions of efficiency in education, with titles like "By What Standards or Tests Shall the Efficiency of a School or System of Schools Be Measured?" By March 1913, the *American School Board Journal* reported that teacher rating scales were used "almost without exception" in large cities. Edward Thorndike, of Columbia's Teachers College, had devised standard tests to evaluate students' achievement in reading, math, spelling, handwriting, and other school subjects, and in 1921 educational sociologist Ross Finney reported that "at the present time scales and tests are used in all but unprogressive schools everywhere." As of 1916, Cubberley reported that efficiency bureaus, which coordinated teacher and student testing, had been established in Boston, New York, New Orleans, Detroit, Kansas City, Rochester, and Oakland; by 1934 about 60 of the larger systems had adopted the school research bureaus.[13] Superintendents, in turn, were being trained for their new role as powerful data-driven managers by many of these same experts at schools like Columbia, Stanford, Chicago, and Wisconsin.[14]

In short, the claims that today's reformers are the first to emphasize accountability or focus on "inputs" over "outputs" are historically shortsighted. Similarities between the Progressive and modern reforms are evident in the *organizational shifts in power*, in the *policy tools* that are employed, in the *faith in science* that guides reform, and in the *pessimistic social and psychological conceptions of motivation* (of teachers and students) that underlie the policy models. Organizationally, in the Progressives' efforts to centralize control of the school system, they shifted power away from locally controlled school boards and toward central administrators, much as state and federal reforms do today. The favored model of change was one of goal setting, measurement, and accountability, a tripod later reinvented under the banner of standards-based reform. The Progressive movement not only shifted power, as is often pointed out, from politicians to "educators" (more accurately, from local school boards to professionally dominated school boards); it also shifted power *among* educators, with testing and accountability used as policy levers that lessened the autonomy of individual teachers and empowered the superintendents at the top of the accountability chain. Reformers then and now see education as more science than art and are not shy about proclaiming the benefits of data to create transparency, motivate teachers and schools, and spread the adoption of best practices. And each, at base level, embraces a Weberian view of schooling as a social system in need of rationalization and a behaviorist psychology that sees teachers and schools as externally motivated and highly responsive to clear outside incentives.

Not surprisingly, as is true today, all of these tenets were challenged by critics; explaining why the reforms were able to triumph over the criticisms requires a more complete account of educational politics than I have provided thus far. But before turning to this task, it is important to emphasize the one major way that the efficiency reforms of the Progressive Era differed from those of today—their emphasis on the social sorting of students according to measured abilities.

## A Different Kind of Efficiency: Curricular Differentiation and Social Sorting

For the Progressive Era reformers, accountability did not mean that the school system was responsible for all students meeting a high standard, as the aim of accountability efforts is defined (at least rhetorically) today. Rather, to them, an efficient system was one in which students were sorted according to their perceived and tested abilities and then directed to the educational track considered commensurate to those abilities. Seeking to meet challenges created by demographic imperatives and economic changes, incorporating new findings from the emerging science of testing, and reflecting the social and cultural emphasis on order that characterized their day, reformers settled on a model of schooling that sought to use the most up-to-date scientific techniques to sort students into tracks that matched their measured abilities and projected future occupations.

Schooling at the beginning of the 20th century was facing the challenge of massive immigration: 14 million immigrants had arrived between 1865 and 1900, and after 1900 they came at a rate of about 1 million per year.[15] The combination of this influx with the normal growth of the student population and the increasing importance of schooling resulted in a growing strain on schools and the finances required to support them. It was in this climate that Leonard Ayres published his 1909 book, *Laggards in Our Schools*, contending that schools were squandering resources by having students, particularly immigrant and minority students, repeat grades and eventually drop out. Ayres classified students as "retarded" if they were over age for their grade level and constructed an "index of efficiency," which measured how effectively schools were moving their students along and how much was being wasted on repeaters.[16] While in the 19th century holding children back had been seen as a sign of high standards,[17] in the new context of an expanded student population and limited resources, it was seen as a waste of valuable tax dollars. The need to find a way to more effectively channel students, particularly newly arrived immigrants, through the schooling process was one impulse behind the move to develop a curriculum that was less academic, more vocational, and more highly differentiated. Junior high schools were invented; they shortened the elementary school from eight years to six and created a period in grades seven through nine during which students could sort themselves into the appropriate tracks. Reformers hoped that a more diverse schooling experience would be more attractive to the wide range of new students and thus solve or at least reduce the problems of dropouts and "retardation."

Curricular differentiation was also a product of a debunking of an older model of learning known as mental discipline. The mental discipline movement assumed that training students in one academic subject with sufficient discipline would develop their reasoning powers, judgment, and logic in such a way that it would be broadly useful. Otherwise pedantic topics like Latin were, because of their difficulty, assumed to be especially useful for the development of mental powers. But a series of psychological experiments by Edward L. Thorndike cast doubt on this theory of transference. Thorndike found, for example, that intensive training on estimating the area of a rectangle did not produce significant gains in the ability to estimate the area of similar shapes of the same size. The mind that Thorndike envisioned, on the basis of his experiments, was less a major muscle that needed to be exercised than a complex machine with thousands of separate functions. For educational reformers like Bobbitt, Thorndike's work suggested that a common academic curriculum was likely to be of little use to that vast majority of students who were not planning to attend college; rather, they should be trained in the specific subjects that they were likely to encounter later in life.[18]

Further impetus for social sorting came out of the emerging IQ movement. Alfred Binet, a Frenchman, had devised the first intelligence tests in 1905, but they came to be used widely in US schools only after the army popularized IQ tests to sort recruits for World War I. Many of the psychologists who were involved in devising and administering the tests in the army became leaders of the intelligence testing movement and eagerly spread their gospel to the schools. For superintendents and principals, the IQ tests became an invaluable scientific tool for assigning students to an appropriate (i.e., efficient) kind of curriculum. While performance on these tests was highly predicted by the family background and immigration status of students, the tests were seen as tools that could identify precocious poor and immigrant children and assure that they were being given a sufficiently rigorous education. In turn, the bell-shaped distribution of ability that these tests showed was used as evidence that schooling should be tracked. While IQ itself was not thought to be amenable to change, a proper course of schooling should be differentiated, so that high-ability students would be challenged and low-ability students would not be discouraged.[19]

Curricular reformer David Snedden, the commissioner of education in Massachusetts beginning in 1912, brought together these various intellectual strands into a tracked, differentiated system of education that could be implemented in the schools. Snedden believed deeply in the importance of a differentiated curriculum that could be used to adapt students to their future pathways. Snedden felt that by junior high school, "differences of abilities, of extra-school conditions and prospects will acutely manifest themselves, forcing us to differentiate curricula in more ways, probably, than are as yet suspected." A curriculum would be designed as strands organized around "adult life performance practices," such as becoming a farmer, a street motorman, or a homemaker. Studies at the time revealed wide acceptance of curricular differentiation—one found that 15 different curricula existed in secondary schools in Newton, Massachusetts, and 18 different curricula in Los Angeles in 1926.[20]

The landmark commission report of that period, the 1918 National Education Association's "Cardinal Principles of Secondary Education," encapsulates the thinking that inspired the movement toward curricular differentiation. The report identified three reasons to move away from an academic curriculum for all: the schools needed to respond to growing industrialization by preparing students for the workplace; high school enrollments had become larger and more diverse; and advances in educational science suggested the importance of "applying knowledge to the activities of life, rather than primarily in terms of the demands of any subject as a logically organized science." The Cardinal Report then identified the major objectives of secondary education as "1. Health. 2. Command of fundamental processes. 3. Worthy home membership. 4. Vocation. 5. Citizenship. 6. Worthy use of leisure. 7. Ethical character."[21] In each of these dimensions, with the possible exception of the second, the goal was to use the high school to inculcate the skills and values students would need to fit into a changing society, more specifically into their future occupational roles.

In sum, despite the many organizational similarities between the efficiency reforms and those of the modern period, the more recent reforms have a spectacularly utopian vision of what schools should accomplish—No Child Left Behind's stated requirement is that *all* students should be proficient to a high standard by 2014—whereas the social efficiency reformers had a much more conservative view of schooling's possibilities. For the efficiency reformers, schooling was intended to fit students to their future occupations, a goal that was seen as self-consciously functional in its implications. The modern movement, then, embraces the basic (and conservative) organizational and motivational model of the social efficiency reformers but ties it to a more liberal set of assumptions about the environmental malleability of students' abilities and the responsibility of schools to push all students toward a high standard.[22]

## The Politics of Efficiency Reforms

### Critics out of Step with the Times

The reformers faced significant opposition on both political and intellectual grounds. In their goals of "removing schools from politics" and centralizing authority in city elites, they not surprisingly faced opposition from the local wards, which were losing power in the centralizing wars. These divisions between city elites and local communities often mirrored divides between classes and between WASPs and immigrant Catholics; the less powerful groups in these disputes were not impressed by the claims of the "professionals" to be removing school administration from politics.[23] William Taggert,

a prominent opponent of the reforms, argued that "this bawling and whin-
ing about the 'degradation' and 'inefficiency' of our schools" comes mostly
"from the old maids in the Civic Club, from a handful of educational cranks,
from the University Clique which is anxious to boss the whole school system,
and from newspapers which are anxious to please powerful advertisers." In
Taggert's view, the movement was intended to replace the common sense of
the working man with theories of the elite: "The real object is an effort of the
so-called status people, who have no faith in the system of boilermakers, car-
penters, painters—in short the bone and sinew, as well as the good common
sense element to be found among our mechanics as well as businessman in all
our wards—to take a hand in the management of our public schools."[24] As the
battles raged, city by city, to consolidate school boards in the hands of business and political elites, opposition from teachers, labor unions, and other
local constituencies was significant and sometimes victorious.[25]

The related desires of reformers, particularly school boards and superintendents, to standardize, measure, and direct the work of teachers and
students through systems of testing and accountability also received political and intellectual criticism. Teachers, for reasons both self-interested and
philosophical, resented their loss of autonomy, the influence of outsiders
in criticizing and rating their work, and the imposition of a factory model
onto the process of learning. The *American Teacher*, the official journal of the
American Federation of Teachers, printed the following message on its front
page in March 1916: "If efficiency means the demoralization of the school
system; dollars saved and human materials squandered; discontent, drudgery
and disillusion—we'll have none of it!" As one articulate teacher opposing
the reforms put it in a 1912 issue of *American Teacher*, the efficiency reforms
represented the commercialization of education, the introduction of a business logic into a sphere in which it did not apply:

> By this I do not mean that the management of schools is motivated by
> an itch for profit.... I mean merely that our educators have yielded to
> the temper of their surroundings.... We have yielded to the arrogance
> of "big business men" and have accepted their criteria of efficiency at
> their own valuation, without question. We have consented to measure
> the results of educational efforts in terms of price and product—the
> terms that prevail in the factory and the department store. But edu-
> cation, since it deals in the first place with organisms, and in the sec-
> ond place with individualities, is not analogous to a standardizable
> manufacturing process. Education must measure its efficiency not in

terms of so many promotions per dollars of expenditure, nor even in terms of so many student-hours per dollar of salary; it must measure its efficiency in terms of increased humanism, increased power to do, increased power to appreciate.[26]

From the eyes of many teachers, then as today, an increased focus on quantification of results and accountability had the potential not only to place blame directly on them but also to narrow the purposes of schooling to what was measurable and neglect education's less quantifiable aspects.

This more intellectual set of criticisms reflected the conception of schooling preferred by what Tyack calls the "pedagogical progressives" and educational historian Herbert Kliebard calls the "developmentalists." These are the forerunners of what we recognize today as progressive education: led by John Dewey and G. Stanley Hall and guided by Rousseau and other Romantics, the developmentalists proceeded from the assumption that education should build outward from children's interests and aid in their growth and development. Although often caricatured as lacking entirely in adult direction and belief in content knowledge (particularly in the 1960s Summerhill version), progressive education as envisioned by Dewey was a process of adults guiding children from their initial interests along a path of development toward a body of knowledge. Progressive educators emphatically rejected the input-output model of education proposed by the efficiency reformers in favor of a model that emphasized growth of children achieved through the active agency of both teachers and students; they were opposed to what they accurately perceived as a behavioral model of systemic improvement.

Finally, the doctrine of a differentiated curriculum that would fit students' probable final occupational destinations drew a wide range of criticism. Liberals, like Walter Lippmann in the *New Republic*, opposed using tests for sorting, both because they were limited and flawed as measurement tools and because they would create a perverse fatalism among educators, who "will stop when they have classified and forget that their duty is to educate."[27] Humanists, who preferred a college curriculum of Greek and Latin for all, were critical of what they saw as the diminishing standards of what it meant to be educated. Unions often opposed the differentiated curriculum, arguing that the children of their members were being assigned to lesser tracks of education than those with greater means. While some progressive educators supported a differentiated curriculum as a way of breaking down an academic regimen that they thought had a stultifying view of learning, others, like Dewey, opposed the prevailing view that education should serve as a means for economic placement. He argued instead that education was an important end in itself: "Who can reckon up the loss of moral power that arises from the constant impression that nothing is worth doing in itself, but only as a preparation for something else, which in turn is only a getting ready for some serious end beyond?"[28] In even broader terms, those with a broadly social progressive bent, Dewey among them, opposed the inherent conservatism of training students for the occupational positions that awaited them and instead argued that schools should act as instruments of social reform.

Despite this array of criticisms and critics, the reformers were largely successful in implementing their reforms. While the centralizers were not always successful in consolidating school boards, on average they were able to reduce the size of the boards and increase their influence over them.[29] Even more successful than their battle for political control was their ability to set the intellectual direction for school administration. Looking back in 1930 at the past quarter century of reforms, George Strayer of Teachers College saw a steady expansion of the principles of scientific management: while in 1900 a "relatively powerful and able group" of administrators had been skeptical of the role of science in education, by 1930, as Tyack paraphrases Strayer, "almost all influential schoolmen had become converts."[30] In short, as Wayne Urban and Jennings Wagoner Jr. put it, "the pedagogical progressives lost out to the administrative progressives."[31] To put it another way, it was the first instance of what Ellen Lagemann describes as the running story of school reform in the 20th century, a contest that "Edward L. Thorndike won and John Dewey lost."[32] The question is why. Why were the administrative progressives triumphant despite the opposition of an array of influential critics, political constituencies and interest groups, including perhaps America's leading educational theorist and the vast majority of the people who would be implementing the reforms?

## A Powerful Elite?

The simplest explanation is to argue that it was an unfair fight, with many of those who had the greatest social, political, and financial resources arrayed on the winning side. There is certainly truth to this, as it is indisputable that the reformers stemmed disproportionately from the upper middle class. Tyack considers four cases (New York, Philadelphia, St. Louis, and San Francisco) of school centralization between 1896 and 1920 and finds that "in each case, the proponents of reforms were members of highly educated civic elites who believed that structural reforms were necessary to create efficient, rational and 'non-political' school bureaucracies."[33] In Philadelphia more than 75 percent of the organizations active for the reformers were listed in either the Philadelphia Blue Book or the Social Register; in New York, 92 of the Committee of 100, which sponsored the reforms, were in the Social Register.[34] Whether their motivations were altruistic or stemmed at least in part from a desire to retain their social status in a rapidly changing society, the reformers comprised many of the most powerful actors—businessmen, foundation officers, and members of the political elite—in these cities.

At the same time, the weakness of an elite reform movement in a democratic society is that it needs votes, and these votes cannot be found solely among its membership. Decisions about abolishing ward boards, for example, had to be made by political bodies that were accountable to voters. To be sure, reformers sought to change venues in order to find the ones most favorable to their intentions. For example, Tyack recounts that in St. Louis, reformers found allies in the Democratic-controlled state legislature, which was eager to reduce the power of the St. Louis Republican city machine. But even so, the people making the final decisions, be they mayors (New York), state legislatures (St. Louis and Philadelphia), or the electorate by ballot (San Francisco), ultimately either were or had to report to the voters in their cities and states. And unlike the kind of iron triangle special-interest politics that often prevails in areas of policy that are largely hidden from public view,[35] the battles to consolidate control over the schools were highly visible and fiercely contested by the ward locals who would lose power under the proposed new arrangements. As a result, *power* had to be complemented by *persuasion*, as it was up to the reformers to convince the broader public of the need for the changes that they recommended.

A second limitation of an approach that emphasizes the power of the elite reformers is that many of the key actors were in universities, outside the direct orbit of the influence of the city elites. The models of social efficiency in educational administration that proliferated so widely were disseminated, not by the city reformers, but by giants in the field of educational administration—Cubberley, Strayer, Bobbitt—who trained many superintendents in their emerging educational administration programs. Of course, they were elites too, but they functioned in an academic world with an academic value system; understanding why they did what they did is in large part a matter of understanding the rules that governed that world.[36] Any explanation that sees the efficiency reforms as simply a corporate power grab of the schooling process has to contend with the fact that many of the leading figures were in universities and hence not as clearly subject to material incentives. A power approach must be complemented by an institutional account that explains why scientific efficiency models came to prevail in educational administration programs.

More fundamentally, a power-centered explanation is limited because it does not explain why the reformers pushed for the models that they did. If questions of persuasion are largely about the strategic value of ideas—how some ideas are more able than others to win the day—then questions about goal setting are about the constitutive purpose of ideas. Constitutive ideas are ideas that become part of actors' identities; in this case, there is no reason to think that both the city reformers and the university professors did not believe in the values of efficiency and science they consistently espoused. For the city reformers, in particular, to advocate a model of greater executive power to the superintendents lessened their direct hold over schooling decisions; it is hard to see this position as reflecting anything but a belief in the efficiency of the executive manager model. In the broadest sense, then, explaining the success of the reforms is a matter of understanding not only why these reforms were chosen over potential alternatives but why the reformers chose to embrace this approach in the first place.

## Paradigms Create Politics: Ideas and the Efficiency Movement

As would be true in later rounds as well, the way in which the problem of schooling was conceived had a significant impact on the events that followed. The experts' efforts at scientific, rational reform were greatly aided by news media that defined the problems of the schools as stemming from corruption, inefficiency, and parochial control. Much as reformers today seize upon international comparisons or national commission reports as evidence of the need for reform, early reformers drew upon the work of muckraking journalists, who exposed the worst aspects of the existing system. The way the problem was defined delimited the terms of the debate, motivated new actors to join in the crusade to reform schools, built public support behind the reforms, and marginalized critics whose views were not in step with the dominant narrative.

### *Muckrakers Define the Problem*

The initial spark for criticism of the schools came in Joseph Mayer Rice's exposé of school practices in 1892. Rice, a doctor by training, traveled to schools in 36 cities over the course of six months and published a nine-part series in *The Forum* criticizing the dullness of recitation as a method of learning and the failure of superintendents to introduce more effective pedagogical methods to the classroom. Rice reserved much of his outrage for teachers, whom he saw mainly as incompetents who had gained their positions through networks, not merit. To these criticisms he added (in a second set of articles published the following year) a comparative research method that sought to explain why third-grade reading and math were taught more effectively in some schools than in others. In the two decades that followed, many of the themes that Rice had initially championed were repeated by other muckrakers, and the idea that the schools were inefficient and corrupt was widely repeated in low-priced, popular magazines, whose combined circulation by 1905 was 5.5 million.[37]

In education reform, as in other fields, the role that the muckrakers played in defining the problem cannot be underestimated. Richard Hofstadter has argued that "to an extraordinary degree the work of the Progressive movement rested upon its journalism."[38] Tyack's work on centralizing reforms in four cities reaches the following conclusions about the patterns of reform: "Like reforms in public health, city government or police and welfare work, urban educational reform followed a familiar pattern of muckrakers' exposure of suffering, corruption, or inefficiency; the formation of alliances of leading citizens and professional experts who proposed structural innovations; and a subsequent campaign for 'non-political' and rational reorganization of services."[39] This is the constitutive role of ideas—defining the goals that motivate a movement.

Having inspired the initial movement for reform, the muckrakers also played an important role in shifting the balance on the playing field toward the reformers. As Tyack writes, "Most of the educational muckrakers—like Rice, Adele Marie Shaw and other writers for popular magazines—agreed that the source of the evils they described was corruption and lack of expertise running the schools, thereby accepting the centralizers' definition of the problem."[40] There was a reciprocal relationship here, in that the muckrakers, who had initially defined the problem, were now confirming the reformers' analysis. Moreover, the reformers used the muckrakers strategically to build support for their position. In the legislative fight over centralization in New York, for example, a senator cited Joseph Rice's indictment of the school system to demonstrate that the results "were far below the standard in other cities; that the methods employed in the classroom were nothing short of 'dehumanizing'; that the whole system was not only antiquated but actually pernicious."[41] Sometimes the muckrakers directly advocated for change in legislation, as when Jacob Riis wrote to New York Mayor Strong urging him to sign the centralization bill. Reformers also used to their advantage emerging information such as Ayres's study of "retardation" in the schools and the dismaying results of army IQ tests.[42] The combination of the muckrakers' stories of corruption and inefficiency and the reformers' proposals for scientific management and efficiency proved a potent force.[43]

In a climate of skepticism about educators' efficient use of tax dollars, outsiders like political and foundation elites gained legitimacy to speak, while those who defended the status quo were perceived as self-interested obstructionists. As we will see, similar patterns exist today. Despite their financial and political resources, teachers unions have been undermined by their lack of legitimacy. Educators in the Progressive period, facing a hostile climate, often chose to backpedal, inviting school surveys or creating their own measures of efficiency before these were demanded externally.[44] Callahan describes the situation thus: "Although some educators undoubtedly believed that the education of children would be improved through the introduction of the various efficiency measures, the primary motivation for adoption by administrators was self-defense."[45] Problem definitions are important not only as constitutive and strategic factors, as described above, but also as regulative forces that determine who can speak legitimately and arbitrate what kinds of ideas are likely to be acceptable. In a climate that one critic of the movement described as "an age of efficiency," pragmatic critics sought more to stem the tide than reverse it.

Finally, the efficiency reformers could also buttress their case by drawing upon the critique of the academic curriculum by the pedagogical progressives, who were well represented in the National Education Association and in the public debates over the schools. Even if not in favor of a growing bureaucracy and administration, they had criticized the existing system as stultifying and not alive to children's interests.[46] Some early leading lights of pedagogical progressivism, such as G. Stanley Hall, supported the idea of curricular differentiation on the grounds that it would reduce the barrier between school and society and better integrate the practical and the abstract. Dewey, although opposed to many of the goals of the administrative progressives, supported the idea that the curriculum should be changed to become more real to the child, eliminating recitation as a method of teaching and using concrete activities to initially engage children's interests. The wider public did not always appreciate this mixed position. As Herbert Kliebard summarizes it: "If anything, Dewey's vague and loosely defined identification as an educational reformer seeking to infuse active occupations into what had become a passive, almost archaic, curriculum, probably served to associate him in the popular mind with the very position he tried to oppose."[47] Progressives like Dewey and Hall were leading educational theorists at the time, with a prominent voice in public debate; to the degree that the efficiency reformers were able to claim the pedagogical progressives' ideas as their own, they strengthened their rhetorical position.

### Drawing on Higher-Status Logics; Finding Solutions That Fit

Having successfully defined the problem as inefficiency and the need to standardize practices across a variety of units, reformers, not surprisingly, were able to enact solutions that emphasized greater centralization and managerial control. Not only did the solution fit the problem; it was buttressed by sources of authority widely accepted at the time. For example, testing in schools drew upon the emerging authority of psychological science as a way of fairly and efficiently distributing an increasingly heterogeneous group of students.[48] The model of school accountability derived much of its traction because it drew upon the widely acclaimed Taylor model and other models of corporate efficiency. The greater status and legitimacy of other fields made them appealing authorities for a field that had been roundly attacked and was seeking to find its way. That the reforms claimed the mantle of objective fact (as encompassed in the critical reports on the schools) and often were sponsored by prominent foundations or by well-regarded academics gave even greater credence to those advocating the reforms.

In addition to fitting the prevailing problem definition and drawing upon powerful sources of authority, the administrative model of schooling also offered organizational advantages for dealing with the rapidly growing school population.[49] Institutionally oriented scholars have emphasized the success of solutions that are administratively feasible; in this case, the expanding complexity and diversity of the school population favored the adoption of a model that rationalized the system governing these students.[50] Particularly from the point of view of the superintendent, the sheer size of the system necessitated some way to monitor the performance of various schools and the teachers within them. In turn, as superintendents created expanding layers of administrators and other professionals to attend to the various needs of the student body, these groups formed professional societies to advocate for their interests.

Critics did not offer comparably workable proposals. As is often true in politics, it is difficult to oppose a set of reforms unless you have a more compelling alternative, and the critics were short on alternatives that both fit the prevailing problem definition and were organizationally feasible.

The pedagogical progressives agreed with one of the central critiques of the administrative progressives: that the schools were largely stultifying places that needed to be made more child-friendly. Their proposed solution, however, was not to add layers of administration, but rather to reform the pedagogy of individual schools. This meant that key pedagogical progressives were not authors of proposals that would govern systems of schools; rather, they focused in their writings (e.g., Dewey's *Schools of To-morrow*)[51] and by example on how to create individual schools to embody their vision of schooling. Politically, however, this school-by-school approach did not offer the comprehensive reform that the perceived underperformance of schools and the rapid growth of the school population demanded. While Dewey spoke out critically against the overuse of testing as a sorting device and against the need for a larger layer of central administration, neither he nor other pedagogical progressives offered a comprehensive alternative to address the perceived crisis of the entire school system.

Teachers and ward locals had what would have been a technically feasible proposal—leave the current system alone! But, as detailed above, they were undermined by a prevailing problem definition that deemed local educators and local school boards largely underperforming, if not downright incompetent or corrupt. Defenders of the school system sought to turn the debate by asking how the university administrators who were purveying the reforms would like it if their college students were measured and their performance evaluated on the basis of student learning.[52] These charges did not stick, however, because the universities were not broadly seen as underperforming institutions. Then, as now, the relatively low status of the teaching profession and its lack of clear internal standards made it an easy target for outside reformers promising to eliminate waste, root out incompetence, and improve performance.

## *The Climate of the Times*

The broader intellectual and political climate of the times was also hospitable to the administrative model of schooling. During the Progressive period, a conservative climate emphasizing social order and the business value of efficiency dominated both rhetoric and action. In the theoretical terms proposed above, this climate played a constitutive role in orienting reformers to focus on problems of inefficiency and to see Taylorism as the solution; simultaneously it played a regulative role in limiting alternative definitions of the problem offered by critics.

An administrative model of schooling, particularly the tracked and differentiated curriculum, provided a way of creating social order at a moment when growing industrialization and urbanization were disrupting long-held patterns of community life. Reformers embraced sociological theories, such as Edward Ross's *Social Control*, which emphasized the school as a beacon of authority and order at a moment when such other long-standing sources of authority as the family, church, and community were declining in significance. As Kliebard has written, "Of the varied and sometimes frenetic responses to industrialism and to the consequent transformation of American social institutions, there was one that emerged clearly dominant both as a social ideal and as an educational doctrine. It was social efficiency, that, for most people, held out the promise of social stability in the face of cries for massive social change, and that doctrine claimed the now potent backing of science in order to ensure it."[53]

In such a climate, those, like Dewey, who saw schools as potential sources of social reform, were vastly out of step with a majority that wasn't demanding social reform, much less looking to the schools to incubate it. The teens and twenties were simply not fertile years for these "social reconstructionists," who made much more headway in the 1930s, when a book like George Counts's *Dare the School Build a New Social Order?* was published to widespread critical acclaim.[54] (That this critical acclaim did not translate to substantial school-level change is a story for another day about the institutional inertia of a newly bureaucratized school system.)[55] Still, by the 1930s the demands for greater efficiency in the school system had died down considerably, and the penchant for importing business models of reform was, not surprisingly, greatly reduced. Nevertheless, the earlier reformers had built a form of social organization of schools that would become the foundation for subsequent reforms.

### *Establishing a New Discipline: Science, Status, Gender, and the University Politics of Education*

While the resonance of the efficiency model in the broader culture was important, no account would be complete without an explanation of how this conception of educational administration came to be favored within a university context. City reformers were essentially parroting the ideas put forward by leading figures of educational administration and through their reforms empowering superintendents as managers; they were also giving greater power to the people trained by these programs of educational administration. Institutional theorists often stress the importance of the goals, norms, and organizational imperatives faced by state actors;[56] similar forces were important here, although in this case the key institutions were university education departments, not state bureaucracies.

At the turn of the century, the field of education was only just emerging as a university subject, usually housed as a subdiscipline within philosophy departments. Faculty within many of the top-flight universities considered the study of education not worthy of the title of either art or science and were particularly skeptical that the largely female-dominated field of teaching was worthy of the professional training accorded to the male-dominated fields of law, medicine, and engineering. As Harvard, President Charles Eliot said, speaking for the Harvard faculty, "The faculty in common with most teachers in England and the United States feel but slight interest or confidence in what is usually called pedagogy." Similar attitudes were found at Stanford, where the Department of Education survived only due to its support from Stanford President David Starr Jordan; Jordan told Cubberley upon his arrival in 1898 that, if the decision had been left to the faculty, the department would have been abolished entirely. At Columbia, President Seth Low was able to persuade the trustees to bring Teachers College within the umbrella of the university, but as Dean of Teachers College James Earl Russell put it, not "as a professional school on par with the others... [but] as the stepchild of the University Department of Philosophy and Education."[57]

Facing this climate of skepticism, such deans and department chairs of education as Cubberley (at Stanford), Russell (at Columbia), and Hubbard Judd (at Chicago) moved to shift the study of education away from its diffuse humanistic focus and toward a more practical and specialized view of educational administration grounded in emerging findings from science. At Teachers College, Russell became "one of the foremost advocates for a professional science of education. He believed that professional knowledge could enhance teaching, an improvement which would, in turn, foster a more generous attitude toward education among both academics and the public at large."[58] To be sure, educational science at the time was extremely thin and in even lower repute than it is today; it would be more accurate to say that administrators were seeking to create such a field and model it after other, more prestigious harder science fields than it would be to say that they drew upon this authority to establish their goals. Education schools at the turn of the century rapidly founded journals and monograph series in an effort to ape what other departments were doing to ensure the rigors of their discipline. The *School Review*, Chicago's journal on secondary education, was intended by Judd to establish the scientific nature of education study and reverse the perception, as Judd succinctly summed it up, that "in academic circles and high school circles it is eminently respectable to be a student of the lowest forms of animal life and a very doubtful distinction to be a student of education."[59]

At Columbia, Thorndike proved extremely attractive to Russell, as Thorndike was the country's leading quantitative behavioral psychologist and was quickly converting a formerly soft field into a harder form of science. While Thorndike himself wanted to create distance between the "academic" work of psychologists and the "applied" science of educational administration, his influence was expanded enormously through his teaching of many Teachers College graduates, and Teachers College in turn benefited greatly from his associated prestige. At Chicago, Herbert Judd sought to professionalize the study of education by eliminating all undergraduate programs and creating a new course of study for all students in research and research training.[60] Judd also recruited many of the men who were prominent in the scientific study of education, including John Franklin Bobbitt, and dropped the courses of figures like George Herbert Mead who advocated a more philosophical approach to education.[61] In shifting away from the generalist, humanistic approach that had dominated education in the past and incorporating findings emerging from science, these administrators were simultaneously accommodating themselves to university-wide changes that favored increasing specialization of research and seeking to shift their shaky discipline and the profession it taught onto the seemingly more objective, rigorous, and less conflict-laden field of science.

In addition to tying their programs to emerging findings in psychology, these departments also developed their own models of scientific administration, which were based on an early version of applied organizational sociology. The increasing enrollments of schools and the increasing power of the superintendent provided an opportunity for education departments to train a new class of professionals. This required its own science, and the departments were eager to oblige. At Teachers College, for example, the number of courses in educational administration increased from 4 offerings in 1911/12 to 29 courses by 1929.[62] At Chicago in 1912/13, there were 2 courses in educational administration; by 1917/18, there were 15 courses offered, including 3 taught by Bobbitt himself. Not only were more courses being offered in educational administration, but more degrees were being awarded in this increasingly critical field. In 1909/10, 73 graduate degrees were conferred at Teachers College, with 13 in the category of administration and supervision; by 1923/24 there were 939 graduate degrees, with 390 in administration and supervision.[63] Students completed degrees in ever more applied topics of school administration. An analysis of 290 doctoral theses in administration between 1910 and 1933 found that a plurality were in fiscal administration (55), followed by business administration (34), pupil personnel (29), personnel management (29), legal provisions (24), and buildings and equipment (19).[64] While critics disparaged this technical emphasis as not befitting academic training, these objections were overwhelmed by an appetite for developing a detailed science of administration, which fit within a university context that was demanding ever more specialized original research.

The training of administrators also provided an opportunity for education departments to train a new class of male professionals whose role was widely being discussed as equivalent to what today would be called a CEO. This offered a way for education departments to see themselves more on a par with professions like medicine, law, and engineering and eliminate the stigma that came with training a largely feminized profession. As Cubberley described it in his classic textbook, *Public School Administration*:

> School supervision represents a new profession, and one which in time will play a very important part in the development of American life. In pecuniary, social, professional and personal rewards it ranks with the other learned professions, while the call for city school superintendents of the right type is today greater than the call for lawyers, doctors or ministers. The opportunities offered in this new profession to men of strong character, broad sympathies, high purposes, fine culture, courage, exact training and executive skills...are today not excelled in any of the professions, learned or otherwise.[65]

Cubberley continued by suggesting that superintendents should be expected to complete college and one year of graduate school, and many should continue to the PhD, while teachers needed only a high school education and a two-year training program. For a university discipline seeking to gain its footing, developing a science of school administration that required extensive training and that would be overseen by a largely male administrative corps provided a way for education departments and schools to claim closer equivalence with higher-status fields like medicine and law.[66]

In so doing, they embraced a hierarchical and differentiated model of research, administration, and implementation, a model that provided much of the template for the accountability movement. A largely quantitative and statistical research program would be carried out by the scientists in the university; they would convey it to the highly trained school administrators, who would implement it, with teachers, the final links in the chain, at the bottom of the totem pole. As Thorndike himself encapsulates this hierarchical approach in his 1906 text *The Principles of Teaching*: "It is the problem of the higher authorities of the schools to decide what the school shall try to achieve and to arrange plans for schools' work which will attain the desired ends. Having decided what changes are to be made they entrust to the teachers the work of making them."[67] It is not surprising that, with this template in mind, what emerged was a program of scientific efficiency that allowed superintendents to supervise, evaluate, and compare the work of different teachers and schools, with the goal of using comparative data and research to establish best practices for improving performance and the efficiency of administration.

Again, Dewey provided an alternative model of the organization of schooling and research, and the failure of his model reveals the strength of institutional imperatives pulling in the opposite direction. In Dewey's famous laboratory school, founded while he was at the University of Chicago in the period before Judd became chair, the school itself served as a primary opportunity for research. In Dewey's words, a lab school should bear "the relation to work in pedagogy that a laboratory bears to biology, physics or chemistry." Research, in Dewey's view, should be carried out in schools; this contrasts with Thorndike's view that time spent in schools was largely a "bore."[68] Further, Dewey did not seek to partition the role of researcher and teacher; he argued instead that both were interested in the same subject—improving learning. Rather than have "one expert dictating educational methods and subject-matter to a body of passive, recipient teachers," Dewey advocated "the adoption of intellectual initiative, discussion, and decision throughout the entire school corps."[69]

We can see in Dewey's ideas an early form of what it might look like to build a profession based on practical knowledge: teachers and researchers working alongside one another to produce new knowledge, knowledge organized in part around practical questions coming from the field rather than entirely out of the heads of university researchers; a healthy and interdependent relationship between basic and applied knowledge; and most of all, teachers treated as people capable of taking "intellectual initiative" and organizing their own work rather than as implementers of the ideas of others.

While Dewey's ideas were widely discussed, his model of research as a function to be shared between researchers and schoolteachers was rejected by university education departments, which were seeking to elevate themselves precisely by distancing themselves from teachers. As Ellen Lagemann puts it, "His position was very much at odds with the hierarchy then developing among educational institutions, a hierarchy in which mostly male university scholars of education would generate the knowledge needed by mostly male school administrators, who would, in turn, be responsible for dictating and supervising the instructional methods to be used by teachers in schools, especially the mostly female teachers involved at the elementary levels."[70]

## Conclusion

The Progressive Era efficiency reforms were a remarkably successful early attempt to impose accountability on schooling. Often simplistically remembered as a period most notable for the shift in power from politicians to "educators," a less noticed aspect of the reforms was that they shifted power *among* educators—away from classroom teachers and toward the administrators who supervised them. By centralizing the control of schooling in the powerful figure of the superintendent, the reformers sought to take a diverse, parochial system and institute measures of standardization, using accountability and testing as the primary means of supervisory control. Superintendents drew upon prevailing Taylorist models to carefully cost out the value of various school subjects (financial accountability) and utilized emerging standardized tests to evaluate teacher and school performance. The efficiency reforms spread rapidly, through advocacy efforts by coalitions of professional reformers, urban superintendents, and college education professors, which often used state or locally commissioned school surveys as the vehicles for outsiders to recommend change. By 1921, educational sociologists had reported that scales and tests were ubiquitous in "all but unprogressive schools." Over the course of one generation, the efficiency reformers had succeeded in turning a diverse set of one-room schoolhouses into a system overseen by a centralized set of superintendents, with the test as the primary vehicle for teacher and school accountability. In so doing, the reformers created both the structure of the system and the cultural template that would underpin future attempts at even more ambitious rationalization.

## 4

# The Forgotten Standards Movement: The Coleman Report, the Defense Department, and a Nascent Push for Educational Accountability

THE LATE 1960S and early 1970s are remembered for many things, but educational accountability is not foremost among them. A time when the nation was ripped asunder by fights over Vietnam, when women burned bras, and when African Americans took to the streets seemed hardly a propitious moment for an educational movement emphasizing technocratic rationality to come to the forefront. Yet although overshadowed in the educational arena by conflicts over desegregation, community control, free schools, and open classrooms, a relatively quiet movement led primarily by state bureaucrats did in fact initiate the beginnings of an educational accountability movement. Between 1963 and 1974, no fewer than 73 laws were passed seeking to create standards or utilize a variety of scientific management techniques to improve schooling.

These efforts at rationalization in some ways followed the same trajectory as the efficiency reforms five decades earlier and the standards movement to follow two decades later. First came the invocation of a crisis, this time born of rising demands for greater equity and increasing dissatisfaction with the quality of the schools. Second, into this void stepped the new logic of rationalizing reform, this time drawn from a set of techniques pioneered by the Rand Corporation and popularized by the Department of Defense, which promised a new approach to defining objectives, measuring goals, and aligning available resources. And third, humanists and educators were once again the primary opponents of the reform, objecting to the quantification of schooling and the limited view of educational improvement that underlay the rationalizing reform. In all of these respects, the now almost forgotten accountability efforts of the 1960s and 1970s resembled the other two accountability movements of the 20th century.

However, the other two movements mobilized a broad range of elites behind their reforms, whereas in this case real political support remained thin. The narrow base of support kept the programs from spreading or being implemented more widely; this effort never gained the kind of power or traction that the earlier and later ones did. But at the same time it was critical in creating the template of state standards, assessments, and accountability that became the framework we use today. In a number of states, the assessments created in this era became the foundation of the accountability system when the issue was revisited in the 1980s and 1990s. The nascent accountability efforts of the 1960s and 1970s created the template for modern standards-based reform and provided the bridge from the district-level rationalization of the Progressive Era to the state and federal accountability movements of the contemporary period.

## Defining the Problem: Equity and Efficiency, Inputs and Outputs

American schools have been under constant assault from external critics since the end of World War II. The period from the 1950s through the 1970s had three major but overlapping crises: the crisis of *standards* (1950s), the crisis of *equity* (1960s), and the crisis of *efficiency* (1970s). The first strand of criticism emerged during the 1950s, when best sellers such as Arthur Bestor's *Educational Wastelands: The Retreat from Learning in Our Public Schools* (1953) and Rudolph Flesch's *Why Johnny Can't Read* (1955) bemoaned the excesses of pedagogically progressive education and urged a return to phonics, standards, and other basics. The launching of *Sputnik* in 1958 seemed to validate these critics and spurred an increased emphasis on math and science education. Meanwhile, civil rights advocates, beginning with *Brown v. Board of Education* and continuing through the civil rights movements of the 1960s, were pointing to the ways that schools had traditionally failed to serve minority students. As the 1960s gave way to the 1970s, an increasing dissatisfaction with the performance of public institutions and a worry about rising government expenditures amid tough economic pressures led to greater demands for efficiency in schooling. Cutting across these crises was a rising distrust in existing patterns of professional control; after all, leaving educators in charge had not brought about schools that met standards, created equity, or spent dollars efficiently.

The consequences of these crises spun out in many different directions. Out of the equity movement came a sustained campaign to desegregate the schools and later a corresponding backlash against these efforts. The equity movement also spawned the Elementary and Secondary Education Act (ESEA), Head Start, and other efforts to help disadvantaged students. The attack on professional control produced calls for control of schools to shift from a mostly white teacher and administrator class to a more diverse parent base. Related attacks on failing city bureaucracies led to early experiments with vouchers in education, as critics argued that money should follow the child and not the school. The antiauthoritarian counterculture of the 1960s also had its heyday in schools, as progressive educators sought to create free schools, open classrooms, and other models that aimed to free the child rather than teach her to conform to social expectations. These are the 1960s we remember and read about in the history books—a period in which the existing order was challenged by movements that demanded greater equality for poor and minority students and greater freedom for all students.

These crises, particularly the combination of the equity and efficiency movements, also produced a more centrist definition of the problem, a definition amenable to the most staid practices of top-down reform. A key precipitating event was the release of the Coleman Report (named after its principal author, sociologist James Coleman) in 1966. Commissioned by the US Office of Education in accordance with the Civil Rights Act of 1964, the study was expected to show that differences in resources available to minority students would explain the differences in outcomes between them and more advantaged students. Instead, the report found that differences in outcomes were more attributable to differences in family background and peer composition than to school resources per se. The study has been called the "most significant educational study of the 20th century"[1], and its impact on policy thinking continues to be felt. The significance of the report, as Coleman himself noted in an essay five years after its release, is that it "has had its major impact in *shifting* policy attention from its traditional focus on comparison of inputs (the traditional measure of school quality used by school administrators...) to a focus on output, and the effectiveness of inputs for bringing about change in output" (emphasis in original).[2] The accountability movement that would emerge in the years that followed took this disjuncture as its raison d'être, seeking to ensure that school spending would efficiently lead to better outputs.

The passage of a host of Great Society efforts accelerated the shift from inputs to outputs. Robert Kennedy, in deliberations over Title I in ESEA, asked whether it would be possible to evaluate whether it was achieving its intended outcomes:

> Obviously I am completely in accord with the objectives of the bill. All I wonder is whether we couldn't give further protections to the child by certain requirements. Now what I ask is whether it would be possible to have some kind of testing system at the end of a year or 2 years in which we would see whether the money that had been invested in the school district of New York City, or Denver, Colorado, or Jackson, Mississippi or whatever it might be was coming up with a plan and program that made it worthwhile, and whether the child, in fact, was gaining from the investment of these funds.[3]

Concerns about federal intrusion precluded the possibility of real stakes for students or teachers resulting from such evaluations, but Kennedy's concerns did prefigure the state accountability movements in the years to come.

The early evaluations of a host of Great Society efforts reinforced these concerns, as they seemed to suggest that spending to create programs did not necessarily engender the expected results. These disappointing outcomes, in turn, lent greater credibility and visibility to the Coleman Report. While the report had been largely buried in the Johnson administration, as officials feared it might be used to undermine Great Society efforts, it became the bible of the Nixon White House.* In a 1970 address, Nixon drew heavily on the Coleman Report: "American education is urgently in need of reform," he began. "A good school," Nixon said, used to be measured by a series of inputs, like whether a school plant was kept in good condition or whether class sizes were reasonable. "This was a fair enough definition so long as it was assumed that there was a direct connection between these 'school characteristics' and the actual amount of learning that takes place in a school. Years of educational

---

* A careful study of the politics of the Coleman report suggests that when the report was released in 1966, the Johnson Administration issued a carefully edited summary intended to soft-pedal the report's most provocative findings. Daniel Patrick Moynihan, however, had read the study and invited author James Coleman to write an essay in the *Public Interest* which more straightforwardly laid out the study's core findings. While the Coleman Report was little discussed during the Johnson administration, it became central during the Nixon years, in part because Moynihan was an adviser to Nixon and in part because the report's findings fit with the emerging conservative mood. See Gerald Grant, "The Politics of the Coleman Report" (PhD diss., Harvard University, 1972).

research, culminating in the Equal Opportunity Survey of 1966, have, however, demonstrated this direct relationship does not exist." Citing the limited gains demonstrated by Head Start and Title I, Nixon thus concluded that expenditures needed to be monitored to assure that they achieved outputs and that teachers and administrators should be held accountable for their students' results.[4]

In sum, the combination of the Coleman Report, the failings of the early Great Society efforts to deliver, and the explosion of social and behavioral science engendered by the social reforms of the Kennedy and Johnson administrations created a definition of schooling as a black box sitting between programmatic inputs on the one hand and test score outputs on the other.[5] With this production-function view in place, it was a short road to developing a system of scientific management that would focus on outputs over inputs, with reformers once again seeing standards, assessments, and accountability as the cure to schooling woes.

## An Unlikely Source of an Educational Logic: Rand, the Defense Department, and the Spread of Systems Analysis

The functionalist definition of the problem paved the way for a second set of efforts to rationalize American schooling. Again a managerial logic came to the fore, and again it came from outside the educational field. The progenitor this time was the Department of Defense, which initially adopted the techniques that would come to be associated with rationalizing education.[6]

Many of these tools, particularly systems analysis and planning, programming, and budgeting systems (PPBS), were developed by the Rand Corporation in the 1950s. Seeking to create a "science of war," the heavily mathematical Rand had devised a series of tools to analyze how best to operate rationally in complex situations with high degrees of uncertainty. While an older strain of "operations research" had demonstrated how to make an existing organization more efficient, the Rand researchers developed systems analysis to try to quantify the "expected costs, benefits, and risks of alternative future systems."[7] Similarly, proponents argued that planning, programming, and budgeting systems would inject rationality into the budgeting process; rather than budget simply by incrementally adding to the prior existing budget, leaders were expected to identify objectives, develop plans and programs, and budget accordingly.

These techniques found a champion in Robert McNamara, who in 1961 was not yet the highly controversial overseer of the Vietnam War but was the newly appointed Secretary of Defense. Early in his career, McNamara had been a professor of accounting at the Harvard Business School. During World War II, the Army Air Force unit contracted with Harvard to have its personnel trained in "statistical controls," which led to a job for McNamara with the AAF, helping the force to optimize the efficiency of their operations around the world. At the conclusion of the war, Henry Ford II hired McNamara and nine other "whiz kids" from the AAF statistical unit for the Ford Motor Company, where they were tasked with applying modern statistical and managerial methods to the troubled car manufacturer. As a result, unlike the usual career trajectory within Ford, by which one moved from plant operations up into the corporate hierarchy, McNamara came into Ford near the top, with little practical knowledge or field experience. McNamara's success at Ford, where he rose rapidly and became president, derived largely from using advanced quantitative techniques to revive the automotive giant.

When McNamara became Secretary of Defense in 1961, he brought a similar mind-set to Washington. Two Rand researchers, Charles Hitch and Roland McKean, had just published a book, *The Economics of Defense*, that promised to use economic thinking to rationalize the dilemmas of defense spending.[8] Economics as a discipline focuses on making trade-offs within constraints, and its application to Defense, they argued, would allow for a similar set of utility-maximizing calculations. McNamara read the book and quickly hired Hitch and another Rand researcher, Alain Enthoven, as assistant secretaries within the department. (Enthoven later recalled that when McNamara and Hitch met, "It was love at first sight.")[9] The Rand researchers provided a way to link the analytic techniques McNamara had used at Ford to the Defense Department. As historian David Jardini writes, "Drawing from his experience at Ford, he conceptualized the national defense establishment as a massive and complex production system, characterized by inputs and outputs that could be rationally organized and analyzed so as to achieve optimal efficiency. As was the case at Ford, he saw centralized control in the hands of a very few expert managers to be the most effective way to pursue that efficiency."[10]

At Defense, these logics had two particular virtues from the perspective of McNamara and John F. Kennedy. First, rule by numbers allowed for the assertion of civilian control over the military, as it diminished the role of field expertise and elevated the role of the number crunchers. Second, the commensurating nature of cost-benefit analysis allowed for what were argued to be rational decisions *across* the major branches of the military. Under the previous system, each major branch of the military was given an allocation, and it was then up to the head of that branch to decide how to spend it. With systems analysis and PPBS, proponents argued, McNamara would be able, for the first time, to ask how much different branches were contributing to a common set of stated objectives and allocate funding accordingly. Such systems would bring order to disorder, substitute logical analysis for political bargaining, and create coherence out of fragmentation—or so its sponsors promised. The dream of governance by Enlightenment rationality had never seemed so alluring.

From the perspective of career military officers, however, the system that McNamara was instituting was long on statistics and short on experience and judgment.[11] It was not lost on them that underneath the veneer of objective analysis was a shift in power, away from them and towards McNamara and his number-wielding assistant secretaries. As one wrote in April 1961:

> [T]he youthful McNamara has launched his own direct-action plan to improve efficiency in the Defense Department...with only cursory consultation with the Joint Chiefs of Staff....It does seem a little odd that the nation's top military men, experts in the art of national defense, are given short shrift in deciding vital defense issues destined to have far-reaching effects on the military establishment. In industry, an error in judgment may result in a financial loss. In the Defense Department a mistake can endanger our future freedom.[12]

Prefiguring many of the arguments that would occur as these techniques spread to other arenas of policy, the debate pitted a commensurating logic of quantifiable analysis, which empowered central decision makers, against a diverse set of field experts, who argued that substantive decisions should be made by those who had expertise derived from experience in the domain.[13]

In retrospect, McNamara's faith in rational modeling, though initially supported, proved unable to bear the weight that was placed upon it, with ultimately tragic consequences. McNamara is widely credited with introducing modern management techniques to Ford, shaking up conventional thinking, and greatly improving the fortunes of the slumbering giant. The initial decision to push the Joint Chiefs to justify their spending in light of overall priorities is credited with forcing the military to move away from pet projects and toward a more efficient allocation of overall resources. All to the good. But at the same time, the idea that the vast military apparatus could be somehow reduced to one large cost-benefit equation proved to be a pipe dream. Over time, it became clear both to McNamara and to the military branches he was seeking to rationalize that the models were highly dependent upon exactly what was included and how highly uncertain costs were estimated and, thus, that it was possible for both sides to make the analyses reach conclusions they previously favored. Even more hubristic was the idea that rational modeling could somehow obviate the need for judgment, wisdom, and contextual understanding when it came to questions of war and peace. McNamara's emphasis on "body counts" and "kill ratios" as metrics for whether the United States was winning the war in Vietnam proved to be as ill fated a usage of quantitative data as has been seen in US history. While quantitative analysis had its place, it could not substitute for the kind of political judgment needed to question the domino theory and extricate the country from Vietnam. As David Halberstam famously chronicled in *The Best and the Brightest* and McNamara himself admitted in the 2004 documentary *Fog of War*, the degree of faith that McNamara and the Kennedy and Johnson administrations placed in well-schooled experts who sought to rule by numbers far outstripped what such quantitative analyses could support.[14]

In 1965, however, none of this was yet apparent to Lyndon Baines Johnson, who, enthusiastic about the success of quantitative techniques in the Defense Department, mandated the use of planning, programming, and budgeting systems across the entire federal bureaucracy. Each department was expected to declare its objectives, quantify how its various inputs were contributing toward outputs on those objectives, and then develop its budget accordingly, with the goal that all of the department's operations would then flow directly towards the prespecified objectives. As Daniel Patrick Moynihan put it, PPBS "colonized the federal establishment." Similarly, HUD Undersecretary Robert Wood argued that the goal of PPBS was that "actual data" and the rational "scientific" method would replace "seat-of-pants judgment" and "political intuition" in departments ranging from State to Health, Education and Welfare.[15]

The debates around the expanded use of these scientific methods in the federal bureaucracy prefigured many of the debates about similar efforts to impose rational ordering on the educational sphere. Leaving aside the broad question of whether rule by numbers was desirable, four more specific critiques of the expansion of these techniques emerged. The first was that Defense was a bad model. Systems analysis in Defense had the benefit of many researchers who had been trained at Rand and had a full decade of experience in developing complex models of different scenarios. No equivalent expertise existed in other fields. Relatedly, Defense was a field with exorbitantly high costs and no opportunities for trial and error. In such a field, critics argued, it may have made sense to put a large sum of money into mathematical analysis, because the costs were still small compared with the overall Defense budget and there was no opportunity to try out different scenarios in practice. In fields with lower levels of spending, the cost of analysis was much higher in relation to the overall outlays, and experience provided an alternative to theoretical modeling.

Second, other fields had much more trouble finding common value measures across which different outcomes could be measured and weighed. In theoretical parlance, they had trouble commensurating their ends. As former Assistant Secretary for Health Education and Welfare William Gorham put it in his congressional testimony on the subject:

> Let me hasten to point out that we have not attempted any grandiose cost-benefit analysis designed to reveal whether the total benefits from an additional million dollars spent on health programs would be higher or lower than that from an additional million spent on education or welfare. If I was ever naive enough to think this sort of analysis possible, I no longer am. The benefits of health, education, and welfare programs are diverse and often intangible. They affect different age groups and different regions of the population over different periods of time. No amount of analysis is going to tell us whether the Nation benefits more from sending a slum child to pre-school, providing medical care to an old man or enabling a disabled housewife to resume her normal activities. The "grand decisions"—how much health, how much education, how much welfare, and which groups in the population shall benefit—are questions of value judgments and politics. The analyst cannot make much contribution to their resolution.[16]

While Defense had at least one clear goal (security), it was clear that in the social spheres, the plurality of ends made comparative analysis much more challenging.

A third and related critique of PPBS was that it privileged experts' notions of what was rational and treated politics as an incursion on rational decision making. Critics argued that this view was essentially upside down: experts were there to serve democracy, not vice versa. These critics argued for a more democratic process of planning and decision making, one in which differences in the public's interests and values were a central part of the process. As we will see, this critique paralleled educational debates to come, where the reign of lowest-common-denominator outcomes (test scores in reading and math) would be accused of crowding out broader perspectives about the purposes of education.

Finally, critics pointed out that systems analysis and PPBS were better for making decisions *atop* organizations than for reaching *down* into the field to create changes on the front lines. Choices about which weapons system to invest in, for example, were largely under the control of decision makers in Washington. But choices about how to organize or support the operations of ground troops were much less amenable to top-down control. As Aaron Wildavsky described it:

> The deeper change goes into the bowels of the organization, the more difficult it is to achieve. The more change can be limited to central management, the greater the possibility for carrying it out. The changes introduced in the Defense Department did not, for the most part, require acceptance at the lower levels.... The kinds of problems for which program budgeting was most useful also turned out to be problems that could be dealt with largely at the top of the organization. The program budget group that McNamara established had to fight with generals in Washington but not with master sergeants in supply. Anyone who knows the Army knows what battle they would rather be engaged in fighting.[17]

This critique proved to be prescient as scientific management techniques spread into other arenas—clarifying objectives could change the priorities of those at the top of organizations but did not, by itself, have much power to change or improve practice on the front lines.

## *Scientific Management Returns to Education*

Despite such critiques, educational reformers seized upon the growing enthusiasm for scientific management techniques, linked them to emerging civil rights concerns, and proposed a system of educational accountability. Generally speaking, the aim was to identify learning objectives, collect data on the fulfillment of these objectives, and evaluate the role that each part of the system was playing in achieving these objectives; the aim was both to exert pressure on schools and to reallocate funding in the hopes of producing better results. At least 73 state laws seeking to create educational accountability were passed between 1963 and 1974. An analysis of these laws reveals that they featured the following techniques of scientific management: planning, programming budgeting systems (PPBS), management-by-objectives (MBO), operations analysis, systems analysis, zero-based budgeting, and program evaluation and review technique (PERT), among many others.[18] At least a thousand districts in more than 30 states attempted to introduce some version of PPBS.[19] A review of the literature in 1974 found that the educational accountability movement had generated more than *4,000* books and articles on the subject, many of them works on how to introduce these techniques into education.[20]

A number of these works explicitly credited McNamara and the Defense Department for popularizing the approaches and then tried to show how such techniques could be applied in the educational sphere. A typical piece was Thomas Koerner's "PPBS: New System Promotes Efficiency, Accountability," written for the National School Public Relations Association in 1972. Koerner begins by asking where PPBS came from and concludes, "It got a big boost when Robert McNamara was asked to take over the Department of Defense." He then notes that Johnson spread it through the federal bureaucracy but that "without the benefit of an executive order," school districts have been uneven in their adoption of PPBS. He then urges proponents to "junk the jargon" and explain to school personnel that the use of the tool will allow school people to begin to think of schooling as a system, one in which goals could be set, data could be collected, and priorities could be set.[21]

US Office of Education Associate Commissioner Leon Lessinger, perhaps the best-known proponent of educational accountability in the early 1970s, outlined the rationale for accountability in terms consistent with PPBS: "Once we have standardized, reliable data on the cost of producing a variety of educational results... our legislators and school officials will at last be able to draw up budgets based on facts instead of on vague assertions. Through knowledge gained in the process of management, we will also be able to hold the schools accountable for results."[22]

Like John Franklin Bobbitt five decades before him, Lessinger saw in industry a model for reform. He writes, "In business we judge the effectiveness of a firm by its profit, by investment return, and by other financial indicators. In a nonprofit agency such as a school, we judge its effectiveness according to the benefits experienced by its clients (or in the case of education, its students)." Resisting claims that professional knowledge or expertise should insulate educators from the judgment of outsiders, Lessinger asserted that professionals are judged by one standard: results. "Ultimately there is only one test of professional competence: proof of results. For example, if an attorney loses as many cases as he wins, he will soon have none but the most ignorant impecunious clients. Neither special education nor experience by itself validates his claim to special wisdom." Channeling Bobbitt and Frank Spaulding, Lessinger advocated a measure that would allow managers to evaluate the costs of educating a student per year per subject: "For example we do not know what the average cost of increasing a youngster's reading ability by one year is: all we know is what it costs to keep him for one year with a textbook and a teacher.... It would make much more sense if we moved from the concept of per-pupil cost to the concept of *learning-unit cost*, and focused on the cost of skill acquisition rather than the cost of maintaining children in schools."[23]

This model viewed schools primarily as organizational entities that could be engineered for higher productivity. Thomas James, an astute critic of the 1960s–70s accountability reforms, wrote in 1968 that a "new cult of efficiency" was emerging, paralleling the Progressive Era reforms.[24] (The best-known book on the rationalization of schools in the Progressive Era was Raymond Callahan's *Education and the Cult of Efficiency*.) James highlighted the role of efficiency experts at the Defense Department and then argued that a "newer priesthood of economists and political scientists" had "joined the engineers in advising government about improving schools.... The models they use are, like those of engineers, adapted from among those long used to describe physical, mathematical, and mechanical relationships." In works with titles like "Education Needs Rational Decision-Making," "The Application of Cost-Effectiveness to Nonmilitary Government Problems," and "Engineering Accountability for Results in Public Education," these authors, in much the same way that Hitch, McKean, and Enthoven had sought to rationalize military spending, argued that education should be subject to the same process: specify objectives, create ways to measure those objectives, estimate costs and benefits of different alternative means for reaching those objectives, and then make decisions accordingly.[25] Five decades after the Progressive Era, scientific management had returned to education; it drew on some new techniques, but in basic form it was largely unchanged.

## A Centrist Logic Draws Support from Different Quarters

Scientific management and accountability, then as now, proved attractive to different constituencies for different reasons. For liberals, school accountability promised greater equity through standardization—the hope being to diminish variations in school quality across poorer and richer areas. Particularly as early evaluations of Great Society efforts showed that results did not measure up to hopes, some saw holding schools and teachers account-able as a way to ensure that poorer students were actually receiving the educa-tion they deserved. The concerns of Robert F. Kennedy in the debate over the passage of ESEA, quoted above, are an early representation of this view.

For conservatives, support was less about standardizing practice than cre-ating accountability. Conservatives prided themselves on their spending dis-cipline and saw in the movement a way to ensure that dollars were not going to waste. Demands for accountability would impose the same kind of disci-pline on the public system that the profit motive imposes on the private sec-tor. Richard Nixon's education reform message, quoted near the start of this chapter, is representative of this view. Taxpayer groups were also among those demanding greater educational accountability.

A third group of supporters came from newly growing state departments of education. These public bureaucrats saw in scientific management and educational accountability a way to use rational techniques of public admin-istration to take control of a large and unwieldy system. Many of these state department officials were liberals. Their belief in scientific management was consistent with the general faith, characteristic of the times, in the ability of government to remake society. As will be discussed more in the pages to come, these state departments of education developed and implemented many of the nascent standards, testing, and accountability efforts during this period.

While there was support from different quarters for educational accountability during this period, it was much thinner than it would be several decades later. Robert Kennedy asked for evaluation of Title I dollars but quickly conceded that evaluating educators for results was politically infeasible. Nixon spoke for educational accountability but concentrated most of his energy on defeating busing. Liberal advocates were fighting in the courts and the legislatures for desegregation, and parents were demand-ing community control of schools. Only state departments of education saw educational accountability as a central priority. Thus, while there was wide rhetorical support for rationalizing schools and significant efforts in state departments to make it happen, there was no strong political backing for the reform program.

## *Efforts to Resist: Teachers and Humanistic Priorities*

Speaking directly against the proposed reforms were teachers and some lead-ers of the educational field. Then as now, teachers argued that accountability measures unfairly evaluate them for outcomes only partially under their control and that an emphasis on testing would narrow the curriculum and undermine important educational goals. A 1974 *New York Times* article about a new accountability program quoted a series of teachers who registered a familiar set of objections. A teacher union representative argued that unless certain conditions were met, "we don't have enough control over the situation to be held accountable for the final product." A teacher said that an accountability program in his district had gotten "the teachers...so involved with testing...that they had little time for anything else. It was a misuse of testing and a misunderstanding of what accountability is all about."[26]

While teachers rebelled against the direct impact of testing on students and themselves, some educators raised profound concerns about the effect of accountability programs on the shape of education as a whole. In an essay titled "Accountability from a Humanist's Point of View," C. A. Bowers of the University of Oregon warned that with accountability movements playing to populist views, the risk was that schools, rather than foster students' abilities to think critically, would simply respond to the most powerful segment of the public. Quantitative accountability was particularly likely to diminish the educational enterprise, Bowers argued:

> I suspect that another reason the advocates of accountability have not talked about education as an intellectual experience is that they have committed themselves to a quantitative system of measurement. There is some usefulness in knowing the rate at which a person can perform a skill. But I am not sure that we can measure objectively and quantitatively what students learn in the social sciences and humanities unless they are rendered lifeless by being reduced to names, dates, and places.... Educational measurement encourages teachers to offer a simplistic view of life, conditions students to look for the right or wrong answer without doing the hard work of thinking and wrestling with ambiguities, and allows the educator to maintain the illusion that he is conducting his enterprise on a scientific basis.[27]

Similarly, University of Florida psychology and education professor Arthur Combs argued that the accountability metrics were too confined: "I don't think anybody can be against accountability. Everyone ought to be accountable. What the humanist is constantly trying to make clear, however, is that accountability, as it is currently being practiced, is far too narrow a concept. And it is this narrowness that seriously injures the educational process." He continues by arguing that human judgment is a critical skill overlooked in the emphasis on objectivity:

> To deal with the humanist aspects of accountability, we have to insist on the validity of human judgment for evaluation. We have sold ourselves a bill of goods in our insistence on being objective. Objectivity is fine when you have it. But judgment is what we use when we are unable to deal precisely and objectively with a particular event.... Judgment is what education is all about; in fact, the goal of education is to improve human judgment. If teachers are not allowed to use judgment to determine what is happening then what we have done is rule out the very quality that makes them most effective in the long run.[28]

Anticipating Deborah Meier's criticism that children need to trust the judgment of the adults they see each day, Combs similarly saw an earlier wave of accountability as misguided in its distrust of those closest to students.

Finally, a third set of critics argued that the methods simply did not have the muster to deliver what they promised. The most thorough of these critiques was authored by Arthur Wise, whose book, *Legislated Learning*, pointed to the limits of external agencies to engineer from afar changes in the inner workings of schools. Wise says that he himself had great hopes for these methods when they first emerged in 1965, even going so far as to take a leave to learn the new techniques. But over time he became disillusioned. The crux of the problem, he argued in 1979, was that the political and legislative remedies appropriate for equalizing resources across schools were not appropriate for improving teaching and learning:

> Policy designed to solve the problem of low academic achievement is quite different from policy designed to solve the problem of unequal educational opportunity. The solution to the problem of low achievement is more technical than political. While it is true that some teachers do not teach and some students do not learn, the cause of low achievement may not respond to the kinds of policy interventions permitted by the current state of knowledge about teaching and learning. And each policy intervention contributes to the further centralization and bureaucratization of education. These are costs which may have no benefits.[29]

While such an approach was understandable for policymakers, courts, and other advocates who were seeking ways to fix schools, Wise argued that the likely consequences would be a more "bureaucratic conception" of schooling, in which "education is seen as serving narrowly utilitarian ends employing rationalistic means." Educators, he argued, were likely to reject this bureaucratic conception, which would have the effect of undermining the reforms. And if educators were to accept this conception of the school, "the more bureaucratic will the schools become *in fact*. Quasi-judicial procedures, rigid rules, pseudoscientific processes, and measurable outcomes can be implemented." In language that is eerie for the degree to which it mirrors the criticisms that have emerged around No Child Left Behind, Wise accurately foresaw the potential limitations and unintended consequences of top-down reform.

## A Nascent Model: The Limited Penetration of Standards and Accountability in the 1960s and 1970s

The most detailed information on the development and use of accountability policies across the states comes from a series of reports by the Educational Testing Service and a consortium called the Cooperative Accountability Project.[30] The picture that emerges is an early phase of a standards-based package. As of 1973, there were 42 state testing programs in 33 states, but most tested only in one or two grades.[31] A section of one of these reports, titled "What's Happening with Educational Accountability?" found that states had consistently completed the early, more informational steps of the accountability model (developing objectives, conducting a needs assessment) but had not moved to the later, more contentious aspects of the model (making consequential decisions on the basis of measured results). The activities in the states corresponded to this division: 38 states determined desired outcomes, and 44 states conducted a needs assessment, but no states fully implemented a model that moved all the way to using data for consequential decision making.[32]

A more detailed analysis of the efforts of the state of Michigan, which had the most developed version of assessment and accountability in this period, will help explain the reasons why proponents were not better able to implement accountability at this time. The Michigan Educational Assessment Program was founded in 1969 in order to measure the progress of the state's students. The program was founded by the research division of the Michigan Department of Education, which was then able to rally sufficient support from the legislature and the Republican governor, William Milliken, to gain program approval. In contrast to contemporary notions of accountability, what the Department of Education proposed was relatively soft and school-friendly: it wanted to use testing to create information on where the school system was falling short of its objectives, with the hope that this would in turn inform school and statewide decision making in terms of targeting interventions and resources.

Almost immediately the program ran into opposition from various sources. Parents found some of the questions intended to measure the background of the students insensitive ("is there a dishwasher in the home?"). Teachers and administrators objected to what they perceived as unfair comparisons of raw test scores, which predictably showed higher levels of performance in more affluent suburbs and worse performance in Detroit and other impoverished areas. One indication of dissatisfaction with the program among administrators was that 42 superintendents threatened to withhold their districts' scores in 1971/72. In 1973/74, the primary Michigan teachers union, the Michigan Educational Association (MEA), with support of the national NEA, contracted for a critical appraisal of the program. The analysis concluded that the program was racially biased, created unfair and simplistic comparisons across districts, and debased education by teaching to the test.

An extremely skillful Michigan Department of Education, led by Superintendent John Porter, himself African American, was able to sustain the program in its early years through a combination of political savvy and strategic concessions and revisions. The background socioeconomic status measures were revised and finally dropped. The tests themselves, which were initially off-the-shelf, norm-referenced tests, were changed to criterion-referenced tests developed by teachers through a process of collaboration and standard setting. While norm-referenced tests measure students relative only to one another, criterion-referenced tests set an absolute standard for progress, lessening the importance of comparisons and making it easier to see success and failure in terms of improvement over previous years. Porter and his staff also publicly defended the tests in forum after forum, framing the debate as one that would enable the public to evaluate how schools were serving poor and minority students and what could be done to improve the schools. Ron Edmonds, also African American and later an important member of the effective schools movement, was a member of the research division at the time; he was described by fellow staff members as a particularly convincing public advocate for the program. Perhaps most importantly, Porter and his staff created what they called the six-step accountability model, which linked testing, standards, and school improvement in one package. Rather than simply treat tests as a tool to measure overall progress, the six-step accountability model, in providing feedback to classroom teachers about which students were failing in which aspects of reading and math, served as a kind of diagnostic tool that teachers could use to assess problems and improve student performance.

Despite these efforts, even this support-heavy vision of accountability was ultimately defeated by its opponents. In 1974, the MEA was able to get the state's Board of Education to put a moratorium on expanding testing to other subjects and grade levels until the program had been assessed further. In 1977, the state board, again at the urging of the MEA, passed a resolution that explicitly prohibited the use of tests for evaluative purposes. While the testing remained in place, the idea of linking these tests to the broader ambition of improving schools was stymied. The reason was straightforward—the state's Department of Education was isolated as it sought to move its agenda forward. This was not an important priority for the business community, and it did not have strong backing from the legislature. The governor, parents, courts, and civil rights actors were in the midst of a huge public fight over desegregation; real support for the accountability agenda was concentrated within the state's Department of Education. Conversely, thwarting external accountability was a critical issue to the MEA and its members. When this battle was joined again in the 1980s and 1990s, the specter of an economic crisis, which widened the conflict and brought in a larger group of political and economic constituents in favor of the reforms, tipped the scales in the other direction.[33]

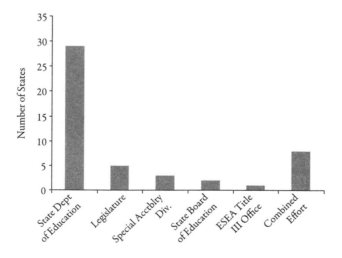

**FIGURE 4.1** Origins of state accountability programs
Source: Hawke et al. (1975)

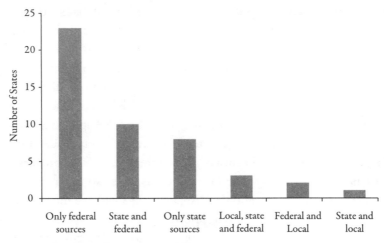

**FIGURE 4.2** Funding of state accountability programs
Source: Hawke et al. (1975)

Survey evidence suggests that in other states, accountability movements were similarly sponsored primarily by state departments of education. Figure 4.1 shows the initiating actor in accountability programs across the states. The vast majority (29) were initiated by state departments of education (also called the State Education Agency or Department of Public Instruction in some states). The legislature was the initiating actor in only 5 states, and in 8 states it was a combined effort across multiple actors, often including a state's Department of Education. Figure 4.2 shows the funding of these efforts, which indicates that in most states the funding came from the federal government or jointly from federal and state governments. It is perhaps not surprising that state accountability systems, which were largely initiated by state departments of education and paid for by the federal government, were unable to gain more traction, as they frequently had neither political nor financial support from the states that in theory were sponsoring them.

## Conclusion: A Bridge from the Past to the Present

The late 1960s and 1970s saw an important, if little remembered, effort to create state-level systems of standards and accountability. This movement, drawing upon scientific management techniques popular in the military and industry, tried to develop statewide objectives, create assessments, and hold schools accountable for reaching designated goals.

The contours of this fight mirrored the earlier and later ones in a number of key respects: a crisis that defined the problem as a need to improve the relationships between inputs and outputs; proponents who argued that the benefits of data, quantification, and objectivity could create standardization across an unwieldy school system; and critics who argued that the measurable was crowding out the meaningful and that managerial systems from above were likely to alienate those actually doing the work in schools. The cleavages of the battle over accountability also mirrored the earlier and later fights, with supporters on both the left and the right sitting in policymakers' seats and resistance coming largely from schools, teachers, and educators supporting humanistic priorities. Again, the dynamics were of outsiders versus insiders, those in the field versus those who sought to rationalize them from above.

While in many respects the standards and accountability movement in the 1960s and 1970s resembled the earlier and later ones, its penetration was not as deep. States did pass laws to create assessments, and thousands of books and articles were written about educational accountability, but the outcome was not the remaking of schools and systems evident in the Progressive Era and the present. The reason was not that those in power heeded the eloquent critiques of Arthur Wise or C. A. Bowers. Rather, the reason was more purely political. Standards and, particularly, accountability in this period were delimited by the inability of proponents to, in E. E. Schattschneider's term, *widen the conflict* and create significant political momentum behind the proposed reforms.[34] The result was that this period was one in which a policy template was created, incubated, but not fully launched.

While the lack of wider political and financial support limited the penetration of this effort, the accountability movement of this period did create a series of assessments and a policy template that would be used and revived when standards-based reform gained political momentum in the 1980s and 1990s. It served as a bridge between the development of the "one best system"—which created a bureaucratically administered hierarchy at the level of the district—and the modern state and federal accountability movement.

The one major difference between this movement and those that came earlier and later is that it was not the most powerful reform movement in its own time. It was clearly overshadowed by explosive nationwide battles over desegregation and community control. As such, it never achieved the kind of broad and deep political momentum needed to really push and alter school practice. All of that was about to change. When the bombshell report *A Nation at Risk* hit the school reform landscape, it propelled a widespread and deep movement to reform, reform that took up many of these more quietly developed policies of the late 1960s and early 1970s.

## 5

# *Setting the Problem: The Deep Roots and Long Shadows of* A Nation at Risk

DEVELOPMENTS IN THE 1960s and 1970s brought schools under fire, but the modern American school reform movement began with the release of the famous *A Nation at Risk* report in 1983. Sponsored by the US Department of Education but largely written by a group of prominent academics, *A Nation at Risk* invoked crisis and framed a narrative so far reaching in its impact that it still governs the way we think about schooling 30 years later. Emphasizing the importance of education to economic competitiveness and the failings of American schooling in comparison with international competitors, *A Nation at Risk* presented a utilitarian and instrumental vision of education. It argued that schools, not society, should be held accountable for higher performance and that performance should be measured by external testing. As will be seen in the chapters to come, these assumptions underlay the state standards movement in the 1980s and 1990s and persist today in federal policy through No Child Left Behind. Much as the muckrakers shaped reform efforts in the Progressive Era and the Coleman Report did so to a lesser degree in the 1960s, *A Nation at Risk* powerfully framed the debate and set off a chain of events that resulted in the largest-ever effort to rationalize American schooling.

*A Nation at Risk* has not been ignored in previous accounts of American educational history: it is often cited as a critical document in American school reform.[1] I seek to build on this literature by examining, in more detail than previous work has, the creation, rhetoric, and reception of the report, as well as drawing on new state-level evidence to explore its impact. I also look deeper into the past, finding a more diverse set of antecedents than is usually identified, and further into the future, seeking to specify more precisely how *A Nation at Risk* affected subsequent reform efforts. While, in retrospect, the publication is often treated as a fait accompli—there was *A Nation at Risk* and then many things changed—at the time there was no reason to expect that a short report would have such a profound effect. There are a number of interesting questions to explore here, including, of all the reports and commissions on education, why did *A Nation at Risk* have such a seismic impact? Why did the authors define the educational problem as they did? Why did their definition resonate so widely? Why were critics unable to dislodge the dominant narrative? Why has the report had such staying power in framing the debate? And how, exactly, did it reshape first state and then federal politics—what was it able to change in terms of goals, actors, assumptions, and policies, and why?

This chapter and the ones that follow take up these questions. In particular, I draw on archival evidence to examine three case-study states—Maryland, Michigan, and Utah*—to explore in detail the way in which *A Nation at Risk* changed the political landscape for school reform. Drawing on this state-level evidence, I find that the paradigm framed in the report recast the goals of education in these states, increased the agenda status of schooling in comparison with other issues, brought new noneducational actors into the education space, and eventually led to consequential new policies, most notably standards-based reform. While previous analyses have highlighted the policy activity that followed immediately after *A Nation at Risk*,[2] here I argue that it is the way in which the authors defined the problem that has been of more lasting significance.

Examining *A Nation at Risk* also provides an opportunity to explore the question of how paradigms or problem definitions get "set."[3] Three perspectives on problem setting can be delineated, drawing on literatures that focus on the social construction of problems, policy feedback and learning, and agenda setting. One perspective, developed by social conflict theorists and social constructionists, suggests that issue definition is a strategic process in which claimants use symbols, indicators, and narratives to favorably define problems and thus create political advantage.[4] A second perspective draws on the literature on policy learning and feedback, as well as on the sociology of science to argue that new paradigms are formed when anomalies become too numerous to be explained by the prevailing paradigm.[5] A third perspective argues that the changing tone of coverage of an issue in the media can prompt a shift in the set of "policy images," which in turn structure legislative debate.[6]

---

* See A Note on Methods for discussion of case selection and analysis.

The case under discussion here suggests evidence for a fourth possibility, selective synthesis, or bricolage, which emphasizes the way in which existing perspectives and changing external circumstances combine to create a new paradigm. From this viewpoint, the paradigm that emerged in *A Nation at Risk* was not one that had strategically been constructed or advocated by any organized interest nor one that simply aped the media definition of the problem. Furthermore, it was not a reaction to the failures of any single existing paradigm; given the decentralization of the American school system and the weakness of federal and state policy, there was no reigning policy paradigm for schooling comparable with, for example, Keynesianism in economics. Instead, the commission established a paradigm by synthesizing a diffuse set of developments into one coherent framework. It was this uniting of different elements into a whole that created the strange bedfellows we see in school politics today: liberals who insist that high expectations in schools are the key to breaking cycles of poverty joining forces with business leaders seeking skilled workers and political conservatives crusading for higher standards or greater efficiency. By adopting a perspective that emphasizes both external events and the selective choices of the report's authors, my account seeks to balance structure and agency, suggesting that school debates are shaped by changing real-world forces but that those forces are mediated by the interpretations of powerful actors.

## A Nation at Risk: *Establishing a New Story Line*

There was no indication in 1982 that the next two decades would witness an explosion of reform strategies aimed at increasing performance in schooling. A serious economic recession, severe state budget deficits, and Reagan's stated intention to downgrade the federal role in education policy all pointed to education remaining a low priority. In their 1982 textbook on the politics of education, long-time education policy analysts Frederick Wirt and Michael Kirst pointed to tax revolts, slow national economic growth, the shrinking share of the population with students in the schools, and a decreasing federal role as factors that likely precluded significant education reform, concluding that "the 1980s will be a decade of consolidating and digesting the large number of innovations from the 1970s."[7]

It was into these seemingly calm waters that *A Nation at Risk* dropped in April 1983. In a short report that employed bold and ominous language, the report assailed the nation's poor performance, famously declaring that the United States was caught in a "rising tide of mediocrity" that imperiled the nation's economic future. In support of its case, it cited a variety of academic indicators, most notably high levels of illiteracy, poor performance on international comparisons, and a steady decline in SAT scores from 1963 to 1980. Quoting analyst Paul Copperman, the report claimed that this would be the first time in the history of the country that the educational skills of one generation would not be equal to those of their parents. Contrasting this declining educational picture with the centrality of skills and human capital in the knowledge-based postindustrial economy, the report linked the future of the nation's international economic competitiveness with the reform of its educational system. The report's recommendations called for a new focus on "excellence" for all, which would be achieved through a revamped high school curriculum with fewer electives and more required courses in math, English, science, and social studies, a combination that the authors called "the New Basics." They also called for a longer school day and school year, more homework, tighter university admission standards, more testing for students as indicators of proficiency, higher standards for becoming a teacher, an 11-month professional year, and market-sensitive and performance-based teacher pay.

The reaction to the report was instantaneous and overwhelming. The report was released in a Rose Garden ceremony in which Reagan, disregarding the report's findings, used it as an occasion to highlight his familiar agenda of school prayer, tuition tax credits, and the end of the "federal intrusion" into education. But the media reports of the ceremony highlighted the claims about the "rising tide of mediocrity," pushing Reagan's agenda to the background.[8] The US Government Printing Office received more than 400 requests for copies in a single hour the following day and distributed more than *six million* copies over the course of the next year. The press interest was insatiable; the *Washington Post* published almost two articles per week on *A Nation at Risk* in the year following the report's release.[9] An assessment in 1984 found that more than 250 state task forces had been put together to study education and recommend changes.[10]

Some critics have charged that the commission "manufactured a crisis" as part of a broader neoconservative agenda for school reform.[11] But a careful look at the composition of the commission and the internal records of its deliberations show that this view does not hold up. At the time the committee was formed, the agenda of the Reagan administration was the abolition of the Department of Education, not an expanded federal bully pulpit demanding educational excellence. The commission was initially formed by Department of Education Secretary Terrel Bell, whose primary assignment from Reagan was to find a way to eliminate his own department. He devised the idea of a national commission to report on the quality of American education and make suggestions for improvement as a way of increasing national attention to the important functions of public education. Finding little support from Reagan's office for the appointment of a Presidential commission amid criticisms that it might generate a greater federal role for education, in July 1981 Bell appointed a commission himself.[12]

The composition of the commission does not support the idea that the analysis was motivated by larger ideological, partisan, or corporate concerns. It was chaired by University of Utah President David P. Gardner and was composed of university faculty and administrators (seven members) and state and local school personnel, including principals, teachers, school board members, and superintendents (seven members), with only one business leader, one politician, and two others.[13] It included some very distinguished educators who presumably would not be easily swayed by political concerns, including Gardner, Chemistry Nobel Prize winner Glenn Seaborg, Harvard physics professor Gerald Holton, and Yale President A. Bartlett Giamatti. Reagan did initially try to set a direction for the committee; one member reported that in an early meeting Reagan suggested that it focus on five fundamental points: "Bring God back into the classroom. Encourage tuition tax credits for families using private schools. Support vouchers. Leave the primary responsibility for education to parents. And please abolish that abomination, the Department of Education. Or, at least, don't ask to waste more federal money on education—'we have put in more only to wind up with less.'"[14] But the commission members did not share the president's interests and, ironically, elevated the priority of educational reform so that the abolition of the Department of Education (created in 1979) subsequently became impossible. The commission engaged in 18 months of fact-finding, commissioning dozens of papers and holding six public meetings, as well as a number of regional meetings with a variety of stakeholders, before producing its analysis. There is no reason to think that its report did not represent the committee's honest appraisal of the state of the school system and what needed to be improved. The fact that Reagan's office largely disregarded the findings of the report in drafting Reagan's remarks for the Rose Garden ceremony indicates that the White House had not gotten a report it wanted.[15]

Internal drafts do show that the report's inflammatory rhetoric about a system in crisis was a conscious choice made by some on the commission in order to increase its impact. An outline of the final report that was approved in September 1982 reveals a version that would have been much longer and more complimentary, including four chapters of text, beginning with a "relatively brief, positive description of the size and scope of American education" and leaving an outline of major problems to the final section.[16] Staff offered drafts of sections of the report in December 1982, which some members of the commission regarded, as one put it, as "not emphatic enough to measure the gravity of the need." In January 1983, Seaborg wrote an outline that more closely resembled the final document. He wrote: "1. Clarion call, call to arms, concise, include 4, 5 or 6 top recommendations. Total of 10 pages (no more than 15 pages). 2. Strident opening sentence or two. (1) If foreign country did this to us we would declare war. (2) 'We have identified the enemy and it is us.'" This theme was picked up by Holton, who voiced his displeasure with the "involuted and complex" versions written by the commission's staff and wrote a February 14 draft that contained much of the heated rhetoric that would serve as the groundwork for the final version.[17] In the end, the good the report offered about American education—high college-going rates compared with international competitors and high scores for top American students on international comparisons of achievement—was buried near the end, a minor qualification to a dominant rhetoric of crisis.

## The New Story Line Triumphs over Its Critics

Not everyone agreed with the claims of *A Nation at Risk*, and its over-the-top rhetoric was a source of much criticism among professional researchers and academics, who argued that the panel's desire to capture attention for its report had led it to suspend the usual standards of scientific scrutiny in order to make its provocative claims. As Harold Howe II, a former US commissioner of education, said in the week following the report: "I think American education has a cold. Most people think it has the flu. It certainly doesn't have the pneumonia the committee suggested."[18] Specifically, these critics noted that the international comparisons were unfair because other countries were more selective about which students took the tests; that measuring a decline in SATs neglected to consider the increase of students, particularly poor and minority students, taking the test; that SAT scores had actually increased since 1980; and that basic skills, particularly among poor and minority students, had been on the rise throughout the 1970s.[19] Educators resented the implication that economic problems should be laid at their feet; critics have subsequently questioned the connection between national educational and economic performance, especially as the American economy rose in the 1990s and the Japanese economy faltered. A *New York Times* article in

September 1983 reported some of the early discontent in a story, headlined "'Tide of Mediocrity' May Not Be Rising As Fast As It Seems," in which it quoted Ernest Boyer, at the time president of the Carnegie Foundation for the Advancement of Teaching, acerbically noting that "what we have is a rising tide of school reports."[20]

These academic qualifications, even when they were reported in the media, had little impact on the dominant story line in the mind of the public or policy elites. Public confidence in schooling, which had already been falling as part of the post-Watergate decline of confidence in public institutions, hit a new low after the release of the report in 1983.[21] States rushed to issue their own reports to evaluate whether they were falling short of the new measures of excellence specified by *A Nation at Risk*. Despite the claims of the critics, *A Nation at Risk* had been the rare report that galvanized not only debate but also action.

Why did *A Nation at Risk* succeed where so many previous high-level reports, including one by the College Board in 1977 that reported the same decline in SAT scores, were unable to rouse more than a moment's notice?[22] Part of it was undoubtedly attributable to the prominence of the report's authors. The fact that it was commissioned by the Department of Education gave it needed weight and authority and assured initial media attention. The conflict between the substance of the report and Reagan's school agenda, particularly over the issue of federal responsibility for schooling, was of early interest to the media. The timing of the report was also important, as it was released in the midst of a recession and offered a seemingly compelling explanation of the relative success of leading international competitors like Japan and South Korea.[23] The analysis was also bolstered by a series of other reports, released shortly thereafter, that also raised concerns about the quality of schooling and emphasized the growing importance of schooling to state and national economic competitiveness.[24] The findings themselves, particularly on the decline of the SAT scores, the levels of illiteracy, and poor international performance were also striking and widely publicized, even if they could partially be explained by the report's detractors.

In addition to the substance of its findings, the report also gained influence by telling a powerful story of decline that resonated with policymakers and the public. More than simply a jumble of numbers, the report contained an identifiable narrative arc that made it both memorable and resonant. This arc was what Robert Putnam, referring to his own work on the decline of social capital in America, calls a "declensionist narrative," or more simply, a story of decline and fall.[25] Deborah Stone notes that decline and fall stories are among the most powerful forms of political narrative: "[The] story of decline [...is] not unlike the biblical story of the expulsion from paradise. It runs like this: 'In the beginning, things were pretty good. But they got worse. In fact, right now, they are nearly intolerable. Something must be done.' This story usually ends with a prediction of crisis—there will be some kind of breakdown, collapse, or doom—and a proposal for some steps to avoid the crisis."[26] For an audience of adults who no longer had firsthand knowledge of the schools, a declensionist narrative, supported by the glaring indicator of dropping SAT scores, proved irresistible.[27] Critics never were able to offer an equally convincing counternarrative that would tie together their assorted criticisms into a compelling story.[28]

Two other important tropes that *A Nation at Risk* drew upon were the contrasts between "excellence" and "minimums" and between "hard" and "soft" visions of educational reform. We have gotten away from "standards," "rigor," and "high expectations," the authors write, in favor of a "cafeteria style curriculum" in which the "*appetizers* and *desserts* could easily be mistaken for the main course" [emphasis added]. The report counterposes ideals of "excellence" to a present reality in which for "too many people education means doing the *minimum work necessary* for the moment, then coasting through life on what may have been learned in the first quarter" [emphasis added]. The arguments here are almost banal—more students should study traditional academic subjects, learning should continue beyond secondary schooling— but the imagery tells a much more powerful story: of a lax educational system that needs to have its screws tightened. (That those "minimums," in the form of minimum competency tests, were a product, not of a Rousseauian education school establishment gone wild, but of an earlier backlash led by many of the same conservative legislators and business leaders who now were demanding high standards was ignored in this master narrative of "hard" and "soft.")

The trope of hard over soft appealed to Nixon's "silent majority," to the plurality of respondents who had always told the Gallup Poll that "order and discipline" were the most important functions of schooling,[29] to anyone who thought that the 1960s had unleashed a soft self-indulgence that needed to be countered with discipline, rigor, and a drive for excellence.[30] One commentator described the approach recommended by the commission as "make the little buggers work harder."[31] *Washington Post* columnist Meg Greenfield diagnosed this mood in May 1983 as follows:

Following the great cackles of the political antipermissiveness crowd when this report was released, I was struck again by how much such people...implicitly view education as a disagreeable thing. It is invariably discussed by them—and with relish—as something between a medicine and a punishment that must be administered to its unwilling little subjects for their own good no matter how they howl. It is not supposed to be fun, they admonish, and children cannot be expected to like it—whatever happened to our moral fiber, and so forth.[32]

Tying the softening of the schools to a Cold War rhetoric of military and economic competition only increased the stakes and reinforced the trope. That empirical research has shown that the actual impact of 1960s progressivism on schools was remarkably limited in comparison with its prominent place in public debate did not diminish its effectiveness as a rhetorical target.[33] While many people and policymakers of all political persuasions were influenced by the report's analysis, particularly that a changing economy and poor international comparisons would require a broad focus on improved school quality, the use of these tropes and narratives gave the report a power that a story of sheer numbers would not have possessed.

## Paradigms Create Politics: The Impact of the Education-Economy Nexus

What was apparent even to a casual observer of American education at the time was the frenetic activity that took place as officials, mostly at the state level, sought to put together their own commissions and ultimately embrace the report's recommendations. Subsequent research revealed that 45 states initiated or increased graduation requirements for course taking and two-thirds of states increased teacher testing.[34] The percentage of students in an academic as opposed to general or vocational track increased from 42.5 percent in 1982 to 68.8 percent in 1994,[35] and the proportion of students studying the New Basics increased from 14 percent in 1982 to 39.1 percent in 1994.[36] Teacher salaries increased 12 percent (in constant dollars) between 1983 and 2000, although this rate of salary increase was slower than that of other college graduates.[37] Proposals to extend the school day or school year or to extend the teacher's professional year to 11 months, which were the most costly proposed reforms, were for the most part not adopted.[38]

While *A Nation at Risk* accelerated these changes, careful research on state policymaking in the early 1980s suggests that the recommendations from *A Nation at Risk*, with the possible exception of course-taking patterns, were not a radical break from policies that states had previously enacted or were already pursuing. A review of state programs in 1982 found that 23 states had curriculum development efforts and that 16 states mandated teacher testing. Thirty-six states required student testing of some kind.[39] All three of my case-study states—Maryland, Michigan, and Utah—had taken steps toward student testing in the late 1960s and early 1970s, utilizing state testing as a means of assessing local school and student performance. As education policy analyst William Firestone concluded in 1990 on the basis of a five-state study contrasting changes before and after *A Nation at Risk*: "The excellence movement may have provided short-term acceleration of state activity and highlighted certain directions, but states did not make fundamental changes. Rather, they usually adopted incremental policies that extended current lines of development or slightly redesigned existing policies."[40]

While *A Nation at Risk* undoubtedly increased the rate of diffusion across the states, its effect on policy was not as significant as the way in which its paradigm reshaped educational politics. With the benefit of hindsight, *A Nation at Risk* created a paradigm that fundamentally recast the terms of the debate around education and, in so doing, altered the relative importance of education on state and national agendas, bringing new actors into the educational policy arena. Figure 5.1 displays the relative importance of education as an issue in governors' state of the state addresses in each of the case-study states between 1973 and 2005. The *y*-axis measures the percentage of the total lines in the state of the state address devoted to elementary and secondary education. Note that in Utah, where the legislature met every other year until 1985, the state of the state address was also a biannual event until 1985.

This graph indicates a clear break in 1983. On average, Michigan governors devoted 4.8 percent of their addresses to education up through January 1983, whereas in the period since *A Nation at Risk* they have devoted 19.2 percent to education. Results are similar in Utah: 4.8 percent of space in the addresses was devoted to education before *A Nation at Risk*, and 21 percent since. In Maryland, where the addresses are on average significantly longer and the number of topics covered greater, the total space devoted to education is less, but the rate of increase is about the same: 2.7 percent before *A Nation at Risk*, and 10.8 percent since.

The shift cannot be explained by partisanship. Table 5.1 provides a breakdown of the share of each address devoted to K–12 education, by governor, both before and after *A Nation at Risk*. Governors of both parties devoted relatively little attention to education before *A Nation at Risk* and have devoted significantly more since. The most striking change was in Michigan, perhaps not surprisingly given that its troubled automobile industry was ripe for the *A*

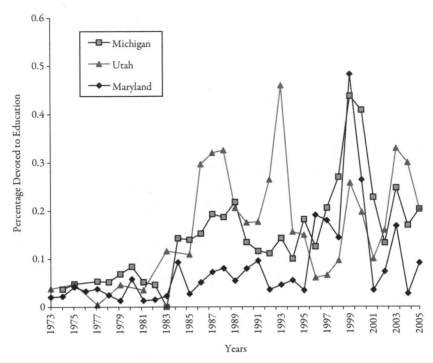

**FIGURE 5.1** Percentage of Michigan, Utah, and Maryland state of the state addresses devoted to education, 1973–2005

*Nation at Risk* message. Republican Governor William Milliken devoted 5.4 percent of his addresses between 1974 and 1982 to education, and Democratic Governor James Blanchard did not devote any of his address to education in 1983. This shifted quickly after *A Nation at Risk*, as Blanchard devoted 14 percent of his address to education in 1984 and 16.6 percent of his total space to schooling between 1984 and 1990. Reflecting the raised agenda status of schooling, Republican Governor John Engler (1991–2002) devoted 20.4 percent of his addresses to education, and Democratic Governor Jennifer Granholm (2003–05) devoted 18.6 percent of her addresses to education. Similar trends are evident in Utah, where greater attention was paid to education in the addresses after *A Nation at Risk* under a string of almost exclusively Republican governors, and in Maryland, where an increase in agenda status after *A Nation at Risk* was evident among the addresses of the state's almost exclusively Democratic governors.

What is particularly striking about these changes is that unlike the period following *Sputnik* or many other crises that temporarily raise the agenda status of an issue, this shift in agenda status was enduring and shows few

**Table 5.1 Percentage of Michigan, Utah, and Maryland state of the state addresses devoted to K–12 education, by governor, 1973–2005**

| Michigan | | Utah | | Maryland | |
|---|---|---|---|---|---|
| Before *A Nation at Risk* | | | | | |
| William Milliken (R) 1974–82 | 5.4% | Calvin Rampton (R) 1973–78 | 3.0% | Marvin Mandel (D) 1973–77 | 3.1% |
| James Blanchard (D) 1983 | 0.0% | Scott Matheson (R) 1979–83 | 6.6% | Blair Lee (D) 1978 | 2.4% |
| | | | | Harry Hughes (D) 1979–83 | 2.4% |
| After *A Nation at Risk* | | | | | |
| James Blanchard (D) 1984–90 | 16.6% | Norman Bangerter (D) 1985–92 | 23.4% | Harry Hughes (D) 1984–86 | 5.7% |
| John Engler (R) 1991–2002 | 20.4% | Michael Leavitt (R) 1993–2003 | 18.4% | William Donald Schaefer (D) 1987–94 | 6.4% |
| Jennifer Granholm (D) 2003–05 | 18.6% | Olene Walker (R) 2004 | 29.9% | Parris Glendening (D) 1995–2002 | 17.5% |
| | | James Huntsman (R) 2005 | 20.3% | Robert Ehrlich (R) 2003–05 | 9.5% |

signs of abating. Comparing, for example, the 11 years immediately following *A Nation at Risk* (1984–94) with the 11 years after that (1995–2005), there is little difference in the relative space devoted to education. Across the three states, 15.3 percent of the earlier addresses are devoted to education, in contrast to 18.8 percent of the later addresses.

These findings on changes in the agenda status of education at the state level after 1983 are consistent with national opinion data findings about the increased priority that voters gave to education after *A Nation at Risk*. Frederick Hess and Patrick McGuinn look at voters' ranking of educational issues in determining their vote for president since 1960, using results from the polls stored at the Roper Center for Public Opinion research. They find that education was dead last among listed issues in 1968 and 1972 and was not listed among voters' issues in 1976. In 1980, education was still in the bottom half of the distribution, ranking 23rd of 41 issues, but by 1984, it had moved to the top third of issues, ranking 17th of 51. Its relative status has remained in the top third since 1984, culminating in its becoming voters' single most important issue in 2000.[41]

The content of the addresses supports the notion that the education-economy link was a key part of what spurred greater political attention. In Michigan, education in the Milliken period is largely characterized as an end that is important in itself rather than as a means to a broader goal of economic development. The 1982 state of the state address, for example, has sections on school finance, educational assessment, compensatory education, special education, and bilingual education, but it has no mention of the economic purpose of education. Instead, the education section, drawing upon the 1969 Governor's Commission on Education Reform, lists the primary objectives for the state regarding education as ensuring equal opportunity, distributing the tax burden equitably, and devising systems of testing that ensure the effectiveness of educational programs.[42] Blanchard's 1984 state of the state address, by contrast, begins to talk of education in human capital terms, opining that if state support for education continued to decline, "this disinvestment in the future, if left unchecked, would undermine our efforts to spur economic development, create jobs and improve our quality of life."

Subsequent addresses reaffirmed this theme, as much of the economic and educational sections of the addresses merged into one another. For example, by 1989 the section on economic development included a lengthy discussion of "developing a skilled workforce," and the education section in turn devoted one-third of its pages to "our workers, our future." Engler continued this theme in his state of the state addresses. Arguing that with the decline of manufacturing in Michigan, building a stronger workforce was a critical part of interstate competition, he titled his 1999 address "The Smart State First in the 21st Century."[43] Given the growing conflation of educational and economic ends, the share of the addresses devoted to education would grow even further if discussion of schooling in the sections on economic development were included in the count. (To allow for comparability over time, the measure used in the charts and figure is limited to the sections that are devoted only to education.) Roughly 30 percent of the 2000 address, for example, was devoted to education if mentions of education in the economic development section are included.

The Maryland addresses show a similar shift, although given that the state is less reliant on manufacturing, the economy-education link is not as pronounced.[44] The 1984 address by Democrat Harry Hughes calls for the "greatest increase in State aid to education in the history of our state." Subsequent addresses include mentions of the need for greater quality and excellence in education, reflecting the concerns of *A Nation at Risk*. However, Maryland did not fully embrace the idea that its state economy was dependent upon the quality of its education system until the 1990s, when Governor Parris Glendening began to discuss the importance of "all our citizens reach[ing] their full potential in the knowledge-based economy of the future."[45] As the economy frame for education became more prominent, the share of the agenda devoted to education increased, providing further evidence for the link between the two.

Similar trends are evident in Utah, except that the discussion of education in human capital terms began to appear slightly before *A Nation at Risk*. Early state of the state addresses focus on the basic goal of expanding access to secondary education: the 1975 address called for making free public education available to all students in grades 9 to 12. In 1981, in the midst of a crisis of a rising school population and diminishing revenues, Scott Matheson's focus was on finding a way to provide minimally adequate funding for the basic upkeep of state schools. In Matheson's address in January 1983, three months before the release of *A Nation at Risk*, he spoke eloquently about the coming changes to a postindustrial society, noting the decline of smokestack industries and the projected growth of professional, managerial, technical, and clerical jobs.[46] He concluded: "Education then—an investment in our human capital—is the key to economic growth in this new era. Utah has long been among the leading states in the literacy of its people.... Our challenge is to sustain our commitment to education and prepare our people to participate in the new technological age."[47] Subsequent state of the states expanded on this theme. In 1989, Norman Bangerter spoke of education as an important part of "our economic development team," making education, along with the economy, efficiency, and the environment the key priorities of his terms as governor.[48] Michael Leavitt similarly embraced education reform as his issue when he took office in 1993, devoting 46 percent of his first state of the state to education. In 1996 he made the economy-education link explicit, declaring that key businesses were settling in Utah because of the quality of its schools. In 2003, Leavitt launched yet another round of school reforms, arguing that "in the economic race of this century, the society with the best-educated people wins. Period. End of conversation."[49] In all three states, linking education to the economy enduringly increased the agenda status of schooling, drawing in more powerful political and business elites for whom improving the quality of schooling was now a central concern.

## Defining the Problem: Synthesizing Strands of the Past, Shaping the Debate of the Future

*A Nation at Risk* drew together into one short document a variety of concerns about schooling that had been accumulating since the late 1960s, synthesizing these concerns into a framework that in turn defined the terms of the debate in the years that followed. This gradual change to the way the problem was defined explains why Utah's Governor Matheson articulated a similar perspective on the economic necessity of schooling even before *A Nation at Risk*, as did several other commissions whose analyses were largely developed before the release of *A Nation at Risk*.[50] It also helps to explain the success of *A Nation at Risk* as a focusing event; by synthesizing these preexisting strands of concern, *A Nation at Risk* was rhetorically bringing together a diverse constituency that was already inclined towards its analysis.

What changes, specifically, did *A Nation at Risk* encapsulate? To preview the argument briefly, change is evident on four related dimensions: 1) an elevation of one *purpose* of schooling, focusing attention on its economic purposes over the many other goals of schooling; 2) the *goals* of school reform, which shifted from moderately improving the lowest-performing students and schools to increasing performance across the board under the banner of higher standards for all; 3) the *responsibility* for addressing the problem of poor school performance, which shifted from a shared family, school, and societal responsibility to a narrower focus on school responsibility, and 4) the *outcome measures* or *site of accountability* for schooling, which shifted from a range of measures set by local school boards to accountability to the state and broader public using quantitative markers of success, generally measured by performance on state and international tests. Permeating all of these dimensions was a crosscutting theme inspired by the rhetoric of decline and international underperformance; namely, a declining view of educators. Educators were not seen as professionals who should be left in charge of their own domain; rather, they were viewed with skepticism, and their ability (or even motivation) to meet the desired standards was distrusted. Table 5.2 provides a summary of the changes in problem definition on each of the dimensions and of earlier currents that fed into the new problem definition.

**Table 5.2 A Nation at Risk and redefining the educational problem**

| Dimension | Previous problem definition | Problem definition in A Nation at Risk | Factors that fed into changing the problem definition |
|---|---|---|---|
| Purpose of education | Diverse; no one purpose dominant | Education a tool of economic development | National perception that education is key for international economic competition; State perception that education is key for economic development; Increase in individual returns to schooling |
| Goals of reform | Categorical programs for disadvantaged groups; increased performance of low performing students (minimum competency movement) | Higher standards for all students; "excellence" | State economic competition, spurring higher standards; Focus on New Basics, a reaction to "cafeteria style" curriculum of 1970s; Standards a reaction to perception of 1960s Progressivism in schools; Excellence a reaction to minimums; Excellence for all an antidote to perceived excesses of equity emphasis |
| Responsibility for schooling | Shared between parents, schools, and government | Educators primarily responsible for schooling | Effective schools research; International comparisons |
| Outcome measure / site of accountability | Qualitative standards set by local school and school board | External tests, accountable to state | Minimum competency testing; Greater state spending, plus perception that increasing spending not producing results; Changing image of teachers as an interest group (unionization, collective bargaining, teacher strikes); Declining public view of schools; low performance on international tests; other dyspeptic reports on American education |

## Shifting Purposes: The Economic View of Schooling

Perhaps the most fundamental shift in thinking that *A Nation at Risk* encapsulates is the elevation of the economic purposes of schooling over its many other purposes. Schooling has traditionally been accorded a wide variety of functions—to create citizens and social cohesion, to promote patriotic values, to incorporate immigrants, to stimulate student growth, creativity, and critical thinking, to provide an avenue for upward mobility—only some of which are consistent with the human capital approach. In Utah, for example, the official state goals and objectives for education, as formulated in 1972 through a process that involved substantial community input, reveal a very different view of educational purpose from the human capital approach, a view that still prevailed as recently as 1982. A state curriculum plan for the years 1982–88 summarizes the overall purpose of schooling as follows: "The education system is seen as a vehicle which provides for the growth of each individual as he searches for meaning and builds competencies in these eight important areas of his life." The eight areas are "intellectual maturity," "ethical-moral-spiritual maturity," "emotional maturity," "social maturity," "physical maturity," "environmental maturity," "aesthetic maturity," and "productive maturity." The complete text of these goals can be found in Box 5.1.

---

BOX 5.1

*State of Utah—Educational Goals and Objectives (1982)*

Man's *intellectual maturity* is exemplified by a continuing desire for understanding, a continuing accumulation of knowledge, and an increasing ability to use his rational powers.

Man's *ethical-moral-spiritual maturity* is exemplified by his use of rational powers and of internalizing, valuing, and emphazing [*sic*] processes in satisfying himself regarding life's purposes; in locating himself in time and space; in revering life; in comprehending death; and in perceiving his relationships to mankind and to the basic forces of the universe.

Man's *emotional maturity* is exemplified by his increasing constructive management of his emotions, of coping with stress and frustration, of accepting himself, and of emphathizing [*sic*] with others.

Man's *social maturity* is exemplified by increasingly exercising freedom with its accruing responsibilities; demonstrating functional leadership and appropriate followership [*sic*]; interacting in the social environment for self-realization and/or an awareness of the needs and values of others; acting within the basic values, institutions, and processes of American democracy; understanding world interdependence and how diverse cultures function.

Man's *physical maturity* is exemplified by his continuing appreciation and respect for the mind and body; his increasing neuromuscular development; his fulfilling experiences through physical activity; and his continuing positive response towards the solution of problems arising from increased leisure and health needs.

Man's *environmental maturity* is exemplified by his seeking constantly to understand his natural environment through rational thinking processes; through demonstrating fundamental skills required in the use of materials, equipment, and information gathered concerning the environment; through exhibiting an awareness of relationships that exist between man and his environment; and through performing acts in the environment that are relevant to his own well being and to that of others.

Man's *aesthetic maturity* is exemplified by his increasing sensitivity in perceiving his environment and acknowledging the human qualities of man; by a more satisfying use of his sense in making aesthetic judgments; by more capably communicating his aesthetic insights through the cultural arts; and through a greater harmony within himself.

Man's *productive maturity* is exemplified by his continuing involvement in the creating, generating, and using of ideas, goods and services beneficial to mankind and satisfying to himself.

Source: *Utah State Office of Education Curriculum Plan 1982 through 1988, pp. 1–2.*

The 1982 goals show a concern with the spiritual, ethical, social, and even existential purposes of schooling, a focus that was to be replaced in 1984 by a more practical, economic, and utilitarian view of schooling's purpose (see Box 5.2). Shortly after *A Nation at Risk*, the state's Board of Education reformulated its aims in a single sentence on the first page of its new "action goals": "The Utah State Board of Education sets as its primary goals the attainment of excellence in education and the improvement of productivity as expressed in

> BOX 5.2
>
> *State of Utah—Educational Goals and Objectives (1984)*
>
> "The
> Utah State Board of Education
> sets as its primary goals
> the attainment of
> excellence in education
> and the improvement of productivity*
> as expressed in
> the following objectives."
>
> * The State Board of Education considers productivity in education to have several definitions, all of which are important in providing excellence in education: (1) teaching an increased number of students for a given amount of money while maintaining current quality, (2) increasing quality for a given amount of money and a given number of students, and (3) increasing quality through increasing expenditures.
>
> Source: *Action Goals of Utah State Board of Education (1984)*

the following objectives."[51] The objectives were familiar *A Nation at Risk* staples, including a core curriculum, more time on task, and career ladders for teachers. A prominent footnote next to the word "productivity" in the above sentence underscored the new emphasis on efficiency: "The State Board of Education considers productivity in education to have several definitions, all of which are important in providing excellence in education: (1) teaching an increased number of students for a given amount of money while maintaining current quality; (2) increasing quality for a given amount of money and a given number of students, and (3) increasing quality through increasing expenditures."

What propelled the elevation of the economic purpose of schooling? Three separate consequences of the changing economy were likely relevant. Most often noted has been the greater role of education in *international economic competition*. This is an issue that *A Nation at Risk* placed squarely on the map, and it has not receded since. In hindsight, *A Nation at Risk* overstated the case—other factors affect productivity, and, before the most recent recession, the American economy had since overtaken many of its rivals, despite little improvement on international school comparisons.[52] But the link between educational success and national competitiveness caught the popular imagination and continues to be a widely used prism in op-ed columns and political speeches.[53] Less noticed but more important in spurring state policy adoption was the idea that improving education was key to *state economic growth*. While international productivity comparisons are influenced by a variety of factors that differ across countries (e.g., infrastructure, regulatory climate, proximity to supply chains) the differences across states in these factors are less significant, making the quality of the labor force more critical. A group of southern governors had already begun reform efforts to improve education under this banner, and *A Nation at Risk* nationalized these state concerns.[54] Finally, *A Nation at Risk* highlighted the increasing *individual returns to education*, which were of widespread concern to parents and students everywhere. In the years since, politicians have largely blurred these various economic advantages to greater educational performance, linking individual, state, and national prosperity to the bandwagon of school reform.

To be sure, individuals have always seen schooling as a key route to economic mobility, and political leaders have always stressed the role of education to our broader economic prosperity. In this sense, *A Nation at Risk* did not provide a new analysis. But the political debate around education does shift from one educational purpose to another—sometimes emphasizing the equity purposes of schooling, sometimes its role as a shaper of social citizenship—and *A Nation at Risk* (like *Sputnik* before it) did play an important role in concentrating attention on the economic functions of schooling. By linking an old set of concerns about the economic role of schooling to a new analysis of international economic competition and the shift to a postindustrial economy, *A Nation at Risk* succeeded in elevating the economic purpose of schooling over its other purposes.

As I show in more detail in later chapters on state policy debates, the elevation of the economic purpose of schooling has restructured the terms of rhetorical debate and the political landscape of schooling. By raising the agenda status of education, the economic emphasis brought in a much wider array of actors, most notably state (and eventually federal) legislators and business groups. To the degree that state legislators and governors of both parties believed the new analysis, it provoked a constitutive change in the attention paid to the issue and the desire to improve school quality. More strategically, the idea of investing in human capital was especially attractive to Democrats, since it provided a way to pitch their traditional concerns about greater resources for schools in the hard language of economic investment.[55] At the same time, the economic view of schooling has proved appealing to Republican legislators eager to please business constituencies, and the market and business-derived reform strategies that followed enabled Republicans to erode the traditional Democratic advantage on education.[56] For both parties, what the economic imperatives meant in educational terms—greater literacy, improved skills in math and reading, more advanced critical-thinking skills— were so fundamental as to be uncontroversial, drawing wide and deep support from the general public. In the past, the parties had largely split over the issues of busing, school finance, and greater federal intervention into schools. In the new environment, both parties had reasons, constitutive and strategic, to pursue reforms that promised to enhance overall school quality.

Losing power under the economic view of schooling are teachers and local-control supporters. As I show in more detail in later chapters, the key cleavages are no longer partisan but institutional—those who sit in state and federal legislatures and see schools as tools for larger economic ends are now in conflict with those who sit in schools and on local school boards and see schools as reflections of educator and community values. Also on the outside of the legislative consensus are those on the outer edges of the left and the right who see schools as more than an avenue for greater skill building— namely, progressives who embrace a view of schooling as a means to personal growth and social justice and Christian right advocates who embrace a religious view of schooling. Both groups have been largely frozen out of the ongoing efforts at school reform. Exercising exit when voice and loyalty fail, they provide many of the nation's homeschooled students.[57]

Finally, the economic vision of schooling also sets priorities in the allocation of resources and attention in school reform. In higher education, as numerous critics have pointed out, more dollars are allocated to economically important areas like technology and science, while traditionally important but less practical subjects like humanities and the arts have been neglected.[58] At the elementary and secondary level, much of the attention has been paid to reading and math, the two areas for which annual testing is required under NCLB, to the neglect of untested areas. Many states have cut funding for music and the arts in order to maximize time and resources for tested subjects.[59] In short, the rise of the economic view of schooling has powerfully reshaped the cleavages of educational politics and has focused the aims of schooling tightly around learning that has economic value.

## Shifting Goals: High Standards and "Excellence for All"

The move toward the widely repeated mantra of "excellence" and "high standards" also continues to shape the debate over education. The specific policy remedies of the "excellence movement" were largely played out by the end of the 1980s, but the desire to improve the core performance of all students and schools, as opposed to creating add-on programs for categorical groups, has remained a defining feature of school reform in the years since 1983. While critics initially perceived a shift in this movement from "equity" to "excellence," in hindsight it appears that the movement for excellence contained within it the seeds of equity. The enduring cleavage created by standards has not been between excellence and equity but between "hard" and "soft," elevating traditionalists and putting progressive educators on the defensive.

*A Nation at Risk's* emphasis on "excellence" and "high standards" drew its power by opposing a series of what the authors saw as unwelcome educational trends during the 1960s and 1970s. Foremost among these trends was the progressive vision of schooling that had gained prominence in the late 1960s. In contrast to the child-centered view of progressive educators, the standards-based view emphasized the importance of material that needed to be mastered. The standards-based view appealed to many who saw the 1960s and 1970s as a period of disquieting challenges to educational order and authority; everything from Summerhill to the new legal protections afforded to students was seen as undermining the ability of adults to create the controlled environment needed for learning.[60] At the same time, excellence was also contrasted with the emphasis on "basics" and "minimums" that had prevailed during the 1970s. In contrast to both the progressive and basics views of schooling, *A Nation at Risk* argued for New Basics, which were an increase in the number of expected years students should study math, English, science, and social studies. This recommendation sat well with many mainstream educational analysts, whose analysis had revealed a decline in standard content courses, such as English, in favor of a proliferating number of electives.[61] Prominent books, such as *The Shopping Mall High School*, decried the high school as having lost its central mission in the face of these ever-expanding options, a problem that *A Nation at Risk* sought to remedy through promotion of the New Basics.[62] Through the process of political boundary drawing, *A Nation at Risk* drew a series of favorable distinctions—order over disorder, maximums over minimums, essentials over electives—that helped win broad public support for its agenda and continues to define the debate today.[63]

The contrast between excellence and equity was more complicated; there were two visions of the relationship between equity and excellence—one that saw them as in tension, and one that saw excellence as encompassing equity. The first, more competitive view predominated initially. For the parents of average and talented children, a renewed focus on excellence promised that policy attention would no longer be heavily focused on disadvantaged or handicapped students and that policymakers would instead turn their attention (and resources) to more advantaged students. This zero-sum view of resources shifting away from less advantaged students also created initial opposition among advocates for poorer children. A coalition of child advocacy groups released a report in 1985, "Barriers to Excellence: Our Children at Risk," that espoused this view: "Policymakers at many different levels talk of bringing excellence to schools and ignore the fact that hundreds of thousands of youngsters are not receiving even minimal educational opportunities guaranteed under law."[64] Underlying both initial support and opposition to the excellence movement was the shared understanding of it as an effort that would redistribute resources and attention away from the most disadvantaged students.

Related concerns were raised by conservative intellectuals, who saw the problem in Tocquevillian terms and thought that the nation's efforts since 1965 to create greater equality had resulted in the lowering of standards across the board. Michigan psychology professor Joseph Adelson argued for this point of view in a 1984 *Commentary* essay: "There is an implacable trade-off between 'excellence' and 'equity' in education." Equity "means leveling, which in turn means intellectual mediocrity; mediocrity is the price we pay for universal education."[65] Taking this view to its logical conclusion, these critics advocated standards as a way to motivate and, ultimately, sort and evaluate students. In a 1983 *Education Week* essay, prominent conservative intellectual Checker Finn argued for a "strategy of setting standards and letting those affected decide how hard to push themselves to attain those standards." This was only fair to students who would soon find themselves judged by real-world metrics. As he argued the case in an *American Spectator* essay, "platoons of educators and child developers . . . would shield youngsters from awareness that the race is to the swift, insulate them from competitiveness, protect them from anxiety." As Counselor to the President Edwin Meese put it in a 1981 speech to California school administrators, "Without competition, there can be no champions, no records broken, no increasing degrees of excellence. Excellence in education demands competition—competition among students and competition among schools." In this view, equity undermines excellence; excellence can be achieved only by raising standards and accepting that some will necessarily fail in school as in life. In a mid-1980s climate of backlash against the excesses of liberalism, a rhetorical emphasis on excellence over equity provided a powerful trope for politicians, particularly conservatives, who wanted to proclaim their support for high standards.

Over time, however, a second view of equity came to predominate. This view, which was held by the authors of *A Nation at Risk,* sees equity as encompassed within excellence. The authors explicitly reject the idea of a trade-off between equity and excellence and instead argue for "twin goals of equity and high-quality schooling." In this view, which continues to hold sway, standards would serve as a way of enforcing high expectations for all students. This goal had the support of traditionalist conservatives, like Diane Ravitch, who wanted to see a much broader swath of students experience the academic curriculum, as well as liberals, like Harvard Graduate School of Education Dean Patricia Graham, who saw it as an important civil rights issue. California State Superintendent Bill Honig championed this vision as early as 1980. It seemed to provide a winning political template for liberals and conservatives alike: who could be against a reform movement that promised to guarantee the American dream for all?

In practice, setting the goal of high standards for all and then measuring the performance of students to achieve those goals almost inevitably meant that policy attention would turn to the students who were not meeting those standards. The process of policy feedback, then, practically ensured the developments that followed—political support for excellence in the 1980s shifted to support for closing gaps in achievement in the 1990s, most prominently in No Child Left Behind. (The discussion of the legislation in the chapters that follow shows this in more detail.) Ironically, experience with state standards suggests some support for exactly what some conservatives had initially feared—by requiring that all students get over a bar, the bar in some states has gradually been lowered to make this possible.[66] So in a sense, the policy has traveled full circle—reforms that were initially pitched as a way of moving away from an earlier emphasis on equity have themselves morphed into a set of policies focused on improving the performance of low-achieving students. In so doing, they show at least some signs of undermining the high standards that the movement initially sought to establish.

The excellence movement set in motion a train of ambition that still marks American education. Reform movements in the years since have been frenetic in their pace and totalizing in the breadth of their ambitions. They have promised to improve the quality of all schools, not simply to increase access or marginally improve the worst off, culminating in No Child Left Behind's pledge that all students will be proficient in reading and math by 2014. A focus on excellence did not mean, as some critics had initially feared, an indifference to the performance of poor or disadvantaged students, who ironically rapidly became more important because they were the ones least able to meet the new standards. In the long run, the legacy of the excellence movement was not a neglect of equity but an approach to fixing schools that was across the board rather than targeted, a utopian level of ambition that ensured continuous efforts at reform, and the elevation of traditionalist over progressive views of educational purpose and pedagogy.

## Shifting Responsibility for Education: Narrowing the Focus

Hidden in plain sight in *A Nation at Risk*'s analysis was the responsibility that it placed on schools as the source of the problem and the solution. By pointing the finger at declining standards and a diffusing mission, the authors placed responsibility squarely on schools to the exclusion of a range of other societal factors. As they write, "We conclude that declines in educational performance are in large part the result of disturbing inadequacies in the way the educational process itself is often conducted."[67] While the report repeatedly mentions the importance of a wide variety of stakeholders, including parents, students, unions, business groups, and legislatures, its call for excellence focused primarily on schools themselves as the prime enforcers of a new set of expectations: "Excellence characterizes a school or college that sets high expectations and goals for all learners, then tries in every way possible to help students reach them." Not surprisingly, the commission's recommendations were also focused on school variables, such as increasing academic course-taking requirements for graduation.

In adopting this school-centered analysis, *A Nation at Risk* implicitly rejected the broader view that school performance is a result of both school and societal factors. A 1977 College Board report, for example, sought to explain the same decline in SAT scores; its analysis allocated responsibility much more widely. Drawing on a variety of different kinds of evidence and offering a much more careful (if necessarily less definitive) analysis, the report concluded that a range of factors, both in school and out, were partially responsible for the decline in SAT scores. Among the nonschool factors cited were the increase in the time students spent watching television, a growth in single-parent families, changes in the composition of students taking the test, and the impact of the tumultuous 1960s and 1970s on the psyche and motivation of individual students. They concluded, "So there is no *one* cause of the SAT score decline, at least as far as we can discern, and we suspect no single pattern of causes. Learning is too much a part of Life to have expected anything else."[68] In a warning to those who sought a simpler analysis, one that would focus attention narrowly on schools, the authors wrote: "[A] ny attempt to isolate developments in the schools from those in the society at large turns out to reflect principally the inclination to institutionalize blame for whatever is going wrong; the formal part of the learning process cannot be separated from its societal context."[69]

Critics have charged that by ignoring the role of these external factors *A Nation at Risk* unfairly scapegoated educators.[70] There is truth to this, but it is also the case that developments in educational research were giving increasing support to the idea that schools did, or at least could, play a powerful role in affecting student outcomes. Research subsequent to the Coleman Report concluded that the idea that "it was all family" was overblown and that by focusing on measurable school resources (books in the library, for example), the Coleman Report ignored the school process variables that differentiated low- and high-quality schools. These researchers, collectively dubbed the effective schools movement, found that high-quality schools generally shared five characteristics: "strong administrative leadership, high expectations for achievement, an orderly learning environment, an emphasis on basic skills and frequent monitoring of student progress."[71] Coleman and his colleagues reached similar conclusions in their prominent studies of Catholic schools, which found that the sense of shared mission and high expectations that characterized these private schools produced higher levels of learning than similar public schools. Sara Lawrence-Lightfoot's book *The Good High School* put less emphasis on order and discipline but also found that the school's atmosphere, principal leadership, respect for teachers, and high expectations were key ingredients in school success.[72] In sum, while the specific characteristics of success were debated and continue to be, there was a growing sense by the mid to late 1970s that schools could make a considerable difference in student learning, even for students who came from highly challenging family situations.

Putting American schools in international perspective heightened the sense that school improvement was not only necessary but possible. That ghetto schools did not fare as well as suburban schools could be attributed to differences in family background, but no such easy rationale was available to explain why American schools were not faring as well as Japanese schools. By advocating not the narrowing of the bell curve, but rather the raising of the American curve to match the curve of other countries, the initial goals of the excellence movement bypassed the debates about race, heredity of intelligence, and the feasibility of improving the test scores of poor children that had plagued efforts for compensatory education in the 1960s. In sum, the combination of crisis created by the dismal indicators in the report and the more optimistic sense that schools could be improved created by the effective schools movement produced a perfect storm of concern and confidence to spur major efforts at school reform.

These efforts, however, were largely limited to schools—a circumscribed approach to reform that fit comfortably into a broader decline in collective responsibility for schooling. By the early 1980s, the desegregation movement, America's most concerted effort to assume broader responsibility for schooling, had long since fallen by the wayside. In light of the failures of busing and the anti–welfare state political climate that it helped to produce,[73] political leaders of both parties became averse to discussing the antipoverty or school integration measures that many critics argued were necessary for real reform. Margaret Weir and Ira Katznelson point to the way that postwar shifts toward suburbanization, aided by government construction of highways and Federal Housing Administration mortgage guarantees, exacerbated racial and socio-economic segregation and eroded collective responsibility for schooling.[74] The consequences of these shifts for schools (and neighborhoods) that remain in concentrated poverty have been disastrous, a point that has been amply documented in a series of social scientific studies beginning with William Julius Wilson's *The Truly Disadvantaged*.[75] Journalistic critics like Jonathan Kozol and Alex Kotlowitz have dramatized the traumatic consequences for children of the growth of high-poverty schools and neighborhoods and the unfairness of this arrangement in a land that promises equal opportunity.[76] But this time, the social scientific consensus and moral claims for fairness were running against the political tide, and political leaders steered clear of anything that could be linked to busing.[77] In this regard, the school-centered analysis offered by *A Nation at Risk* provided a comfortable template for risk-averse political leaders—it put responsibility squarely on the schools and, consistent with the broader political temper of the times, did not ask for redistribution of resources or otherwise challenge the structural inequalities of schooling.

The analysis of *A Nation at Risk* placed a set of boundaries around the responsibility for improving schooling that have continued to mark the debate in the years since. The calls for educator accountability that have become prominent in recent years take as their premise the idea that schools are, at minimum, substantially responsible for student outcomes. This premise, with its roots in the effective schools movement, has been reinforced in subsequent years by research on the importance of teacher quality and the success of some charter schools serving low-income populations.[78] This emphasis on school responsibility has created a fundamental cleavage that has persisted through the subsequent battles over school reform, with many teachers arguing that it is unfair for them to be judged on outcomes that are at least partly out of their control and political reformers preaching the mantra of accountability and "no excuses." Again, the lines are teachers versus politicians and parents as opposed to left versus right, as many school reformers on the left and center-left have welcomed greater educator accountability as a means to use schools to break cycles of poverty.[79] At the same time, embracing an essentially managerial effort to improve schools performance precludes a broader discussion of structural reform (combating poverty, improving housing and employment) or societal responsibility for improving schools (desegregation). In this regard, the debate over schools reflects a rightward shift away from comprehensive efforts to improve high-poverty schools and neighborhoods.

## Increasing Demands for Accountability: From "Professionals above Politics" to "Results or Else"

Perhaps the change from *A Nation at Risk* that continues to have the greatest influence on education politics and policy is the move toward seeing educators as accountable for quantifiable results.[80] In the previous chapter, we saw the inklings of the beginning of this movement in the call for standards in the 1960s and 1970s, but in a way that call was still somewhat cautious about imposing real external accountability.

*A Nation at Risk* did not specifically recommend the idea of state (or federal) testing and accountability systems—this would begin slightly later, in the early 1990s. Rather, what *A Nation at Risk* did was to juxtapose its dismal view of American achievement with its aspirations for what Americans needed to be able to do to successfully compete in the global economy. Combined with its emphasis on the importance of schools (as opposed to society) in producing educational outcomes, the commission made clear that in the new era that it was defining, results would be paramount, and educators would be expected to produce them. The climate of crisis and emphasis on outcomes took priority over long-standing objections to testing; namely, that it would narrow the curriculum or deskill teaching. This ethos of bottom-line results has effectively captured the school reform movement in the years since, as improving test scores has become the sine qua non of good educational policy. The report's indictment of the school system also crystallized a tone of skepticism about the performance of educators, a view that undergirds many of the more recent pushes for school and teacher accountability.

*A Nation at Risk* sounded the clarion call for accountability, but in so doing it built upon a foundation of educator criticism that went back nearly two decades. As discussed briefly in the previous chapter, the desire to hold educators more accountable had been increasing gradually, replacing the long-standing view that educators should control their own domain. Beginning in the 1960s, the existing monopoly on professional expertise began to be undermined as educators came under attack from a variety of sources. This increasing skepticism of professional control in turn sprang into a full-throated accountability movement in the wake of *A Nation at Risk*.

The first blow against the monopoly on professional expertise was the community control movement of the late 1960s, displayed most spectacularly in the New York confrontation at Ocean Hill–Brownsville. Spurred by the slow pace of integration and the unresponsiveness of big city bureaucracies, the community control movement sought to target the white power structure and assume greater power over the schools. Books like Jonathan Kozol's *Death at an Early Age* criticized the bureaucracy of big city school systems as both overtly and subtly racist.[81] National and city power brokers, as well as key institutions, like the Ford Foundation, were eager to sponsor experiments in greater decentralization and community participation, which they hoped would simultaneously improve practice and quiet the winds of dissent. The turn-of-the-century movement to centralize control of the schools became the problem: in this new age of local accountability, centralized school boards came to be viewed as distant from local concerns. Teachers who, at the turn of the century, had largely resisted the move towards centralization were now a firmly entrenched part of the establishment. In Ocean Hill–Brownsville, the move of the newly localized school board to transfer 19 educators sparked a seven-week teacher strike, as the largely white teachers argued for the protections of due process in the face of a black community demanding the right to control their schools.[82] In a period of rising expectations fueled by the civil rights movement, educators' claims to power on the basis of their "expertise" were severely diminished; schooling came to be seen as part of a wider struggle for power and social justice. In this struggle, teachers were no longer seen as the champions of children but as part of an unresponsive educational bureaucracy.

As the 1960s gave way to the 1970s, broader swaths of parents and taxpayer groups replaced community control activists, but their demands for accountability were strikingly similar. In part, this was driven by the same bad news about the schools that fueled *A Nation at Risk*: declining SAT scores and reports from employers and the military that entering workers and soldiers needed heavy remediation. These statistics were amplified by indictments in the popular press. A 1980 *Time* cover story, for example, intoned, "Like some vast jury gradually arriving at a verdict, politicians, educators and especially millions of parents have come to believe that the U.S. public schools are in parlous trouble."[83] Public opinion about the schools was also becoming less favorable. The percentage of Gallup Poll respondents assigning an A or B rating to the schools declined from 48 percent in 1974 to 34 percent in 1979.[84] A 1983 Harris poll reported that only 29 percent of the public had "a great deal of confidence" in the nation's educators, less than half the number that had reported similar confidence in 1966.[85] The combination of these declines in perceived performance with increases in spending (four times the rate of inflation since the mid 1960s) brought the ire of parents and taxpayer groups and put educators on the defensive. As Frederick Wirt and Michael Kirst describe the shift, "In short, parents became much more than the old PTA clique which had unquestioningly supported professionals prior to the mid-1960s.... It no longer worked to keep them busy with a cake sale to raise money for a classroom projector. The traditionally unchallenged use of public authority that had been tendered to school professionals was being reexamined—and the professionals were widely regarded as failing."[86]

Not only was overall spending increasing without similar improvements in performance; state spending was increasing in comparison with local spending. The shift increased the calls for accountability from state legislators. The 1970s featured the expansion of state movements for school finance reform, with an associated sharp increase of state aid to local districts. Figure 5.2 shows the changes in the share of total spending from local, state, and federal sources from 1980 to 2000.

In total, state spending increased by 10 percentage points from 1970 to 1980; it surpassed the share spent by local districts for the first time in 1980. As states began to pour more dollars into schools but saw no gains (and often declines) in the results, the demands for school accountability intensified.

While the standards and accountability movement in the late 1960s and early 1970s was perhaps a bit ahead of its time and struggled to find its footing, by the mid to late 1970s a simpler push for accountability, in the form of minimum competency testing for students, did diffuse. Spreading across the states in the late 1970s, the movement reached 37 states by 1979.[87] These tests that students were expected to pass before graduating were usually rudimentary in what they asked students to do. One analyst at the time thus described the motivations behind the movement: "The reason for the interest was straightforward: Elected officials usually want to know what they are getting for the public's dollar. Legislators wanted some measure of school outputs, particularly when quality was declining."[88] Accountability in this case was focused on

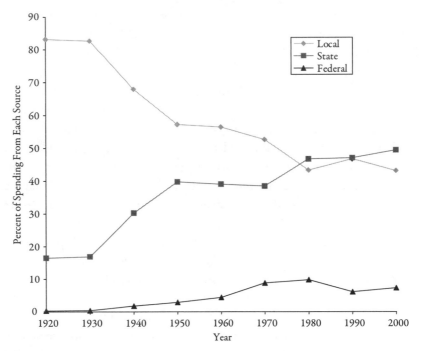

**FIGURE 5.2**  Local, State and Federal Share of Education Spending, 1920–2000

students rather than schools, but the general idea that schooling should show an external measure of validation to other constituencies, most notably the public and the business community, had been established.

At the same time that the public was increasingly putting pressure on the schools to produce, teachers were slowly undermining their image as trustees of students' interests by pursuing their own material interests through collective bargaining. What had been a largely docile (and feminized) profession through the 1950s rapidly changed its tactics beginning in the early 1960s. As the formerly administrator-dominated NEA sought to compete with the more militant AFT, unionization rates increased dramatically, and strikes became increasingly common. Between 1960 and 1965, the total number of teacher strikes nationwide numbered 25; between 1975 and 1980, there were more than a thousand strikes involving a million teachers.[89] By the mid-1970s, with nearly 90 percent of teachers members of either the AFT or the NEA, education was the most unionized occupation in the nation.[90] As teachers strengthened their bargaining position, their wages, pensions, and benefits did improve but at a cost to their professional self-image and moral power, and legislators began to see them more as the interest group that they were in the process of becoming.[91] It is not surprising, then, that a movement for accountability that had initially manifested itself through the testing of students (using minimum competency tests) was ripe for transformation into the educator accountability movement that we see today.

It is not hard to see how this changed view of educator accountability has structured subsequent reforms. Most fundamentally, it has created a climate of distrust of educators that underlies reforms, like standards-based reform, that use systems of incentives and sanctions to motivate and monitor local educators.[92] Critic Deborah Meier captures this ethos: "The dominant American attitude toward school these days…is a fundamentally new level of distrust. We don't trust teachers' judgment, so we constrain their choices. Nor do we trust principals, parents, or local school boards. We don't trust the public school system as a whole, so we allow those furthest removed from the schoolhouse to dictate policy that fundamentally changes the daily interactions that take place within schools."[93] What Meier calls distrust (or what movement proponents would call skepticism) is also paired with a desire for external measurement, which has been the leading theme of subsequent reforms. More broadly, this might be seen as an example of a "technology of distance," a label that scholars have given to reforms that deny the power of those on the scene to make qualitative judgments of worth in favor of quantitative measures that can be wielded by those not present at the local site.[94] In both of these ways, a new conversation about educator accountability directly prefigured the movement towards standards-based reform.

## Conclusion: Deep Roots and Long Shadows of A Nation at Risk

*A Nation at Risk* has had remarkable power in shaping a 30-year movement to reform American schooling. With the benefit of hindsight, its lasting impact has come less through its proposed solutions and more through its shaping of the problem: by linking educational and economic concerns it created broad and deep political momentum for school reform; by emphasizing high standards for all, it shifted the discussion from high-poverty students to all students; by focusing on the failings of school and not society, it narrowed the scope of potential reforms to focus exclusively on school improvement; and by measuring schools by quantifiable results, it accelerated a trends towards test-based accountability that continues unabated. In all of these respects, the school reform conversation in 2013 looks much as it was framed in 1983.

At the same time, *A Nation at Risk* was not fashioned out of whole cloth; rather, it synthesized a number of different strands into one catalytic document. Concerns about national economic competitiveness built upon the concerns of state political and business leaders about state economic competitiveness, as well as the concerns of individual families about the importance of schooling to economic success. Its focus on high standards drew upon dissatisfaction with what had come before, successfully positing new goals of excellence in contradistinction to both the emphasis in the 1970s on "basics" and "minimum competency" and the emphasis in the 1960s on equity and child-centered schooling. Its emphasis on school rather than social reform reflected both new strands of research on the potential efficacy of schools and a more conservative political climate wary of broader social intervention. Its desire to measure schools by test scores built upon the growing distrust of educators and the calls for accountability accumulating since the 1960s. The commission synthesized these varied strands into one framework, effectively building a diverse constituency behind its analysis.[95]

Understood this way, the example of *A Nation at Risk* suggests the importance of a more synthetic approach to problem setting. Ideas did not mask power; the ideas in the report did not reflect the agenda of President Reagan, Secretary Bell, the business community, or any other organized constituency. The commission notably disregarded the advice of President Reagan, who urged support of vouchers, prayer in school, and the abolition of the federal Department of Education, instead calling for a greater state and national role in the central problem: improving educational quality. Thus, while social conflict or social constructionist perspectives would have us focus on the way dominant actors are able to provide a definition of a problem that furthers their interests, the evidence in this case suggests, rather, that a winning problem definition is like a woven tapestry, integrating and crystallizing a number of seemingly unrelated strands into one powerful framework. It also emphasizes the constitutive as opposed to the purely strategic function of ideas; while the commission's overheated rhetoric was clearly fashioned to increase its impact, there is no reason to believe that the substance of its analysis did not reflect the authors' underlying views about what was wrong with American education and what should be done to fix it.

In retrospect, of all of the consequences of *A Nation at Risk*, perhaps its most significant has been the privileging of one purpose of schooling over its many other functions. In the years since *A Nation at Risk*, such values of schooling as personal growth, critical thinking, social justice, and character education have lost ground to a skill-building vision of schooling. Progressive educators have lost ground, as an emphasis on mastering material on state tests has superseded student creativity, teacher autonomy, and other important values. Reading and math, the most clearly economically valuable subjects, have been designated for testing, leading schools to shift resources away from music and the arts and sometimes from other academic but nontested subjects as well. The elevation of an economic view of schooling has ensured wide political support and continued priority in budgetary allocations, but it has also privileged the external uses to which schooling can be put over the intrinsic purposes of schooling. Richard Hofstadter described an earlier round of school reform as one in which "the ruling passion of the public seemed to be for producing more Sputniks, not for developing more intellect"; the same instrumental view of schooling prevails today.[96] In the wake of *A Nation at Risk*, the primary schooling debates are about different ways to improve test scores and increase the stock of useful human capital; the preeminence of this economic view has largely foreclosed a broader debate among competing educational visions over what schooling should ultimately seek to accomplish.

# 6

# A "*Semiprofession*" in an Era of Accountability

While changes in the way that education was defined were key to subsequent policy debate, the movement toward educator accountability also drew its impetus from a broader movement toward the rationalization and lay control of professionals that has affected medicine, law, higher education, and many other fields.[1] Viewing educational politics through this broader lens of the sociology of the professions explains why similar movements toward accountability arose simultaneously across fields, as well as why the teaching profession was particularly vulnerable to these external demands.

Previous scholarship on the educational accountability movement has largely ignored the perspective offered by the sociology of the professions on the dynamics of reform. Political scientists who seek to explain the movement toward educational standards and accountability have focused on state and particularly federal legislative history, seeking to understand the key decisions that have propelled education reform.[2] They have paid little attention to similar movements toward accountability in other fields or to how the "semi-professional" status of education may have affected the dynamics of reform.[3] Sociologists who study schooling have noted what they perceive as a trend towards the deprofessionalization of teaching, but their interest is less in the causes of deprofessionalization and more in its consequences for teachers' work.[4] They also have shown little concern with the question of how professionalization affects the politics of reform or, more sociologically, of what explains the success or failure of teachers' attempts to increase the professionalization of their practice.[5]

This chapter seeks to fill this void and address a series of questions about the movement toward educational accountability from the perspective of the sociology of the professions. This perspective brings several key questions to the fore: Why has there been an increasing demand for accountability across the professions? How does the low status of K–12 education in comparison with other professions affect the demands made by external reformers? How have teachers sought to increase their professional status and power in light of these external demands? And finally, how successful have teachers been in their efforts to professionalize their practice, and what explains their success or lack thereof? Answering these questions provides an important backstory for the later chapters on the legislative debates over accountability, because the inability of teachers to professionalize their practice shaped both what was asked of teachers and how they responded.

## Professions under Attack

Public opinion data show a clear decline in trust in public and private institutions, including all of the major professions, beginning in the mid-1960s. National survey data bear out the popular perception that the strife of the 1960s, followed in the 1970s by the oil crisis, the Watergate scandal, and recession and stagflation, produced a substantial decline in the level of trust accorded major public institutions.[6] For instance, the portion of the public that agreed that "you cannot trust government to do right most of the time" increased from 22 percent in 1964 to 78 percent in 1980.[7] In their systematic examinations of trends in public opinion, Seymour Martin Lipset and William Schneider combine all available national polls for each of six periods between 1966 and 1986 to track changing confidence in major American institutions (see Figure 6.1). Lipset and Schneider find that the percentage of Americans who say they have "a great deal of confidence" in the leaders of each of the country's major institutions has declined by at least 10 percentage points, for many professions by as much as 20 or 30 percentage points. They find that the percentage of Americans who say they have a "great deal" of confidence in the people running medicine, for example, declined from 66 percent in 1966–67 to 41 percent by 1978–80. Those with a great deal of confidence in the people running the military dropped from 59 percent in 1966–67 to 29 percent by 1978–80; trust in the heads of major companies declined from 51 percent in 1966–67 to 29 percent in 1978–80.[8]

Education saw a similar change, as the confidence in its leadership declined from 59 percent in 1966–67 to 34 percent in 1978–80 and then to 29 percent in March 1983. The relative prestige of the different professions remained mostly unchanged; medicine, for example, still earned the highest degree of confidence of the ten institutions measured in 1980, but all professions experienced a substantial decline in public confidence.

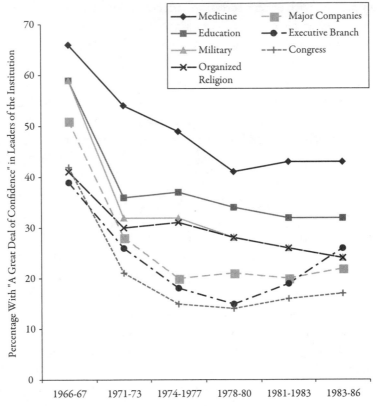

**FIGURE 6.1** American confidence in major institutions, 1966–86

*Source*: Lipset and Schneider (1987)

In addition to the major political and economic events that shook the public's confidence in the country's most important institutions, a more specific set of forces combined to put the professions on the defensive. Three characteristics widely seen in the literature as defining traits of professionals came under attack: 1) monopoly over knowledge in their field of expertise; 2) status as guardians of the public good; and 3) ability to set the standards of practice within the profession.[9]

Professionals' claim to a monopoly of knowledge in their subject areas came under fire for a variety of reasons. As early as 1973, sociologist Marie Haug identified the rising education levels of the public, the increased availability of specialized information through technology, and the growth of consumer movements as three forces that undermined professionals' claims to monopoly over expertise.[10] In subsequent years, the availability of information and easy research on the Internet and the legalization of direct-to-consumer advertising (in medicine) greatly shifted the balance of power in the relationship between consumers and professionals. While the consumer movements and self-help groups of the early 1970s have largely vanished,[11] their function has been taken in recent years by web sites that allow easily accessible comparisons among providers, as well as by new consumer groups that advocate for consumer rights. Print and electronic media have also frequently taken on the role of consumer advocate.[12] In terms of schools, this trend is reflected in the growth of a number of nonpartisan groups, such as the Education Trust, that push for more publicly accessible data from schools, as well as by web sites, like www.schoolmatters.org, that provide comparable test score data for all schools in a given area. An ethos that can be either left (when, like Ralph Nader, it demands government regulation of markets) or right (when it demands more individual choice through market mechanisms), it is always fundamentally populist in its orientation, challenging the claims of professionals to expertise and empowering consumers to demand improved performance. In short, *consumer logic* has made significant inroads in challenging a formerly dominant *professional logic*.[13]

Professionals' status as guardians of the public good has also come under increasing attack. Scholarly studies of the professions, which had, since Parsons, taken the functionalist view that the professions were owed greater pay, prestige, and autonomy in return for their expertise and ethical commitment to solving public problems were supplanted by new studies emphasizing how particular professions had skillfully won their dispensations through mobilizing for their members.[14] As Eliot Freidson describes the shift, "Writing has shifted from analyzing the professions' special knowledge and ethicality to examining their concern with establishing and maintaining a specially favored market position, and investigating their relationship to the power of the state, patrons, and clients."[15] Organized professional associations were increasingly perceived as more interested in protecting their members than in improving their practice, and the number of malpractice and negligence suits increased significantly. The introduction of Medicare in 1965 meant that many more physicians were paid with government funds, increasing (at least initially) doctors' salaries; this development in turn drew significant skeptical publicity during the following decade, in which recession and stagflation limited the income of most Americans. Conservative intellectuals wove an ideological critique out of these disparate elements, arguing that the professions were a "new class" seeking to milk a recently expanded welfare state for its own profit.[16] This critique bore some fruit, as a series of legislative and judicial decisions sought to spur price competition by eliminating professionals' ability to fix prices collectively.[17] Professionals enmeshed in public bureaucracies, schoolteachers at the forefront among them, faced similar neoconservative criticisms. Here the focus was less on their compensation and more on the inefficiency and complacency produced by a state-controlled rather than a market system.[18] Professionals, in turn, have responded in recent years by emphasizing what Steven Brint calls "expert professionalism" in place of the "social trustee professionalism" that previously prevailed.[19] In a more cynical climate, professionals staked their claim less on the honor of their intentions and more on the specialized nature of their expertise. This shift, however, has further disadvantaged the already weak profession of teaching. Since educators have been unable to convince the public that a specialized body of knowledge is required for teaching, their authority, more than most professionals', depends on a perceived commitment to helping their students. Overall, professionals' aura as protectors of the public good was diminished by new empirical research, changing public perception, and polemical ideological critique. This conjunction of developments diminished the power of professional logic and elevated *market logic* in its place.

A third and perhaps most significant challenge has been to professionals' ability to set the standards of practice in their professions. This eroding sense of control is partly attributable to the growing size of the organizations in which many professionals work. Gone are the days of the individual proprietor in law and medicine; these professionals have mostly become part of larger practices. Universities, accounting firms, and a variety of social agencies have also grown in size and complexity. Enlarged scale has led to additional levels of monitoring, although since in many cases those who do the monitoring are also professionals, some scholars argue that the result has been a greater stratification in the division of labor within the professions. At the same time, increased state spending on the professions (particularly medicine and education) and the greater exertion of capital and shareholder control in for-profit professional settings have further multiplied the external groups demanding accountability. *Capital control* and *state control* have increased, and professional control has become increasingly embattled.

Table 6.1 summarizes the sources of attack on the professions and the consequences of these shifts for professional authority. If the period from the end of the Second World War to the mid-1960s could be characterized as the golden age of the professional, the period since has been marked by increasing challenges to professional expertise, as a more educated and skeptical public has sought to impose greater consumer, market, capital, and state control over the professions.[20]

**Table 6.1 The professions under attack: Causes and consequences**

| Characteristic of profession | Sources of attack | Consequences |
|---|---|---|
| Monopoly over knowledge | • Rising education<br>• Greater mass availability of professional knowledge (Internet)<br>• Consumer movements | • Increased demand for transparent data<br>• Less deference to professional authority<br>• More consumer control |
| Social trustee status | • New class criticism / populist ideology<br>• Loss of trust / scandals / changing image of professions | • Diminished protection of monopoly status<br>• More market control |
| Ability to set standards for practice | • Growing size<br>• Growing state fiscal responsibility<br>• Growing investor pressure | • Reduced ability to set standards for practice<br>• More state control<br>• More capital control |

## The Making of a Semiprofession

In the face of these broad forces attacking the professions, teachers are particularly vulnerable because they have not achieved full professional status. As was discussed in Chapter Two, like the similarly feminized semiprofessions of nursing and social work, teaching never developed the characteristics that defined the more traditional professions.[21] For instance, the ability of law and medicine to limit the supply of practitioners is one of their most important sources of power, but because the demand for teachers has always exceeded the supply, teachers have not been able to achieve similar social closure over their ranks. Over the course of the 20th century, the profession has gradually tightened licensing requirements, but such efforts have frequently been undermined by the need to grant emergency credentials in order to staff classrooms. Teachers have also been unable to establish a defined body of knowledge considered essential to becoming a teacher. Much of the most relevant knowledge belonged to other disciplines, like psychology, and the status of pedagogical knowledge and educational research has been notoriously low within the academy and with the public. Consequently, teachers have been unable to convince the public that a lengthy course of study is required or necessary for good teaching; this liability has become more significant as other professions have recast the source of their authority in mastery of technical knowledge. Finally, because 90 percent of schools are public, most teachers do not have a private market for their services. This limitation reduces the power of teachers to set the rules for prospective clients, as many other professionals do, particularly when their work is fee for service.

In addition to the traits that differentiate teaching from other professions, the historical patterns under which teaching developed also help explain its subordinate position. Teaching in the Progressive Era was incorporated within a bureaucratic-management model: teachers reported directly to administrators and established little professional control of their own. Important to this arrangement was the NEA, which for its first 100 years (1858–1958) was largely an administrator-run organization, with little voice granted to the interests of teachers. During this period, the NEA argued for a model of a unified profession—teachers and administrators working together for the sake of the students—that in practice preserved the Progressive Era division of labor that left individual teachers with little power and low pay. Beginning in 1962, the AFT successfully challenged administrator dominance by organizing teachers to fight for wages, and the NEA, in reaction to this competition, rapidly shifted from administrator to teacher control. However, by embracing an antagonistic model of bargaining almost exclusively on wage and benefit issues, teachers' claim to authority on the basis of social trustee status steadily diminished.

## A Comparative Case: Higher Education at Risk?

The weakness of school teaching as a profession is apparent when it is contrasted with American higher education. The latter, which operated in the 19th century through a hierarchical managerial model in which trustees and presidents made final decisions on curriculum and hiring, evolved during the first half of the 20th century into a model that grants significant power to faculty over these substantive areas. As disciplinary associations and academic journals proliferated, higher education took the form we see today, with scholars working in a self-regulating profession uniquely charged with judging the work of fellow academics.[22] Higher education is professionalized in all the ways that secondary schooling is not: professors have the power to exclude unqualified practitioners; they have a lengthy training regime and have mastered a technical or specialized body of knowledge that wins broad respect and deference; and they have market power, with easily transferable credentials and a significant share of universities in the private sector. The result is that colleges and universities, even public ones, are granted considerable institutional autonomy, and within those institutions administrators need to show some deference to faculty power.

Contrasting a 1984 Institute of Education report seeking to achieve "excellence in higher education" with *A Nation at Risk* illustrates how similar concerns for improving quality can lead to very different prescriptions in fields that vary in their levels of professional power. The 1984 report, *Involvement in Learning: Realizing the Potential of American Higher Education*, reflects many of the same concerns as *A Nation at Risk*. (A foreword to the reports says that the commission was formed with the explicit intention of extending the analysis of *A Nation at Risk* to higher education.) The report cites a parallel set of indicators to *A Nation at Risk*'s falling SAT scores, noting that student performance on 11 of the 15 major subject area tests of the Graduate Record Examinations declined between 1964 and 1982. These declines in GRE scores, above and beyond what could be explained by declines in students' SATs, were seen by the commission as critical "warning signals" that "must be recognized and addressed."[23] Colleges and universities were also criticized for their insufficiently rigorous academic standards, which emphasized the number of course credits over the quality of the courses for which those credits were received.[24] Finally, colleges and universities were taken to task for ignoring problems of declining quality and for failing to develop formal assessments of student learning.

The unifying themes of the recommended goals for higher education, laid out in a section titled "Conditions of Excellence in Higher Education," also had much in common with *A Nation at Risk*. Specifically, the report notes that colleges and universities had traditionally been judged by a variety of inputs—endowment and expenditures, breadth of curricular offerings, degrees held by the faculty, test scores and selectivity of entering students—that were at best proxies for the important outputs of learning. In stark language, the report points to the limitations of this input-oriented focus: "None of them [inputs] tells us what students actually learn and how much they grow as a result of higher education. None of them tells us anything about educational outcomes. As a result, we have no way of knowing how academic institutions actually perform."[25] Given this shifting focus, the report argues that excellence in higher education requires 1) "...*demonstrable improvements* in student knowledge, capacities, skills and attitudes between entrance and graduation...; 2) That these demonstrable improvements occur with *established, clearly expressed, and publicly announced and maintained standards of performance* for awarding degrees...; 3) That these improvements are achieved *efficiently*, that they are cost-effective in the use of student and institutional resources of time, effort and money" (emphasis in original).[26] The parallels to *A Nation at Risk* are striking, specifically in the shift from inputs to outputs, the need to clarify and focus energy around standards, and an ethos of bottom-line efficiency in achieving these ends.

However, when the report shifts to recommendations for achieving these goals, the differences in institutional power between elementary and secondary education and higher education become immediately apparent. Take, for example, the idea that more challenging standards need to be set, a theme in *A Nation at Risk* that is also emphasized in *Involvement in Learning*. The key difference between the two reports is that *Involvement in Learning* asserts that the individual institutions should determine the standards, as opposed to the state or other outside bodies. The rationale for this decision is grounded in the presumed expertise of colleges and universities to run their own affairs: "It is not our aim to dictate particular and highly detailed sets of knowledge, capacities, skills, or attitudes that students should develop in the course of their undergraduate education....Our reason is simple: the responsibility for defining specific standards of content and levels of student performance and college-level learning in undergraduate education must fall on academic institutions themselves, *or those standards will have no credibility*" (emphasis added).[27] In contrast with secondary schooling, for which states have repeatedly tried to specify instructional standards, in higher education the presumption is that those outside the institutions are not in a position to tell those inside what should be learned.

The recommendations concerning assessment follow a similar pattern. After repeatedly stressing the importance of measurable indicators of progress, the report leaves it to individual institutions to decide whether they want to adopt systems of assessment and, if so, to design the assessments to fit the values or the special needs of each institution. Not only are colleges and universities to be free of state mandates for assessments; the assessments themselves should be designed with the participation of the full faculty: "The best way to connect assessment to improvement of teaching and learning is to ensure that faculty have a proprietary interest in the assessment process."[28] Involving professors in the design of assessments, the report continues, would help faculty to clarify the expected outcomes of their courses and to match their teaching to achievement of those ends. What is striking about these recommendations when compared with those in *A Nation at Risk* is the level of trust accorded to the professionals who are doing both the teaching and the assessing. (An earlier draft of the report was titled "A Matter of Trust," and although the title was eventually changed, the introductory section of the final report bears that heading.) Whereas in discussions of K–12 schooling it is common, particularly in conservative circles, to see the idea of teachers setting assessments as equivalent to the fox guarding the henhouse,[29] the assumption in higher education is not that practitioners need to be monitored by tests, but rather that assessments will be utilized as resources for internal improvement.

The two reports differ in other important ways as well. Even given its emphasis on outcomes, productivity, and efficiency, *Involvement in Learning*—much more than *A Nation at Risk*—spells out an educational vision as opposed to an economic one. In contrast to the view in *A Nation at Risk* of schooling as a critical tool of economic development, here the authors take the opposing view, that an economic or preprofessional emphasis has undermined liberal education. Looking at the period from 1971 to 1982, the report laments the growth of vocational and professional degrees at the expense of degrees in arts and sciences. Decrying the loss of liberal ideals, the report concludes: "[T]he college curriculum has become excessively vocational in its orientation, and the bachelor's degree has lost its potential to foster the shared values and knowledge that bind us together as a society. To a large extent, our recommendations seek to reverse the trends implied by these indicators and to restore liberal education to its central role in undergraduate education."[30] The authors acknowledge the importance of a college education to individual economic prospects in a postindustrial economy but do not infer from this shift a greater need for preprofessional or vocational training. Instead, they argue, the new economy will expect students to be able to adapt to unforeseen changes, a need requiring students in all fields to learn how to "think critically, synthesize large quantities of new information, and to master the language skills (critical reading, effective composition, clear speech and careful listening) that are the fuel of thought.... To fulfill them is to achieve a liberal education."[31]

Why did *A Nation at Risk* subordinate educational concerns to economic ones and *Involvement in Learning* do the opposite? Part of the difference could be attributable simply to the predilections of the authors, but it is reasonable to hypothesize that the greater standing of higher education as a professional enterprise is also at least partially responsible. Higher education is treated as its own "practice," to use the term of philosopher Alasdair MacIntyre, a sphere with its own internal standards of what constitutes excellent work.[32] (The medical field's Hippocratic oath is an obvious example of a practice's internal standards.) While both reports acknowledge that education is becoming increasingly important to economic outcomes, *Involvement in Learning* counterposes those economic values with a vision of higher education as an enterprise intended to produce a liberal arts education. Lacking a similar foundation for elementary and secondary education, *A Nation at Risk* chose instead to encompass educational goals within broader economic ones that were widely shared.

Finally, the most glaring difference between the two reports is their respective views of students. If the ethos of *A Nation at Risk* was to "make the little buggers work harder," the mantra of *Involvement in Learning* was, not surprisingly, that student "involvement in learning" was the first precondition of successful reform. Students are seen less as inputs upon whom reform strategies are tried and more as critical participants in the process of schooling. The authors of *Involvement in Learning* conclude, "We could offer hundreds of recommendations to college officials and faculty on the best ways to increase student learning, and they could implement all of our suggestions— all to no avail if students themselves do not respond."[33] The implications of this fundamental premise are many and various: teaching should become less didactic and involve students more actively; more students should become involved in campus life through work and student organizations; students should become involved in research projects and experience disciplines from the point of view of the scholars; more interchange should take place between faculty and students; and student evaluations should be incorporated into efforts for institutional improvement. In other words, students should be seen as partners in their own education, active learners whose interests can be stimulated and knowledge refined, stakeholders in shaping the institutions in which this learning would take place. The progressive origins of this view are obvious—students are seen as participants in their own learning. What is less apparent is that it also reflects a highly professional model of schooling. Rather than unwilling employees who need to be motivated and monitored (the managerial model), students are seen as one part of a professional community that is engaged in the "practice" of education. The problem is that too few students are choosing to actively participate in this community, and the remedy is to make the community more attractive and inclusive.

Overall, *Involvement in Learning* illustrates how the dialogue around improving educational quality is conducted in a context that is much more highly professionalized. Partly out of deference to institutional and faculty power, partly out of respect for professional expertise, the report's recommendations are largely advisory and exhortatory. The prevailing ethos is one of trust, specifically trust that institutions are best situated to assess and direct their own improvement. The role of the state is largely to avoid interfering with this self-regulating process. As the authors conclude, "The integrity and autonomy of colleges are critical to the establishment of an environment conducive to learning and growth."[34] While the authors recognize an almost inexorable increase in the demands for external accountability for results, they argue that universities and their voluntary accrediting agencies should get out in front of the movement in order to protect the critical values of professional self-regulation: "If voluntary accreditation associations themselves do not insist on seeing standards realized in outcomes and assessments, external forces may eventually do so. We prize the self-regulating tradition of higher education too much to allow this to happen."[35]

To be sure, in the years since, the significant growth in the demands for external accountability in higher education has somewhat diminished the ideals of professional autonomy so heavily stressed in *Involvement in Learning*. Public systems have come under significant pressure in the states, in large part because increasing costs for elementary and secondary schooling and Medicaid payments have exacerbated the difficulties of balancing budgets.[36] In addition, an antiprofessoriate ideology has been an important part of the debate in some states. The consequences of increased pressures have often included declines in real wages for faculty, greater use of low-paid adjunct professors who are not represented in institutional decision making, and greater funding of sectors of universities that are profitable or can be easily justified to the public to the detriment of the humanities or the arts.[37] However, even acknowledging these trends, U.S. higher education continues to withstand more intrusive calls for accountability because of its high level of professional and institutional power. Proposals have been floated to make institutions of higher education accountable for tuition increases or even to model a system of testing along the lines of No Child Left Behind. But these proposals, which have been strongly opposed by the lobbying groups representing institutions of higher education, have thus far gained little traction,[38] at least in the United States.*

---

* Accountability has penetrated more deeply into higher education in England, perhaps in part because there universities are more directly dependent upon the state for financial support. The point is not that professionalization is always a bulwark against external accountability; rather, it is one buffering force, although it is not necessarily always dispositive. In England too, accountability came first and in more invasive form to primary and second education. See Andreas Hoecht, "Quality Assurance in UK Higher Education: Issues of Trust, Control, Professional Autonomy and Accountability," *Higher Education* 51, no.4 (2006): 541–563.

## A Renewed Call for Professionalism

In the wake of *A Nation at Risk*, there was a renewed push among some educators to "professionalize" the field.[39] Ironically, leading the newfound calls for professionalism was AFT President Albert Shanker, long a militant unionist and the organizer of the 1962 New York City teacher strike that had sparked the collective bargaining movement. In April 1985, two years after the release of *A Nation at Risk*, Shanker stunned many in the education community by calling for a new era of teacher professionalism. In an address to the Niagara Falls teacher convention, he said: "[W]e have not been able to achieve all that we had hoped for through the bargaining process, and it is time to go beyond it to something additional and quite different. We can continue working away only at collective bargaining. But if that is our decision, I predict that in 10 to 15 years we will find we've been on a treadmill." Shanker asserted that making the profession more attractive was necessary to draw more talented undergraduates to teaching and to increase the status, prestige, and power of the profession. He argued (presciently) that if teachers continued to block efforts at reform, they would not only undermine their own credibility but might actually encourage further flight from the public schools, supported by vouchers and tuition tax credits: "Unless we go beyond collective bargaining to teacher professionalism, we will fail in our major objectives: to preserve public education in the United States and to improve the status of teachers economically, socially and politically."[40]

The professionalism agenda was given a significant boost by the Carnegie Foundation's Task Force on Teaching as a Profession, which released its report, *A Nation Prepared: Teaching for the 21st Century*, in May 1986. The task force was the first major initiative of the newly formed Carnegie Center for Education and the Economy, which allocated $3 million for the production and distribution of the report. Lewis Branscomb, the chief scientist at IBM, chaired the report, and the commission's membership included Shanker, NEA President Mary Futrell, California Superintendent Bill Honig, the ubiquitous former North Carolina governor James Hunt, and New Jersey Governor Thomas Kean. Not surprisingly, given its prominent authors and its august institutional backing, the report quickly became the touchstone for much of the debate around teacher professionalization.[41]

*A Nation Prepared* accepted the central premises of *A Nation at Risk*—that human capital would be critical in the emerging global economy and that the quality of American education needed to be improved to create a more skilled workforce. But to these premises *A Nation Prepared* added a new idea: professionalizing teaching was the best hope for realizing excellence in education. The way to improve schooling did not lie in more time in school for students, increased testing, or stricter course requirements, as *A Nation at Risk* had argued, but rather in refashioning teaching into a more professional occupation.

## Teacher Autonomy and Discretion

What would it mean to professionalize teaching? One theme that ran through the Carnegie report was the idea of moving away from the model of hierarchical bureaucratic accountability that had traditionally characterized teaching and shifting toward a system in which teachers would have greater control and discretion regarding their work. The authors argue that teaching still bears the imprint of its historical origins as a part-time occupation for women; as a result the conditions of the field "more nearly resemble those of semi-skilled workers on the assembly line rather than those of professionals."[42] If the goal was to recruit more talented people, the field would have to be refashioned, as had other attractive occupations, to offer the kind of autonomy and discretion characteristic of professions: "Professional work is characterized by the assumption that the job of the professional is to bring special expertise and judgment to bear on the work at hand. Because their expertise and judgment is respected and they alone are presumed to have it, professionals enjoy a high degree of autonomy in carrying out their work."[43] By these standards, teaching was clearly wanting—"rules made by others govern [teacher] behavior at every turn," the report avers[44]—and without change, the profession could not expect to attract talented new candidates, especially as professional options for women were rapidly proliferating in other fields.

Particularly in an era where students were expected to master complex content and become autonomous learners who could adapt to the ever-changing requirements of the global economy, the teaching role needed to become more discretionary and less bureaucratic. As the Carnegie authors put it: "Teachers must think for themselves if they are to help others think for themselves, be able to act independently and collaborate with others, and render critical judgment."[45] Ironically, the report argues, the reforms stemming from *A Nation at Risk* have moved away from this needed discretion and toward more belt-tightening from above.[46] For example, the education code had reached more than 10 volumes in some states.[47] Top-down reform is contrary to the principles of professionalism, the authors argue: "Bureaucratic management of schools proceeds from the view that teachers lack the talent or motivation to think for themselves." Successful reform could not come about unless this situation was reversed and teachers were included in the reform process. As the commission reasoned: "[R]eal reform cannot be accomplished despite teachers. It will only come with their active participation."[48]

In contrast to a top-down set of initiatives, the report called for a revamped reform agenda that would give teachers greater control of their work. Scholars in the 1980s dubbed these bottom-up reforms the "second wave," following the first wave of *A Nation at Risk*.[49] State and federal regulations should be drastically cut back, and teachers and principals should have much greater discretion over how to spend money within their schools. "Within the context of a limited set of goals set by state and local policymakers," the report argued, teachers should have much greater discretion in determining how to reach these goals. Teachers should be able "to make—or at least strongly influence—decisions concerning such things as the materials and instructional methods to be used, the staffing structure to be employed, the organization of the school day, the assignment of students, the consultants to be used, and the allocation of resources available to the school."[50] The report cited Ted Sizer's Coalition of Essential Schools as an example of a networked group of schools that had put these principles into practice, with teachers developing their own curricula and goals and administrators working with teachers in the development of strategies to meet those goals. This bottom-up approach, which was one version of what came to be known as "site-based management," became a key rallying cry for teachers and their unions in the years following the Carnegie report.

## Professional Control over Entry

If one emphasis of the Carnegie report was bottom-up control of schools, an equally important related theme was the need for educators to define and raise the standards that governed the profession. The report argued that at a moment of low confidence in the teaching profession, setting standards was the first step toward reversing the vicious cycle in which highly prescriptive reforms alienated talented teachers, weakening the teacher pool and inviting even more prescriptive reforms in the future. As the authors put it: "Raising standards for entry into the profession is likely to give the public confidence that the teachers they hire will be worth the increased salary and worthy of the increased autonomy we advocate."[51]

The report's authors saw gaining control over the certification of qualified candidates as perhaps the most important step in teaching's becoming a profession on a par with others. Drawing on the notion of expert professionalism, the report notes that education is unlike many other highly respected professions in not creating this standard:

> Virtually every occupation regarded by the public as a true profession has codified the knowledge, the specific expertise, required by its practitioners, and has required that those who wish to practice that profession...demonstrate that they have a command of the needed knowledge and the ability to apply it.... They capture that knowledge in an assessment or examination and administer that examination to people who want a certificate saying they passed the assessment.[52]

To fill this function, the report advocated the creation of a National Board for Professional Teaching Standards (NBPTS), which would certify teachers as highly qualified. Through a range of assessments, the NBPTS certificate would serve as a stamp of the profession's approval, much as the bar and medical school boards do in law and medicine. The committee's hope was that the high standards set by NBPTS, while initially voluntary (so as not to alienate the hundreds of thousands of practicing teachers), would become incorporated in state standards and thus become de facto requirements for entry to the profession.

## Professional Responsibility for School Quality

A third part of the Carnegie agenda encouraged teachers to take greater responsibility for school quality. Echoing Shanker, the Carnegie reformers argued that the model of industrial-style bargaining, which had served teachers well in the past as they fought for higher pay, better working conditions, and enhanced benefits, was insufficient to confront the key challenges facing teachers in an era of results. The key to progress would be to "overcome a legacy of conflict and confrontation" that had characterized adversarial bargaining. Instead, the commission argued, "Unions, boards and school administrators need to work out a new accommodation based on exchanging professional-level salaries and a professional environment on the one hand, for the acceptance of professional standards of excellence and a willingness to be held fully accountable for the results of one's work, on the other."[53] In practice, adopting this new model would mean a range of more specific changes: accepting greater responsibility for school quality through site-based management; creating a differentiation of roles for teachers that would resemble the career trajectories found in other professions; and shifting compensation away from a system based on seniority and continuing education credits and toward a system based more heavily on job responsibility and productivity. Systems of peer review, in which master teachers would evaluate the work of other teachers and recommend dismissal for the least competent, were not mentioned in Carnegie but became prominent in subsequent years among those who endorsed the Carnegie approach.[54]

Linking all of the recommendations was a three-pronged vision: 1) that improved practice in schools would come from shifting power downwards to teachers, 2) that teachers needed to take greater control in defining standards of entry and good practice in the profession, and 3) that teachers needed to move beyond industrial bargaining and embrace a more professional conception of pay and responsibility for local practice. By co-opting much of the rhetoric of *A Nation at Risk*, the report aimed to build on the growing momentum for school reform but to turn the tide away from top-down regulation and external interference and toward greater teacher autonomy and professionalism.

## The Politics of Professionalization

This three-part agenda has achieved limited success since it left the confines of the Carnegie Foundation and entered the contested field of school reform politics. The professionalizers faced external resistance from skeptical legislators unwilling to relinquish control over schooling and internal resistance from a teaching force still wedded to the protections of industrialized unionism. In the sections that follow, I consider each of the three parts of the professionalism agenda described above, beginning with the professionalizers' call for greater teacher autonomy and discretion.

### Power to Which People? The Allure and Ambiguity of Bottom-Up School Reform

In the calls to reduce central administration red tape and give greater authority to teachers in schools, the Carnegie Commission's recommendations neatly paralleled both a rising ideological tide against governmental bureaucracy and the recommendations of management theorists who advocated a decentralizing shift. The work of the management theorists, including W. Edwards Deming, Peter Drucker, and most notably, *Reinventing Government* gurus David Osborne and Ted Gabler, effectively legitimized the need to reform government beyond the conservative antigovernment critique, particularly among centrist Democrats seeking to broaden their base. In Osborne and Gabler's narrative, the large bureaucracies formed in the industrial age were anachronistic in a rapidly moving, consumer-driven, information-age economy. Much as the Progressives had reformed government to combat patronage and corruption, a new generation of politicians aimed to reshape government to become the entrepreneurial force modern life demanded. In an era marked by tax revolts and low confidence in government, they argued, government needed to show that it could achieve more with less to sustain its critical role and defend itself from its many critics.[55]

Decentralization of authority was one key to improving performance. Granting greater power to frontline workers would allow them to respond more quickly to changing circumstances. The villains in Osborne and Gabler's book are frequently rule makers from above; they make it impossible for local actors to exercise common sense to solve problems on the ground. Bureaucratic structures, in this telling, resist innovation and impose a one-size-fits-all solution that is not adaptable to local conditions. Not only do frontline workers have more information about local conditions; granting them greater authority would also improve morale, generate ownership among employees, increase commitment, and raise productivity.[56] In all of these recommendations, Osborne and Gabler's views mirror those of the Carnegie report, which repeatedly emphasizes the importance of teacher ownership of reform and the destructiveness of regulations that produce a situation in which "everyone has all of the brakes and none of the motors."[57]

Political actors embraced this critique of top-down regulation as well but coupled it with a demand for greater results and accountability. The 1986 National Governors Association report, *Time for Results*, famously promised "some old-fashioned horse-trading," where the government will "regulate less, if schools and school districts will produce better results."[58] The governors "invited" educators to "show us where less regulation made more sense" and declared they would "fight for changes in the law...*if* schools and school districts will be held accountable for the results" (emphasis in original).[59] This emphasis on reciprocal exchange was renewed in the 1989 Charlottesville summit of governors with President George H. W. Bush. The group promised that state and federal statutory and regulatory provisions would be waived in return for greater accountability for results. From the beginning, the Carnegie agenda of bottom-up professional control was only partially endorsed by a political establishment intent on maintaining control of the reins of accountability. "Trust us," the educators said; "quid pro quo," the legislators responded.

A second outgrowth of the movement away from centralized bureaucracy was a renewed emphasis on community control. Osborne and Gabler, for example, labeled one of their chapters "community-oriented government" and gave a range of examples detailing how local oversight and involvement were improving the quality of social services in everything from education to policing to job placement programs. The most notable example of community control of schools came in Chicago. Grassroots Chicago reformers, organized by a nonprofit education watchdog organization, Designs for Change (DFC), embraced the critique of unresponsive downtown bureaucracy and the need for power to devolve to local school sites under the heading of "site-based management." Beginning in 1988, 560 local school councils were established, each comprising six parents, two community residents, two teachers and the principal. But while this movement shared a decentralization emphasis with the Carnegie report, it did not share its emphasis on professional control, as local grassroots reformers were able to win approval for the plan over the objections of teachers' unions and city hall.[60] Like the community control advocates of the 1960s before them, the reformers sought to make a profession they perceived as failing their children accountable to the local community. The paradigm of the need for external accountability remained decisive. Under site-based management, teachers were able to purchase some greater freedom from central bureaucratic control but only at the price of greater community accountability. Decentralization as professional control remained an elusive chimera.

Finally, in the minds of many political actors, decentralization was linked to greater market accountability, in the form of public school choice, vouchers, and eventually charter schools. Milton Friedman had introduced the idea of school vouchers as early as 1955, and the idea of school choice picked up steam in the favorable political climate of the 1980s. Much of the impetus came from the right, as Reagan and Thatcher mounted an ideological assault on state bureaucracies, drawing on the foundation built by Friedman and Austrian economist Friedrich Hayek. Conservative think tanks that had proliferated in the 1970s saw their work coming to fruition in federal and state initiatives for vouchers and tuition tax credits.[61] Democrats remained wary of vouchers and tax credits, but public school choice became increasingly popular among Democrats as a way to spur innovation within the public system. Charter schools, which promised to free educators from the bureaucratic oversight that governed regular public schools in return for some form of performance accountability, were introduced in Minnesota in 1991 and have since spread to 40 states. For a "New Democrat" like Bill Clinton, embracing public school choice and charter schools was consistent with the Osborne and Gabler philosophy of creating a more effective and responsive government; it also provided political dividends by laying claim to a reform agenda.[62] The movement to free schools from bureaucratic oversight and turn them into competing units was consistent with the zeitgeist emerging across the political spectrum that married market accountability to deregulation. Choice was endorsed both in the 1986 NGA *Time for Results* report and at the 1989 Charlottesville summit. As Chester Finn put it in a 1990 essay: "[C] hoice is the nearly inevitable companion of…the 'second reform movement' in U.S. education, [which is] a 'bottom-up' effort to improve the enterprise by restructuring it, devolving more decisions to the building level and enhancing the professionalism of teachers and principal."[63]

While these wider currents toward market accountability strengthened the movement toward decentralization, the competitive view of improvement was anathema to many teachers and their unions. Both the AFT and NEA have consistently opposed vouchers, have expressed "skeptical support"[64] for public school choice, and have either opposed charter schools (NEA) or insisted that legislation authorizing them include provisions that require collective bargaining (AFT).[65] Charter schools, in particular, have been caught in this crossfire, as union leadership remains skeptical or opposed on the grounds that charters often do not have the same protections for employees as do regular public schools,[66] while some teachers and educational leaders have embraced the greater autonomy afforded by the charter model.[67]

In sum, teachers' calls for greater autonomy in the conduct of their work gained a political hearing because they were often linked to a deregulation agenda that had much broader support. Political views of deregulation, however, were inevitably coupled with demands for accountability to the state, community, or market, a view that in many ways conflicted with the Carnegie report's emphasis on teacher autonomy as a key component of professional control over practice. The "second wave" of reform that would counter the top-down nature of *A Nation at Risk* with a bottom-up strategy of teacher empowerment thus never really got off the ground. To the degree that greater discretion was granted, it would be circumscribed by heightened expectations of performance accountability. New forms that emerged in the 1990s—including charters and standards-based reform—incorporated both the criticisms of bureaucratic management and the demands for accountability into frameworks that proclaimed increasing discretion over school level operations in return for greater accountability for results.

## Who Should Guard the Gates? Professionals
## versus Markets in an Era of Results

The second part of the Carnegie professionalism agenda focused on gaining greater professional control over teacher training and licensure. The ensuing dispute—between those in the profession who would raise standards and lengthen training along the lines of other professions and critics outside the profession who would abolish existing requirements and move toward a laissez-faire system of selecting teachers—goes to the heart of the debate over teaching as a profession.

### Organizational Power and Institutional Support:
### Professionalism Gains Ground

In the years since the Carnegie report, professionalizers have relied upon a "three-legged stool" to establish professional standards: 1) standards for advanced mastery of teaching practice; 2) licensure for beginning teachers; and 3) standards for teacher preparation institutions.[68] The first effort was the National Board for Professional Teaching Standards (NBPTS), discussed above; it was established to create standards to oversee the voluntary credentialing of master teachers. Credentialing involves passing advanced tests on disciplinary subject matter and pedagogical knowledge, presenting a portfolio of student work, and submitting videotapes of teaching. More than 100,000 teachers have been board certified, roughly 3 percent of the nation's teaching force.[69] Forty-nine states have been persuaded to recognize or assist with NBTPS certification, either by paying for the cost of the certification process or by awarding greater status or pay to those who have achieved this designation.[70] Second, to create higher standards for beginning teachers, the Interstate New Teacher Assessment and Support Consortium (INTASC) was launched in 1987. INTASC seeks to establish model standards of what beginning teachers should know both in pedagogy and in particular subject areas. INTASC standards, built largely on NBPTS standards, are consistent with those developed by the major subject matter groups. Thirty-six states participate in INTASC, and as of 1999, 15 had moved to incorporate its standards into their certification and licensure systems.[71] The third leg of the stool has been the reassertion of control over teacher preparation programs through the NCATE (National Council on Accreditation of Teacher Education), a group that was founded in the 1950s but expanded its reach considerably in the 1990s. As of 2002, eight states require that teachers attend NCATE-accredited institutions, and NCATE has partnerships in 46 states.

In total, 540 of the nation's 1,300 teacher-training institutions are accredited by NCATE. These institutions train 70 percent of the nation's teachers. Perhaps reflecting this growth, in 2002 the *U.S. News and World Report* rankings for the first time included NCATE accreditation as part of its rankings of teacher preparation institutions.[72]

All three of these initiatives were pushed by a coalition that included the NEA and the AFT, as well as a variety of organizations representing higher education and teacher preparation programs. Each of these initiatives was endorsed and given a boost by the National Commission for Teaching and America's Future (NCTAF), which authored a 1996 report arguing that a quality teacher was the "birthright" of every child. Not surprisingly, given that NCTAF was largely composed of the above-mentioned groups, it defined quality teaching in a way that was highly sympathetic to the professionalism agenda, calling for NCATE accreditation of all teacher preparation programs and the creation of 100,000 NBPTS-certified teachers.

While these initiatives have not succeeded in establishing the kind of tight control over credentialing that marks law and medicine, they have made considerable progress in getting states to adopt the professionalism agenda. Three major reasons account for this success: the power of the agenda's backers, institutional configurations favorable to the policies, and the way that proponents were able to link the professionalism agenda to the broader standards movement. The greatest advantage that the professionalizers had was the organizational backing of the AFT and the NEA. Teachers' unions represent 90 percent of the nation's teachers and supply the single largest block of delegates to the Democratic Convention. (The Democratic-controlled Congress provided federal start-up funds for the NBPTS in 1987, and the Clinton administration endorsed many elements of the NCTAF agenda.) Additional support has come from the teacher preparation institutions, state agencies responsible for overseeing training and licensing, NCATE itself, and foundations such as Carnegie and Rockefeller, which provided initial financial backing.

The power wielded by these groups is magnified by a favorable institutional terrain, as decisions about licensing and accreditation are made by a diverse array of state actors, including governors, legislatures, state boards of education, state education departments, and professional standards boards. This decentralized arrangement is conducive to the decentralized power of professionalism's proponents, who have advocates in each of the many venues where policy decisions are made. Critics charge that some of these venues have been subject to regulatory capture: professional standards boards that advise on teacher certification policy, for example, frequently include teachers, administrators, and teacher-preparation-program representatives.[73] The professionalism approach also builds upon decades of policies that have accreted to create the current approach to licensing. Continuing to tinker with this approach by raising requirements for accreditation or licensing requires only incremental policy change; other approaches, such as alternative certification, demand a more radical overhaul of existing arrangements.

These interest group and institutional advantages might have come to naught if the efforts for teacher professionalism in preparation and licensure were not perceived as congruent with the emerging student standards movement. The teacher standards movement had a clear and compelling rationale that fit with the broader current of the times—if standards were enacted to clarify expectations for what students should be able to do, then there should be accompanying standards that specify what teachers should know to teach students to those standards. In more recent years, the professionalism advocates have also tried to position themselves on the right side of debates over accountability, as teacher preparation programs and those who accredit them have moved away from an input-oriented focus to assessment and have increasingly focused on whether these programs improve student learning.[74] By linking their goals for professionalism with broader efforts to impose standards and accountability, the advocates were able to gain wider acceptance for their ideas. As Andrew Rotherham and Sara Mead describe it, "Teacher professionalism allowed teachers unions to use the rhetoric of 'higher standards' to advocate improving teacher quality in ways that were not a threat to their organizational goals, but rather advanced them."[75] In short, the professionalism agenda was able to make some progress by incorporating the goals of accountability for results into its call for higher teacher standards.

### Professionalism under Fire: An Alternative View Emerges

While the initiatives sponsored by the professionalizers have proliferated, critics have simultaneously become increasingly vocal in their criticism of the entire underlying model of professionalism. These critics, led by the Fordham Foundation on the right, and the Progressive Policy Institute and the National Council on Teacher Quality in the center, argued that the professionalism agenda had not proved that it could boost student results and just concentrated power in precisely the institutions that had created the educational crisis. Lacking evidence (in the critics' view) that teacher preparation programs produced measurable gains in student learning, the rhetoric of professionalism was seen as a screen for monopoly control over entry into the profession. Worse, by boosting the requirements for credentialing, potentially talented teachers, particularly those who were interested in switching to teaching midcareer, would be dissuaded by state licensing requirements that had little to do with effective teaching. In a climate of teacher shortages, especially in math and science, stiffened requirements for credentialing would only exacerbate the difficulty of finding new teachers to fill classrooms. NCATE was assailed on the grounds of offering accreditation more on the inputs that teacher preparation programs provided (facilities, resources, books, faculty degrees) than on any demonstration that the training improved student learning. The standards offered by NBPTS and INSTAC were criticized as vague and overly influenced by student-centered constructivist pedagogy. Education schools, long a favored whipping boy among traditionalists, were criticized for lacking rigor, and college-based certification programs were derided for overemphasizing pedagogy and multiculturalism at the expense of solid grounding in subject matter. Pointing to the lack of a clear knowledge base for teaching, critics argued that the medical model was not applicable, as there was no similar body of scientific knowledge that preparation institutions could promise to convey. Encompassed by this critique were education's many failings in its efforts to become a full-fledged profession: the weakness of its knowledge base, the lack of popular acceptance of its preferred pedagogy of constructivism, the low status of its preparation institutions, and the high demand for teachers, which undermined efforts to toughen credentialing. Critics were also aided by an emerging view of teachers as focused more on their professional interest than on the public good; in this skeptical climate, claims that teacher professionalism was a cover for monopoly control over entry seemed increasingly plausible.

In place of the monopoly professionalism model, the critics offered a deregulatory alternative: potential teachers would bypass existing licensure requirements and undergo alternative certification. Here the deregulatory ethos worked against the teacher professionalism agenda, as in this case the professionalizers were depicted as the ones embracing regulatory control. A Fordham Foundation "manifesto," which provides the clearest statement of opposition to the professionalism agenda, offers deregulation as its leading rationale:

> We conclude that the regulatory strategy being pursued today to boost teacher quality is seriously flawed. Every additional requirement for prospective teachers—every pedagogical course, every new hoop or hurdle—will have a predictable and inexorable effect: it will limit the potential supply of teachers by narrowing the pipeline while having no bearing whatever on the quality or effectiveness of those in the pipeline.[76]

A better approach, critics argued, would be to minimize or eliminate course-based requirements for licensure and test beginning teachers on the subject matter they were expected to teach. Rather than have teacher preparation programs as the primary gatekeepers, individual principals would have the power to decide which teachers to hire. Skeptical of the constructivist pedagogy dominant in education schools, the critics argued that content-based subject tests were a more effective means for evaluating potential teachers than completion of a teacher preparation program. Former Bush Secretary of Education Rod Paige summarized the arguments for this view in the 2002 *Annual Report on Teacher Quality*, which urged states to streamline their systems of teacher certification, open alternative routes, reduce educational coursework requirements, and eliminate "bureaucratic hurdles" to becoming a teacher.[77]

Alternative certification has proliferated in the years since *A Nation at Risk*, although the motives for its enactment have not always been as hostile to teacher preparation programs as those of the critics quoted above. The modern push for alternative certification began in New Jersey in 1984. The aim was to find ways to bring nontraditional candidates into teaching that were more effective than simply issuing emergency teaching certificates until teachers could earn regular ones. New Jersey designed a program to recruit liberal arts graduates and provide them with training, mentoring, and formal instruction while teaching. Teach for America and Troops for Teachers became well-known alternative certification programs in the 1990s. Overall, the number of states that have alternative certification increased from 8 in 1983 to 48 in 2010. While the vast majority of the nation's teachers have acquired certification by the traditional route, approximately one third of new teachers now enter the profession via alternative certification.[78]

The debate between the professionalizers and the proponents of alternative certification has been wide ranging and often vitriolic.[79] As one alternative certification partisan put it in a reflective article, "Members of these two camps disagree about the skills and knowledge that aspiring teachers need, how to cultivate good teaching, what effect various licensing provisions have on the quality of applicants, or what the evidence says on these questions."[80] Studies debate the effect on student achievement of alternative and conventional certification, with partisans on both sides claiming that evidence supports their conclusions.[81] Teach for America has come under criticism from some of the professionalizers, who argue that the teachers are unprepared in comparison with traditionally certified teachers.[82] In addition to arguing over evidence, the two sides have staked competing claims to accountability, the professionalizers seek to incorporate performance-based

standards into NCATE and NBPTS, and alternative certification proponents argue that new approaches should be evaluated against old on the
basis of gains in student test scores. The groups have also argued vehemently
over who can claim to represent the public good, with alternative certification advocates depicting professionalizers as a cartel protecting the interests
of their members and professionalizers asserting that the market-oriented
approach their opponents favor would cause inequities likely to punish the
least advantaged children.[83] A professionalizer like Linda Darling-Hammond
has also tried to recapture the high ground on deregulation; she argues that
better preparation could create conditions for greater deregulation at the
school level: "If policy-makers and the public are convinced that educators
are well-prepared to make sound decisions, they should find it less necessary
to regulate schools against the prospect of incompetence. Assuring quality in
the teaching force is actually, we believe, the best way to support decentralization and local control in education."[84]

Overall, the debate of the two sides mirrors the larger debate over professionalism. Defenders of professionalism uphold the traditional view
of teachers as those committed to serving the public who need training in
the established knowledge of a discipline; critics arguing for a deregulatory
agenda that would remove the profession's power over training and entry
reflect a market- and consumer-driven vision of how to produce quality.[85]

### *Agnostic on Professionalism: Policymakers' Concerns Orthogonal to Professionalism Debate*

While professionalizers and their critics have vigorously debated the utility
and applicability of the professionalism model, policymakers have largely
sidestepped these debates. Rather than choose sides, they have provisionally
endorsed both models as potential means to meet their primary objective:
improving student outcomes. Although contradictory theories of action
underlie professionalism and alternative certification, politicians of both parties have been content to elide this dispute and support a diversity of strategies. Secretary of Education Richard Riley said in a 1999 address:

> As state and local leaders consider new strategies to improve teaching, I
> ask them to avoid the "either/or" mentality that is dominating the cur-
> rent debate on teaching. One side argues that the current licensure and
> compensation system keeps talented people out of the profession, does
> not ensure quality, and provides few incentives to improve their prac-
> tice. Others contend that teachers need proper training and rigorous

standards for entering the profession. My friends, both sides are right. We need to lower our voices, get practical and think in a new way.[86]

Riley's view did not simply mark Clintonian "split the difference" triangulation; it reflected a pragmatic political reality: leaders of both parties were unlikely to oppose either "higher standards" for professional training or alternative routes designed to get talented candidates into teaching. For this reason, the strategies have proliferated simultaneously. Since *A Nation at Risk*, 49 states have recognized or assisted NBPTS-certified teachers, and 48 states have adopted alternative certification. While there is a partisan aspect to the debate (particularly at the federal level), with Democrats endorsing the professionalizing agenda of Carnegie and NCTAF and Republicans more comfortable with market approaches to certification, on the whole both parties have supported both approaches, particularly at the state level. As Rotherham and Mead describe it in their survey of the teacher politics landscape, "For most state elected officials...teacher-certification issues have less to do with ideology or partisanship than with the realities of operating a system of schools and meeting the public demand for teachers."[87] Policymakers punted on this question again when crafting federal legislation. They endorsed the idea that all children should have access to a "highly qualified teacher" but left considerable wiggle room by giving states discretion to decide what that might mean in terms of certification policy.

In addition to the professionalism and deregulatory strategies, policymakers' efforts to improve teacher quality have also resulted in support for a third approach, which one scholar has dubbed the "overregulation" agenda.[88] Reflecting the continuing distrust of teachers and the institutions that prepare them, this approach underlies the push for teacher testing that has gripped the states in recent years. In 1987/88, for example, only 35 percent of public school districts required a teacher test of basic skills; by 1993/94 the number had increased to 50 percent. Over the same period, the percentage of districts requiring a subject matter test for teachers increased from 25 to 40 percent.[89] Legislators have also sought to intervene in teacher preparation programs, often in directions opposite to the professionalizing reforms, by limiting the amount of coursework in pedagogy, specifying acceptable majors for certification, and even stipulating the number or content of required courses.[90] In 1998 the desire for accountability from teacher preparation institutions came to a head in the debate over reauthorizing the Higher Education Act. Amid reports that nearly three-fifths of teachers failed the new Massachusetts licensing exam and research showing that many states were overlooking the problem of out-of-field teaching,[91] Congress pointed the finger at teacher preparation institutions. Democratic Representative George Miller accused teacher preparation programs of "perpetuating a fraud on the public because they are graduating teachers who aren't prepared to teach" and proposed cutting federal aid to the programs if a federally designated percentage of their graduates did not pass the state licensure exam. Objections from higher education associations eventually derailed this proposal, but Title II of the Higher Education Act was amended to add requirements for informational accountability. Under the amended law, all teacher preparation institutions now had to publish the percentage of graduates passing state licensure exams.[92] Again, the key cleavages were not partisan but institutional, as legislators, led by a Democrat, sought to impose accountability on a profession that, in legislators' eyes, had not proved itself trustworthy to handle its own affairs.

In sum, while the initiatives of the professionalizers have proliferated in the years since the Carnegie report, the professionalizers have not succeeded in getting legislators to adopt the professionalism agenda as their own. Critics have fiercely challenged the underlying rationale of professionalism, but legislators have largely sidestepped this debate and supported a variety of approaches, with improvement in student test scores the bottom line. As Penelope Earley nicely summarizes this dynamic, "In general, decision-makers do not care how teachers are prepared or about definitional matters that are important to the profession. Instead, they see teacher education as a tool to achieve broader, presumably more important policy goals."[93] In one sense, this stance is unremarkable, as presumably all sides of the professionalism debate advance their positions at least in part on the basis of their expected contribution to student success. In another sense, the legislators' attitude illustrates the ongoing weakness of teaching as a profession. As Marilyn Cochran-Smith points out, no other profession is expected to justify itself on the basis of the outcomes of its clients.[94] Legislators' ongoing demands for accountability, by testing of teachers and their preparation institutions, make clear that policymakers remain skeptical of the education profession and grant it autonomy only to the degree that it produces quantifiable results.

## Taking Control of Practice: Resistance from Within

The third aspect of the Carnegie professionalism agenda asked teachers to collectively assume responsibility for the quality of schooling. Shanker was the first major union figure to embrace a new kind of "professional" unionism with his famous Niagara Falls speech in 1985. In the years since, commissions such as Carnegie and the National Commission on Teaching and America's Future have urged a similar stance, as has NEA president Bob Chase. Some union local leaders, particularly but not exclusively within the AFT, also support reform unionism. The specific initiatives under this umbrella have included peer assistance and review (teachers mentoring and evaluating other teachers), performance-based pay, management of charter schools by unions, and collective bargaining contracts that explicitly create joint responsibility of administrators and teachers for school quality. The common thread running through these initiatives is an increased emphasis on school quality over protection of union solidarity, justified by a broader conception of teachers as professionals who should take responsibility for practice.

No single speech better captures the differences between "old" and "new" unionism than NEA President Bob Chase's 1997 National Press Club address: "Not Your Mother's NEA: Reinventing Teacher Unions for a New Era." While lauding the progress of industrial style unionism in winning better salaries, benefits, and working conditions for school employees, Chase argued that "while this narrow, traditional agenda remains important, it is *utterly inadequate* to the needs of the future.... Industrial-style, adversarial tactics are simply not suited to the next stage of school reform." Embracing many of the charges that critics frequently lobbed at the NEA, such as its protection of job security and the interests of its members above all, he offered some "blunt truths" in an effort to "clear the air":

> The fact is that, in some instances, we have used our power to block uncomfortable changes... to protect the narrow interest of our members, and not to advance the interests of students and schools....
>
> The fact is that while the vast majority of teachers are capable and dedicated... there are indeed some bad teachers in America's schools. And it is *our* job as a union to improve these teachers or—that failing—to get them out of the classroom.
>
> The fact is that while NEA does not control curriculum, set funding levels, or hire and fire, we cannot go on denying responsibility for school quality. We can't wash our hands of it and say "that's management's job." School quality—the quality of the environment where students learn and where our members work—must be *our* responsibility as a union.
>
> The fact is that, too often, NEA has sat on the sidelines of change... naysaying... quick to say what won't work and slow to say what will.[95]

Chase pledged the NEA to a "new unionism" to counter these deficiencies of the old. Drawing again on the Carnegie report's rhetoric of institutional autonomy from external regulations and the work of the "reinventing government" management gurus, Chase called for teachers to move from "production workers" to "full partners" or "co-managers" of their schools. Pointing to examples from a few enterprising NEA locals, he offered the vision of a future in which the traditional collective bargaining contract would be replaced by a joint labor-management constitution, giving teachers comanagerial responsibility for a school district. Perhaps most heretical to the traditional unionists and most encouraging to their critics, Chase argued that unions should use peer review to counsel and, when necessary, dismiss their least effective members. This provocative position advocated a shift away from the long-standing union practice of using its power to protect members from dismissal.

In pushing for a more professional unionism, both Shanker and Chase were responding to a changed political environment. Their new positions illustrate the interplay of regulative, strategic, and constitutive ideas in bringing about change. The increased external emphasis on reform made a bargaining-style unionism seem increasingly obsolete, undercutting the legitimacy of industrial unions as major players in school politics (the regulative role of ideas). In response, Shanker and Chase sought to redirect their rhetoric and some of the union's positions, a repositioning that they hoped would afford the union a greater and more legitimate voice in ongoing debates over reform (the strategic use of ideas). Shanker, for one, changed his position quite dramatically after *A Nation at Risk*. Shanker had been such a notoriously obstructionist unionist early in his career that in the 1973 movie *Sleeper*, Woody Allen predicted that the world would be destroyed "when a man named Albert Shanker got hold of a nuclear warhead." Shanker maintained this stance right up until 1983. The AFT was not initially encouraging of Toledo's program for peer evaluation in 1982, and it opposed a career ladder plan offered by Tennessee governor Lamar Alexander in 1983.[96] But all of this changed after *A Nation at Risk*, as Shanker came to endorse shared decision making at the school level, peer review, and career ladder plans in Tennessee and elsewhere.[97]

Chase's "new unionism" speech in 1997 was similarly pitched as a way to adapt teacher union politics to a changing external reality. After Bob Dole publicly attacked the teachers' unions in his speech accepting the presidential nomination at the 1996 Republican Party convention, the NEA commissioned a study of the public's views of the NEA. The study concluded, "The NEA is now painted as the number one obstacle to the nation's public schools."[98] In responding to criticism from local unions that the speech had effectively undermined long-standing union prerogatives and legitimized the position of its critics, Chase cited results from the survey as evidence that the organization needed a fundamental makeover: "NEA is not viewed by virtually anyone in the education, political, social environment as a creative, positive, and influential leader in making America's public schools better....Even worse than being seen as irrelevant, we are seen as part of the problem....I believe it is folly to continue demanding that NEA think and function the same way as in the past, while the education industry itself is verging on collapse."[99] Adam Urbanski, the dynamic leader of the Rochester AFT, succinctly summarized this view as unions either will "reform or be reformed."[100] From the perspective of these union leaders, changing external circumstances demanded a strategic shift from industrial to professional unionism.

What these leaders have not been able to accomplish, at least thus far, is getting their memberships to embrace this shift from industrial bargaining, either as a matter of strategy or, more constitutively, as the proper role for teachers' unions in a new era of school quality. While there are no hard numbers on the number of districts that have adopted peer review or shared responsibility for management, even the most supportive accounts of professional unionism usually cite only a handful of the nation's more than 14,000 districts as examples.[101] Adam Urbanski's network of districts committed to reform, TURN (Teachers Union Reform Network), started in 1995 with 21 AFT and NEA locals; its ranks had grown to only 31 by 2006.[102] Despite the emergence of high-profile experiments, like performance-based pay in Denver, seniority-based pay and transfer policies continue to be the norm. Collective bargaining contracts that lay out in considerable detail the rules and regulations under which teachers will be governed—covering everything from the length of the school day and year to allotted time for bathroom breaks—also continue largely unchanged, with the kind of flexible comanager contracts envisioned by Chase few and far between.

At the national level, the AFT has been committed to the standards agenda and some of the new unionism reforms. The AFT has supported peer review since shortly after *A Nation at Risk* and in recent years has supported some experimentation with pay for performance. The presidents who have followed Shanker, Sandra Feldman (1997–2004) and Edward McElroy (2004–08), have continued his general support for standards and accountability, but neither has become a public spokesperson for reform in the same way that Shanker was. It is too soon to judge current AFT president Randi Weingarten's tenure, although she appears to be more in the Shanker mold of seeking to put the union behind reforms that would move away from the worst excesses of industrial unionism and professionalize teaching.[103] The national AFT continued to maintain general support for standards and accountability even after No Child Left Behind, urging midcourse corrections but not fundamentally challenging the basis of the law.[104]

Despite Chase's support for "new unionism," the NEA has with few exceptions rejected the move toward professional unionism. Chase was the first to embrace reform unionism in 1997, but his position was often not supported within the larger NEA. In a victory for Chase, the NEA did add its support for local experimentation in peer review in 1997, but its representative assembly soundly rejected an endorsement for performance-based pay in 1999. An *Education Week* assessment of Chase's efforts to "reinvent the NEA" at the end of his two terms in 2002 concluded that he "appears likely to be remembered more for the conversations he started than for the deeds of the union he led."[105] In subsequent years, under the leadership of Chase's successor, Reg Weaver, the NEA has repudiated much of Chase's effort to move toward new unionism. Overall, even scholars who have been the most sanguine about the possibilities for reform unionism have had to concede that the unions remain largely conservative forces. As Julia Koppich put it in "The As-Yet-Unfulfilled Promise of Reform Bargaining": "Whatever the reasons…at this moment [summer 2005] neither the AFT nor the NEA is positioning itself to pursue much of a union reform agenda."[106]

The reasons for this resistance to a more professional unionism are complicated and more various than they are usually portrayed. For a union critic like Terry Moe, there is little to explain: teachers' unions exist to protect the interests of teachers, not students, and when the interests of students and teachers diverge, unions are expected to protect the rights of teachers.[107] This is not, in Moe's view, a value judgment about the character of unions and their leaders but simply a recognition that the purpose of a union is to ensure the employment protections of its members. Moe and other union critics cite a litany of examples in support of their view. For instance, unions continue to support seniority-based pay and transfer policies, which critics see as undermining the ability of districts to pay on the basis of performance and place teachers in the schools where they are needed most. Union protections also impede the ability of districts to dismiss teachers they deem ineffective, at considerable cost to the school system. Collective bargaining contracts that specify in detail the maximum number of hours teachers will work also reflect protection of union members' interests. From the critics' perspective, union resistance to accountability measures is only to be expected, in that they impose external evaluation on teachers who have been largely free of it.

As union critics Frederick Hess and Martin West put it: "Teachers unions favor existing arrangements that protect jobs, restrict the demands placed on members, limit accountability for student performance, and safeguard the privileges of senior teachers, not because they benefit students, but because they benefit existing members."[108]

In one sense, self-interest provides a compelling explanation for union behavior: it accurately predicts what most unions do most of the time. But in another sense, this perspective only begs the more interesting question, which is why industrial-style bargaining continues to trump professional unionism. Like all other workers, teachers care about wages, benefits, and working conditions, but they also care about professional goals, such as helping their students to learn and working in effective organizations that give them a sense of efficacy and success. Given this dual focus, why do union positions, particularly in the NEA, continue to emphasize material self-interest over other, more professional concerns? Why does this emphasis persist, even in a changing environment in which high-profile leaders are urging the unions to adopt a greater focus on professional concerns or risk sacrificing all legitimacy in policy debate?

Research on this question suggests that the obstacles to change are cultural, institutional, and political.[109] Culturally, focus groups with teachers reveal that many see teaching as primarily an individual task, resisting the idea that teachers should take broader responsibility for the practice of teaching. As two union scholars summarize the views of teachers, "most teachers work in semi-isolated classrooms and think little about the bigger picture, except when the union calls a meeting."[110] Charles Kerchner and Julia Koppich, who have done some of the most thorough research on reform unionism, report that union staff say they have considerable difficulty in getting teachers to engage with them in efforts for reform.[111] Teachers, for their part, say that they are concerned about problems of teaching and learning but that they do not see the unions as the vehicle for addressing these concerns. In the view of many teachers, the role of unions is to increase pay and to ward off external influences (be they local school boards or federal mandates) so as to widen latitude for individual professionals. This perspective grows out of the historic division of labor within the school system: "loose coupling" preserves teacher autonomy inside the classroom but assigns responsibility for the quality of schooling to the district, not the unions. Here two parts of the professionalism agenda collide, as professionalizers who seek to have teachers enforce standards of practice through peer review or other mechanisms are opposed by another group also claiming the mantle of professionalism through the preservation of individual autonomy and freedom from external review.

In this environment, a cleavage emerges between union leadership and rank-and-file teachers. Surveys suggest that teachers do not share the perception of crisis widely accepted by policy elites. As union leaders try to maintain legitimacy in a policy environment emphasizing increased accountability, local teachers feel no similar compunction to adjust their long-standing views. This cleavage helps to explain some of the differences in the national policies of the AFT and the NEA. The AFT, the more centralized of the two organizations, has given Shanker and his successors considerable leeway to set national AFT policy. By contrast, with a 9,000-member representative assembly voting on policy changes at yearly meetings, the NEA's local districts are much more empowered. The fact that the NEA also draws more heavily on rural and suburban districts, which are less obviously troubled than the more urban districts represented by the AFT, leads, not surprisingly, to an NEA stance that is more resistant to reform.

Institutional inertia and lack of organizational capacity also militate against change. Perhaps the most enduring finding of scholars who study institutions is that they change very slowly, if at all, and teachers' unions are no exception.[112] These unions have been organized since the 1960s to recruit members and to advance their interests against their employers; thus they are populated by people who share that perspective and have a limited capacity to organize around quality. In terms of attitudes, Kerchner and Koppich report that it is not uncommon to hear union leaders say, "We just want to represent teachers; we've no interest in running the district."[113] In terms of organizational capacity, research suggests that unions may be able to create contracts that create joint management over districts but do not have the capacity to oversee the implementation of these contracts. School administrators also exhibit institutional conservatism in their commitment to an industrial unionism that preserves their power to make decisions on matters of school quality. When the Rochester union and district pioneered a plan for comanagement of schools, Rochester administrators sued to stop it.[114] Adversaries at the bargaining table, administrators and union members share a commitment to an industrial model that limits the union role to bargaining for teachers' material interests.

Finally, to many union members, the traditional role of unions in safeguarding members' interests is not only still relevant but essential to protect teachers in an ever more hostile political environment. From this perspective, compromise simply legitimizes and abets those who seek, at best, to take external control of the profession, and at worst, to destroy it. Four Wisconsin teacher union locals expressed this position in a letter to Chase after his new unionism speech:

You must understand our reality. We have a governor and a legislature committed to wiping out the rights of our members, curtailing collective bargaining rights, attempting to shift precious resources from our schools to private and religious schools.... There is no reason to accommodate the privateers, those who would destroy the essence of bilateral determinism against those who wish to destroy us. It is, at best, naïve to believe the people who are attempting to destroy our union for ideological and economic gain will be assuaged because of your pledge to get "the bad teachers out of the classroom." Because you were a social studies teacher before you became President of NEA, you should understand the results of appeasement in Eastern Europe in the 30s and 40s.[115]

In both language and argument, the Wisconsin unions' letter represents the view of teachers under siege. From this perspective, the enemy is at the gates, and to do anything other than fight would be to lose everything.

Similar reasoning motivated the NEA's rejection of the pay-for-performance measure and its continued opposition to NCLB. According to *Education Week*, on the vote on pay for performance, "many delegates feared the changes would set them on a slippery slope toward initiatives for compensating teachers based on factors outside their control." Even among those who do not equate advocates of accountability to Hitler, there is a clear fear that union support may legitimate measures that might carry the appearance of professionalism but would actually confer greater power on administrators and others external to schools. Teachers are also particularly skeptical of plans that would measure their performance on the basis of student performance, which many still argue is at least partially outside the control of teachers. One teacher who opposed the pay-for-performance measure merged these two concerns in voicing his opposition to the plan: "Do we want to send the message to our state legislators and boards of education that we are willing to negotiate or worse, initiate, pay for performance? I do not wish to be evaluated or paid on my students' achievement, but on the fact that I do my job well each day and every day to the best of my ability."[116] Opposition to NCLB has followed similar lines.

## Conclusion: A Semiprofession in an Era of Accountability

Increasing demands for educational accountability are one manifestation of a broader challenge to professional control. Since the height of professional power in the mid-1960s, professionals in many fields have found themselves increasingly challenged from above and below. Growing distrust of major institutions, the rising educational levels of the public, and advances in technology have all undermined deference to professional expertise. Consumer movements, from both the left and the right, have taken a populist stance and sought to hold businesses and professionals accountable from below. Ideological attacks, challenging professionals' commitment to the public good, have charged that the "public good" is simply a screen for protecting professionals' monopoly status and for swelling profits. Enlarged organizational size, growing state spending, and the rising influence of capital and shareholder control in for-profit institutions have all multiplied the number of external stakeholders seeking to direct or standardize the practice of professionals. Overall, deference to professional control has diminished considerably, as a growing number of claimants have sought to exercise market, consumer, state, or capital control over professional practice.

Teachers are particularly vulnerable to external reformers because they did not develop the power of other professions. The high demand for teachers has undermined their ability to control who enters the profession, and the lack of a codified knowledge base has made it difficult to justify the long regimens of training that mark other professions. Teaching is also a highly feminized profession and one that serves children, two characteristics that weaken the power and status accorded it. In part because of this low status and feminization, teaching in the United States was institutionalized in a bureaucratic management model, which gave teachers little formal power over the practice of schooling. Collective bargaining, beginning in the 1960s, increased teacher pay and improved working conditions but did not fundamentally alter this division of power. From the perspective of the sociology of professions, school teaching at the time of *A Nation at Risk* was a "semiprofession," lacking the training, status, or knowledge base that would give the profession power to resist external reforms.

Part of the challenge for those who would professionalize teaching is that the whole notion of professionalization is increasingly under attack. As David Angus writes in his monograph *Professionalism and the Public Good*: "[T]he professional model has itself become suspect. The very professions that educators seek to emulate, notably lawyers and physicians, have become targets for criticism based on fears that their interests conflict with those of the public. ... Simply asserting that greater expertise and professionalism will lead to improved education will not work this time around."[117] In this context, professionalizers' arguments for increased teacher autonomy and use of professional discretion have been circumscribed by political demands for accountability. Teachers have been able to gain a hearing for the benefit of greater autonomy in management of school affairs only by linking their position to a broader movement for deregulation, pushed by neoliberals and "reinventing government" gurus like Osborne and Gabler. Professionalism advocates were able to gain political support for some of the reforms they advocated, such as site-based management, but were never able to get the broader political world to accept the professionalism agenda as an important end in itself. Greater school- and teacher-level autonomy continues to be seen by politicians as a means to the end of better outcomes. Not surprisingly, political impatience with the flat or slow rate of progress over the course of the 1980s has led states to move away from site-based management and toward external standards and accountability in the 1990s, a movement which has diminished the space for professional control and discretion.[118]

*　*　*

Taken together, the last two chapters can explain the proliferation of strategies for school reform in the early 1990s. Public school choice, charters, vouchers, community control, and standards-based reform have all either been invented or had their prominence grow significantly over the past 20 years, despite the fact that they reflect very different theories of school improvement. From one point of view, all of this activity is incoherent or even contradictory. Market-based theories of change assume that the problem is state control of education and that competition is the elixir that will motivate improvement. Standards-based reform, by contrast, assumes that more government standard setting and pressure is the key to reform, a position that is strongly opposed by libertarian groups who perceive a big government takeover. Chicago-style community control assumes that neither the state nor the market is the right vehicle for change but that public involvement from parents is the key to improve practice.

The developments described in the last two chapters can help to explain the simultaneous flourishing of these seemingly contradictory strategies of reform. *A Nation at Risk* created a rhetorical space for policy entrepreneurs who had a solution that fit within their definition of the problem. Successful solutions would need to be school-focused rather than society-focused, ambitious enough to promise wholesale improvement, centered on outputs rather than inputs, and with test scores as a key outcome of schooling and metric of success. Despite their differences, all of the major school reforms of the 1990s fit within this overarching framework. The reform strategies also reflected and fed off increasing distrust for the professional expertise of teachers. The decline of professional control has launched a thousand ships of school reform, each promising to demand a form of accountability—state, market, or community—from an underperforming, untrustworthy school system. When policy did move to create greater school-level autonomy—in charter schools or through standards-based systems that set ends but left schools free to devise means—this autonomy was exchanged for clear measures of external accountability that allowed policymakers and the public to monitor and evaluate school practice.

The question remains how, among these viable options, standards-based reform became the primary template of state and then national reform. Why did No Child Left Behind (and the Improving America's Schools Act before it) anoint standards-based reform as the solution to the nation's schooling woes rather than vouchers, charters, community control, or public school choice? And why did states embrace the standards-based strategy before the federal government required it? To answer these questions requires joining this macro account of the broad shifts in the educational agenda and the professional status of teachers to a micro account of why specific policies were selected in particular legislative contexts. We turn to this next.

# 7

# E Pluribus Unum: *How Standards and Accountability Became King*

IN THE YEARS following *A Nation at Risk*, a storm of educational reform activities swept across the states, as governors and state legislatures tried everything they could think of to improve their schools. But beginning in the late 1980s and continuing through the 1990s, one idea became more popular than the rest. Standards-based reform—setting standards, creating assessments, and imposing accountability—became the most widely preferred school reform strategy; it was enacted in 42 states before federal legislation began to encourage it in 1994 and in 49 states before it became required under No Child Left Behind in 2001. Furthermore, since norms against federal involvement in education made it difficult for Congress to act in the absence of a state-level consensus, understanding how this consensus came to be formed is critical to understanding how standards-based reform became federal law as well.

When a policy spreads across the majority of states in the absence of strong federal requirements, it is reasonable to hypothesize that diffusion processes are at work. Some states develop models, and their success begets adoption in other states. There is some evidence of such a process at work here, particularly in the case of later-adopting states copying some of the leaders. But the possibility of adopting a diffusing policy template still begs the question of state politics—why, exactly, did so many different states choose to put their eggs in the standards-based-reform basket?

In this chapter I argue that the key to the widespread success of standards and accountability is the way that the policy crossed ideological divides. Democrats and Republicans, who had long been divided over issues such as vouchers and increased aid to schools, found themselves on the same side of the fence when it came to standards-based reform, if not always for the same reasons. The pages that follow trace the trajectory of three very different states in moving toward standards-based reform—blue Maryland, where a coalition of Democratic reformers championed standards as a way to gain leverage on failing schools in high-poverty districts; purple Michigan, where a mixed coalition of left and right came to support the same policy for different reasons; and red Utah, where an angry Republican legislature saw in standards-based reform a way to hold a recalcitrant educational establishment to account. The ability of the policy to appeal to such varied constituencies for different reasons enabled it to flourish in a variety of states that otherwise had little in common.

The dynamics of these accountability movements are consistent with the theoretical ideas presented in Chapter Two and with previous efforts at rationalization. The paradigm established by *A Nation at Risk* defined the terms of the debate: schooling is critical for economic development; schools overall are underperforming and require across-the-board solutions; failures of student performance lie with schools and not broader social factors; and the success of solutions will be measured by test scores. As this definition, particularly the economic rationale, took hold in the states, powerful actors—most notably governors, state legislators, and economic groups—became increasingly involved in an arena formerly ceded to state boards or departments of education. In this context, the idea of standards and accountability was appealing because it was consistent with the definition of the problem—it promised across-the-board improvement, it focused on outputs over inputs, it focused on schools, and it could be measured by test scores. Again, the primary opposition came from teachers and, particularly, their unions, which argued that such reforms undermined claims to professional expertise and held teachers accountable for results that were largely outside their control. But the unions' commitment to an industrial bargaining model undercut their legitimacy with legislators: their substantial political and financial power was decisively undercut by their lack of moral power.

Across the cases, we will see that while the lead *actors* varied, the underlying *ideas* were constant—both the *logics* supporting the reforms and the *problem definition* that governed the situation were shared across the states. Thus while the reform ball was carried at different times by governors, state legislators, state superintendents, and business and other advocacy groups, they were all essentially reading from the same playbook in terms of the nature of the problem and its most appealing solution. Clearly, ideas can complement explanations that emphasize interest group power or the power of state actors by accounting for why those actors came to take the positions that they did. That the states, however varied they might have been on other dimensions, largely came to see themselves as responding to the same problem was a critical factor in developing a widespread consensus behind the reforms.

It is also worth emphasizing that the state story recounted here had a parallel federal story. In 1989, President George H. W. Bush convened the governors at the Charlottesville summit, where the governors collectively pledged to measure progress in improving their schools; then Congress, to encourage the states to move forward on standards, passed Goals 2000 and the Improving America Schools Act in 1994; and then the passage of No Child Left Behind in 2001 required states to adopt more robust standards systems. These federal developments are discussed in the next chapter; for now it is enough to say that the detailed state-level evidence presented in this chapter suggests that state policy was not much affected by federal developments until the advent of No Child Left Behind. In the 1990s, it was more that states forged a consensus enabling later federal action than that federal action created a state consensus.

To research the creation of this consensus, I sought to maximize diversity among the case study states, in order to understand how very different states could come to adopt the same policy. The chosen states varied considerably on a number of factors thought to affect education politics, including geographic region, demographics, partisan context, level of local control, and timing of adoption of standards-based reform.[1] I trace these states from the origins of their standards-based policies through the passage of No Child Left Behind, although I occasionally look further into the early years of NCLB—to see how state politics were affected by the adoption of the powerful federal law.[2]

## Maryland: Standards-Based Reform from the Left

### Origins: The Impetus for Maryland's Move to Accountability-Based Reform

The impetus for standards-based reform in Maryland was a 1989 commission report, the Sondheim Report, named after its chair, Walter Sondheim. Released six weeks *before* President George H. W. Bush gathered the governors to discuss education reform at the Charlottesville summit, the report was one of the first in the nation to direct a state toward what would become known as standards-based reform. The report called for a public accountability system for all of Maryland's schools, driven by high standards set by the state, to be enforced by a system of accreditation that would evaluate whether each school was meeting those standards.

The motive driving the commission was a concern about providing equity in a new economy. Belying arguments of a business-driven movement, the initiators of the agenda were State Superintendent of Education David Hornbeck and Democratic Governor William Donald Schaefer. Schaefer appointed and provided the charge to the commission, but an internal memo from Hornbeck shows that the language Schaefer employed was identical (in sentiment and often in wording) to that offered by Hornbeck in a 1987 memo. Hornbeck (and later Schaefer) argued that while Maryland's average scores on the SATs and on national norm-referenced tests were well ahead of most other states, these averages masked a crisis in the performance of Maryland's lower-ranked students characterized by high dropout rates, absenteeism, drug use, and lack of academic skills. As Hornbeck expressed candidly in an interview, he had been seeking greater funding and more action to improve city schools since he had taken office; the goal of the task force was to provide a broader mandate for action. Accountability would be a quid pro quo for funding, Hornbeck said, because the legislature, after years of pouring city and state funds into the city schools, would not support more action without more accountability.[3] Hornbeck's internal memo concluded: "This effort is potentially so significant that it could be the catalyst that places Maryland in a new and different reform context. Excellence *and* equity can be achieved with high standards by *all* kids (including kids at risk)" (emphasis in original).[4] In Maryland, the charge for standards came from outside the legislature and from the left, as a state superintendent sought to jar what he saw as a complacent system into action by creating a commission that he hoped would improve the poorest- and lowest-performing schools in the Maryland system.

The composition of the committee suggests that Hornbeck and the governor were seeking a panel of agents who would reform the system but not one dominated by business interests. The committee of eleven included three educators (a teacher, a principal, and a superintendent), three representatives from business (one of whom was also a former school board member),[5] two legislators, one representative from higher education, a Catholic priest, and Sondheim, a longtime Baltimore civic leader. Notably absent from the list were representatives from the teachers unions, which would later be portrayed by Schaefer in the press as protectors of the status quo. As Sondheim said at the time, the exclusion of the "interest groups" of the school system was necessary to avoid a "lowest common denominator" report: "If we're wrong, we're wrong, and let them say it. But let them say it after we have something out there."[6] The committee was staffed by the Maryland State Department of Education, most notably lead staffer Joe Schilling, who would succeed Hornbeck as the state superintendent of schools and be initially responsible for implementing the committee's recommendations.

The policy approach of the committee was framed by the prevailing problem definitions offered in *A Nation at Risk* and *Time for Results*. Schaefer's charge to what was officially named the Commission on School Performance demanded that it "define the major elements of accountability for determining school and school system performance." The committee's recommendations for a performance accountability system followed from this definition of the problem.[7] In line with *A Nation at Risk*, the committee recommended a shift from norm-referenced to criterion-referenced tests, in an effort to move away from basic skills and toward higher-order thinking. The commission identified the school as the critical unit of accountability, as opposed to the student-accountability approach that Maryland's minimum-competency testing had utilized in the past. This shift made adults responsible for improving the performance of the schools, another key idea of *A Nation at Risk*. The idea of high standards also permeates the report. More than ten years before President George W. Bush sought to end the "soft bigotry of low expectations," Sondheim argued that "low expectations are the curse of our educational system. Kids will certainly live up to low expectations. And that's the worst thing that could happen to us."[8] Reflecting the "tight on ends but loose on means" thinking of *Time for Results*, the committee also recommended that accountability for performance be linked to deregulation of the schools, specifically "the elimination of rules, regulations and other strictures that constrain school staffs in applying their professional abilities and creativity to the task of teaching children."[9] In line with the prevailing climate of accountability, the commission suggested that rewards and sanctions, including the possibility of "corrective action" and closure within three years, be assigned to schools depending on the findings of the accreditation team.[10]

The thinking of the committee was also informed by a set of national policy experts whose views were consistent with standards and accountability. Those asked to testify before the committee or comment on the report included Michael Cohen, the lead staffer at the National Governors Association and the governors' point person at Charlottesville; Marc Tucker, the president of the National Center on Education and the Economy; Susan Fuhrman, the director of the Center for Policy Research in Education; and Hornbeck himself. As is described in more detail in the next chapter, these policy experts would be critical influences in the federal movement toward standards-based reform. Feedback from Cohen on a draft of the report, for example, suggested that the goals be more clearly aligned with the accountability measures (a demand that would become a rallying cry for standards-based reformers). He also suggested that the accreditation system "may be unnecessary" if "there is an effective state assessment system" to create accountability, and that implementing accreditation in each of Maryland's schools would strain state administrative capacity.[11] While Cohen's advice would not be heeded in full in the committee's final report, it would prove to be prescient, as state department of education officials shifted the program away from accreditation and toward performance-based assessment in the years to come.

The debate around the report reflected the new political cleavages created by a politics of accountability. It was embraced by the business community and emphatically opposed by the teachers unions. Reflecting both self-interest and institutional perspective, a survey by the Maryland State Teachers Association (Maryland's largest teachers union and the state affiliate of the NEA) found that its members thought the proposed accountability and accreditation measures had "limited value" and that a better approach would be to remove disruptive students, provide help for clerical chores, and free teachers from tasks such as monitoring lunchrooms. Reflecting an industrialized union model, the teachers also strongly opposed the proposal for greater deregulation, arguing that such loosening of strictures could jeopardize the terms of teachers' contracts.[12] MSTA leader Jane Stern publicly challenged the merits of the program in a joint appearance with Sondheim on the *Today* show shortly after the report was released. In Stern's telling, the primary problem was resources; accountability was a way of dodging legislative responsibility. Politicians "have it backward," she said in her yearly address to the MSTA in November 1989. "When they tell us that there's no more money for education, we should tell them they're not really trying and that they should try harder."[13]

These calls fell on deaf ears among legislators because of prevailing assumptions that had developed over time and were crystallized in *A Nation at Risk*. Two interrelated assumptions that influenced the reception of the report were that resources were not the primary key to school improvement and that teachers were resistant to change and demanded only greater funding. Schaefer repeatedly portrayed teachers in the media as agents of the status quo. On the day the report was released, he said, "Whenever you try to shake up education, you immediately run into a lot of problems because people love the status quo. I just hope the report shakes up education and sends us in a new direction."[14] This was not simply public grandstanding. Sondheim voiced a similar perspective in a private letter to Robert Embry, the president of the Abell Foundation, one of Baltimore's largest philanthropies, and a powerful advocate for the city's disadvantaged youth. Embry had written to Sondheim chiding the commission for emphasizing accountability at the expense of greater resources. Sondheim endorsed the need for "proper funding" but went on to say that funding should not be the only concern:

> It seems to me that fundamental as that issue [funding] is, we should not be so obsessive that we fail to recognize that there are other matters that should concern us, particularly when they have an inescapable relationship to funding, as does accountability for performance (whether or not one welcomes that relationship)....My own impression is that elected officials believe that the educational establishment has a recent history of asking for steadily increasing financial support without any inclination to install a process for accounting for its use of a substantial portion of public funds. Rightly or wrongly, there is a feeling that educators are saying, "Just give us the money. Trust us to spend it wisely." There seems to be a growing lack of patience with that attitude.[15]

In a climate of ongoing underperformance of schooling, funding without accountability was no longer on the table.[16]

As editorials in the *Baltimore Sun*, the *Evening Sun*, and the *Washington Post* endorsed the commission's recommendations using similar reasoning, the education community was further rhetorically isolated and the reformers emboldened.[17] The *Baltimore Sun* wrote that the report's recommendations were "so common-sensical they are bound to be controversial. Educators, after all, are often distinguished by professional arrogance," which has "put them increasingly at odds with the politicians who hold the purse strings." The *Evening Sun*, picking up the resources theme, argued that "*how* money is spent can be as important as *how much* is spent." Support from the media reinforced the prevailing problem definition and weakened the position of the teachers and their unions.

A final push came from the Charlottesville summit. Governor Schaefer trumpeted it as evidence that Maryland was ahead of the curve on performance accountability.[18] The summit was significant in Maryland because actors external to the commission (but shaped by many of the same ideas) validated the report's backers and undercut the legitimacy of its critics. Not surprisingly given the reigning climate of ideas, the proposal to endorse the committee's recommendations was unanimously passed by the Maryland State Board of Education in December 1989.[19]

## The Maryland State Department of Education Transforms the Sondheim Report: The Role of State Bureaucrats

The pathway from the commission report's adoption to its implementation would not prove to be a straight one. The primary means of accountability in the Sondheim Report were the visits of the accreditation teams. Accreditation was the theme covered in the initial newspaper accounts of the report, with the most newsworthy item focusing on the consequences of receiving bad ratings. Criticism from the MSTA focused on the potential of the ratings to stigmatize schools, and Sondheim himself said in an interview that he expected accountability through accreditation to be the primary impact of the report.[20]

But when the Maryland State Department of Education (MSDE) began to formulate its implementation plan, it realized that such an initiative would be far beyond its capacity. Thomas Rhoades, an MSDE official who had been project director of the Sondheim Report in 1988/89, explained the problem: "There are 1200 schools. If you visit one every three years, you visit 400 a year; it's 180 days in the schools...so you are visiting three a day. How many teams will it take?" Even if somehow the visits were conducted, the Sondheim Report had envisioned that the next step would be external technical assistance from the department, which would also be beyond its capacity: "Look at the number of scores that end up in the [lowest category of accreditation] that have to be visited and monitored. The question is where do all these staff come from?"[21] The department was faced with a lack of capacity to carry out the reforms, much as Michael Cohen had predicted.

Instead, the department, led by its experts in testing and assessment, fashioned another approach between the fall of 1989 and the spring of 1991. Rather than accountability through accreditation, accountability would come through testing. Publicly released data would show how well each school fared on the tests, and sanctions or recognition would be based on this performance. What was innovative about the program was the nature of the tests, which would not be the norm-referenced, multiple-choice tests of the past. The Sondheim commission had asked for criterion-referenced tests in order to set an absolute standard, but the department's goals were even more ambitious: it wanted to revolutionize the type of teaching practiced throughout the state. If what was tested was what got taught, department officials reasoned, they would create tests that would be worth teaching to. Unlike traditional multiple-choice tests, these tests would require open-ended responses. Unlike individual paper-and-pencil exams, the tests would involve active and cooperative learning. Students on a science test, for example, might work together to do an experiment before answering questions. The lengthy and time-consuming nature of the exams meant that a given student would not cover enough material to produce an individual score, but that was not seen as a problem, because the purpose was to create accountability for schools rather than students. The tests were deliberately designed to be quite difficult; they set a high absolute standard to reflect the department's emphasis on higher-order skills. The expectation was that over time schools would improve until students could cross this higher bar; the stated goal at the outset was that 70 percent of students would be proficient by the year 2000. In all respects, this approach was consistent with the Sondheim Report's emphasis on higher-order skills (following from *A Nation at Risk*), and it promised to be more in line with the kind of cooperative and critical thinking that the modern workplace was said to require. Pedagogically progressive and informed by authentic assessment techniques, the Maryland Student Performance Assessment Program (MSPAP, pronounced *miz-pap*) linked the political demand for accountability to a constructivist pedagogy favored by education experts.[22]

## The Institutionalization of Standards-Based Reform

### *The Process of Legitimation*

When MSPAP initially debuted in 1991,[23] it was not without problems or critics. The first runs of the test predictably found teachers and students confused about the directions, and a test item in the program's second year that involved a picture of a nude bar became a topic of considerable criticism. MSTA President Jane Stern, who charged that a number of the items were inaccurate, concluded that "the problems involved in this year's test are so severe that there's no way to score them."[24] Stern sought to broaden this critique in a 1993 op-ed in the *Baltimore Sun*, arguing that testing was a repeatedly tried and failed approach to school reform: "Insanity has been defined as doing the same thing over and over again, and expecting a different result. Yet the 'test-pushers' seem undeterred, convinced that if we can just get the 'right' testing program, we can solve educational problems."[25] In its place, she argued for the familiar package of teacher autonomy built on the management principles of deregulation. Citing Total Quality Management guru W. Edwards Deming, she argued for greater frontline control and a move away from a command-and-control top-down model: "Teachers want to transform our public schools from assembly-line factories, offering crowd-control pedagogy, into academic communities capable of giving students the personal attention and follow-up to be successful."[26]

These arguments largely fell on deaf ears with the state school board, the legislature, and state school superintendent Nancy Grasmick, who was the face behind the program. The combination of supporting ideas for accountability and powerful backers was too much for the MSTA to overcome. State legislators whom I interviewed suggested that they largely deferred to Grasmick, who was quickly building a national reputation as an effective state schools chief. Traditions of local control were weak in a small state with only 24 districts, and Grasmick was described as constantly on the road selling the program to the district superintendents and the districts. The Maryland Business Round Table, a statewide coalition of 120 leading employers formed in the years following the Sondheim Report, provided a consistent voice advocating for the program, arguing that the higher-level skills it emphasized were exactly what would be needed in the new economy.

One important opportunity for critics came in the 1994 governor's election. Initially, Democratic candidate Parris Glendening was not entirely sold on standards-based reform. He was skeptical of the program's commitment to hold teachers accountable for student performance in high-poverty areas, like his own home region of Prince George's County, and also thought that teachers should have greater input in designing the program. But newspaper accounts suggest that the policy community persuaded him to continue to support the reforms, particularly as Maryland was quickly becoming a national model for standards and accountability.[27] Glendening announced his support for the program in an appearance in front of the Maryland Business Roundtable, reflecting the prominence of its role as a supporter of reform.[28] The framing of the issue in the media again supported the reformers. The MSTA was depicted as an interest group seeking to thwart a reform that would be in the general interest: "[The MSTA's] political power can bend a candidate's opinion about the tests, especially if the results have recently raised doubts about the educational progress achieved in his or her own county. But a candidate who takes pride in putting policy before politics ought to evaluate the program on its own merits before making commitments to an organized interest group."[29] By the election's eve, both candidates were supporting the program, and it had become a nonissue in the campaign. Grasmick was again a key player; she gave Glendening a C− in an article in *Baltimore* magazine before he came out in support of reforms.[30] Despite the fact that there was no love lost between Grasmick and Glendening (Grasmick's husband had been a major financial supporter of Schaefer), Grasmick's stature in the state was such that she was able to hang on to her position and the reforms she championed even after Glendening was elected.

With a mainstream consensus supporting standards and accountability, critics that challenged the program, other than the union, were few in number and frequently marginalized in their arguments. Republican Delegate Janet Greenip and a small band of followers offered a critique from the social conservative right. Her objections were that the program promoted "higher-order skills" without attention to the "basics" and that testing in general marked state control in a domain that should be left to local districts. This opposition was also rooted in a broader conservative critique of the presumption of expertise by the education profession and the government, an entitled class of "educrats" whose values were suspect. As Greenip put it: "The arrogance, this mind-set is what's causing most of the problem. Too many educators have the attitude that 'I know what's best for your children.'"[31] The anger, even paranoia, of conservative critics was further fueled by the state's unwillingness to release past tests (on the grounds that tests were costly to create). In interviews, Greenip and another opponent of MSPAP expressed particular frustration with the *Sun*, which had not been supportive of their position editorially and, they implied, shared the mind-set of the educrats. However, this position was unable to win much support from either the legislature or the public. Repeated bills to alter or kill the test in the (Democrat-dominated) legislature failed, and protesters organized by Greenip numbered fewer than 40.

Key to sustaining the momentum behind the tests was the positive perception of the program's impact. After the first few years, when the kinks were worked out, teachers became more acclimatized to the tests: "My anxiety level is fairly low," said one teacher in the fourth year of reforms. "I have lived through this and seen the children live through the test."[32] Newspaper coverage, which in early years had focused on snafus in test item construction, began to focus on the human-interest aspects of the novelty of the tests. For example, a 1994 *Baltimore Sun* story began by tracking teachers to the store as they bought raisins and paper towels to be used during the science portion of the tests.[33] *Education Week*'s annual evaluation of state standards and accountability programs rated Maryland's among the best in the nation. Perhaps most important, scores gradually rose: each year's results produced newspaper headlines trumpeting gains over the previous year in the majority of the state's districts. Faced with a climate that was supportive of MSPAP, the MSTA in 1999 stopped calling for the end of testing and suggested incremental changes to the testing regimen instead.[34] Proponents had largely co-opted their critics, building an elite consensus behind reforms that legitimated what had been a highly nontraditional approach to testing. Who would have foreseen that within three years MSPAP would be on its way out, even as standards-based reform firmly established itself for years to come?

*Losing the Battle but Winning the War: The Demise of MSPAP, the Triumph of Standards-Based Reform*

The first serious public breach in the consensus around MSPAP came in fall 1999, when it was revealed that scores had fallen for the first time. In 15 of Maryland's 24 districts, including all of Baltimore's suburban districts and all the Washington-area suburban districts, scores declined.[35] These results suggested that the MSDE's ambitious proficiency goals for the year 2000 were not going to be met. The initial reaction to the decline was support for MSPAP from the political leaders and interest groups who had backed the program. Governor Glendening, for example, said, "We do not change policy based on one year."[36] Experts who favored standards, like the Center on Education Policy's Jack Jennings and Education Trust's Kati Haycock, weighed in to argue that Maryland should not make the mistake of other states and lower its standards. Democratic State Senator Barbara Hoffman, one of the strongest advocates for finance equalization in the Maryland legislature, picked up this theme when she said, "The reaction is that we've got to do a better job. I don't think that we're going to decrease our standards."[37]

But as scores continued to plateau in subsequent years—no district met the goal of 70 percent proficiency that the department had set as the target for 2000, and Baltimore city schools, although showing gradual improvement, still had a pass rate of 20 percent[38]—critics of the program proliferated. One problem for proponents was that despite the "tight-loose" rhetoric of the Sondheim Report, MSPAP claimed not only to be measuring results but also to be creating the means to achieve those results by stimulating new teaching techniques. The consequence was that when the results weren't there, the central agents could not simply blame those farther down and tighten the accountability strings; rather, it was their program that was on the line.

Increasing doubts about the program was a study sponsored by the Abell Foundation. Abell's president, Robert Embry, was the one who had initially written to Sondheim about the need to add funding to accountability, and he was also the president of the state's board of education when it approved what would become MSPAP in the early 1990s. By 1996 Embry had grown concerned with the content of the tests, although he was still a strong advocate of the overall approach, revealing an interesting intraleft cleavage between the pedagogical progressives in the MSDE and equity liberals outside it. In a memo dated Christmas Eve 1996, Embry raised a number of concerns about the program, most fundamentally whether it should produce scores for individual students and test knowledge instead of "application of knowledge." Embry offered to pay for an outside review; after some haggling with the state department over who would be appropriate for the task, Williamson Evers, of the Hoover Institute, was selected to chair the review. The review of Evers's team, although confidential because it mentioned particular test items, was leaked to the *Sun*. It blasted MSPAP along many of the same lines that Embry had, arguing that it was far too geared to process rather than content and that the standards for what would count as a right answer were far too lax. The department responded that the evaluators were politically biased against Maryland's performance-type assessment, preferring a more traditional content-based exam. State testing director Mark Moody said it was "unprofessional in tone" and equivalent to "creationists reviewing the theory of evolution."[39] The department also cited numerous other evaluations that had found the tests to be in good standing. But the report, whether it was fair or not, cast doubt on the neutrality of the tests; it created two legitimate sides to what had been a virtually uncontested issue. No less a figure than Walter Sondheim called for an independent panel to review the Evers study and the department's claims because, he said, the dispute "has developed into two armed camps."[40]

The declining test scores also created a powerful enemy for the program, as Montgomery County Superintendent Jerry Weast found his high-scoring district on the hot seat. Home to some of the state's (and the nation's) best public schools, with high percentages of students attending Ivy League colleges and winning National Merit Scholarships, Montgomery County showed declining MSPAP scores in 1999 and, even more markedly, in 2001. The drops in Montgomery and other counties in 2001 were significant enough that Grasmick commissioned an external review of the administration and scoring of the tests, but the review concluded that the scoring of the tests was valid. While in the past superintendents had backed the program, in this case Weast publicly questioned it, calling the results inexplicable. Given the success his schools were having on other measures, why were they not faring better on MSPAP?[41] Weast was not opposed to standards or testing, but he questioned whether MSPAP was a valid measure of performance.[42] The department initially continued to back its measure publicly, and some criticized Weast for blaming the messenger rather than address real problems in his district. But the damage to the program had been done. As one reporter described it, critics who had for years been "outside the education establishment," had now expanded their ranks to include some of the most powerful educators in the state.[43]

As more powerful public leaders began to question the program, many of parents' long-standing concerns with the program became magnified. The length of time it took to complete MSPAP had long been a complaint: because of its unusual format, it took five days each spring. Parents had also asked repeatedly why their children did not receive individual scores from the exam, particularly given the amount of time spent on it. In addition, observers questioned whether eighth-grade students would take the exam seriously if it did not reflect on them individually. By February 2002, 85 percent of the respondents to an MPT electronic pulse poll wanted to do away with MSPAP.

Facing a climate of discontent, in 2001 Grasmick appointed a 40-member "Visionary Panel" to recommend the next steps for the testing program. Heading the testing subcommittee was none other than Jerry Weast, joined by such longtime standards experts as Michael Cohen and Jack Jennings. The committee, several of whose members had close ties to the Washington developments around No Child Left Behind, recommended that the state move to a simpler tool that would emphasize content, use more multiple-choice tests, and provide individual scores for each student. Released within weeks of the passage of No Child Left Behind, the report cohered nicely with the emerging federal requirements, which also demanded individual results. In addition, the federal program demanded annual testing for grades 3 through 8, meaning that the sheer volume of testing needed would favor the adoption of commercial tests or at least of tests that were simpler to create and score than MSPAP. This decision raised the ire of some within the MSDE, who felt that Grasmick was simply bending to the political winds by abandoning the constructivist instrument the department had pioneered. While MSPAP had fallen victim to a rebellion from below against its pedagogical constructivism, the broader agenda of standards-based reform had prevailed.

## Maryland: Summing Up

The Maryland case shows how a governing paradigm can set the terms for a reform debate. The problem definitions set by *A Nation at Risk* and *Time for Results* were reflected in the governor's call for a commission on accountability and in the commission's recommendations for a system of performance accountability. The emphasis on accountability in turn shaped the political cleavages around reform, with political and business elites in support and teachers unions opposed. The prevailing image of a school system in crisis and teachers unions defending the status quo provided legitimacy for the accountability program and was essential to sustaining it. In this context, critics eventually had to narrow their barbs to focus only on the nature of the specific test rather than the idea of test-based accountability. Despite their success in eliminating the test, they were unable to shake the broader foundations of standards-based reform.

While it is sometimes alleged that standards and testing are tools of corporate interests, the Maryland case shows that standards-based reform can be championed from the left. Hornbeck, Schaefer, Sondheim, and the Democratic Maryland legislature were the primary sponsors of the reforms, which they saw as a way to gain increased leverage over schools that were badly failing poor children. In accreditation first, then later in testing, the reformers sought to ensure that all schools would reach a common floor, a standard they hoped would level the playing field for more and less advantaged schools. While business groups became important backers of the reforms, the initiative came from left-leaning advocates seeking better schools for poor children.

The means the reformers employed reflected the technology available to those who sit atop a system and seek to create greater standardization across it. Administrative considerations were clearly important, as a more time-intensive system of accreditation and technical assistance was shelved in favor of a cheaper and less resource-intensive methodology of testing through MSPAP. These means proved initially capable of lifting scores, but ultimately they were too weak to create significant change and sustained improvement in Maryland schools. The limits of the strategy in failing to achieve what it promised almost brought down the overall reform effort, but proponents were able to save the program by changing the tests and effectively resetting the clock to zero.

The Maryland case also reveals how "standards" are a content-free vehicle, one that different pedagogical visions can utilize. The MSDE had a fairly strong vision of constructivist pedagogy, which it sought to infuse through the state using an unconventional set of assessments that it hoped would model and drive practice toward higher-order skills. That the state education department was able to pioneer such an approach confirms that state administrative actors play an important role in shaping technical aspects of policy. But the department's preferred constructivist pedagogical approach was supported only to the degree that it was able to link itself to a broader narrative of improving tested abilities; when test scores faltered, the department was forced to abandon its preferred approach and adopt a more traditional testing program that had more popular legitimacy. In part because of the perceived failings of the previous program and in part because of NCLB, standards-based reform in Maryland in the 2000s would come to look much less radical and much more like reforms in the rest of the nation—individual scores, multiple-choice tests, and an emphasis on basic skills.

## Michigan: "Standards-Based Reform" from the Middle

### A Nation at Risk and the Initial Steps to Standards

Not surprisingly, given the prominence of the automobile industry in the state, *A Nation at Risk* hit home in Michigan. As was briefly discussed in Chapter Five, themes of educational crisis, the economic importance of schooling, and the need to move away from a failing status quo were widespread in Michigan in the years following *A Nation at Risk*. A prominent 1987 Michigan commission on school finance, composed of leaders from business, industry, agriculture, labor, education, and government, reflected the prevailing sentiment in suggesting that "the quality of education, in general, must be significantly improved."[44] *A Nation at Risk*'s metaphor of decline permeated the Michigan commission report: "Michigan has a long and honored tradition of providing quality, equitable educational services for all of its people. This tradition is now in jeopardy."[45]

The newly dominant economic view of schooling directly affected who was empowered to act in educational policy. Legislators were not willing to defer to the state board or state department of education when it came to something as important as the state's economic future. As one legislator dismissively put it in discussing education reform in the 1990s: "The state Board of Education wasn't a player. The Department of Ed wasn't a player."[46] The players, in the view of this legislator, confirmed by almost all of my respondents, were now the governor, followed by the legislature, followed by the Michigan Education Association, a powerful state chapter of the NEA.

This reshaped political landscape led to the passage of a bipartisan standards bill in 1990. The new law, Public Act 25, created a statewide but voluntary core curriculum, requirements that schools prepare report cards and develop improvement plans, and a state accreditation program to ensure the quality of local schools. This law started Michigan down the road toward standards-based reform, even though by the criteria of a full-fledged accountability movement, what the law required was rather minimal. The bill was supported both by Democratic Governor James Blanchard and gubernatorial

challenger and State Senate Republican leader John Engler. Each of them, having failed in the larger task of restructuring Michigan's school finance system,
was looking for a way to address issues of school quality. The Greater Detroit
Chamber of Commerce supported the bill because it promised to increase the
quality of the workforce without raising taxes or spending more state money.
The MEA favored the legislation and advocated that the state go a step farther
and mandate the core curriculum. (Some saw this as a genuine desire by the
MEA to improve and standardize the quality of school curricula; the more
cynical said that the MEA saw the mandated core as a jobs program, since
it would increase the need for teachers in subjects that some schools might
otherwise decide they could do without.) The only real opposition came from
local-control conservatives, who argued that this was the first step toward a
state takeover of matters that properly belonged to school boards. However,
in the context of a state and national imperative to improve school quality,
their voices had less impact than they once did. According to aides involved in
the development of the bill, in the end the legislation was not very controversial; the decision to make the core curriculum *voluntary* muted much of the
opposition. Public Act 25 passed by overwhelming margins in both the house
and senate and was signed by Governor Blanchard in March 1990.[47]

The second step came three years later, when the Michigan legislature, in
a move to make the core curriculum mandatory, created statewide standards.
The mandatory core was only one part of a much larger piece of legislation
that addressed Michigan's long-standing inequities in school finance. The
new legislation abolished property taxes, increased the sales tax, and largely
shifted the burden of paying for the schools from the districts to the state. In
another move to improve school quality, the law also created charter schools in
Michigan. Two rationales were given for the greater state role in ensuring school
quality. As suggested in Chapter Five, one reason that underlay the large-scale
state movement into education was the shifting of spending from localities to
states. Legislators in Michigan who were interviewed at the time offered a similar rationale, arguing that assuming a much greater share of the spending on
education entitled them to be more invasive in their policymaking.[48] Said one
Democratic legislator, "Frankly, the issue is when you're talking about putting
10 billion—*billion*—dollars into education, we have a right to make some of
those decisions. Far more now I think than we did in the past when we weren't
the major funders of the schools. So I think that was a very legitimate discussion for us to have."[49] Second, legislators suggested that since they were reforming the finances of schools, they wanted to tie that restructuring to some effort
to reform quality—so that, as one put it, they wouldn't simply be "rearranging

chairs on the deck of the Titanic."[50] Especially given that the new measures were going to necessitate a tax *increase*—potential death for Democrats and Republicans alike in an election year—legislators wanted to assure the public that they were doing everything possible to get a good return on the dollar. One legislator said, "We're not supporting any new taxes unless we get some assurance of improved quality in education."[51] The problem definition established by *A Nation at Risk* was again controlling—schools were failing; old solutions hadn't proven effective; accountability for public dollars was paramount.

The parties shared the above rationales, but there were diverging views of how best to boost school quality. For Democrats, the way was through the creation of a state core, which would provide a means to diffuse high standards across Michigan's hundreds of districts. For Republicans, the concern was less with standards and more with accountability, to be created through either the state or the market. Republicans said the magnitude of the legislation provided an opportunity for significant progress on school quality, a chance to confront a resistant educational establishment. In the words of one Republican legislator, "The schools are not going to change unless change is forced upon them."[52]

In the final legislation the divergent visions compromised, within a shared commitment to improving school quality. Democrats were supportive of the mandatory core (standards) and were able to get it into the legislation in return for supporting charter schools, Governor Engler's top priority. Democrats interviewed at the time said they were determined to pass a significant quality measure so as not to be portrayed as either obstructionist or unwilling to demand accountability for public money. With support from the MEA, the Democrats championed the mandatory core curriculum because, unlike the Republicans, they did not have to placate a social conservative wing opposed to the core on local-control grounds or a libertarian wing that saw it as an unwanted bureaucratic intrusion. In a state with more than 500 districts and a high level of local control, adopting a mandatory core was a substantial step but one legitimized by a demand for state-level action to solve a perceived educational and economic crisis.

### Interest Groups and the 1993 Reforms

Interest groups also played a role in the legislation, each taking the expected side in a post–*Nation at Risk* context. Legislative aides said that for the first time in their memory, various parts of the business community came to the table with more than gripes. They advocated a model core curriculum, assessments aligned with that curriculum, privatization of school services, interdistrict choice, and charter schools. Both publicly through the media and in meetings with the governor and legislators, the business community countered the position of the unions and others who defended the existing system and demanded increased performance for results. The leaders of the Detroit and Michigan chambers of commerce coordinated meetings on school quality between CEOs of several of Michigan's largest companies and legislators. This was the first time CEOs had directly lobbied on an issue that did not affect the bottom line. Another important group was Michigan Business Leaders for Educational Excellence (MBLEE), formed in 1990 by the CEOs of Kellogg, Whirlpool, and a number of other of Michigan's largest companies as the local branch of the Business Roundtable. Their agenda was standards-based reform: beginning in 1991, they advocated consistently for a combination of high standards set by the state, curriculum and testing aligned with those standards, and strong accountability measures for schools that fail to live up to them. This agenda was developed outside the business community by a group of four academics from Michigan and Michigan State universities in the years when the CEOs had identified school quality as a problem but were still searching for a solution.[53] The Michigan business groups did not advocate choice or vouchers; they were the only state interest group to focus solely on standards-based reform.

Although the business community had adopted a standards-based agenda, some legislators and aides were skeptical about its knowledge and commitment to reform. While legislators were impressed that the CEOs themselves would travel to Lansing, the CEOs were also described as underprepared and not up to speed on some technical or political issues the legislation encompassed. One Engler aide expressed frustration that business was not a stronger player on education issues: "In politics, there are chickens and pigs. They [the business community] were definitely more on the chicken side. They would drop an egg, but that would be about it. But the people on the other side, people that are part of the status quo, they were completely committed."[54] By all accounts, the business investment in educational matters was minor compared to its lobbying on more traditional tax and regulatory issues (one aide estimated the ratio at about 100 to 1). Calling the business community "chicken" might overstate the case, but it would be fair to say that legislators did not perceive the community to be as committed to educational issues as it was to those that directly affected its bottom line. Rather, its key function—by denouncing the failures of the system and calling for greater accountability and reform—was to support legislators and the governor in a public relations battle with what Republicans perceived as an entrenched status quo.[55]

The 1993 reforms also showed the declining influence of the MEA in a context that was increasingly unfavorable to its long-standing demand for more resources without a quid pro quo of reforms to improve school quality. This was a striking development since, even among teachers unions, the MEA was seen as a particularly powerful industrial-style union. The MEA was the largest contributor to the Democratic Party in the state; its financial resources, combined with its significant voting block, had long made it a powerful player in legislative politics.[56] Republican legislators in particular had feared the MEA's willingness to fund candidates in primary races. Said one, "They were threatening because *they could get you* ... They could finance your opponent with thousands of dollars in political action money."[57]

But despite the MEA's material power, the 1993 reforms indicated that politicians were no longer willing to defer absolutely to the union. Its power was counteracted by the broader public interest in school quality. One legislator said at the time, "I have told them that I feel that they ought to be more of a proactive participant in supporting changes as opposed to simply being obstructionist from fear of these changes. And I wouldn't say that they sustained that status quo preservation mentality throughout all of this, but they were too resistant; and as a consequence, diminished their own role in some negotiations."[58] Engler was able to create a distinction between teachers, to whom he pledged respect and admiration, and teachers unions, which he fought as an enemy of excellence and free enterprise.[59] A September 1993 *Free Press* poll found that 58 percent of the Michigan citizenry either strongly or moderately agreed with the statement that teachers unions were too powerful.[60] In the end, the MEA was able to win when its interests were consistent with the emerging emphasis on school quality, as in the instance of the mandatory core, but lost when its interests opposed the new consensus, most notably on charter schools. To put it in more theoretical terms, the MEA's raw interest group power was diminished, and its success in the new environment was largely contingent on linking its proposals to the broader concern for boosting school quality.

## Standards Challenged but Survive

One of the most interesting features of the state debates over standards-based reform is that the demands for standards were constantly challenged and sometimes revised but never in a way that disturbed the underlying movement toward state-driven reform. One such challenge came after the 1994 elections gave the Republicans control of the Michigan governorship, both houses of the legislature, and the state board of education. Much as the Gingrich Republicans fought to repeal the just passed Goals 2000 legislation after winning control of Congress in 1994, the Michigan power structure favored deregulation, with no countervailing force to stop it.

In 1995, Republicans narrowly passed the revised school code legislation, which erased numerous regulations from schools. Most significantly, it created a "general powers" clause, which ensured that local districts could engage in activities unless the code prohibited them, instead of limiting activities to those the code explicitly permitted. It also eliminated the mandatory core curriculum only two years after its adoption. The core was portrayed as a dictatorial state intrusion on local control; in addition, some argued that it was an unfunded mandate that would make the state liable to district suits. Social conservatives also favored the elimination of the core; they saw it as vague or as promoting sexual education or socialist values.

None of these arguments dissuaded the business community, Democrats in the legislature, or the editorial page of the *Detroit Free Press* from pointing out that the legislature was abandoning its commitment to standards almost before implementation had begun. No Democrat in either the house or senate voted to abolish the core; the legislation to eliminate the core passed on straight party-line votes. House minority floor leader Pat Gagliardi issued a press release that cited support for a mandatory core by business groups and the governor in the past. He argued, "The public wants it, parents want it, the business community wants it, and the children need it."[61] The *Free Press* denounced what it called "Christian right activists" and "'local control' cliché mongers" for thwarting the will of employers, parents, and taxpayers, all of whom wanted the mandatory core.[62] House Democratic leader Curtis Hertel argued in a letter to the *Free Press* that the conservative majority was dangerously out of touch with the will of the people of Michigan. He pointed to a state board of education survey that showed that 87 percent of Michigan residents believed that the state should set standards for schools, a view which he interpreted as support for a core curriculum.[63] Groups like the Michigan Business Leaders for Educational Excellence continued to advocate systemic standards-based reform, although seemingly to no avail.

However, a close look at the legislation reveals that even at a moment when Republicans were strongly antigovernment, they still embraced many core assumptions of *A Nation at Risk*. In return for not having a state-mandated curriculum, districts would have to adopt core academic curriculum content standards, and state accreditation of schools would include pupil performance on state tests. However, both Engler and the state department of education argued that enforcing the core curriculum standard would be bureaucratically cumbersome; state tests could achieve the same result, with accreditation dependent in part on student test performance. The revised school code also included a provision that required students to pass a test for a "state-endorsed" diploma, another state safeguard to ensure quality. In response to critics of the elimination of the mandated core, Republican legislator William Bryant pointed to the state testing program and the endorsed diploma. If schools go too far astray, he argued, they won't do well on those external measures, "and parents will hang the school boards."[64] In the longer view, while the 1995 legislation marked a modest shift away from the growing appetite for state power, the movement for standards-based reform simply changed its instruments and continued largely unabated.

## Beyond Standards: Accountability through Accreditation

The early 1990s legislation had planted the seeds for accountability through the state accreditation system, and the late 1990s featured intense political fights over how to apply accreditation criteria. The political cleavages were now the mirror image of the fight over the core curriculum: Republican legislators and Governor John Engler pushed for tighter test-centered accountability, while Democrats and the MEA fought for a looser system of accountability that allowed for progress over time and included measures other than test scores.

The first volley on the accreditation standards came from the governor and from critics on the right. When the state department of education first determined accreditation in 1995, it awarded "summary accreditation" (full passing marks) to 163 schools, "interim accreditation" (partial pass) to 2,762 schools, and no accreditation to 93 schools, a number that was later revised downwards to 8.[65] This outcome engendered a number of criticisms, most notably that the distribution included many schools in the middle with few at the bottom and the top.[66] In part at the prompting of the governor, the department prepared a new plan to significantly stiffen the requirements for different kinds of accreditation and move the process closer to a system of standards-based reform. State Superintendent Arthur Ellis, an Engler appointee, stated in a 1999 memo that the new requirements would support the education community's efforts to define what students should know and be assessed on and "would hold schools and districts accountable for high levels of achievement [and] workplace readiness," as well as other factors. The new accreditation standards, approved by the state board in May 1999, included a mixture of absolute and overtime performance measures, including high academic achievement, lack of disparity between disaggregated groups, and adequate yearly progress.[67] For the moment, Engler's emphasis on accountability had prevailed.

But before his plan could go into effect, it was derailed by changes in the partisan landscape and a revelation about the likely consequences of the accreditation system. Just as stricter standards were about to be imposed in spring 2001, a public outcry arose when the *Detroit News* revealed that 600 to 900 schools were likely to be unaccredited. The new state superintendent, Tom Watkins, with the support of a now Democratic state board of education, removed the accreditation standards before the results were even released. Over the course of the next six months, Watkins and the department of education developed a new system (Education YES!) that was much more sympathetic in its ratings. Specifically, it moved away from a narrow focus on test scores and significantly broadened the ways that schools would be evaluated. The second round went to the Democrats.

The new results, released in 2003, revealed that many of the worst-performing schools had given themselves the highest scores on the self-rating part of the accreditation and thereby had avoided losing accreditation. Predictably, the business community raked Watkins and the department over the coals for this new system. In addition, given the requirements created by No Child Left Behind, the accreditation system seemed redundant to many: NCLB had its own set of requirements for improvement and its own set of consequences for failing to meet them.

One interesting subplot in the development of the accreditation system is the role education groups played. In 1991, after the initial move to standards, the MEA had expressed skepticism about the effects of standardized testing, particularly on minority students, and "encourag[ed the] curtailment or elimination of group standardized, aptitude or achievement assessments until such time as a critical appraisal of current testing programs [has] taken place." The MEA also asserted that "teachers must have a say in determining who will be assessed, when, and on what; which assessments to use and why." As we have seen, this strategy of resisting testing and valorizing professional expertise had proved a loser in the transformed political context. Taking a different stance, educational organizations, led by the Michigan Association of School Boards, called for a "culture of accountability." In two reports of the Michigan Accountability Task Force, the group, while acknowledging the importance of holding teachers accountable, argued that other entities, including school boards, the legislature, and universities, needed to be accountable as well.[68] On accreditation, the task force specifically advocated multiple measures of school quality, including progress on tests over time, parental involvement, student engagement, and curriculum alignment. While it is impossible to prove that the task force was directly responsible for the substance of Education YES!, State Superintendent Tom Watkins attended many of its meetings, and the program he adopted was very similar to the one the group had advanced. In short, by shifting their rhetoric (and to some degree their recommendations) to better align with the prevailing problem definition and affirmatively offer an alternative solution, the education groups were able to secure a modest victory on accreditation.

## Michigan: Summing Up

Michigan shows how standards-based reform can develop from the center. *A Nation at Risk* transformed the political landscape for education reform in Michigan, as it motivated a shift in control from local districts to a state legislature that saw education as critical to economic development. It also sparked the creation of a business coalition supporting reform and left teachers unions defending a failing status quo. Standards-based reform was the chosen policy solution both because it was congruent with the definition of the problem and because it was able to win support from left and right. Democrats were drawn to *standards*, in the form of a mandated model core curriculum, a position supported by the teachers unions and the professional educational establishment, while Republicans were drawn to the *accountability* inherent in testing, applied in this case through a state accreditation system. The result was an often-revised policy that shifted in the partisan winds, always maintaining an emphasis on either standards or accountability but never knitting the two cleanly into a coherent policy template.

## *Utah: Standards-Based Reform from the Right*

### The Slow Movement to Standards-Based Reform

In Utah just as in Michigan, standards-based reform developed incrementally. The first move came shortly after *A Nation at Risk*, when the state adopted a core curriculum. More specific than previous state standards, the core curriculum provided a clear metric of what teachers would be expected to teach. It was largely embraced by teachers and given high marks by the AFT. Next came the state's early attempt to introduce accountability for results. In 1990, the legislature mandated that all 5th, 8th, and 11th graders take national tests and that districts' performance on these tests would be made public. Meanwhile, the State Office of Education (the Utah equivalent of a state department of education) had pioneered the creation of criterion-referenced tests to measure how well students were learning the Utah curricula. These tests, expensive to create and score, were given to only a portion of Utah's student population (500,000 criterion-referenced tests were given in 1996, up from 200,000 in 1989).[69] During the 1990s, the office of education also developed a writing assessment and a portfolio project, methodologies consistent with the developing conviction in professional education circles about the importance of evaluative instruments other than multiple-choice tests. The result of these various efforts was that by the late 1990s, Utah had many of the pieces in place for standards-based reform, although it did not have an accountability-based system. No stakes were attached to doing well or poorly on the required tests; schools were neither aided nor closed if they performed poorly, and the tests were not aligned to the state curriculum.

That Utah did not move sooner to an accountability model is consistent with the idea that perceived underperformance is what inspires change. A 1984 analysis that sought to measure how well Utah was faring on the indicators of *A Nation at Risk* found that the state was not at risk on many of the indicators the national report had cited. High percentages of Utah students were gifted, student performance in basic reading and math skills had increased since 1975, and Utah students did not suffer from the high remediation rates that *A Nation at Risk* had cited.[70] Comparisons to other states were also highly favorable: Utah generally scored above the median on national test scores. As of 1998, Utah was one of 15 states with a 90 percent graduation rate and had the nation's fifth-highest passing rate on advanced placement exams.[71]

All of these accomplishments came despite the fact that Utah, because of its high Mormon population, had more students per taxpayer than other states and consequently ranked last among states in per pupil funding. Perhaps because of limited funds, Utah also had the lowest share of school money spent on administration, a reality that further reduced the possibility of an expensive state testing and accountability program. State testing director Barbara Lawrence highlighted this factor in 1997 in responding to a report that gave Utah low marks on standards and accountability in comparison with other states: "Utah has every type of assessment that they describe, but we don't administer them on a large-scale basis," she said, arguing that Utah's system was of high quality considering the number of students and available funding.[72] Overall, given that Utah was already perceived to be highly successful in its ratio of learning to inputs, and that it had a tight budget for school administration, it is not surprising that the clamor for a new program of standards-based reform was relatively muted in comparison with that in other states.[73]

## Utah Adopts Standards-Based Reform: Diffusion and Increasing Demands for Accountability

At the same time, developments in the state and the nation were slowly increasing the pressure for greater accountability. Utah scores had been flat or dropping in the years leading up to 1999; fifth graders' reading and language scores had fallen below the national median in the late 1990s.[74] Another factor was the poor ranking of the state on national measures of standards and accountability. It received low grades from *Education Week*'s rankings of the states, which were covered in the local newspapers and created pressure for improvement.[75] Without engaging in a tautology—that is, states adopted standards because states adopted standards—it does seem fair to say that an S curve diffusion process was taking place in which the adoption by early and then midpoint states increased the pressure on other states to follow suit. The fact that almost all states had some form of standards and testing in place increased the legitimacy of state rankings. If a state had already adopted this approach in part, then why shouldn't it be assessed on the quality of its standards or the comprehensiveness of its system?

Into this context came a policy entrepreneur championing standards, supported by a legislator who demanded accountability. The policy entrepreneur was John Bennion, a former Utah state superintendent. Bennion traveled to Maryland, Texas, Kentucky, and Chicago to talk to local officials about the implementation of their standards-based programs. He wrote up his findings in an influential white paper, which concluded that Utah already had many of the needed elements of a standards-based system but that it needed to align its assessments to its standards, create school accountability for results on the tests, and provide assistance to schools that fared badly. The Bennion paper would be widely cited by legislators and the media in the debates that followed, indicating the power of a respected policy entrepreneur to bring a preferred policy solution into a debate.

One person whose eye was caught by the Bennion paper was Republican State Legislator Tammy Rowan. As was reported in the *Deseret News* and confirmed by numerous respondents I interviewed, as Rowan watched her own daughter pass from grade to grade despite her weak reading skills, she became convinced that the school system was unduly lax in its standards.

Rowan initially argued for an end to "social promotion," suggesting that her concern was less with a particular mode of accountability than ensuring that the schools held each student to a given standard. But over time Rowan began advocating a Texas-style system of accountability, which she hoped would encourage the school system to push every student toward his or her potential.[76]

A legislative task force on standards and accountability was convened in 1999 to study the experience with standards-based reform in other states and make recommendations for the creation of such a system in Utah. The lines of rhetorical debate reflected many of the divisions that had become familiar in arguments over accountability policy; their resolution reflected the shifting climate of ideas described in the previous two chapters. Two debates were paramount. One was whether schools could rightly be held responsible for results. In the task force's initial meeting, Republican State Senator Howard Stephenson, its co-chair and a longtime proponent of taxpayers' rights and more choice in schooling, argued that a greater emphasis on results was needed: "We've done a lot...but where are the results?" he asked.[77] Republican Governor Mike Leavitt supported this view at a conference sponsored by the commission, stressing that "we see the results in the inputs but not the results we want to see in the outputs."[78] Educators took the other side, arguing, in what was becoming a familiar appropriation of their opponents' favorite word, that legislators needed to be "held accountable" as well. Phyllis Sorenson, president of the Utah Education Association (state affiliate of the NEA), made this argument repeatedly: "For me, the bottom line is: If they want to hold schools accountable, then, by darn, legislators should be held accountable for the amount that is spent on education. Utah is getting the best bang for its buck with the amount given to schools."[79] Teachers also argued that scores would simply reflect the backgrounds from which students came. "This can be compared to students being graded according to their height and father's yearly income, and it is unfair," said sixth-grade teacher Amy Martz. "Your threats...will only disrupt students, demoralize teachers and disable communities."[80]

A second set of arguments revolved around whether teachers merited control of their profession. In a meeting of the task force that invited public comment, teachers were not shy about voicing what they felt was an unneeded abrogation of their authority. "You people need to quit threatening us and come into the classroom and see what it is we do," said Deanna Johnson, a teacher at Sandy Elementary School.[81] "I would never tell a doctor or lawyer how to run his practice. You need to come spend more time in the classroom."[82] Democrats on the committee supported the teachers. In a *Deseret News* op-ed, Democratic Representative Karen Morgan married arguments about teacher professionalism to the notion that school performance was partially out of teachers' control:

> How do we rate doctors? By the number of patients who achieve full recovery or by the skill of the medical care delivered? Should they turn away those with a terminal illness because it would lower their success rate?…Though many of us have had a bad experience at some time with a health-care professional, does that mean we should start rating them on patient outcomes, much of which is out of their control? Labeling teachers and schools based on test scores of students will hurt a system already struggling with low morale and a teacher shortage.[83]

But critics like Rowan, using the "no excuses" framework, were not mollified by the appeal to professional expertise. "The task force's ultimate goal is to no longer make or accept excuses about why children can't learn but instead to do whatever it takes to help every child learn the basics of math, reading and language," wrote Rowan in the *Deseret News*. "This is the very minimum of what we should expect from our schools."[84]

Ultimately, the Republican-dominated legislature decided to institute a standards-based program, although it was slightly weaker than proponents wanted.[85] Criterion-referenced tests would be required at all grades in all basic subjects, creating more informational accountability and substantially greater alignment between the assessments and the curriculum. The proposal's passage on a largely party-line vote in the legislative task force and the legislature suggested that the emphasis on accountability in Utah would initially come largely from the right. With no civil rights community clamoring for reforms, Democrats supported the position of teachers (and teachers unions): opposition to the reforms. Although the problem definition had created broad support for the idea of standards-based reform, this debate was entirely about accountability and testing, with no promise of increased funds or other capacity-building efforts. As a result, many Democrats saw little reason to support it.

## UPASS Meets NCLB: States' Rights and Constitutive Change

While the debates over standards-based reform in Maryland and Michigan came before the adoption of No Child Left Behind, the debate in Utah persisted even after the federal mandate, with the state threatening (but not following through on its threat) to pull out of NCLB entirely. Following the debate in Utah through the first few years of NCLB allows an analysis of the most prominent challenge to the federal program during that time and sheds further light on the forces that opposed standards-based reforms and those that sought to institutionalize them.

The primary rationale for the opposition to No Child Left Behind in Utah was states' rights. In a state that had a long and proud history of independence from Washington, the idea that the federal government was going to take responsibility for local schools was viewed as federal overreach. Leading the charge was Republican State Representative Margaret Dayton, who in an interview with me said that preserving state autonomy was her primary rationale for opting out of No Child Left Behind. In a memorable legislative session that I attended in April 2005, Dayton argued that when Utah joined the Union in 1896, it did so under an agreement that it would be responsible for educating its citizenry, a power now being wrongly abrogated by an overly intrusive federal government.[86] To punctuate her point, Dayton picked up the more than 1,000 pages of text that constitute the No Child Left Behind act, along with another large stack of accompanying federal regulations for the bill, and asked whether Utah should be subject to these regulations from afar. Others joined her call. As Republican Representative Steven R. Mascaro said, "I wish they'd take the stinking money and go back to Washington."[87] When I asked Dayton and other Republican legislators why they would oppose a program put in place by a conservative president whom they otherwise supported, the almost unanimous reaction was that it was President Bush who had abandoned his conservative roots by supporting federal expansion; they were the true conservatives in favoring limited government.

The State Office of Education supported Dayton's stance. Given that Utah did not adopt standards-based reform until 1999/2000, the office was trying simultaneously to launch Utah's program, UPASS, and to figure out how to implement the federal guidelines for No Child Left Behind. State Superintendent Patti Harrington attended the hearings with Dayton and supported the outspoken legislator's stance: "We have our own ways of running Utah's schools," she told the *New York Times*. "NCLB goes beyond intrusion; it's a federal takeover."[88] The Utah chapter of the NEA was also supportive, as it sought to link the states' rights rationale proffered by Dayton to its broader critique of the harmful effects of testing and accountability.[89]

Support for continuing involvement in No Child Left Behind came from advocates for minority students, including Duane Bourdeaux, the lone

African-American legislator in the state, and administrators and parents of students in Title I schools that stood to lose considerable funds if Utah withdrew from the federal program. These advocates not only wanted to maintain the funding that came with NCLB; they saw accountability as critical in giving them, as outsiders, a lever to compel the school system to improve the quality of education for poor and minority students. Bourdeaux, for example, said of the locally highly unpopular federal law, "There are a lot of problems with No Child Left Behind, but for the first time the federal government has taken a stand to say, 'We have an achievement gap that needs to be dealt with.'"[90] National groups, including the Education Trust, helped prepare testimony and marshal data that showed that Utah minority students were not faring well by national standards. University-based academics were split, with some joining Bourdeaux and claiming that No Child Left Behind had forced Utahns to pay attention to the failings of minority students in their communities, while others were critical of testing as dumbing down the learning process.

Caught in the middle were the governor and many state legislators and school board members who were strongly sympathetic to the idea of resisting federal mandates but also worried about the financial costs of taking the bold step of quitting the federal program. "We don't support repeal of NCLB because we might well jeopardize federal monies that we cannot afford to lose," state school board Chairman Kim Burningham said in 2004.[91]

Ultimately, a compromise was reached in 2005. Wary of the significant funds that would be lost by pulling out of the program, the legislature instead supported a resolution that would prioritize Utah's education goals over the national ones. This bill passed unanimously in the house and by a 25–3 vote, with one abstention, in the senate, as a tide of states' rights advocacy and local pride brought nearly universal support. The hope among state legislators and the governor was that the bill would free the State Office of Education and the schools to focus on the goals set by UPASS without forfeiting federal funds.

In the longer view, what is interesting about Utah's battle with the federal government over No Child Left Behind is that what was at stake was only *which level of government would implement standards-based reform*, not whether standards-based reform was the appropriate vehicle for improving education. Even as they decried the federal mandate, legislators and the state superintendent championed their own standards-based plans for closing the achievement gap. Indeed, State Superintendent Patti Harrington, who assumed the job in 2004, was primarily known as a state leader on standards, pioneering a program that aimed to close the achievement gap in Provo, where she had previously been superintendent. To be sure, minority advocates criticized the

Utah program as less stringent in its requirements than the federal program, and it may turn out that these policy details make a considerable difference in implementation. But looked at over a 25-year time horizon, the bigger story is that while Utah continues to look warily at the federal mandates for standards, an even more fundamental change has happened at the level of state policy. A Republican majority has embraced the idea of standards-based reform and, more recently, of using it to close the achievement gap. In a sense, the federal law has accomplished constitutively what it has sometimes struggled to do by mandate—bring states to see the closing of the achievement gap as an important issue of their own.

## Utah: Summing Up

Much as had occurred in other states, in Utah, *A Nation at Risk* created the context for change. As was described in Chapter Five, the report substantially narrowed educational goals to focus on the measurable and useful. In Utah the push for policy change came from the right; a Republican legislature championed the mantra of "no excuses" and looked skeptically on teachers' claims of professional expertise over practice. Mirroring what happened in Maryland, Democrats were initially opposed to what they saw as the railroading of teachers, with little support or funding to offset the demands for accountability. When the federal government sought to supersede the state's program with NCLB, roles were reversed: now Democrats argued for the importance of data and external accountability to protect the interests of minority children, and Republicans were in opposition on the grounds of states' rights. Over time, both parties came to support a standards agenda; they disagreed only on which level of government should implement it.

The central actors in Utah were legislators and a former state superintendent. Business was not described by any of my respondents as an important player in Utah during the time in which standards were developed; indeed there was no employer education coalition at all. State bureaucrats did play some role in developing the criterion-referenced tests that would eventually be utilized in UPASS, but the primary impetus for reform came from the state legislature. Thus a business- or state actor–driven explanation of the changes is not as persuasive as one that gives primacy to the central ideas motivating the key actors.

Finally, diffusion was important in the Utah case. Former state superintendent John Bennion's white paper brought to the attention of Utah legislators the efficacy of standards-based reform in Texas, Maryland, Kentucky, and

Chicago. A legislative committee also was dispatched to study how standards worked in other states. In addition to the diffusion of the policy model, the growing support for standards across other states and the presence of national rankings that compared states on their standards also served to increase pressure for the adoption of standards-based reform. At the same time, external pressure bore no fruit in Utah until internal state developments—declining test scores and rising demands for educator accountability—whetted legislators' appetites for accountability-centered reform.

## Conclusion

Despite the considerable differences across the three states, over the course of the 1990s all three came to adopt standards-based reform. In each state, after *A Nation at Risk* castigated the American education system for a "rising tide of mediocrity" that imperiled its economic future, powerful legislative actors began to advocate reform in an area previously left largely to local or purely educational actors. This movement was most pronounced in Michigan, where the failings of the auto industry resonated with *A Nation at Risk*'s story about the need for more highly trained workers, but the state of the state evidence in Chapter Five shows that reform rose on the agenda of governors of all three states. What had been a sleepy backwater of state politics mostly delegated to state boards of education and state superintendents was all of a sudden a critical issue for mainstream legislative actors. The perceived growing economic value of schooling also brought in business groups in Michigan and Maryland; they began to see their interests in a new light, no longer opposing reform because of its potential to increase the tax burden but instead seeing quality education as essential to training workers.

Not only did the changed problem definition shift the landscape of *who* was involved in school reform; it also affected *which* ideas would be given credence. Legislative debates in all three states revealed the impact of the assumptions created by *A Nation at Risk* and *Time for Results*. All of the states called for a greater emphasis on higher-order skills, all saw school reform as possible and necessary absent broader social reform, all assumed that success would be measured by performance on state and national tests, and all expressed skepticism about educators' claims of professional expertise. In all three states, Democrats and Republicans shared these assumptions, creating broad support for accountability-centered reform.

In this context, standards-based accountability, with its appeal to different constituencies for different reasons, became the most widely adopted template of school reform. In Maryland the push came largely from the left, as a state superintendent sought to use standards and tests as a lever to effect change in a long failing Baltimore city school system. In Michigan different elements of standards-based reform were supported by different constituencies: Democrats supported standards in the form of a mandatory core as a way of diffusing professionally derived standards to all districts throughout the state; Republicans supported accountability provisions as a way to generate pressure on what they viewed as a highly resistant educational establishment. In Utah the legislative pressure initially came largely from the right, as Republican legislators sought to use standards and tests as a way to create accountability from a public system that they perceived as failing children.

Not only did standards-based reform draw support from the political left and right; it also proved to be an all-inclusive template, one able to generate support from actors with differing pedagogical approaches. In Maryland a pioneering state department of education was initially able to implement an assessment that favored open-ended responses over multiple choice tests and used test questions that actively modeled the pedagogical practices they hoped to see in the classroom. Michigan and Utah used more conventional assessments, a model that Maryland moved to as well after opposition to MSPAP from parents and even some teachers. While standards-based reform is usually portrayed as hostile to progressive pedagogical practice, the Maryland case shows that such reform can incorporate constructivist ideas about learning, an eclecticism that explains in part how it was adopted in very blue states as well as very red ones.

The combination of the program's elite backers, its fit with the governing problem definition, and its ability to be revised without conceding its basic approach has sustained standards-based reform in the face of opposition. The Maryland case illustrates this point well. Teachers unions gradually had to narrow their criticisms from blanket opposition to standardized tests to more modest objections to the testing instrument then in use. When opposition to a particular instrument grew, the state superintendent replaced it with a more traditional assessment, but the broader idea of standards-based reform went unchallenged. In Michigan an antigovernment movement led to the abolition of the statewide core curriculum, but accountability was maintained through continuing use of state assessments. In Utah an objection to federal mandates seemed to some to prefigure a grassroots uprising against the standards-based paradigm, but the state legislators leading the charge were themselves committed to a standards-based approach at the state level. Even when criticisms have forced incremental adjustments, the prevailing idea of demanding external accountability from schools through testing has largely gone unchallenged, and the core approach has been preserved.

Perhaps it is not surprising that an idea-centered view can explain how 49 states came to adopt a similar policy before No Child Left Behind effectively made standards-based reform a federal requirement.[92] Given the diversity of cases, from one perspective there are almost as many ways to such reform as there are states. In Kentucky, for example, a court decision paved the way for reform; in Texas a business group led by Ross Perot was key; in Maryland the impetus came from a state superintendent; in Michigan and Utah, from the state legislature. Any attempt, therefore, to identify one set of actors as responsible is likely to come up short. But what looks like theoretical chaos from the perspective of *who* is pushing the solution looks much more ordered when the focus is on *which ideas* are pushed. Ideas, by their very nature, know no state boundaries, and so it is not surprising that when the question is convergence across many states, shared ideas supply the answer.

# 8

## *The Transformation of Federal Policy: Ideas and the Triumph of Accountability Politics*

EVEN WITH THE movement of the states toward standards-based reform, there was no reason to think a similar movement would, or even could, take place at the federal level. The defining characteristic of American education was its decentralization: the Republican Party habitually called for the elimination of the Department of Education, and the Democratic Party confined the federal role to providing aid to disadvantaged students. But over the course of fewer than 20 years, all of this was transformed, culminating in the most far-reaching federal education law in the nation's history, passed under a Republican president no less. What explains this transformation?

Three sets of changes need to be explained: how political actors were realigned, how policies were chosen, and how institutions changed. To begin with the political: How did the Republican Party, which had long been philosophically opposed to a federal role in education and had called for the abolition of the Department of Education as recently as 1996 come to support the biggest nationalization of education in the nation's history? Why did Congressional Democrats, who in 1991 had strongly opposed a proposal by George H. W. Bush for national standards and testing as unfair to minority students, shift by 2001 to embrace a similar proposal offered by another Republican President, George W. Bush? In short, how did an overwhelming bipartisan political consensus form in favor of policies that had been opposed by large majorities in both parties only 10 years earlier?

A second set of questions relates to policy choices. Of all the available policy tools, what explains the choice of standards-based reform as the primary federal response to this perceived crisis? The bipartisan embrace of tough accountability in No Child Left Behind seems particularly hard to account for by conventional interest group explanations, given that teachers unions are consistently rated the strongest players in educational politics and have historically been opposed to greater demands for school or teacher accountability. Why were standards and accountability the chosen policy vehicle, and why did they triumph over interest group opposition?

A third set of questions relates to institutional change. What had been for 200 years a realm of state and local control, with only modest federal intervention on behalf of disadvantaged students, was rapidly transformed into a realm in which the federal government set the parameters of reform for all public schools. Institutional theorists generally stress how institutional configurations delimit the possibilities for change; one important task for this chapter is to use shifts in education policy as a case study to explore the question of how institutional change takes place. What accounts for this institutional transformation?

This chapter suggests that the power of ideas and the weakness of the educational field can help us understand these puzzles. The change in problem definition sparked by *A Nation at Risk* shaped the context in which federal developments took place in a number of ways. By framing the question as one of urgent economic need, it legitimized the role of federal action with respect to all schools. By stimulating standards-based reform at the state level, it provided a template for what workable reform could look like and built a state consensus upon which federal action could build. Two of the key presidential actors, Bill Clinton and George W. Bush, were former governors whose state education records were built in large part on developments that flowed out of *A Nation at Risk*; they carried what they had learned in the states into the federal context. The framing of the problem also put the teachers unions on the defensive and created strategic opportunities for politicians to take advantage of the new context. The paradigm shaped the thinking of a number of otherwise disparate actors—business groups, civil rights organizations, state governors, policy experts—in a similar direction; they then provided much of the policy direction and interest group support for the reforms. In this context, standards-based reform again emerged as the winning template because of its fit with how the problem was defined and its ability to appeal across the policy spectrum, uniting equity liberals with conservatives who wanted to hold the educational establishment accountable.

Of course, other factors were important as well. In particular, shifts in the broader political context for both parties happened to fit well with the emerging problem definition in education. For Clinton, education provided a way to reinforce his claim to being a New Democrat, one focused less on pouring money into programs (inputs) and more concerned with measuring results (outputs) and protecting the public's money by holding those delivering the programs accountable. For Bush, education provided the central evidence for his claim early in his term to be a "compassionate conservative," repositioning the Republican Party to take away some of the Democratic advantage in helping the needy (particularly children), while doing so in a way that drew upon traditional Republican strengths of efficiency and accountability.

The major difference between the federal story and that of the states is the strength of the institutional norms against federal action. These forces have had some effect in structuring the policy content of the reforms. However, in contrast to the static prediction of institutional or path-dependent theories, these institutional boundaries have gradually shifted as the implementation of the standards agenda at the state level facilitated federal reform. Presidents have played a critical role in shifting these boundaries. President George H. W. Bush first legitimized standards as a topic of federal conversation; President Bill Clinton was able to tame opposition from the left and pass the first legislation linking federal policy to state standards-based reform; and President George W. Bush completed the transformation by championing reform and bringing aboard conservatives previously resistant to a larger federal role.

Particularly intriguing is the way in which this widespread consensus around standards-based reform masked an underlying disagreement between two different visions of standards and accountability. In one version, which we could label *expert professionalism*, the problem was that teachers lacked the needed knowledge to consistently teach at high levels; the role of standards was to systemically guide the organization of different pieces of the field in a way that would enable better practice. The emphasis here is on building the capacity of teachers, enabling higher-order thinking skills for both teachers and students; the pedagogical stance is largely constructivist. In the other version, which we could label *lay accountability*, the problem was that the educational establishment was unaccountable for producing results; stronger incentives needed to be created to motivate improvement. The emphasis here is more on motivating teachers and schools, ensuring coverage of basic skills, and providing clear lines of accountability. No Child Left Behind represents not only the triumph of standards over the objections of its critics but also the triumph of lay accountability over expert professionalism; much of what has followed, for better or worse, is a result of this choice.

## From Devolution to National Goals: A Shifting Federal Commitment

If Reagan's goal, even after *A Nation at Risk*, was to diminish federal involvement in education, George H. W. Bush saw education as a perfect issue on which to stake his claim to lead a "kinder, gentler nation." Much as his son would utilize the issue 12 years later, the elder Bush saw education as a highly popular issue that could cut into the Democratic advantage on domestic policy. Bush's strategists hoped that Democrats, as the party of the teachers unions, would be vulnerable to the charge that the Democrats were the party of the status quo, while allowing Bush to claim the mantle of reform. Viewing education as both an economic policy and an antipoverty policy, Bush's stump speech stated, "I'd like to be the education president. See, I believe as I look into the future—our ability to compete around the world, our ability to solve problems of poverty that are unsolved in this country...whatever it is, education has got to be the priority. Better schools mean better jobs."[1] Substantively, Bush promised not to cut federal spending on education and pledged to create a number of new federal programs, including $500 million for an incentive program to reward "merit schools" and $50 million to sponsor experimentation with new models of reform.[2] While the scale was modest in both ambition and price tag, these programs marked a clear departure from Reagan's efforts to reduce the federal role in education.

In one sense, this shift reflected a temperamental and philosophical difference between the two presidents. Reagan was a proud Sunbelt Goldwater Republican, who saw government as an obstacle to free enterprise and federal social policy as encroaching upon states' rights. The elder Bush was an Eastern Establishment moderate, less inclined toward sweeping ideological visions and always viewed as suspect by the more conservative wing of the party. But to attribute the shift solely to the personal inclinations of the two presidents would be to miss how changes in the broader educational landscape affected Bush's choices. Changes to educational politics after *A Nation at Risk* had elevated education to the top third of voters' concerns in the national election. For the first time, one of the presidential debates was devoted exclusively to the issue of education. In a public climate that was increasingly demanding political action on schools, Reagan's rejection of any federal role in education was becoming an electoral liability; a poll in 1988 revealed that Democrats were favored over Republicans on the issue of education by a two-to-one margin.[3] For a candidate looking to soften the GOP's image with moderate voters, education reform proved the perfect issue. It was an economic development strategy. It provided a way of speaking to the anxieties of middle-class parents, who feared that their children would not be upwardly mobile. It was even an antipoverty strategy, the GOP's silver bullet to all the charges that it did not care about the social problems plaguing the nation.

The changed paradigm around education not only raised the political status of education; it also shaped how Bush discussed the issue. Coupling *A Nation at Risk*'s account of underperformance with the National Governors Association's *Time for Results* paradigm of a "horse trade" of accountability coupled with flexibility, Bush argued in a June 1988 speech to the National Press Club, "[O]ur schools are absolutely not as good as they must be.... [T]o achieve quality results, we must set and enforce standards, provide incentives, and permit the freedom and flexibility on the local level to experiment with new ideas."[4] That these were now mainstream positions among both Republican and Democratic governors shows how significantly the landscape had shifted since *A Nation at Risk*. At the same time, as the first Republican president to embrace these priorities on a national stage, Bush was challenging the GOP's long-standing view that the federal government should leave education to the states. Bush, then, was both a carrier of ideas about education that had been developing since *A Nation at Risk* and a political entrepreneur who changed the national debate by indicating that Republicans were, for the first time, ready to discuss school quality at a national level.

## The Charlottesville Summit

The first vehicle for these changes was the Charlottesville summit, a meeting convened by Bush with the nation's governors to discuss education reform. The ultimate product of the summit was the statement of National Education Goals, a rhetorical agreement that helped frame the drive for reform in subsequent years. While past scholars have debated whether the agreement was a top-down one imposed by Bush or a bottom-up agenda created by the governors,[5] the "paradigms create politics" perspective offered here suggests that the agreement on goals was created by a convergence of all of the actors around the problem definition created by *A Nation at Risk* and *Time for Results*.

The immediate impetus for the meeting was Bush's campaign promise to call for a summit on education, which would convene the nation's governors, college officials, and business leaders to discuss education reform. The idea of goals appears to have come from the governors: a memo by National Governors Association staffer Mike Cohen before the first meeting with the

Bush administration in December 1988 argued that the governors' preferred agenda for the summit was a jointly developed set of long-range goals for educational improvement. Cohen wrote, "The intent here is that the Governors and the President establish a vision of the nature of the education and the results it must produce by the beginning of the 21st century. The goals should be viewed as national rather than federal, and should encourage local governments and the private sector, in addition to the federal government and state governments, to find ways of supporting their attainment."[6] Cohen included several "targets" in the memo, including reducing the dropout rate, increasing instruction in science, and improving performance on tests of higher-order skills, all of which eventually became priorities in the National Education Goals that were adopted after the summit. Cohen argued that pursuing such a strategy would "focus public attention and support" on education and would have the ancillary benefit for governors of strengthening and reinforcing their central role in education reform. Bush agreed to this approach, and the governors and Bush eventually agreed to meet in Charlottesville in September 1989 for a summit focused on creating national goals.

While this approach appeared to have originated outside the White House,[7] it received a friendly hearing within the administration because the president was as concerned as the governors about measurement and results. The problem definition provided by *A Nation at Risk* and *Time for Results* had created a context in which setting goals and comparing outcomes had gradually become ubiquitous for a wide variety of actors. Terrel Bell had notoriously begun making comparisons in 1984, creating an infamous "wall chart" that compared all of the states based on SAT and ACT scores. States generally saw these comparisons as unfair because they did not account for state-to-state differences, such as the widely different types and proportions of students in each state taking the tests. But ironically, the very flaws of the wall chart increased the state appetite for better comparative measures. If the states were going to be publicly compared, they wanted to be compared using measures they considered fair. The Council of Chief State School Officers approved the use of state comparisons of student achievement in 1984. A 1986 commission on the NAEP, chaired by Tennessee governor and NGA chair Lamar Alexander and former Spencer Foundation president H. Thomas James, called for greater state-level comparability of data, a recommendation that was adopted, in trial form, by Congress in 1988. The 1986 *Time for Results* report asked each governor to report annually on progress toward the collective goals they had agreed upon. In short, a problem definition that emphasized results stemming from *A Nation at Risk* led to a demand for goals against which progress could be measured, diminished long-standing taboos against state comparisons, and sparked a variety of different bodies to undertake goal-setting efforts.

Not only were different groups simultaneously undertaking efforts to set goals; what they devised revealed a similar kind of groupthink. Table 8.1 compares five goal-setting efforts between 1988 and 1990. The first set is made up of the goals offered in 1988 by the Southern Regional Education Board, a group that had been influential in calling attention to problems of school quality in the early 1980s and was looking to establish goals for its member states by 2000. The second set comprise the goals of the congressional Democrats, who were unhappy at being excluded from the Charlottesville summit and released their own set of goals for education on the eve of the summit. The third and fourth sets are the Democratic governors' and the Bush administration's proposed goals before the summit, and the fifth, the National Education Goals agreed to by the governors and the president in February 1990.[8]

What is striking is the similarity of the goals offered by Democrats and Republicans, by Congress, governors, and the president, indicating the influence of reigning ideas of the moment. All emphasized preparing children to begin schooling. All but one sought to reduce the dropout rate. All stressed reducing illiteracy. All stressed higher achievement in content subjects, particularly math and science. Directly reflecting the frame of *A Nation at Risk*, all the attempts to set national goals defined achievement in terms of doing better on international comparisons.[9] The influence of *A Nation at Risk* was also notable in what was *not* on the agenda of any of the documents: an emphasis on increasing funding or reducing funding inequities or in achieving goals for schooling that went beyond a skills-based vision. These goal-setting documents, no matter who was issuing them, were largely working within a paradigm that emphasized outputs over inputs and that saw American schooling largely in terms of its inadequacies in meeting the pressures of global competition.

The influence of these paradigms was particularly clear in the creation of the national goals. Although the discussion at Charlottesville featured some of the usual partisan and intergovernmental wrangling, particularly over issues of federal spending and provision of preschool programs, overall the governors and the president were able to find common ground because of their shared assumptions. The joint statement issued by the Bush administration and the governors at the close of the summit opened by laying out the economic rationale for creating performance goals:

**Table 8.1 Convergence around an agenda: National goals for education**

| Southern Regional Education Board, 1988 (selected goals) | Congressional Democrats, presummit | Democratic governors, presummit | Bush administration (OERI), presummit | National education goals, 1990 |
|---|---|---|---|---|
| 1. All children will be ready for the 1st grade. | 1. All "at-risk" 4-year-olds served by 1995. | 1. All children ready for the 1st grade. | 1. All 6-year-olds ready for 1st grade. | 1. By 2000, all children in America will start school ready to learn. |
| 2. The school dropout rate will be reduced by one-half. | 2. High school graduation rate improved annually; illiteracy reduced. | 2. Dropout rate reduced dramatically. | 2. Average scores on national literature and history tests at 90%. | 2. By 2000, high school graduation rate will increase to at least 90%. |
| 3. Student achievement for elementary and secondary students will be at national levels or higher. | 3. Student performance in math, science, and foreign languages improved until it exceeds students of other industrialized nations. | 3. Student achievement rises to internationally comparative levels, especially in math and science. | 3. First among industrialized nations in science and math. | 3. By 2000, all students will leave grades 4, 8, and 12 having demonstrated competency over challenging subject matters in a wide range of subjects.* |
| 4. 90% of adults will have a high school diploma or equivalency. | 4. Basic skills of all students raised to grade level; minority-to-white test score gap reduced by 1993. | 4. Percentage of high school graduates going on to higher education will be increased enough to create opportunities to get good jobs with growing wages. | 4. Illiteracy eliminated for students entering high school in 1997. | 4. By 2000, US students will be first in the world in math and science. |
| 5. 4 out of 5 students entering college will be ready to begin college-level work. | | 5. Illiteracy virtually eliminated. | 5. All students have opportunities for learning a second language. | |

(Continued)

**Table 8.1 (Continued)**

| Southern Regional Education Board, 1988 (selected goals) | Congressional Democrats, presummit | Democratic governors, presummit | Bush administration (OERI), presummit | National education goals, 1990 |
| --- | --- | --- | --- | --- |
| 6. The percentage of adults who have attended college or earned a 2-year, 4-year, or graduate degree will be at national levels or higher. | 5. College attendance, particularly by minorities, increased; reducing imbalance between grants and loans reduced. | 6. Disparities in achievement levels of students of different races and economic backgrounds will be reduced dramatically. | 6. Every student mastered the "skills," "attitudes," and "habits" necessary for full participation in society. | 5. By 2000, every adult American will be literate and will possess knowledge and skills to compete in a global economy and exercise the rights and responsibilities of citizenship. |
| 7. All states and localities will have schools with improved performance demonstrated by results. | 6. More teachers recruited; other steps taken to upgrade the status of the profession. | 7. Schools will have the well-trained teachers and the modern technology they need to be competitive. | 7. Every student should engage in meaningful voluntary service. | 6. By 2000, all schools will be free of drugs, violence, weapons and alcohol. |

* The subjects are English, mathematics, science, foreign languages, civics and government, economics, arts, history, and geography

*Source:* All but the national education goals are drawn from Vinovskis (1999). The national education goals I take from Jennings (1998).

*Notes:* I have paraphrased some of the goals because of space considerations. I have also changed the order of the goals on some of the lists to make them easier to compare; the order of the national education goals is unchanged. The Southern Regional Economic Board had 12 goals; I have presented the most relevant 7, also because of space considerations. The 6 national education goals adopted in 1990 were supplemented by 2 more goals added by Congress in 1994.

The President and the nation's Governors agree that a better educated citizenry is the key to the continued growth and prosperity of the United States.... [A]s a Nation we must have an educated workforce, second to none, in order to succeed in an increasingly competitive world economy. Education has always been important, but never this important because the stakes have changed: Our competitors for opportunity are also working to educate their people.... We believe that the time has come, for the first time in U.S. history, to establish clear, national performance goals, goals that will make us internationally competitive.[10]

The communiqué then listed four areas of agreement reached at the summit, including "establishing a process for setting national goals" and, drawing directly on the *Time for Results* horse trade, "seeking greater flexibility and enhanced accountability in the use of federal resources to meet the goals."[11] The document concluded by stating that as "chief executive officers we expect to be held accountable for progress in meeting the new national goals, and we expect to hold others accountable as well."[12] In its language, rhetoric and assumptions, the communiqué is a document of its time, reflecting the political dialogue around schooling that had been developing since *A Nation at Risk*.

As with *A Nation at Risk*, the creation of the goals proved to be more important for its ability to define the problem than to prescribe a solution. As discussed in the previous chapter, the influence the national goals had on state policymaking was quite weak: governors, who were trying to negotiate with state legislatures, meet budgets, and satisfy interest groups, did not see the national goals as a high priority. Unlike *A Nation at Risk*, the national goals did not even try to recommend specific policy strategies for achieving their ends; the closest they came were the accompanying "objectives," and these quickly disappeared from public dialogue. The group that was put together to oversee implementation, the National Education Goals Panel, was fraught with political infighting and was disbanded by Congress in 2002. However, observers generally agree that despite having little institutional or programmatic legacy, the national goals document played an important role in that it publicly committed the nation to improve its performance and measure that performance on the basis of outputs.[13] On the part of the governors, this step marked a willingness to move away from state control and see the national government as a potential partner in school reform. For Bush it marked a new Republican commitment to a federal role in improving school quality. Left unresolved were the more difficult and specific questions: what policies would be chosen to meet these new performance goals, which level of govern-ment would house them, and how would they be paid for?

## An Early Attempt at National Standards: The Failure of America 2000

With the end of his term approaching and having failed to pass any education legislation, the self-proclaimed "education president" introduced his most ambitious school reform legislation, "America 2000," in April 1991. America 2000 embraced the National Education Goals. It declared that in order to meet them, an ambitious set of national standards in five core subjects would be created and that new achievement tests tied to these standards would be developed. The proposed legislation also included the creation of 535 "break the mold" schools, as well as private-school-choice demonstration projects (vouchers by another name).

In pitching the legislation, President Bush sought to link his proposals both to the bipartisan momentum created by the National Education Goals and to the international competitiveness paradigm of *A Nation at Risk*. The administration's proposal begins, "America 2000 is a long-term strategy to help make this land all that it should be—a nine-year crusade to move us toward the six ambitious national education goals that the president and the governors adopted in 1990 to close our skills-and-knowledge gap."[14] The rationale for the proposal, laid out in a section called "The Challenge," ominously warns that little progress has been made since *A Nation at Risk*. It charges that "education trend lines are flat" and "our country is idling its engines, not knowing enough nor being able to do enough to make America all that it should be." Real spending on schooling is up 33 percent since 1980, the document asserts, with little evidence that this spending is producing bet-ter results. International competitors continue to charge ahead, as demon-strated by international test comparisons, and the United States will stay at the "back of the pack" unless we make "radical changes."

Given this definition of the problem, it is not surprising that national stan-dards and tests were prescribed as the solution. Policy entrepreneurs whose positions were congruent with *A Nation at Risk* analysis were empowered, and many recommended national standards as the solution. For instance, education analysts concerned with international underperformance were increasingly pointing out that one critical difference between the American system and many of its international competitors was that these competitors had education ministries that set national standards for what students were expected to achieve.[15] Several groups with heavy business and gubernatorial representation endorsed the idea of national testing, including the President's Education Policy Advisory Committee, chaired by Alcoa CEO and future treasury secretary Paul O'Neill. These advocates took advantage of several other developments that seemed to lend support to national testing. A widely cited report from the National Academy of Sciences argued that the appearance of local control in American schooling actually masked a de facto minimum national curriculum created by textbook manufacturers. If we already had a national curriculum, advocates argued, why not have one based on high standards? The National Council of Teachers of Mathematics, a teachers' subject-matter group, had produced a highly respected set of content standards in 1989, a development that seemed to suggest that creating national standards was feasible. For all of these reasons, Bush's initial introduction of the proposal received significant support from those in a wide variety of quarters, including Albert Shanker and a cross-section of business leaders.

The reception proved significantly cooler in Congress, where neither party ultimately accepted either Bush's definition of the problem or his proposed solution. Congress had not been a part of the Charlottesville summit and had limited representation on the National Education Goals Panel. Unlike the governors or state legislators, Congress had not had a significant role in the post-1983 school reform movement. As a result, the legislation continued to be viewed in Congress largely through the prism of older problem definitions. For conservatives, this lens reflected a continuing commitment to limiting the federal role in education. Bush sought to finesse this concern by claiming that the standards would be voluntary and "national and not federal," but these concessions did not appease much of the conservative right. While conservatives initially did not voice these concerns prominently to avoid criticizing an initiative of their own president, Senate Republicans' commitment to local control reemerged later in the process as a critical factor in the defeat of the bill. For congressional Democrats, who controlled Congress at the time, the role of the federal government was largely to provide resources to create greater equity for poor and minority students. The Bush bill offered nothing to address what many Democrats in Congress (particularly in the House) viewed as gross discrepancies in resources between more and less advantaged districts. In broad view, the way that *A Nation at Risk* had defined the schooling problem—economic competitiveness, excellence for all, schools as centers of reform, accountability for results—had not yet penetrated the halls of Congress. Rather, two powerful and long-standing alternative views continued to hold sway: the notion, dating to Jefferson and Horace Mann, that schools would be locally controlled and the notion, dating to the 1960s and the original ESEA, that the federal role was to provide greater resources for poor children. Despite Bush's best rhetorical efforts, at the critical level of *defining the problem*, Congress was not swayed.

Many members of Congress, particularly but not exclusively Democrats in the House, also had considerable reservations about Bush's *proposed solutions* of standards and, particularly, testing. Kingdon has argued that new proposals require a period of gestation, in which criticisms are dealt with and opponents slowly warm to the new idea.[16] In this case, the rapid emergence of national testing sparked a considerable backlash, and the idea's defenders had not yet worked out their rebuttals to the critiques. The most vocal opponents of testing were in the House. Two days of House hearings on national testing in March 1991 provide the best window into where the House debate on testing stood when America 2000 was introduced.[17]

Among Democrats, particularly those who represented districts with high poverty or minority concentrations, there was considerable concern that testing would simply quantify once again the poor performance of high-poverty students and schools while providing little to address their problems. Major Clive Owens, a Democratic representative from New York, captured the sentiment in his statement:

> Though some of its proponents may be utterly sincere, I cannot help but view this new wave of interest in testing with great suspicion. I fear it is yet another effort by the White House and the right-wing to substitute symbolism for substance in education policy making and is designed to divert our attention from the urgent need for a greater Federal investment in our children's education. As they sit in overcrowded, dilapidated classrooms, children in New York already spend an average of four weeks every school year taking various standardized tests. There is something ridiculous about the idea that what they most need now is to have another, still more exotic test shoved under their noses in the name of holding them accountable for their performance. Our preeminent concern at this moment should instead be with holding politicians and policy-makers at every level accountable for their consistent failure to give our children and our schools all of the resources they need to succeed.[18]

A number of the witnesses at the hearing supported Owens's view. Trevor Sewell, the acting dean at the Temple College of Education, contrasted the

family and community resources in many affluent communities with the
"other America" whose social problems far exceeded school problems: "There
is another social reality into which a large percentage of America's children
are born. It is a world in which their lives are battered by poverty, social isolation, and often racial and ethnic inequities. It is grim. It is a world in which
taking and doing well on standardized tests is often irrelevant and sometimes
impossible."[19] Sewell summarized the view of many in the civil rights community by warning against the use of high-stakes tests to set consequences
for minority youth. He argued that creating a high-stakes graduation test, as
many employers wanted, would effectively screen out many poor and minority youth from potential opportunities at the beginning of the life cycle. To
do so without providing more resources for improving schools was patently
unfair to these students. A letter organized by FAIRTEST and signed by a
number of civil rights groups, including the NAACP, was read into the record.
It urged significant caution in a move toward national tests. Greg Anrig, the
head of the Educational Testing Service and a prominent liberal, advocated
against imposing a new national test, in part on the grounds that it might
replicate the history of testing as a means of sorting students. He argued: "We
should vigorously guard against creating a new system to sort and label children, especially those born into poverty who start childhood with educational
disadvantages not of their own making." All of these concerns reflected a consensus that had emerged in the 1970s and 1980s among advocates and school
reformers on the left: that the key problem to be remedied was the lack of
resources in poor urban schools, that testing would at best reconfirm what we
already knew and at worst be used for sorting or tracking, and that high-stakes
tests closed off opportunities for poor and minority youngsters.[20]

These equity concerns got the most play, given the dominant positions of
the Democrats on the committee, yet the hearings also raised even more basic
questions about how national testing would spur school improvement. This
critique was bipartisan, represented most prominently on the Republican
side by Pennsylvania's Representative Bill Goodling, who was the ranking
Republican on the committee as well as a former teacher, superintendent,
and school board member. Goodling warned against a "pell-mell rush to
jump on the bandwagon" of national testing and read into the record a letter
from Donald M. Carroll, Pennsylvania Commissioner of Education, outlining seven reasons why testing would not improve schooling. At the heart of
Goodling's objection was the idea that a national test had little relationship
to the other factors needed for creating successful schools: "Will a test drive
teachers to teach better? Will it drive parents to parent better? Will it drive

students to try harder? Will it attract the best and brightest to the profession? Will it change teacher-training institutions? If it will do all those things," he continued, "then I'd be all for it." One educational testing expert summarized this view in labeling Bush's plan "voodoo education policy."[21] Goodling's concerns were shared by Democratic Chairman Charles Kildee, who was also a former educator. Kildee argued that using national testing at the end of the educational process was unlikely to improve educational practice. Where testing could be useful, in his experience as a teacher, was as a diagnostic tool early in the educational process, when it had allowed him to adjust his strategies to make the material more comprehensible to his students. The national testing experts called before the panel raised a similar set of concerns: that testing by itself had little ability to create improved practice; that testing was better used for diagnosis than for accountability; that testing imposed from the outside would not have the support of teachers; that testing would create teaching to the test; and that a national test would most likely be a lowest-common-denominator test, which would not reflect good pedagogical practice. In all of these concerns, both Congress and the testing experts were reflecting the long-standing experience of the education community with standardized tests.[22]

With Congress sharing neither the president's definition of the problem nor his enthusiasm for the proposed solution, it is not surprising that America 2000 went down to an unceremonious defeat. Liberals in the House stripped the testing and choice provisions from the bill and produced a version that emphasized standards (which continued to be supported by teachers and their unions) but not national testing. They also eliminated several aspects of the legislation that did not relate to testing but were central parts of the Bush America 2000 proposal, such as the "break the mold" schools. They mandated that states create "delivery standards," which would later become known as "opportunity-to-learn standards"; they required that states provide greater resources to try to ensure that students could meet the new standards. This provision in particular was strongly opposed by Republicans, who saw it as a federal imposition on how states should spend their money. Secretary of Education Lamar Alexander called the House version of the bill "worse than awful" and publicly encouraged Bush to veto it.[23] The bill finally died a quiet death at the hands of Senate Republicans in fall 1992. Seeing an expansion of the federal role in education but little accountability or choice, Senate Republicans saw little reason to support the bill. Some have also suggested that Senate Republicans killed the bill to prevent Bush from having to issue a veto on his own education legislation in the months before the election.

While in one sense the death of America 2000 can be attributed to the usual partisan squabbling and long-standing differences between the parties on issues of choice, it also reflected the tenuous foothold of standards, testing, and accountability in 1991 and 1992. George H. W. Bush's initial proposal was a mishmash of elements intended to improve educational outcomes: unlike his son 10 years later, he was unwilling to sacrifice vouchers in order to win passage of a standards-and-testing proposal. And even if he had been willing to stake his political capital on standards and accountability, he lacked a widely accepted policy template for testing-centered reform, a model that explained, even in theory, how standards, assessments, and accountability could be linked to improve educational practice. Absent such an issue-shifting template, Bush's proposal was unable to upend either long-standing partisan divisions or older congressional problem definitions. As a result, the status quo prevailed, and America 2000 was defeated.

## *The Creation and Diffusion of a Policy Template*

While the political infighting over America 2000 grabbed the headlines, what would in retrospect prove to be a much more important set of developments was taking place within the policy community. (These developments have also been considered less frequently by other scholarly accounts, which have focused more heavily on legislative events.)[24] Over roughly this same period, 1989–92, the policy community gradually coalesced around the idea of "standards-based" or "systemic" reform. This template would be adopted by a wide variety of key groups in the years that followed, including the National Governors Association, the Council of Chief State School Officers, and the Business Roundtable, three groups that included many of the critical actors in advancing the standards movement at the state and federal levels. Standards-based reform would become the template for Goals 2000, the Improving America's Schools Act, and later, No Child Left Behind, as well as the rapidly growing state standards-based reform movement. Understanding *why* this template came to be favored by the policy community and *how* the policy community was able to diffuse this template to a wide variety of powerful actors is critical to explaining the legislation that followed.

Figure 8.1 offers a visual overview of the creation and diffusion of the standards-based reform template. The left side of the diagram summarizes much of the previous discussion of America 2000 and the National Education Goals. In brief, *A Nation at Risk* raised the economic importance of education, bringing in business support and creating a context

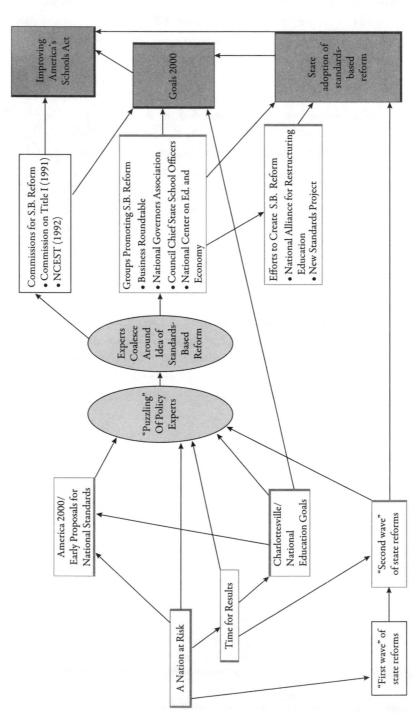

**FIGURE 8.1** "Standards-based reform" created, becomes favored policy template

that motivated the governors and the Bush administration to set national goals. This action, in turn, spawned the America 2000 legislation to create voluntary national standards. At the same time, governors had moved into the education reform business after *A Nation at Risk*; a second round of decentralizing reforms were fleetingly taking hold in the states as governors sought to implement their 1986 horse trade of reduced regulation in return for greater results. However, despite all of this activity, there was, according to *Education Week*, no clear sense of what would come next. A 1990 questionnaire sent to many of the nation's top education thinkers asking for predictions about the decade ahead revealed a wide range of possibilities, including greater choice, more "fragmentation" and school-level control, and greater accountability.[25]

## "Puzzling" toward Standards-Based Reform

Out of this morass, a group of policy experts in a variety of venues produced the template that became known as "systemic," or standards-based, reform. Responding in part to what the experts perceived as incoherence in the reforms of the 1980s, standards-based reform aimed to focus all of the actors in the system around a set of standards. Standards-based reform presumed a trio of elements that would coordinate reform: *standards*, which specified the academic expectations for the system; aligned *assessments*, which measured the ability of students to meet those expectations; and *accountability*, which assessed schools' and teachers' ability to achieve the goals. While the state would determine the assessment framework, schools would be unregulated in deciding how to meet the reform goals. Standards would also coordinate other key elements of the system, such as teacher training and licensing and professional development.[26]

The process of creating this policy template is akin to what Heclo has called the "puzzling" of policy experts.[27] While a 1991 article by Marshall ("Mike") Smith and Jennifer O'Day is commonly credited with providing the first crystallization of this view, it sprouted up simultaneously in a variety of places from 1989 to 1991, as a well-networked set of policy experts talked with one another and sought to draw lessons from ongoing efforts in the states. Although virtually unmentioned in previous accounts, the Pew Forum on School Reform was named by a number of my respondents as a central venue for this puzzling. The group, formed in 1991 to explore the idea of creating a set of reforms around standards, was codirected by Robert Schwartz at Pew and Mike Smith, then dean of the Stanford Graduate School of Education and later undersecretary of education in the Clinton administration. In the Pew Forum were a number of figures who either had been or would be important in the standards movement, including

- Gordon Ambach, the executive director of the Council of Chief State School Officers;
- Albert Shanker, the head of AFT;
- David Hornbeck, a former Maryland state school superintendent and the principal architect of the 1990 Kentucky reform act;
- Mike Cohen, the lead advisor to the NGA at Charlottesville and later undersecretary of education in the Clinton administration;
- Marc Tucker, president of the National Center on Education and the Economy;
- Chester Finn, a leading conservative expert on reform;
- Kati Haycock, who would become the executive director of the Educational Trust;
- Thomas Payzant, then the superintendent of the San Diego Unified School District and later undersecretary of education in the Clinton administration;
- Jack Jennings, general counsel for the House Committee on Education and Labor and later a prominent congressional backer of standards-based reform;
- Michael Timpane, the president of Columbia's Teacher College; and
- Linda Darling-Hammond, who would become an important voice in efforts to professionalize teaching.

While some went further in their thinking than others,[28] the members of the seminar describe it as a process of puzzling, at a time when the policy direction was far from clear. As Schwartz describes it, the forum was "a learning organization and professional development seminar with no expectation around product."[29] The seminar combined the intellectual concerns of its members with on-the-ground lessons from the states. Schwartz says it brought the members together "to learn from going around the country and looking at emerging policy and practice. Let's see if we can come to some shared sense of what a more aligned system would look like, that would...combine more top down instructional guidance with more flexibility at the school level."[30] The Pew Forum worked to do collectively what many seminar members had been doing individually: delineate what taking a new standards-centered approach to reform might mean.

Why did the policy community come to favor standards-based reform? As it turned out, it appealed to different analysts for different reasons, a multiplicity that would serve the template well when it sought to find political backers.

## Four Strands: The Many Rationales for Standards-Based Reform

The first strand, most prominently represented by Marc Tucker at the National Center on Education and the Economy, saw the problem primarily in economic terms. While *A Nation at Risk* had told a "story of decline" that was not supported by data available at the time, Tucker said to me in an interview that, looking toward the future in 1988, he was certain that the skills of the bottom 70 percent of American workers would need to increase if their wages were to rise and the country were to compete.[31] Tucker then founded the National Center on Education and the Economy; it proceeded to study the education and training systems of American competitors who did better on international tests. The results of this analysis were released in a report titled *America's Choice: Higher Skills or Lower Wages.*[32] The report concluded that despite the vast cultural differences among the countries studied (Germany, Japan, Sweden, Denmark), all had embraced a standards-based system in which a central authority specified the expectations for learning and the assessments by which students would be judged. The best of these assessments differed from American tests in a number of important ways, ways the report judged critical to their success. The tests were criterion-referenced as opposed to norm-referenced; that is, they measured student achievement against a national standard set by experts rather than against the performance of other students. Because assessments were explicitly aligned to the curriculum, student energy would be focused on the academic outcomes the curriculum had prioritized. Using assessments that measured curriculum mastery also sent a clear signal to students about the importance of effort, unlike the SATs, which purport to reflect innate student aptitude. Finally, the assessments were not multiple-choice tests but open-ended instruments that measured complex thinking skills. The best of these models, Tucker said, were like "college bluebook exams," asking students, for example, to compare two historical periods from the perspective of a given set of writers. Unlike multiple-choice exams, which promote teaching to the test, Tucker said, to "do well on that kind of exam, you really need to know the material in the course [or in the curriculum]."[33] While there was no obvious way the decentralized US system could replicate the national ministries of education found in other countries,

NCEE advocated a similar standards-based system at either the national or state level.

A second strand came from equity liberals within the education policy community, including some civil rights advocates and a state superintendent like David Hornbeck. For these professionals, whose longtime interest had been improving outcomes for poor and minority students, the economy provided a useful hook to get the broader public interested in their issues. In a 1991 volume coedited by Hornbeck, *Human Capital and America's Future*, the opening lines of the first essay make this case: "The United States finds itself today at a unique historical moment. For the first time in our history, the nation's social agenda and its economic agenda seem to have converged. Policies to deal with poverty, drug abuse, employment discrimination, and related problems, which formerly could be justified only in terms of morality or political expediency, have now come to be seen as essential for the nation's economic progress, as critical investments in its 'human capital.'"[34] Standards provided a critical piece of that vision, because they provided a public commitment to the idea that all children can learn at high levels, a promise to fight against the long-standing practice of assigning challenging curriculum to only a select group of students. In an interview Hornbeck, who had been Maryland superintendent from 1976 to 1988, traced a continuous line from Project Basic, his 1977 initiative that measured whether graduating seniors could do basic reading and math, to the much more advanced challenges contained in the 1990s version of Maryland testing, MSPAP. Hornbeck says:

> I think that what has been really quite remarkable is the straight line implementation in Maryland for what is in effect 28 years, with no break. Never mind, MSPAP versus Project Basic, but the core idea that's embodied in that stuff is all exactly the same.... It all began and unfolded driven out of policy considerations in one sense from inside the education community. Those of us—from the inside we wanted to do this stuff. We wanted to do it primarily for equity kinds of reasons—commitment to poor kids and believing, as I strongly have always believed, that standards-based reform is the greatest equity sword that exists.

Speaking out of frustration with the glacial pace of change in schools that serve poor students, Hornbeck advocated not only standards and assessments to set high expectations but incentives and accountability to spur change. A public system offers few rewards for high performance or penalties for low performance, he writes: "[I]f an institution fails badly, most often nothing of significance occurs. Students cannot read. Children are taken from their families or left in their families and then abused. Poor performance can continue year after year with no consequence."[35]

A third strand came from governors and policy experts seeking a way to reconcile the benefits of top-down and bottom-up change. Smith and O'Day begin their influential 1991 article by reviewing the history of school reform since *A Nation at Risk* and finding limits in both the top-down and bottom-up strategies pursued in isolation. Drawing on researchers' evaluations of the first wave of reform, they find "only minor changes in the typical school, either in the nature of classroom practices or in achievement outcomes." They agree with many of the "second wave" critics that the "first wave" reforms represented an "intensification" of current practice that made little effort to "change the content of instruction, to directly involve teachers in the reform process, or to alter the reigning notions of teaching and learning." But to this familiar critique they added the notion that ceding responsibility to schools was also unlikely to bring about systemic change: "While reliance on school-based initiative (even that stimulated by states) may be more likely to produce significant changes in classroom practice than have edicts from above, a strictly school-by-school approach makes it difficult to generalize such changes from the small number of initially active schools to the well over 100,000 education institutions across the country." Bottom-up change was also unlikely to produce the upgrading of skills that was needed; such a change would require that teachers themselves learn a substantial amount of new material and how to teach it. "Site-based management, professional collaboration, incentives, and choice may be important elements of the change process, but they alone will not produce the kinds of changes in content and pedagogy that appear critical to our national well-being." Systemic reform promised to address these shortcomings by giving teachers considerable autonomy at the school level but using the power of the state to ensure widespread reform. High student standards would ensure that reform was pitched at an appropriate level, assessments and accountability would bring every school into the loop of reform, and teacher standards would guide changes in teacher education and professional development to ensure that teachers mastered the new content. For governors and state policymakers unhappy that a blizzard of reforms in the 1980s had produced little gain in student achievement, Smith and O'Day's 1991 proposal provided an attractive and coherent paradigm. It seemed to address the limitations of the first and second waves of reform by linking all the elements of the system to improving results.[36]

A fourth strand drew those who saw the educational system's lack of accountability as the most pressing problem. The roots of this viewpoint were largely conservative, although the perspective would come to have broader appeal. Conservatives had long been concerned with standards. This was most prominently reflected in Allan Bloom's *The Closing of the American Mind*, which charged that a variety of forces in modern life were undermining the commitment to academic rigor. Such prominent conservative figures as E. D. Hirsch, William Bennett, Diane Ravitch, and Lynne Cheney advocated standards as a means to restore the place of the academic curriculum (and often the Western canon) in the face of movements for equity, multiculturalism, and self-esteem. To this concern for standards, which had developed in the 1980s, the promise of corresponding assessments and accountability spoke to another part of the conservative mind-set, the part that saw the lack of accountability of the system as its major problem.

Chester Finn, who was one of the few conservative members of the Pew Forum and is perhaps the most influential conservative thinker on education reform over the past 20 years, expressed this view in his 1991 book, *We Must Take Charge*. Finn emphasized that the primary problem of the system was that incentives were not designed around results. He quoted favorably a line by then Secretary of Education Lamar Alexander: "Teaching is the only profession in which you are not paid one extra cent for being good at your job." Painting with a broad brush, Finn argued that schools are like other public-sector enterprises—slow, inefficient, and focused more on not rocking the boat than on creating innovative practice.[37] Unlike private schools, which were accountable to their students and parents, public schools were accountable only for regulatory compliance, not for producing student learning.[38] Finn contrasts academics to athletics, arguing that in the latter sphere, high performance is generated through clarity of goals, accountability for results, and an embrace of effort as the primary key to success.[39] Underlying this range of arguments is a view of human nature as largely motivated by external incentives: "When it comes to academic learning, I believe that external consequences are the main determinant of how hard most of us work and how much we accomplish."[40] Although foreign to many educators, this worldview resonated not only with business people but also with many legislators, who were used to utilizing the various carrots and sticks at their disposal to create the outcomes they desired. Even among Democrats committed to public schools and opposed to private school choice, the idea of setting goals, creating measurable indicators of progress, and holding frontline workers accountable for progress seemed like a natural and rational way to solve a pressing public problem.

All four of these strands shared a definition of the problem shaped by *A Nation at Risk* and *Time for Results*. Poor performance on international assessments imperiled American economic competitiveness. Emulating other nations' systems of national standards thus provided the best hope for making progress. Domestically, the problem was not inequitable funding or an anti-intellectual culture, but declining standards within the schools. Not surprisingly, a program of higher standards and corresponding assessments was prescribed as a solution. *Time for Results* accelerated this trend by its emphasis on outcomes. As Mike Cohen said of the report in an interview, "You scratch the surface of the accountability part [of *Time for Results*] and it presumes a set of standards. Wasn't highly explicit about it, but it presumed it."[41] *Time for Results* also stressed greater frontline discretion. This emphasis was reflected in the idea that standards-based reform would integrate external standard setting with the freedom to innovate on how to achieve those standards at the school level. Perhaps most critically, *A Nation at Risk* described the problem as one that was all-encompassing, a definition that created favorable terrain for a solution whose hallmark was its promise to integrate everything that came before it into one package of "systemic reform."

While in one sense standards-based reform was an example of "policy feedback" in that it drew upon the lessons of the first and second waves of reform to create a new template, it also illustrated a more general lesson about the intersection of problem definition and policy feedback: *which lessons are drawn depends largely on which problem reformers are trying to solve.* If the goal had been creating qualitative change in how some schools were managed or run, then continuing efforts to build on the second wave might have been recommended. But since the goal was improvement in *all* schools, not surprisingly the school-by-school strategy of the second wave was judged inadequate. The *Nation at Risk* definition of the problem as wholesale failure won the day and with it came a presumption in favor of wholesale reform.

## Seeing like a State: The Importance of Institutional Vantage Point

Varied as they were, all of the reformers also shared a particular institutional vantage point that shaped their views on reform. Either they were entirely outside the system acting as policy analysts or advocates for reform, or they were operating from the top layers of the system as governors, legislators, or chief state school officers. From this perch, it is not surprising that they saw the obstacles to creating a more rational system in fundamentally Weberian terms. This problem definition led to an approach of clarifying goals and setting incentives from above. Reformers repeatedly decry the "fragmentation" of the policy system as a "fundamental barrier" to reform and propose "systemic reform" as the antidote.[42] The comparisons here to the Progressive reformers are striking: they too constituted a bipartisan set of elites from business, politics, and academia; they too had foundation support; they too wanted higher levels of administration to set standards, give tests, and hold accountable those lower in the hierarchy; they too were influenced by Weberian models of rationalization and extrinsic notions of motivation; they too were trying to create order and coherence out of disorder and educational anarchy. When reformers argued that "politically motivated squabbles at the state level" are "the greatest deterrent to an improved school system," they could easily have been mistaken for Progressives demanding that schools be removed from politics.[43] Not coincidentally, the first major effort at standards-based reform took place in Kentucky, when the courts invalidated the state's school system and ordered up an entirely new template. What more could a social engineer ask for than a blank slate?

As was true in the Progressive period, the cleavages created by this viewpoint were less between left and right and more between an amorphous group of reformers sitting outside the schools and teachers and reformers emphasizing building-level change.[44] In 1993, *Education Week* asserted that "reform strategists can be roughly divided into two camps: those who believe that schools must change from the ground up, one building at a time; and those who believe that federal and state policies should provide the stimulus and the conditions for building-level change."[45] Included in the first camp were those who were trying to develop networks of schools pursuing a particular approach (varying in pedagogical terms from highly traditional to highly progressive), including such prominent figures as Ted Sizer, Robert Slavin, and James Comer. As was true for Dewey, such individual reformers gained significant acclaim and influenced the schools in their networks, but they were largely overwhelmed by a tide of more powerful reformers seeking to create systemic change.

## Two Templates in One: Expert Professionalism versus Lay Accountability

Similarities among the systemic reformers in their shared institutional vantage point and their common definition of the problem created wide support in the policy community for the standards-based approach to reform. But it also concealed an important fault line among the reformers that would emerge in the legislative battles over standards-based reform. While most

## Table 8.2 Two models of standards-based reform

|  | Expert professionalism (Smith and O'Day 1991) | Lay accountability (Finn 1991) |
|---|---|---|
| Trust placed in | Leaders of the profession | Public, legislators |
| Problem with teachers | Capacity | Motivation |
| Commitment to school-level site-based management | Stronger (but still limited) | Weaker |
| Pedagogical agenda | Progressive | Traditional |
| Strategy for reform | Increasing teachers' knowledge base | Holding teachers accountable |
| Role of testing | To stimulate the teaching of higher-order skills | To create accountability |

accounts of the movement have discussed standards-based reform as if it were one template, two visions of standards-based reform lurked below a surface of agreement: a softer one, which sought to increase teachers' skills and schools' capacity; and a harder one, which placed greater emphasis on accountability for results as a reform strategy. These were not merely differences in emphasis; they reflected significant substantive differences in assumptions about who should be trusted to reform the system, what pedagogical agenda should be pursued, and whether the fundamental issue was one of motivation or lack of skill and knowledge (see Table 8.2).

The Smith and O'Day view of standards-based reform represented one pole, which might be labeled *expert professionalism*. Smith and O'Day placed their faith in the leaders within the profession, the people who would develop standards that incorporated the latest in research and who would stimulate change from above. They did not see the problem at the classroom level as one of teacher motivation but of a lack of knowledge and familiarity with complicated material and advanced pedagogical technique. (As Harvard professor Richard Elmore frequently summarized this view, if teachers knew how to teach better, they would do it.) Past reforms such as minimum competency testing had been successful at achieving their limited aims because they did not ask much of anyone in the system; this round of reforms would require much more fundamental change. As Smith and O'Day put it, "Such a reorientation is not likely to happen on a widespread school-by-school basis among educators who have themselves been schooled in a philosophy and settings that embody fact-based conceptions of knowledge, hierarchical approaches to skill development and a near total reliance on teacher-initiated and teacher-directed instruction."[46] The authors' pedagogical approach here is progressive and directly challenges traditional teacher-directed modes of instruction. They argue instead for more "active involvement for the learner" through "group activities," "cooperative learning," and "activities that do not have a 'right' answer" and "demand sustained and imaginative problem solving."[47] There is some support for site-based management—"teachers should have an important decision-making role"—but also considerable skepticism about the ability of rank-and file-teachers to accomplish what is being asked of them: "Most teachers, at present, do not have the knowledge, skills, and time necessary to do a competent job carrying out their roles in a shared governance system or in jointly developing curricula that are integrated across grades within a school."[48]

The role of the experts is to fill this vacuum at the school level by providing higher-quality curricula and enhanced preservice and in-service professional training. Assessments and accountability are the final piece, not as a motivating device, but as a mechanism for stimulating pedagogical change at the building level: "While current standardized and minimum competency tests reinforce teaching toward an emphasis on isolated facts and basic skills, state-of-the-art examinations based on well-designed curricula frameworks could help encourage instruction toward higher-order learning goals.... Thus if students taking a science examination are expected to produce science— that is, to write, analyze text, to manipulate the necessary tools, to solve problems—teachers are more likely to emphasize these capacities in their classes."[49] In sum, the Smith and O'Day view was one of professionally led top-down change, wherein the leaders of the field define the standards and skills of the profession and then use a variety of policy levers to diffuse that knowledge to the rank and file.

The other vision of standards-based reform, advocated by conservatives as well as many equity liberals, is what we might call *lay accountability*. Here the problem is seen to lie fundamentally in the profession (or the educational establishment), a circle that can include higher education as well as state departments of education. What needs to happen is that this failing establishment needs to be held accountable by the public, either through choice or, in standards-based reform, by the legislature. Students should be challenged to learn higher-order skills but not at the expense of learning content, a position that is backed by the public but frequently subverted, in this telling, by a profession infatuated with constructivist pedagogy. Arguments about "capacity," while hard to deny in the abstract, in practice simply work to undercut a commitment to judge schools on the accountability of their results. The purpose of assessments and accountability is to create the needed incentives to produce results.

The battle between these two models of reform would prove to be critically important in defining the nature of the standards-based reform movement in the years that followed. While the primary cleavages defining school reform continued to be between standards-based reformers of all varieties and teachers and school-based reformers, a secondary and ultimately equally important battle was taking place *among* the standards-based reformers for the soul of the movement. As will be seen, No Child Left Behind represented the victory of the hard version of standards-based reform over its softer cousin, an outcome that explains not only why we have a national program of standards and accountability but also why it looks the way that it does.

## From Talk to Action: Networks of Experts and the Diffusion of Standards-Based Reform

Having coalesced around a template, this wide-ranging set of policy entrepreneurs began pushing to put standards-based reform into practice. Taking advantage of a policy climate ripe for systemic solutions, one that promised across the board increases in test scores, these policy entrepreneurs were able to implement their template in a wide variety of venues. Table 8.3 shows the convergence around systemic reform in five critical venues in 1990 and 1991: the Consortium of Policy Research on Education, a leading research policy group that included many prominent education school researchers, including Smith and O'Day; the Business Roundtable, which became an important umbrella organization for business concerns; the National Governors Association; the National Center on Education and the Economy; and the Kentucky Education Reform Act of 1990, which marked Kentucky as the first state to adopt standards-based reform in its modern incarnation.

Each of these groups had embraced the key elements of the standards-based vision: a presumption that all children could learn to high levels; that the curriculum should be based on higher-order skills; and that some decentralization of decision making should be coupled with more centralized assessments and accountability. While partisan considerations and fear of a national curriculum were sinking America 2000, standards-based reform was, under the

**Table 8.3  Convergence around a solution: "Systemic reform" sweeps across the landscape**

| Consortium of Policy Research on Education | Business Roundtable | National Governors Association | National Alliance for Restructuring Education (part of the NCEE) | Kentucky Legislature |
|---|---|---|---|---|
| Systemic School Reform (Smith and O'Day 1991) | Nine Essential Components of a Successful System (1990) | What Restructuring Is (1991) | Seven Components of the Restructuring Process (1991) | Kentucky Education Reform Act (1990) |
| This proposal addresses two fundamental problems with American education: the lack of a coherent long-term set of policies to improve the system and the basic-skills emphasis in instruction. | 1. New system committed to four assumptions: • All students can learn at higher levels. • We know how to teach all students successfully. • Curriculum content must lead to higher-order thinking skills. | Restructuring…is a systemic approach [that]…shifts the focus of reform from mandating what educators do to looking at the results their actions produce. Restructuring requires many pieces of the system to change, including the following: | The goal of restructuring the education system is to raise the performance of all students to world-class standards. • **Leadership and strategic management:** Leading…a restructuring effort requires communicating a vision for systemic change, a long-range strategic plan that orchestrates all the elements. | Kentucky has adopted a bold plan…[that] reflects the belief that all students can learn and nearly all at high levels.…Key components are • high educational goals • an assessment process to measure whether the goals are being reached by all students |

- The purpose of this strategy is to put the pieces of reform together in a coherent system that combines the vitality and creativity of bottom-up change with an enabling and supportive structure at the district and state levels. States should develop challenging curriculum frameworks. Districts should determine how best to teach the content.

- Every child has an advocate.
2. The new system is performance or outcome based.
3. Assessment strategies must be as strong and rich as the outcomes.
4. School success is rewarded and failure penalized.
5. School staff plays major role in instructional decisions.
6. Major emphasis placed on staff development.
7. High-quality prekindergarten program is established.

- **Curriculum and instruction** must be modified to promote the acquisition of higher-order, not just basic skills. School goals and assessments must reflect these higher-order skills.
- **Authority and decision making** must be decentralized so the most important decisions are made at the school site.
- **Accountability systems** must clearly link incentives and rewards to student performance at the building level.

- **Performance-based accountability system:** A performance-based...system requires high standards and...world-class curriculum that are demanding and varied, new performance assessments that measure higher-order skills, incentives for continuous improvement for students and educators, and consequences for persistent failure to improve.
- **Decentralized decision making:** Decisions must be made at the most appropriate level: instructional...decisions must be made at the level closest to the action engaging the student.

- an accountability system to reward schools improving their success and to intervene in schools failing to make progress
- school councils, made up of educators and parents, to make decisions on curriculum, instruction, and school management
- early childhood education programs for at-risk students
- a new funding system to correct the financial disparity between wealthy and poor districts

(Continued)

# Table 8.3 (Continued)

| Consortium of Policy Research on Education | Business Roundtable | National Governors Association | National Alliance for Restructuring Education (part of the NCEE) | Kentucky Legislature |
|---|---|---|---|---|
| Systemic School Reform (Smith and O'Day 1991) | Nine Essential Components of a Successful System (1990) | What Restructuring Is (1991) | Seven Components of the Restructuring Process (1991) | Kentucky Education Reform Act (1990) |
| • coordinate teacher professional development with the curriculum framework.<br>• coordinate student assessment with curriculum frameworks. | 8. Health and other services are sufficient to reduce barriers to learning.<br>9. Technology used to raise productivity. | • **Comprehensive service systems** must be developed to help children and families access the support they need. | | |

*Source*: All but the Kentucky Education Reform Act (KERA) are drawn from the National Governors Association, *From Rhetoric to Action* (Washington: National Governors Association, 1991). KERA is drawn from the Legislative Research Commission, *The Kentucky Education Reform Act: A Citizen's Handbook* (Frankfurt: LRC, 1991). Some of the documents have been abridged or paraphrased because of space considerations. This is not intended to be a comprehensive list of organizations that backed standards-based reform.

radar, in the process of capturing many of the groups that would prove critical for future policymaking.

A key factor in the diffusion of the template was the relatively small network of actors who staffed these various organizations. Table 8.4 shows the considerable influence that this small group had in directing the agenda of many of the most powerful organizations interested in school reform. Initially it might seem surprising that such a wide range of actors with almost nothing else in

Table 8.4 Networks of policy experts and the diffusion of standards-based reform, 1990–94*

| Purveyor of standards-based reform | People involved |
| --- | --- |
| NCEST Report (National Council on Education, Standards and Testing) | Carroll Campbell and Roy Romer (cochairs), Chester Finn, Gordon Ambach, David Hornbeck (chair, implementation task force), Marshall "Mike" Smith (chair, standards task force), Lauren Resnick, Mark Musick, Albert Shanker; a background paper by Susan Fuhrman and Jennifer O'Day informed the thinking of NCEST. |
| Commission on Chapter One | David Hornbeck, Kati Haycock, Diane Piche, Sharon Robinson, Mike Smith, Marc Tucker, William Taylor |
| Kentucky Education Reform Act | David Hornbeck |
| National Center on Education and the Economy | Marc Tucker, Mike Cohen, Lauren Resnick |
| Southern Regional Education Board | Mark Musick |
| Consortium of Policy Research on Education | Richard Elmore, Susan Fuhrman, Jennifer O'Day, Mike Smith |
| Chief State School Officers | Gordon Ambach, David Hornbeck |
| NGA | Lamar Alexander, Carroll Campbell, Bill Clinton, Mike Cohen (staff), Richard Riley, Roy Romer |
| Business Roundtable | David Hornbeck |

*(Continued)*

**Table 8.4 (Continued)**

| Purveyor of standards-based reform | People involved |
| --- | --- |
| Pew Forum | Bob Schwartz and Mike Smith (conveners), Gordon Ambach, Mike Cohen, Linda Darling-Hammond, Chester Finn, Kati Haycock, David Hornbeck, Jack Jennings, Thomas Payzant, Michael Timpane, Marc Tucker |
| AFT | Albert Shanker |
| Education Trust | Kati Haycock |
| Citizens' Commission on Civil Rights | William Taylor, Diane Piche |
| Bush administration | Lamar Alexander, Chester Finn |
| "Dear Hillary" letter | Marc Tucker (author), Mike Cohen, Mike Smith, David Hornbeck, Bob Schwartz |
| Clinton administration | Bill Clinton, Richard Riley, Mike Cohen, Mike Smith, Thomas Payzant, Sharon Robinson |

* This is not intended to be an exhaustive list either of who was important at these organizations or who was important in pushing standards-based reform. It is intended simply to illustrate the overlapping nature of the expert network that pushed standards-based reform from a variety of venues.

common—business leaders, governors, chief state school officers, state legislatures, the AFT, and the Bush and Clinton administrations—would back a single policy approach. But it is less unexpected if we consider that they shared a core of advisors with similar views of the problem and of the proposed solution. In theoretical terms, the changing problem definition had created an opportunity for policy experts who had a solution that fit the problem, since the various parties involved in school reform wanted to act but did not necessarily know how to. The policy experts filled this niche with the template of standards-based reform. To be sure, leaders of these organizations might not have taken this advice if it had not fit with other aspects of their political or organizational agendas. But the beauty of standards-based reform was that it drew upon a variety of rationales and thus created a wide base of potential support.

The policy entrepreneurs also proved to be creative in seeking ways to broadly establish standards in an institutional climate not particularly hospitable to the idea of national standards. Mike Smith had come out in favor of national standards in 1990; on the other side of the political spectrum, Chester Finn had called for them in the lead up to America 2000. But it became clear relatively quickly that establishing national standards and tests was not going to be politically palatable, given long-standing presumptions in favor of local control. A committee composed of governors, legislators, and policy experts was dispatched in 1991 to advise on the feasibility of national standards. The committee, officially called the National Council on Educational Standards and Testing (NCEST), also included many leading members of the standards-based reform movement, including David Hornbeck, Mike Smith, Lauren Resnick, and Chester Finn. If the Pew Forum was a place for puzzling over policy, then NCEST was essentially a place for puzzling over politics. The group devised a way to make standards and assessments politically feasible. The committee ultimately recommended creating voluntary model national standards and assessments, which states could adopt or not, as they chose. This compromise was sensitive to long-standing institutional constraints; at the same time, it gradually advanced the conversation toward the reformers' agenda of widespread standards-based reform.

The reformers also pursued their preferred policy ends through a variety of other strategies that worked around existing institutional constraints. Marc Tucker's organization, the NCEE, funded two initiatives that aimed to create movement toward standards at the state level. Funded by Bob Schwartz at the Pew Forum, the New Standards Project, under the leadership of Lauren Resnick, worked to develop assessments that states could use as alternatives to multiple-choice tests. A second initiative, called the National Alliance for Restructuring Education, directed by David Hornbeck and Mike Cohen, worked with states and districts to try to implement standards-based reform. The Business Roundtable, perceiving that the action for reform was in the states, formed BRTs in a number of states to prod and pressure them toward reform. Many a state BRT in turn produced a "gap" analysis, which measured the distance between the state's programs and the BRT's Nine Components of Successful Reform (standards-based reform). O'Day and Smith continued to advocate the diffusion of state systemic reform, which they argued "would be a uniquely American adaptation of the educational policies and structures of many of the world's highly developed nations."[50] At the federal level, Hornbeck put together a Commission on Chapter One, which laid out a template for how the traditional Title I emphasis on equity should be retooled to focus on helping all students within a Title I school achieve to high standards. After Clinton was elected in 1992, Marc Tucker assembled a team of the reformers, including Hornbeck, Smith, Cohen, and Schwartz, and produced a letter to Hillary Clinton (who was on the board of NCEE) arguing for a standards-based approach to labor and education reform. (This letter later entered the public domain and has become infamous among conservatives, who see Tucker's "Dear Hillary" missive as the smoking gun in a liberal conspiracy for a federal takeover of schools.) In sum, through a variety of formal and informal channels, these policy entrepreneurs pressed their case. Belying institutional theories that see institutions as all-encompassing constraints, this account suggests that policy entrepreneurs are themselves conscious of the institutional configurations they confront and can actively strategize to advance their agendas in a way that is sensitive to these constraints. Over the longer haul, policy entrepreneurs can sometimes even shift these institutional boundaries, as would happen over the next decade.

## Standards-Based Reform Goes Federal: Goals 2000 and the Improving America's Schools Act

This background work came to fruition with the enactment of two pieces of legislation during the first two years of Bill Clinton's first term: Goals 2000 and the Improving America's Schools Act (IASA). Goals 2000 funded the development of state standards, and IASA, which was the 1994 reauthorization of the Elementary and Secondary Education Act, predicated the delivery of Title I funds on the development of state standards-based reform. The substance of both pieces of legislation can be attributed in large part to the influence of the standards movement's policy experts, who were well represented in the Clinton administration and in the interest groups influencing reform.[51] At the same time, the template of *state* standards-based reform was both gaining credence as a workable model of reform and providing a way to sidestep the difficult battle over national standards. These policy developments were coupled with an important set of changes in the political arena, as Clinton was able to bring in the critics on the left who had defeated America 2000.

### Goals 2000

When Clinton was elected in 1992, the idea of standards-based reform gained a powerful backer in the White House. President George H. W. Bush and Ross Perot had also backed standards in education during the campaign, but Clinton was both a state and national leader on the subject, having pushed reforms in Arkansas and acted as one of the lead governors at the Charlottesville summit. When Clinton assembled his policy team, much of its expertise came from those who had been extensively involved in the standards movement, including Secretary of Education Richard Riley, the former governor of South Carolina; Undersecretary of Education Mike Cohen, who had been the NGA's lead education staffer at Charlottesville and was former copresident of the National Alliance for Restructuring Education; and Mike Smith, the coauthor of the systemic reform framework. Not surprisingly, the proposal this team put forward, Goals 2000, reflected the experience of Clinton and his team with state standards-based reform in the early 1990s. It would codify the national goals, and it offered money to states to develop challenging content, performance, and delivery standards. In addition, it would create a new national body to certify the state standards and to develop model national standards. Learning from Bush's experience, the framers of Goals 2000 did not propose national testing and did not include other reform elements that might jeopardize the legislation.

Three constitutive and strategic considerations underlay Clinton's commitment to Goals 2000, which was the first piece of legislation he proposed after assuming office. First, it reflected his experience as a governor with standards-based reform. From Clinton's vantage point as a former governor, states were far ahead of the federal government in the area of reform; the purpose of Goals 2000 was, in Mike Cohen's words, to try "to get the feds on the same page as the states" when it came to school reform. Second, Goals 2000 incorporated the best thinking of the policy community as to how to stimulate national school reform while avoiding the most obvious political landmines. As the NCEST had recommended, Goals 2000 did not propose a national test. Instead it suggested that while a body appointed by the National Education Goals Panel would produce model national standards and certify state standards, ultimately it would be up to the states to develop their own standards and assessments. Goals 2000 also drew upon the final version of America 2000 (S.2), which had advocated standards-based reform, had passed the House, and had attracted majority support in the Senate before being killed by filibuster. Third, it drew upon Clinton's commitment to be a New Democrat. If the long-standing story about the Democratic Party had been that it pumped too much money into programs with no proven record of effectiveness, Clinton was bent on establishing a new narrative that was more focused on outputs than inputs. He had promised repeatedly on the campaign to "overhaul America's public education system from top to bottom," and Goals 2000 was to be the beginning of this effort.[52] By offering money to states to pursue standards-based reform, the administration hoped that Goals 2000 would be the first step toward realizing an output-based vision.

As Secretary of Education Richard Riley wrote, "We were determined that Goals 2000 become the prism through which all our new legislation...would be considered."[53] With the template of standards-based reform in place, the administration hoped that the subsequent reauthorization of the Elementary and Secondary Education Act—a much bigger program with many more dollars in play—could be retooled away from its longstanding emphasis on pouring dollars into poor schools and towards an emphasis on encouraging whole school reform around standards.

Despite the fact that it built upon these previous templates, Goals 2000 faced considerable resistance in Congress. The same groups which had opposed America 2000 were the primary stumbling blocks: Democrats in the House who saw the problem in terms of providing greater equalization of resources, and Congressional Republicans who were concerned about increasing the federal role in education. Ultimately, however, Clinton was able to get the Goals 2000 legislation through. What explains why Goals 2000 succeeded where America 2000 had not?

The political success of the bill depended upon the long-term trends that established the problem and built support for the bill's ideas and upon some political dealing in the short term to get the policy passed. Take the long-term focus first: *A Nation at Risk* had started the ball rolling toward output-oriented school reform. Policy experts had selectively drawn upon this experience and constructed the template of standards-based reform, which in turn became widespread at the state level and among major interest groups backing reform. By offering to aid the growth of this *state* standards-based reform, Goals 2000, unlike the national testing mandates of America 2000, proposed to build upon this progress and thus had the general support of the National Governors Association and the Council of Chief State School Officers. Intellectually, the ground had been paved for standards-based reform: many in Congress had become more comfortable with the approach as it became a widespread template for reform at the state level. For example, Jack Jennings, the counsel to the House Labor and Education Committee, had initially been skeptical of the approach but came to favor it; he eventually wrote one of the most influential books advocating such reform. The Chamber of Commerce, the National Alliance of Business, the Business Roundtable, and other business groups were also now experienced proponents of this approach; they played an important role in reassuring moderate Republicans of the need for reform. Finally, the template itself was one with bipartisan appeal—it had been pursued by governors of both parties at the state level and had rationales that appealed to both parties. Democrats continued to see it as an important tool for creating equity, and committee Republicans were supportive because it responded to their concerns—dating back to *A Nation at Risk*—about declining standards in the schools.

If these long-term trends created the potential for the passage of the bill, a more immediate set of political choices explain why it was able to gain final passage.[54] Unlike America 2000, Goals 2000 did not include any other reform proposals (America 2000 included vouchers); that fact shifted the debate toward the overlapping consensus on standards and away from divisive partisan issues. The bill also proposed building on the state standards movement as opposed to creating national tests, a position that Clinton believed in as a former governor and had the added advantage of minimizing the federal role in school reform. As Clinton would find out later in the 1990s, when a Republican Congress repeatedly rebuffed him in his push for national testing, this was a line he wasn't going to be able to cross. By acceding to long-standing institutional constraints about the proper federal role in education rather than directly challenge them, the Clinton administration was able to win support from moderate Republicans, who were concerned about standards and the economy but were unwilling to support national testing.

Ultimately, the most significant obstacles to passage of the bill were not Republicans but Democrats. While the administration had taken congressional support for the final version of America 2000 as an indication that there would be similar support for a nearly identical proposal in Goals 2000, this support was not to be forthcoming from House Democrats. Cohen, who was the administration's point person in shepherding the bill along, recalls that the House Democrats said that their counterproposal during America 2000 was "more a press release than a proposal." What these Congressmen wanted from their new Democratic president was a significant resource commitment to schooling, particularly for poor students and high-poverty schools, and they did not get it in the $420 million Goals 2000. Reprising their earlier concerns, Democratic legislators argued that strong opportunity-to-learn standards were critical to ensuring that students not be held accountable unless accompanying resources were forthcoming. While Clinton's initial proposal had included these standards, along with content and performance standards, the House wanted a stronger approach at the state level. On a party-line vote, the House passed an amendment, by Rhode Island Democrat Jack Reed, that required states to take corrective action if districts were not meeting opportunity-to-learn standards.

The controversial Reed amendment was opposed by congressional Republicans, by business groups, and by many governors. House Democrats' insistence upon it threatened to derail the entire bill. Congressional Republicans argued that requiring the states to adopt opportunity-to-learn standards was effectively telling them how to distribute their money, a provision by which, they argued, the federal role would greatly overreach. These standards might also lead to lawsuits, conservatives feared, as civil rights lawyers would use the states' inability to provide opportunity-to-learn as a hook to ensure greater resources. Governors, for their part, saw the standards as a threat to their autonomy. Republican NGA chair Carroll Campbell, in a letter to Riley, suggested that the governors were no longer supportive of the legislation, "for the federal government cannot seem to help without wanting to control."[55]

At this point, Clinton himself entered the fray with a public letter urging that the bill be passed in its initial form—specifically, without any amendments that would create opportunity-to-learn standards. Clinton wrote: "Amendments which require states, as a condition of federal support, to commit to specific corrective actions for schools that fail to meet [opportunity-to-learn] standards go too far. These requirements will impede states' efforts to focus accountability on results.… [T]his type of requirement will be a disincentive for states to participate in reform efforts. I urge you not to support amendments that expand the definition or role of opportunity-to-learn standards."[56] By weighing in against the changes, Clinton effectively isolated the House Democrats, linking himself to the positions of the NGA, moderate Republicans, and business groups. Here Clinton was acting both out of conviction on the merits of the amendment and with the broader strategic motive of keeping the legislation alive. As a former governor, he was well aware of the problems that requiring opportunity-to-learn standards might cause, including the possibility that states or localities might have to take the highly unpopular step of raising taxes to meet their commitments. As a New Democrat, he worried that opportunity-to-learn standards threatened to shift the debate back to inputs, the old paradigm he was trying to move away from. As a standards-based reformer, he was concerned that if content and performance standards were to be premised on the provision of adequate resources, as some on the left urged, it would be practically impossible ever to get any standards in place.[57]

House Democrats were in a weak position to defend opportunity-to-learn standards because they had lost two separate but related battles over problem definition. The first debate was about the role of "inputs" in the schooling process. Skepticism of inputs dated initially to the Coleman Report and was bolstered by the perception that the compensatory education reforms of the 1960s had not achieved goals commensurate to their spending. The findings of the effective schools movement, which focused less on resources and more on nonstructural variables like leadership, high expectations, and a disciplined school culture, also suggested that resources were not necessarily the key to improvement. Reformers tied these various strands into a simple mantra—"outputs" over "inputs"—and charged that those who opposed them were supporting "old wine (all we need is more money) in a new bottle (opportunity to learn standards)."[58] House Democrats were also on the losing end of a broader debate over liberalism; Clinton and the New Democrats successfully argued that many of the problems with both the Democratic Party and the government lay in an overemphasis on spending and pleasing interest group constituencies. These tropes were picked up by the media, whose coverage was largely unflattering to the House Democrats and portrayed the struggle as one between progressive reformers and defenders of an entrenched status quo. As *U.S. News and World Report* summarized the debate, "Just when it looked as though we would get a serious school-reform bill through Congress, House Democrats have moved in and mugged it beyond recognition."[59] With no supporters of their position other than the NEA, the House Democrats had little ground upon which to stake their arguments about the importance of opportunity-to-learn standards.

This rhetorical climate enabled the Clinton administration to persuade the House Democrats to excise the most objectionable parts of their opportunity-to-learn standards. This compromise in turn preserved the broad coalition, creating the necessary conditions for passage. After some wrangling on unrelated social amendments, the bill passed the House by a margin of 307 to 118, with 249 Democrats voting in favor and 2 against, and 57 Republicans voting in favor and 116 against. Passage in the Senate went much more smoothly because Senate Democrats did not push for opportunity-to-learn standards. The critics in the Senate again came from the far right, but the combination of Democrats and moderate Republicans created a coalition to pass the bill by a 63–22 margin in the Senate. The longer-term changes created by *A Nation at Risk* had finally come to fruition in a piece of federal legislation that for the first time shifted the federal responsibility away from its traditional focus on disadvantaged and disabled children and toward school reform aimed at improving the education of all students. While proceeding cautiously so as not to entirely upset long-standing institutional norms about federal control of education (the word "voluntary" appeared 70 times in the legislation), Goals 2000 also signaled an important shift in institutional responsibility. It marked the entrance of the federal government onto ground that had previously been reserved for the states.

## The Improving America's Schools Act

Goals 2000 was only the first piece of the Clinton administration's strategy to move the federal government in the direction of standards-based reform. If Goals 2000 provided money for states to develop standards, the larger set of carrots and sticks to adopt standards would come in the reauthorization of the Elementary and Secondary Education Act. First adopted in 1965 to provide compensatory funding for high-poverty students, the ESEA was the central vehicle through which the federal government channeled billions of dollars to the nation's school districts. By predicating renewal of this aid on the willingness of states to adopt standards-based reform, the Clinton administration's proposal, the Improving America's Schools Act, aimed to use the federal government's limited (but still substantial) dollars and institutional foothold to leverage large-scale change.

The Clinton proposal sought to revamp the ESEA along a variety of fronts to support state standards-based reform. The proposal required states to develop content and performance standards for all students. Reflecting the new emphasis on higher-order thinking, multiple choice tests were to be replaced by new assessments that were aligned with state standards, and Title I money would no longer be allowed to teach low-level skills. The administration's proposal also sought to discourage the use of "pull-out" programs to tutor individual Title I students, seeking to make it increasingly possible for money in highly disadvantaged schools to be used for whole school reform.[60] The proposal also included the stipulation that states should make adequate yearly progress toward meeting these goals, a provision that was not enforced but would provide a critical part of the template for No Child Left Behind.[61]

The surprising thing about the reauthorization is that despite its larger dollar amounts and the greater leverage it provided the federal government to oversee state and district practice, its central provisions went largely without debate in comparison with the passionate debates over Goals 2000.[62] The cleavages over the proposal were the same as with Goals 2000: the conservative Right feared greater federal incursion, and House Democrats wanted greater provisions for opportunity-to-learn standards. But having just been through a similar debate over Goals 2000, it was relatively clear to all sides that the House Democrats did not have enough support to introduce opportunity-to-learn standards and the Senate Republicans did not have enough votes to kill the legislation. The House Democrats did introduce opportunity-to-learn standards along with performance and content standards, but these provisions were dropped in the conference committee after it became clear that including them would endanger the entirety of the legislation. Many on the right who were concerned with federal intrusion voted against the bill, creating the most partisan reauthorization since the ESEA's inception, but the coalition of Democrats and moderate Republicans was enough to ensure passage.

The one new area of serious disagreement was over Clinton's proposals to consolidate programs and reduce long-standing regulations. Clinton's position, which ultimately won out, was informed by his experience as a governor dealing with federal regulation and by the problem definition established in *Time for Results* and in *Reinventing Government* and other New Democrat manifestos. House Democrats again played the minority role. Having passed many of these regulations themselves, they were not inclined to see them as unnecessary red tape. The key cleavage was again one of institutional perspective: from the point of view of the school principal or state education department, federal rules impede flexibility, whereas from the point of view of some policymakers, federal rules are needed to ensure that resources go to the people and programs for which they were authorized.[63] Congressional Democrats, who had seen Reagan use devolution as a means to dismantle the federal role, had another reason to be skeptical of a deregulatory approach. Ultimately, however, the deregulatory position of the New Democrats prevailed. Clinton's support and the increasing acceptance of a new paradigm—accountability for results as opposed to compliance with rules—proved decisive. The legislation reduced rules and regulations by two-thirds.[64]

In the longer view, the Improving America's Schools Act benefited greatly from the fact that support for standards-based reform had diffused through the policy community and the interest group landscape, creating support from the NGA, the CCSSO, the business community, and the AFT. The 1988 reauthorization of the ESEA, itself influenced by the problem definition of *A Nation at Risk*, had emphasized greater accountability for results and more emphasis on advanced as well as basic skills. Several reports in the early 1990s, most notably the Hornbeck-led Commission on Chapter One, had argued that the program's emphasis on providing remedial skills through "pull-out" programs for poor students was ill suited to new goals of providing higher-level skills for all. The Hornbeck report was received with considerable fanfare by the press, and both it and the congressionally mandated *Reinventing Chapter I* report[65] were cited by Clinton officials as important influences in formulating their proposals.[66] These reports also laid the groundwork for the reform proposals with Congress. Despite the magnitude of the changes, Congressman Dale Kildee (D-MI) called the new ESEA legislation "the most well thought-out reauthorization proposal that I have seen in my 17 years in Congress."[67] The policy community had successfully brought together a wide variety of actors behind its template. As Marshall Smith summed up: "The agenda of the standards, state standards in Title I, and having the Title I curriculum and so on was never an issue: everybody was going to support it, the entire Congress.... The passage was overwhelming, but more important the concept was never directly attacked. Nobody wanted the old way of doing it; everyone wanted the new way."[68] Given this broad consensus around programmatic structure, the majority of the debate focused on other issues such as school prayer and the allocation of funding across districts. Once these issues were resolved, the bill passed by a 262–132 margin in the House (with only 31 Republicans in favor), and 77–20 in the Senate (with 21 Republicans in favor and 20 against).[69]

## Completing the Transformation: No Child Left Behind and the Triumph of Accountability

The final act in the movement to a federal system of standards-based reform was the passage of No Child Left Behind in 2002. The act built upon the 1994 ESEA—an "evolution" not a "revolution," as one scholar put it[70]—but it significantly increased the stakes. The federal role would still work through state standards-based reform, but now all students in grades 3 through 8 would be tested annually in reading and math. Schools that did not meet the measure of adequate yearly progress for all of their students or a subgroup of their students would be subject to escalating consequences, including funds for student tutoring from supplemental service providers, intradistrict school choice, and eventually the closing and reconstitution of failing schools. States would also be required to have a "highly qualified teacher" in every classroom by 2006. Championed by President George W. Bush on the campaign trail as a way to end the "soft bigotry of low expectations," after a year of often torturous negotiations the act passed in December 2001 by overwhelming margins: 381–41 in the House and 87–10 in the Senate. President Bush signed it into law in January 2002.

The politics behind the passage of the act are consistent with the idea-centered view developed here. The problem definition from *A Nation at Risk* and *Time for Results* continued to hold a dominant role; it shaped the positions of interest groups, promoted policy entrepreneurs whose views were congruent with the problem definition, and influenced which lessons were drawn from experience with past reform. These long-term factors were joined to important short-term factors critical for actually passing legislation. The most important was President Bush's decision to champion the issue; it co-opted the Republican Congress much as President Clinton had swung congressional Democrats behind standards seven years earlier. I first consider the long- and short-term developments with respect to politics and then turn to policy.

## Politics over the Long Term: Setting the Groundwork for Reform

Without doubt, the most important supporter of No Child Left Behind was President Bush, who had championed accountability-based school reform as the centerpiece of his claim to be a "compassionate conservative" in his run for president. In one sense, Bush's support can be explained by rational choice or the median voter theorem, as Republican strategists were determined to close the gap with Democrats on the issue of education. In 1996, when the Republican platform once again declared support for eliminating the Department of Education, Clinton trumped Dole in polls among voters on education by a 59–30 mark. By championing his support for improved educational quality but linking that support to hard-nosed emphasis on reform, Bush was able to largely erase that 29-point gap, trailing Gore in opinion polls by a statistically insignificant 44–41. Not only had Republicans made up ground on Democrats on education; closing this gap had increased electoral significance, as in 2000: for the first time, education ranked as the electorate's top-ranked issue. That Bush moderated his position and moved toward the center to try to capitalize on its electoral significance is exactly what the median voter theorem would predict.

But what the median voter explanation misses is how longer-term developments shaped both Bush's résumé and the electoral context in which he was running. Bush's claim to be a "reformer with results" was based largely on the Texas school accountability system, which was put in place shortly after *A Nation at Risk* and which Bush continued when he became governor in 1994.[71] The first mover, then, was not the 2000 election or even Governor Bush's embrace of education reform in the mid 1990s; rather, it was changing state politics that demanded educational reform beginning in 1983. Similarly, education's rising agenda status at the federal level was also sparked by *A Nation at Risk*, as the issue shifted from 23rd out of 41 issues in 1980, to 17th of 51 in 1984, to 5th of 24 in 1992, and then to 1st of 11 in 2000. Thus when Bush and his strategists looked at the political landscape in 1999 to shape a campaign against the vice president of a popular two-term Democratic president, these longer-term developments made education a natural issue on which to try to stake a centrist claim.

If Bush's proposals fit within a problem definition shaped by *A Nation at Risk*, he, like his father, also acted as a critical issue entrepreneur by pushing these issues as a Republican at the federal level. Theoretically, one critical mechanism by which new problem definitions ascend is through the *signaling* of powerful actors. Particularly as an issue moves to a new venue, where existing problem definitions are challenged by a new view, powerful actors have considerable influence in terms of which position is adopted. In this case, a long-standing Republican view that education was not a federal concern ran directly into Bush's contention that the schools were in crisis and required greater external accountability. Although both views appealed to different aspects of the Republican worldview, the former had long been the dominant view; it is safe to say that without Bush's championing of the issue, congressional Republicans would not have supported an expanded federal role. Goals 2000 and the IASA had passed before the 1994 election with limited Republican support, but the tide turned against a federal role, as more conservative Republicans took control of Congress in the 1994 Gingrich revolution. In 1996, the majority Republican Congress repealed aspects of Goals 2000 that smacked of too much federal involvement; for example, eliminating NESIC—the National Education Standards and Improvement Council—which was to be the national body that would "certify" state standards. This Republican stance softened somewhat after Clinton's trouncing of Dole in 1996,[72] but no national Republican leader had embraced a significantly expanded federal role until Bush did so in the run-up to the 2000 election. With education established as Bush's major domestic priority and polls indicating that Bush had erased much of the Democratic advantage on education,[73] a majority of the Republican leadership fell into line behind the new president, including ranking Education Committee Republicans John Boehner (in the House) and Judd Gregg (in the Senate), both of whom had been longtime, outspoken opponents of a federal role in education. As one staffer said of the legislation, "Many more Republicans voted for the bill very reluctantly because the president was so passionate about getting the bill passed. Had it been President Clinton offering the same bill, I think the vote would have been very different."[74]

If President Bush convinced congressional Republicans to embrace an increased federal role in standards-based reform, most Democrats were already on board because of their experience under Clinton. Considerable convergence between the parties was evident by the 2000 campaign, as Gore also advocated greater accountability for schools, specifically proposing that schools that did not show progress on state tests be reconstituted. The October 2000 debate illustrated this convergence, as the candidates competed to see who could propose more comprehensive testing and accountability models. Bush trumpeted the Texas model and charged that Gore's voluntary national testing would not provide real accountability; Gore responded that he was in favor not only of voluntary national testing but also state and local testing, as well as teacher testing.[75] Despite the differences between the candidates on many issues, on education test-based accountability had become the mainstream position of both parties.

This new consensus among most Democrats around testing marginalized the objections from those on the left who were not on board with the new paradigm. Minnesota Senator Paul Wellstone, for example, argued in a 2001 editorial that without greatly increased resources, more testing would simply set up poor children to fail.[76] While most Democrats were sympathetic to the concern for more resources, they no longer believed that accountability should be predicated on such funding. An amendment introduced by Wellstone that would defer new annual testing requirements unless Title I funding was tripled failed; voting against it were not only New Democrats like Joe Lieberman and Evan Bayh but also liberal lion and Senate Health, Education, Labor and Pensions committee chair Edward Kennedy.[77] As one congressional aide said, "[House Education Chair] George Miller and Kennedy from the start said they believed in testing children frequently. When they did that, they left the critics on the left with nobody to turn to."[78] In essence, the ground had shifted to the right: In 1994 opportunity-to-learn standards had been intensely debated and had virtually derailed the legislation; by 2001 these standards were not even on the agenda. In part, this was a function of a political shift of power from Democrats to Republicans, but it was also the result of a new consensus among many Democrats about the importance of accountability-centered reform.[79]

Support for accountability among legislators of both parties was strengthened by the prevailing analysis of the impact of the 1994 reforms. A 1999 report from the Citizens' Commission on Civil Rights sharply criticized the lack of implementation of the 1994 ESEA. Their analysis revealed "wide variance in the degree to which states have complied with the new Title I," with some states still resistant to adopting standards-based reform. Arguing that these states were subverting the intention of the law, the commission noted, "Many states and local officials have received the impression that the new Title I is largely a deregulation law that will free them from bothersome federal conditions, and have failed to understand that the tradeoff in the law is higher standards and accountability for results."[80] The Department of Education came in for particularly scathing criticism for its unwillingness to take a harder line with recalcitrant states.[81] From the perspective of many in Congress, the lack of state and local implementation of the 1994 ESEA suggested the need for a harder line on accountability in the reauthorization. This analysis also had the effect of uniting Congress as a legislative body behind accountability measures, with legislators of both parties on one side and those who failed to implement them in states and localities on the other.

The political center around standards and accountability also received considerable support from an array of interest groups on the left and right. The positions of these interest groups were again a product of the longer-term developments in the problem definition stream, as many took the same positions as they had in 1994. Strongly supporting the legislation were a variety of business groups, including the Business Roundtable, the National Alliance of Business, and the Business Coalition for Excellence in Education.[82] Several prominent groups in the civil rights landscape were also intimately involved in producing the legislation and were vocal in their support of its accountability-based approach, including the Education Trust and the Citizens' Commission on Civil Rights. And much of the centrist Washington-based policy community was either influential in writing the legislation or supportive of its contents, including the Progressive Policy Institute on the center left and the Fordham Foundation and the Education Leaders Council on the right.

The cleavages that did emerge were more institutional than partisan. One group that came out wholeheartedly against the legislation was the National Conference of State Legislatures. The NCSL argued that the proposed legislation was "an egregious example of a top-down, one-size-fits-all federal reform" that ignored the diversity of successful approaches to testing at the state and local levels. (As David Shreve, the education point person at NCSL said to me, the problem with NCLB is that it was written by a "bunch of 25 year-olds in Washington" who know nothing about states or schools.)[83] In taking this stand, NCSL was, not surprisingly, resisting legislation that seemed to cut them out of the educational policymaking process, as the proposed reforms would feature federal legislation setting the requirements and timetables, state and local districts and schools implementing the reforms, and state legislators losing much of their influence. The National Governors Association, for its part, also raised concerns about the possibility of unfunded mandates and advocated that the federal government pay a greater share of the cost of new test development. However, thanks to the long-range forces that had generated momentum for standards-based reform in the states, the governors were not generally opposed to the content of the legislation; their fight was a narrower one about who would pay for reform.

In a climate that demanded accountability, those who were inclined to oppose the law because of their institutional positions were on the defensive. The most important and powerful prospective opponents were the teachers unions, whose members would be the ones called to account under a new regime of federal accountability. But facing a climate hostile to their interests, these groups mostly decided to hold their fire. The AFT, continuing the tradition established under Shanker, was generally supportive of the law. The NEA, reflecting the views of its constituents, passed a resolution in its general meeting in 2001 against mandatory testing. However, the NEA as a whole did not, in the end, oppose the legislation—in part, some have speculated, because Kennedy personally implored them not to. In the bigger picture, the changing climate around accountability made it difficult for either of the teachers unions to exert their considerable clout. As Jack Jennings, the longtime House staffer and close observer of federal education politics put it, "Clearly, the unions are the most powerful force in elementary and secondary education, but the tenor of the times is to demand more accountability... so they were fighting the spirit of things."[84]

## Politics over the Short Term: Strategy, Contingency, and the Politics of Enactment

While longer-term developments in the politics stream had created propitious conditions for reform—agreement around a problem, interest group support—they did not ensure passage of the legislation. Short-term factors mattered as well, some of which were shaped by these longer-term trends, and some of which were entirely external or contingent.

Perhaps the most important short-term factor in ensuring that the legislation passed was Bush's willingness, in a closely divided Senate, to take a bipartisan approach and to compromise on the more partisan aspects of the conservative agenda. Even at the initial meetings to present the plan, Bush included members of both parties, most notably the ranking Democrat of the Education and Workforce Committee, George Miller. Miller, himself long a proponent of accountability, became one of the most important backers of the legislation. Bush also proved willing to compromise on key provisions that would have alienated Democrats. Bush's initial proposal had included a provision that students attending consistently failing schools would receive vouchers, which they could use to attend either public or private schools of their choice. This provision was a deal breaker with Democrats, but unlike his father, the younger President Bush was not willing to hold up passage of the reform over vouchers. As Under Secretary of Education Eugene Hickok stated, the president did not wish to "sacrifice accountability on the altar of school choice."[85] Despite the protests of party leaders, including Majority Leader Dick Armey, who sponsored an amendment for choice in the House, once it was clear that vouchers did not have the votes in either chamber, Bush stopped pushing them. (The final bill did contain a provision that allowed students at persistently failing schools to purchase supplemental services from an outside provider of their choice.) A similar pattern played out in the debate over "Straight As," a Republican proposal that would have block-granted much of the federal money to the states. Democrats were similarly unyielding on this proposal, which they felt would strike at the heart of the commitment to targeting Title I money to high-poverty schools. Bush again sided with the moderates, personally intervening to avoid the introduction of Straight As on the floor of the House in order to preserve bipartisan support for the bill. These compromises caused considerable grumbling among conservatives— "This is no longer a George W. Bush education bill. This is a Ted Kennedy education bill," said one[86]—but they were not going to buck their new president. Overall, while longer-term developments created the potential for a compromise around accountability, Bush's willingness to adhere to the center ensured the bill's passage.

The structure for considering the bill also contributed to its passage. Democratic and Republican leaders actively sought to preserve the legislative center while minimizing outside influences. As NCSL education director Shreve described it, "There weren't two dozen people who had a clue what was in that bill."[87] The ranking members initially responsible for the bill were Kennedy and Republican moderate James Jeffords in the Senate and Miller and Boehner in the House.[88] When Jeffords switched parties in late May 2001, the Senate moved from majority Republican to majority Democratic, further elevating the role of Kennedy and moving Republican Senator Gregg into the ranking minority position on the Senate Education Committee. The new Big Four—Kennedy, Miller, Jeffords, and Gregg—were responsible for shepherding the legislation. With each party now possessing two trustworthy representatives to the negotiations, wider debate was minimized, and many of the key decisions over the complicated bill were left to these experienced negotiators. Interest groups were also largely frozen out of the process during much of the summer and fall as the bill developed; even the NEA was unable to see a draft of the bill until it was nearing the final stages. This strategy preserved legislative unity and was critical to hammering out a workable compromise.

In addition to these strategic factors, several contingent factors also played an important role in explaining No Child Left Behind. The first and most important of these was Bush's narrow victory over Gore in the 2000 election. While Bush and Gore had taken similar positions on education reform, Gore had come to them after Bush on the campaign, and there was a sense in the Washington policy community that Bush, given his experience as a governor, was more invested in standards-based reform than Gore. Andrew Rotherham of the Progressive Policy Institute said to me that he thought "Bush had more in common with Clinton than Gore did"[89] when it came to education because of Bush and Clinton's shared experience as governors. And even if Gore had introduced similar legislation, there is no reason to think he would have been able to pass it, given Clinton's failures in the previous Congress. The shift of the Republican Congress on the federal role in education is clearly attributable to Bush's championing of the issue; therefore it seems unlikely that No Child Left Behind in its current form would have passed under a Democratic administration.

A second contingent factor was the bipartisan legislative resolve that arose in response to the September 11 terrorist attacks. In my interviews with respondents and in other accounts of the development of the legislation, there is a clear sense that the parties wanted to come together to pass a bipartisan bill as a way to support the president and show that the country had not been derailed by the attacks. Timing was clearly important. Had the bill been heard later in the presidential term, in all likelihood there would have been much less bipartisan spirit to support its passage. While substantively the longer-term developments would still have sustained the potential grounds for compromise, partisan machinations on both sides might have derailed the legislation.

In sum, the politics of No Child Left Behind bring together the longer-term perspective, developed here, around how paradigms shape politics with the more immediate considerations, suggested by Kingdon and other scholars, of policy enactment. The creation of a new educational paradigm raised the agenda status of education and created a centrist problem definition that was amenable to standards-based reform. Bush seeking to capitalize on this opportunity, built on his experience in Texas, which in turn was a result of earlier developments created by the same problem definition. This centrist consensus created the possibility for reform and served as a constraint on which solutions were considered and which were considered out of bounds (e.g., opportunity-to-learn standards). The actual passage of the legislation was determined by both strategic and contingent shorter-term factors, leaving room for both individual agency and chance in explaining outcomes. In a social world not governed by Newtonian mechanics, such an explanation accurately captures many facets of the process of policy change while allowing for the role of chance and contingency in the policy process.

## Policy Choices: The Triumph of Accountability

What this account of the politics leaves out is the substantive content of the policy. Why, specifically, does No Child Left Behind take the policy stances it does? Two streams of thinking were critical to shaping the legislation. The first was the continued influence of the idea of a horse trade of accountability in results for flexibility in means. Bush's primary education advisor, Democratic Leadership Council member Sandy Kress, emphasized that "accountability" for "flexibility" would be the cornerstone of the administration's approach.[90] This approach was gaining increasing support in Washington on both sides of the aisle. The GOP's proposal for "Straight As" in the previous Congress was not an unrestricted block grant, as Reagan might have advocated, but instead offered unrestricted money to states in return for a promise to deliver performance over time. New Democrats, for their part, had long been committed to this approach (which some called the "tight-loose" framework), as it was consistent with Osborne and Gabler's vision of reinventing government. Seeking to bridge the gap between the demands of Democrats for greater resources and of Republicans for more choice, a bipartisan group gathered by Senators Slade Gorton (R-WA) and Joe Lieberman (D-CT) began to meet in 1998 to outline a centrist approach to reform. One outgrowth was a white paper by Andrew Rotherham, at the Progressive Policy Institute, titled *Toward Performance-Based Federal Education Funding*. Invoking the New Democrat metaphors of Osborne and Gabler, Rotherham argued that the federal government should shift from a "command and control" management role to an "investor and catalyst" role focusing on results. Seeking to incorporate the advantages of flexibility while retaining some programmatic priorities, Rotherham argued that the various programs of the ESEA should be consolidated into five broad areas. More money should be targeted to needy schools and districts, but this funding should be accompanied by tough national standards and corrective action for districts that failed to achieve those goals. This white paper became the basis for a similar proposal introduced in 1998/99 by Lieberman as the Public Education Reinvestment, Reinvention, and Responsibility Act, which became known as the Three Rs. Although it won only 13 votes at the time, it became one of the central influences on the Bush blueprint for reform; "they plagiarized our plan," one Lieberman aide complained shortly after the fact. Fifteen years after Lamar Alexander had proposed a "horse trade" of accountability for deregulation at the NGA, he was still being widely "plagiarized," as that image was still the metaphor guiding reform.

The second stream was one of policy feedback from the 1994 reforms. In policy terms, the 1994 reforms were the moment of real innovation, establishing the elements that would persist in No Child Left Behind—specifically the federal ESEA, which built on state standards and assessments and required districts to provide informational accountability on tests and states to create indices of adequate yearly progress. Shaping the 2001 authorization was a particular reading of what had gone wrong with the previous reforms—namely, that they had not been implemented as Congress had intended and that more accountability was needed, as the Citizens' Commission on Civil Rights (CCCR) report had argued. On the Democratic side, there was increasing impatience with the slow (or nonexistent) progress of reform; no evidence existed of a national improvement in aggregate scores or in closing achievement gaps. CCCR and other civil rights groups and the Education Trust and other advocates for poor and minority children were pushing greater external accountability to spur change. Drawing on this analysis, a bill (H.R.2., the Student Results Act) that would have reauthorized Title I of ESEA in 1999 included many of the provisions that later found their way into No Child Left Behind, including expectations of progress toward proficiency, subgroup accountability, and consequences for schools that failed to make progress. Miller was a central supporter of this bill, and Democratic Senator Jeff Bingaman, with technical assistance from the Education Trust, was a leading proponent of subgroup accountability.

Of course, policy feedback is not a mechanical process. Given the lack of progress on improving test scores in the 1990s, it would have been just as logical to conclude that the standards approach was not working as it was to conclude that a greater dose of the same was what was needed. But in a climate that emphasized the need for comprehensive change and the inability of schools to produce that change, analyses that argued that malingering schools and districts were the problem and greater accountability the solution found a sympathetic audience in Washington. One Bush department of education official said, "A consensus developed around accountability—there was a certain point at which everyone was trying to out-accountability everybody else."[91] Institutional vantage points again played an important role. For policymakers far from the schoolhouse doors, demanding accountability was both one of the few available tools to bring about change and a highly visible way to demonstrate action in the face of public demand for improvement.

In addition to these strands of policy thinking, the content of the legislation was also a product of old-fashioned bargaining among the parties. Policies that can appeal to different constituencies for different reasons have the best chance of surviving this bargaining process, and accountability proved to be such a policy. As had been true in the states, some of those on the right saw it as an opportunity to squeeze the educational establishment and ensure that resources were used to maximal effect, whereas for many on the left it provided a new way to provide equity from afar. Vouchers and block grants were more partisan issues; they did not survive the bargaining process. For those on the left who were not persuaded by the equity rationale of accountability, a bargain was struck in which greater resources were provided in return for greater accountability. Conservatives were able to insert supplemental service providers as a substitute for vouchers. Overall, while a shared problem definition had brought both parties to the table and created the grounds for compromise, the normal processes of strategic bargaining played an important role in determining the content of the final legislation.

Institutional constraints continued to shape the federal role even as it was greatly expanded under the new legislation. Specifically, conservative fears about national standards meant that the law did not include any federal role for developing standards or certifying state standards. In what would look like an odd compromise from the perspective of a country that did not have the American tradition of decentralized education, the federal government would set the timetable for reform and the consequences to schools for failing to improve, but the standards to which schools would be held and the assessments by which they would be measured would be chosen by the states. While states would have to participate in the NAEP biennially as a check on state standards and assessments, no consequences would attach to poor performance, as again the fears of a national test reigned supreme. Thus while the policy entrepreneurs had successfully diffused their paradigm to the states and then persuaded the federal government to build on top of it, they were still not successful in creating a national system of standards like the ones that exist in other countries.

What is perhaps most interesting and least recognized about the content of No Child Left Behind is how it represents a victory for the "hard" wing of the standards-based reform movement. Annual testing, which Bush had imported from Texas, was central to this vision. Underlying it was a sense that the key problem was motivational and that by tightening the strings, incentives would be clarified and school personnel would find a way to increase scores—or else. This is the *lay accountability* vision described above. Largely excluded and unrecognized were many of the policy experts who had laid the initial framework for systemic reform. The *expert professionalism* view they had championed fell by the wayside, because experts were seen as part of the education establishment. Specifically, many of these "soft" reformers decried the overemphasis on tests, particularly the multiple-choice tests that were the easiest way to meet the high demand of annual testing, and the underemphasis on reforming other elements of the system, which might lead to genuine improvement. As Richard Elmore, one of the best-known figures in the expert professionalism school, argues, "Never, I think, in the history of federal education policy has the disconnect between policy and practice been so evident, and possibly never so dangerous. Thus the federal government is now accelerating the worst trend of the current accountability movement: that performance-based accountability has come to mean testing, and testing alone." Elmore continues by contrasting this vision of test-centered accountability with what he sees as a richer vision of standards-based reform. "In the early stages of the current accountability movement, reformers had an expansive view of performance that included, in addition to tests, portfolios of students' work, teachers' evaluations of their students, student-initiated projects, and formal exhibitions of students' work." Elmore concludes by arguing that NCLB represents dangerous Washington naïveté about good practice and is rather a set of choices "based on little more than policy talk among people who know hardly anything about the institutional realities of accountability and even less about the problems of improving instruction in schools."[92]

These comments are revealing in that they reflect the exclusion of a key segment of the policy community that had previously been a critical supporter (and developer) of standards-based reform. Triumphing was the "hard" view of standards-based reform that had been developed in Texas, that was supported by the Education Leaders Council, and that was championed by a president whose every action seemed designed to legitimate his desire to be perceived as a hard leader. Defeated was the "softer" view, exemplified by Maryland and Vermont, which used performance-based assessments and emphasized that the key was not simply accountability but professional development and outside intervention to give teachers and schools the capacity to achieve results. While both conservatives and many equity liberals united behind a law that delivered the accountability they sought from a system that in their view had never been held to account, a new cleavage was emerging *within* the standards-based movement between those who emphasized accountability and those who saw building greater capacity as the next key step for the standards movement.

## Conclusion: How Paradigms Create Politics

The adoption of No Child Left Behind marks the capstone (thus far) of a series of changes that amount to a major shift in federal policy and institutional responsibility. This shift over time was created by an ideational context in which both parties saw emphasizing centrist education reforms as advantageous. As the agenda status of education rose, the imperative for politicians to act grew with it. The paradigms created by *A Nation at Risk* and *Time for Results* appeared again and again, specifically the primacy of education to economic competition and the need to couple accountability with flexibility. As the theoretical model emphasizes, this shift in the problem definition not only focused the subject of debate; it also changed the political landscape, bringing in more powerful political and business actors and putting teachers unions on the defensive. Legislative shifts came in a series of gradual steps, as Congress, which had not been party to the education reform movement of the 1980s, was initially resistant to a greater federal emphasis on standards. Presidential leadership was key to the process. The first President Bush legitimized the federal discussion of the issue; President Clinton was able to corral House Democrats; and President George W. Bush, in a "Nixon to China" maneuver, was able to bring in congressional Republicans. The movement clearly benefited from the election of two presidents who themselves had experience with leading standards-based reform in their states; in the longer view, however, the fact that they had state experience with standards and accountability is itself attributable to the state changes sparked by *A Nation at Risk* more than 20 years ago.

The content of the policy chosen was shaped both by this problem definition and by the active efforts of policy entrepreneurs working within it. The emphasis on across-the-board improvement that could be verified by external measures empowered a group of policy entrepreneurs who proposed solutions that were consistent with that problem. These policy entrepreneurs coalesced around state standards-based reform in the early 1990s. They worked effectively to diffuse this template to powerful organizations affecting education reform, as well as directly to the Clinton administration and state legislatures. The appeal of standards-based reform was various, attracting experts with differing values and presumptions: it promised economic competitiveness, as it was modeled after the countries that the United States trailed on international measures; it promised equity, for those who wanted both to raise standards and to create adult accountability for schools serving poor and minority students; it promised a systemic strategy, for reformers who worried that the first two waves of reform were not achieving sufficient results; and it promised accountability, for those who saw the education establishment as lax and unaccountable. This multiplicity would serve the template well when it entered legislative politics, as it proved to have appeal to a diverse set of political backers.

The accountability template also created new political cleavages, uniting those who were holding the accountability strings (legislators) against those who would be called to account (teachers). In the new politics, the primary cleavages were no longer "horizontal cleavages" between left and right but "vertical cleavages" between teachers and legislators and, as the previous chapter indicated, between states and the federal government. In an interesting shift, legislators in this view are no longer seen as primarily influenced by party, ideology, or the median voter; rather, they are constituted by their very status as legislators, which influences them to see problems in terms of the tools available to them. It is hardly surprising that legislators sitting far from the schoolhouse doors have chosen external standards, tests to measure what has been achieved, and accountability to spur action as their policy levers of choice.

This transformation also belies static institutional accounts, instead offering an argument about gradual institutional change. As Manna correctly emphasizes, the American system of federalism can provide opportunity as well as constraint, as it affords policy entrepreneurs multiple venues in which they can try to advance their agendas.[93] This research suggests that policy entrepreneurs were very aware of the institutional constraints they faced and consciously worked to contravene them through activity at the state level and through incremental means that moved federal programs toward standards-based reform. Institutional change in this case was, not a matter of sudden change, as the punctuated equilibrium framework would suggest,[94] but rather a matter of a gradually shifting boundary of legitimacy, with each movement making possible subsequent moves that would not have been possible initially. The impetus for change was a new problem definition, which created the opportunity to displace long-standing institutional norms. What facilitates the change is the signaling of powerful actors who have the credibility to gradually shift the debate. Each of the three presidents in this period acted as an issue entrepreneur in this regard, gradually stretching the boundaries of a legitimate federal role. At the same time, institutional constraints have persisted, and federal legislators were not successful in passing standards-based reform at the federal level until they devised a way to avoid most directly challenging these norms.

The emphasis on the power of ideas offered here provides an important complement to rational choice, interest group, or historical institutionalism approaches. Rational choice theories can explain why Clinton and the younger President Bush chose to emphasize centrist reforms, but they do not explain the context of longer-term changes that made these the "rational" choices. Interest group explanations are right to point out that a number of powerful actors were important in pushing for the changes, but an idea lens shows how disparate actors came to see the problem the same way and recommend the same solution. The greatest puzzle from an interest group perspective—why were teachers unions unable to slow the pace of reform?—is less puzzling when you consider that the climate of ideas put unions on the defensive at a time when "everyone was trying to out-accountability everyone else." Historical institutionalism can help to explain the institutional constraints on reform, while ideas help us to understand how institutional boundaries can shift and why particular policies were chosen.

Perhaps the most powerful consequence of the idea-centered model is the way it limits the possibilities for debate over time. The problem definition that emerged from *A Nation at Risk* more than 20 years ago continues to frame the debate, fueling the move toward a greater emphasis on standards and accountability. Legislative decisions add momentum to the movement, institutionalizing new programmatic ideas and further delimiting possibilities for reform. Alternative approaches, such as opportunity-to-learn standards, that were powerfully debated in the mid 1990s were, once defeated, entirely off the agenda in the next go-round in 2001. In a dynamic similar to path dependence, earlier decisions do, at least for a time, limit the possibilities for future debate.

Finally, No Child Left Behind represents the completion of the dream of rationalization begun by the progressives more than a century ago. What began as a movement from one-room schoolhouses to CEO-managed urban districts has extended its reach through federal law to create a system of goals, measurements, and consequences for every public school in the country. But even as it has grown, many questions remain. With the benefit of a century's experience, what should we make of rationalization as an educational strategy? What has it achieved, what are its limits, what does it "see," and what does it miss? And how do those lessons inform what we should do next?

# 9

# *Rationalizing Schools: Patterns, Ironies, Contradictions*

ACROSS THE 20TH century and now a decade into the 21st, reformers have repeatedly seen the rationalization of schooling as the solution to the nation's educational ills. Reformers have repeatedly claimed that by setting standards, using tests to measure progress towards those standards, and holding teachers accountable for progress, student achievement would improve and schools would better satisfy the goals of their external constituents. Conversely, educators have repeatedly countered that such a mechanistic model imposes a set of business values that should be foreign to schools; assigns responsibility to schools that belongs in part with families and neighborhoods; and in the name of science, squeezes out critical humanistic priorities of schooling. Round and round we go, with no end in sight.

This chapter steps back from the details of such movements to look at the broader patterns, lessons, and implications of the repeated efforts to rationalize schools. One set of questions is about causes and patterns. Why, despite modest results, has so much energy been repeatedly expended in trying to rationalize schools? What patterns are common across time? Are the sources particular to education, or are there common causes that explain the rise of accountability movements in medicine, higher education, and other fields? And why have educators been comparatively less able to resist external accountability than practitioners in other fields?

A second set of questions concerns the deeper assumptions embedded in efforts to rationalize schools. Choices we make about how to reform schools reflect a broader set of values about what we want for our students, how we regard our teachers, and what our vision of educational improvement is. More specifically, what are our assumptions about individual psychology, organizational sociology, and human nature? Why, at least in recent years, has the school reform movement combined such an optimistic, even utopian vision of what is possible for students with such a pessimistic, behaviorist view of how teachers need to be incentivized and motivated?

A third set of questions concerns the consequences of rationalizing schools. While such discussions are usually limited to student test scores (discussed briefly below), school accountability movements also have implications for the *teaching profession*, for *educational justice*, and for the *educational field* as a whole. These continue to be complicated issues; they divide people of different political persuasions, because multiple stances seem potentially plausible. On the teaching profession: Is the contemporary rationalization of schools yet another effort to disempower teachers and treat them as mere instruments in a Taylorist system? Or as has been recently claimed, can school accountability be the linchpin by which teachers assert responsibility for their work and transform teaching from a semiprofession into a full-fledged profession? On justice and equality: Is school accountability, as its proponents say, the civil rights legislation of our generation—asserting public responsibility for ensuring greater equality of opportunity? Or is it, as others say, sham equality, promising ambitious goals it lacks the means to deliver? Finally, what are the consequences of rationalization for education as a whole? What purposes are elevated or diminished, and what educational values are gained or lost in the rush to rationalize schools?

Taken together, answers to these questions allow us to offer a fuller account of the virtues and costs of efforts to rationalize schools. As we move from the past to the future, I hope that this account can inform a broader agenda for school reform, one drawing on the best ideas of current reformers but also recognizing the problems with their efforts. We turn to those future-oriented questions in the next chapter; for now, we focus on the lessons from past efforts to rationalize schools.

## *Cycles of Rationalizing Schools*

There is no "iron law" of school rationalization. It is not inevitable, it is not the only approach that has been tried for school improvement, but it is a very prominent recurring thread in the last century of American school reform. While each generation has had its own set of reformers, several long-standing features of the American school system have set the stage for repeated cycles of school rationalization.

Most prominent among them is the contrast between the high hopes we invest in our schools and our weak ability to realize the hopes. The American ideology around schooling—in narrative, if not reality—is that America differs from the Old World in its belief in the power of education as a route to social mobility. Henry Perkinson chronicled this history in a 1976 book, *The Imperfect Panacea: American Faith in Education 1865–1976*, and it remains only more true today. The long-standing ideological faith in education was bolstered in the 1960s by the civil rights movement, which forcefully demanded that the promise of equal opportunity be extended to all of the nation's citizens. Born of the 1960s was the educational mantra that "all children can learn," a sentiment that became legislatively crystallized in the goal of having "all children proficient" by 2014.

In contrast to these almost utopian expectations for schools is a school system that has been systematically unable to deliver on these promises. There are at least three reasons for this. First, precisely because of America's aversion to a stronger welfare state, levels of child poverty are much higher in the United States than in its western European counterparts, a situation that makes the task of creating good schooling more difficult here. For urban areas, these challenges have only been heightened across the second half of the 20th century, as changing economic and demographic patterns led to increasing levels of concentrated poverty and joblessness in urban areas. Second, as David Cohen and Susan Moffitt recently emphasized, the fragmented nature of American federalism makes it difficult for centralized authorities to provide the supports and infrastructure needed to produce high-quality schooling more consistently.[1] State and local control over education also ensures that there will be wide variation in the level of performance across units of schooling. This variation in outcomes in turn provides grist for the mill of reformers, who seize upon it as a rallying cry for greater standardization.

Third, the institutionalization of teaching as a semiprofession in the early years of the 20th century continues to haunt the field. Teaching has been institutionalized within a hierarchically administered bureaucracy, one that leaves teachers and schools at the bottom of an increasingly long chain of implementation. Within such a structure, loose coupling has come to be seen as the problem; tightening these links through a regimen of rationalizing schooling has repeatedly been seen as the solution. This structure has also bred norms of isolation and individualism within teaching, modes that have hampered efforts of the profession as a whole to establish common norms and standards of good practice. Lacking these mechanisms has both impeded the ability of the field to produce high-quality practice and limited the field's ability to collectively counter the demands of external reformers.

Within this long-standing context, each reform movement has followed a remarkably similar trajectory: 1) the declaration of a crisis of quality that destabilized the existing educational status quo; 2) the elevation of an external "technocratic" logic of efficiency, backed by the knowledge base of a higher-status epistemic community; 3) the rallying of ideologically diverse powerful actors external to the schools behind a commensurating logic that promised control and improvement over an unwieldy school system; and 4) failed efforts of teachers and their representatives to resist these movements, for many of the reasons stated above.

In the Progressive Era, the crisis was sparked by muckraking journalists, most notably by Joseph Mayer Rice's exposé of the dullness of recitations, the incompetence of patronage-hired teachers, and the wide variation in the effectiveness of the teaching of reading and math. These criticisms, circulated in low-price popular magazines, were frequently cited in subsequent legislative debates. The emergence of Taylorism promised a way to increase standardization and boost efficiency. Taylorist logic was imported by newly powerful figures, among them school superintendents Ellwood Cubberley and John Franklin Bobbitt, who sought to use methods of accounting to compute how to teach more for less and to measure the rate of learning for each teacher as part of an early performance management system. Politically, the rise of these new superintendents was made possible by an alliance of political and economic elites that sought to move away from largely ward-based governance and install new CEOs as effective managers of the school system. This movement was resisted by teachers, who saw in it the values and visions of the factory being misapplied to the educational sphere, but their protests went unheeded.

In the longer term, the success of the reformers in the Progressive Era resulted in a shift from one-room schoolhouses to urban school systems, in which schools were expected to follow the directives of a central manager in a district office. This effectively institutionalized teaching, not as a profession under the control of its frontline practitioners, but as an activity performed within a bureaucratically controlled hierarchy. Teachers and schools, at the bottom of an implementation chain, were responsible primarily for implementing the ideas of central office managers.

In the 1960s and 1970s, state education officials sought to extend the reach of this system from the city level to the state level. Again, education was found to be underperforming. The vehicle this time was a massive social science survey, the Coleman Report. The Coleman Report showed, contrary to the expectations of its creators, that the problem was not in the uneven distribution of resources (inputs) but rather in the differences in outcomes that schools, peers, and families were producing (outputs). These findings meant different things to different people, but a group of state-level reformers took them to mean that the system needed a clearer set of goals, assessments, and consequences so that each school would know the level it needed to achieve. This time the borrowed logic came from the Defense Department, which had pioneered "systems analysis" as a way of seeking to tighten the relationship between inputs and outputs.

More than 70 laws were passed and thousands of articles were written about standards, assessments, and accountability, but at the end of the day, state education officials were not able to erect the full systems they sought. In contrast to the pattern in preceding and subsequent movements, officials were unable to widen the coalition and build a significant political or economic base behind the movement. Overshadowed by struggles over desegregation and community control, state efforts for school accountability became a fight between increasingly powerful teachers' unions and weak state education departments. As a result, these early efforts for state standards-based reform largely did not come to fruition, but they did create a policy template that would be utilized in the years that followed.

A third round of rationalizing schools has extended from the 1980s to the present, and it has succeeded in lengthening the reach first of the state and then of the federal government. The spark for this movement was the famous *A Nation at Risk* report. As its predecessor documents had, it made a powerful case for the inadequacy of American schooling. Critically, it tied the fate of the nation's economy to the fate of its schools, a connection that was already becoming more salient with the shift to a postindustrial knowledge economy. The economic importance of schooling widened the conflict and brought state political and business actors into the educational arena. State education departments shook the dust off the plans they had developed for standards in the 1960s and 1970s and, now with much wider political support, were able to put them into action. The supporting efficiency-centered logic came this time from the management sector as, yet again, setting clear targets and holding people accountable for reaching them was hailed as a way to take control of an unwieldy and underperforming system. And yet again, teachers argued that this approach was placing the measurable ahead of the meaningful. They largely opposed the movement, to no avail.

The framing of the problem under *A Nation at Risk* created support for the reforms on both the left and the right. Democrats saw in standards and accountability a way to try to create greater equity of outcomes between rich and poor schools and in disaggregated data a way to track whether schools were delivering on their promises to poor and minority students. Republicans saw in the reforms a way to make the educational establishment accountable to elected representatives, to weaken the power of teachers' unions, and to follow commonsense business ideas about the importance of results. With this dual framing, the reforms were able to win support in both Democratic and Republican states, an outcome that allowed for broad diffusion of the standards template. The movement under Clinton and, finally, Bush to incorporate standards into federal legislation built on these state efforts, culminating in No Child Left Behind. This federal act completed the century-long dream to use governmental power to try to rationalize schools across the land.

## Theory: From Interests to Ideas, From Power Politics to Moral Legitimacy

In theoretical terms, the argument presented above suggests a shift away from the usual lenses of interest groups, partisan explanations, and the conventional version of historical institutionalism. Instead, this account brings to the fore a complementary cultural set of lenses that emphasize ideas, commensurating logics, fields, moral power, and professions. Interest group and partisan explanations center on which actors matter, but in this case the actors varied widely across the periods: good government reformers and schools of education in the Progressive Era; state departments of education, state legislators, and taxpayer groups in the 1960s–70s reforms; and presidents, governors, state and federal legislators, foundations, business groups, and civil rights groups in the most recent round. Legislators of both parties supported the reforms in all three periods. What was common was not *who* was pushing the reforms but rather the *ideas* that they were pushing—ideas about both the nature of the problem and the form of the solution.

Ideas about the nature of the problem effectively reshaped the political landscape in each case. These dominant problem definitions, or paradigms, shaped the *nature of the educational debate*, which *actors were involved*, and in which *institutional context* they would be debated. New paradigms provided *strategic* opportunities for aligned actors, created *constitutive* change by reshaping actors' identities and goals, and served a *regulative* function by delimiting the boundaries of legitimate argument. Ideas complement more traditional perspectives: interest groups still matter, but ideas can help explain how interest groups come to take the positions that they do. Institutions are also still important, but ideas can help to explain how institutions change and why particular policies are chosen.

The preferred solution for those who wanted to rationalize schools could be described more generally as a *commensurating logic*—they emphasized the ways in which quite various entities (schools) could be both guided and measured by a simple set of metrics that would be visible from outside the school. Rationalizing schooling is a form of what James Scott calls "seeing like a state"—namely, a way of making an extremely messy reality into a set of legible categories that can be externally measured and potentially manipulated.[2] Not surprisingly, these types of reforms created a consistent set of cleavages—between the various external actors seeking to reform schools and those inside schools being called to account.

These commensurating logics generally stemmed from other fields—industrial production, the military, modern business—that have greater social and epistemic status than education. In Bourdieu's terms, what we have witnessed across the 20th century is a *struggle among fields*, one in which the educational field has repeatedly found itself on the losing side. While it is not accurate to say that business *actors* took the lead in each case, it is true that a business *logic* came to the fore time and again. The long-standing high level of respect for business in American culture has facilitated this process; not coincidentally, two of the most successful movements for rationalizing schools have come during periods (the Progressive Era and the 1980s to the present) when business was riding particularly high. Perhaps more surprisingly, in each case many of those implementing these external logics have been within the educational field. This suggests that some educators willingly embrace and serve as carriers of these external ideas. The consequence, some argue, is that education has become subject to a set of external metrics that are not consistent with the highest standards of the educational field.

In battles over which ideas would prevail, *moral power* has proved as important as financial or political power. Particularly in the recent struggles, the ability to position oneself as a defender of civil rights and a champion of poor or minority students has been critical in determining who has standing to speak. Small groups with high degrees of moral power, such as the Education Trust, have had more influence than much larger groups, such as teachers' unions, whose large constituency and funding power are undermined by the widely held perception that they are not interested in what is good for children. More generally, this case suggests that politics can sometimes be a sphere in which actors' technical expertise and moral legitimacy are as important as their votes and dollars in determining how much say they have in outcomes.

Finally, as emphasized above, the way that the *teaching profession was institutionalized* has shaped these reforms throughout. While historical institutionalism tends to emphasize the way in which political institutions are configured, here it is the way in which the profession was organized that has shaped subsequent reform efforts. The Progressive Era reforms established a split between legislators, researchers, and administrators (those who devised and oversaw reforms) and teachers (those who implemented the reforms). These roles were formalized into a bureaucratically administered hierarchy at the district level with the creation of the "one best system"; subsequent rounds of reform built on the base created by earlier efforts. The way in which knowledge, power, and authority were organized within the profession and between the profession and external actors has endured; it serves as the unquestioned foundation for rationalizing reforms today.

## From Cycles to Trends: Explaining the Rise of Accountability Movements across Fields

If these internal-to-education dynamics can explain cycles of school accountability, how do we account for the rise in demands for external accountability across a number of fields? In policing, nursing, higher education, and medicine, to take four examples, recent decades have seen a growth in the degree to which these various fields are expected to show quantitative results that demonstrate the efficiency of their services. What explains these shifts, and if there is a common force promoting accountability across the professional world, then is the above education-specific explanation still convincing?

Michael Power, in *The Audit Explosion*, argues that we should understand the accountability movement as part of a broader emergence of neoliberal conservatism in England and the United States, beginning with the Thatcher/Reagan revolution in 1979/80.[3] In this telling, the emphasis on markets, measurement, and monitoring was a way in which ascendant conservative governments, skeptical of the role of the public sector, developed a method of social control over what they regarded as the bloated public sphere. Others have emphasized the ways in which neoliberal privatization has accelerated the trend of imposing market logic on formerly public functions.[4] Some recent writing on higher education has also emphasized the replacement of an academic logic by a consumer- or market-oriented logic.[5]

These explanations provide some insight, but they miss certain key dynamics of modern accountability movements. The first is that widespread calls for accountability across fields originated earlier than the 1980s and 1990s; they date at least to the late 1960s and early 1970s. In health care, for example, efforts to monitor and regulate the scope of Medicare spending began almost as soon as Medicare itself was enacted, with early proposals for what became HMOs emerging in the early 1970s. The second is that it is hard to say that these accountability movements have been about privatization of public services; in fact, one could argue that it is the expansion of the governmental role and ambitions for what the state can accomplish that have presaged demands to see whether government is getting what it pays for. (This pattern has been apparent in both health care and education.) In a sense, the Texas two-step of expanding ambitions and, initially, spending for government functions, combined with a conservative skepticism and retrenchment in available dollars, produces the kind of accountability movements we see today.

Central to this alternative view is how declining trust in a range of professional fields spurred demands for increasing external accountability. As reported in Chapter Six, each of the major professions has seen the level of public trust fall since its high in the mid-1960s. With this loss in trust, the state increasingly began to ask what it was getting for its money, and rising consumer movements encouraged citizens to assess the responsiveness of the institutions that were supposed to be serving them. Ironically, with the state being asked to protect citizens against the failings of the state, a vertical politics was created, with legislators and departmental agencies on one side and frontline practitioners on the other. In field after field, from health care to police to education, this is the pattern of accountability politics.

Of course, fields differ in the degree to which they are vulnerable to these external movements. The systematic comparison of higher education with K–12 education in Chapter Six reveals how differences in professional power and how professions have institutionalized are critical in determining how they are treated by external actors. Higher education institutionalized into a model of faculty governance; the lengthy training and mastery of disciplinary knowledge of its practitioners engender considerable external respect. In contrast, K–12 education institutionalized within a bureaucratically administered hierarchy, and the knowledge base for teaching is seen as thin or nonexistent. Scholars have grouped K–12 teaching with nursing, social work, and other highly feminized "semiprofessions," while higher education is seen as more akin to the signal professions of law and medicine. As a result, while recent decades have seen greater calls for state accountability in both K–12 and higher education, the higher education movements have been much more respectful of the importance of the knowledge and norms that govern academic exchange and university life. Primary and secondary education has not been afforded similar protections; the weakness of the K–12 profession has enabled legislators to enact far-reaching laws to try to remake schools from the statehouse. Teachers' unions, despite their power in money and votes, have been unable to stop this tide because their bread-and-butter industrial representation further weakens the moral legitimacy of the profession in the eyes of legislators and thus actually increases policymakers' determination to impose reform.

These explanations offer a window into why accountability movements not only cycle but trend. Educational accountability has cycled across the 20th century, but the demand for external accountability has increased across a variety of fields since the mid-1960s, as declining trust in the professions, increasing hopes for what these fields would accomplish, and ever more delimited public funds have come together to produce an explosion of external accountability demands. From a comparative perspective, demands for external accountability in K–12 education are overdetermined: Teaching is a weakly professionalized, highly feminized field, whose knowledge claims are frequently doubted; it is central to a variety of public concerns and commands a large chunk of the public budget. Not surprisingly, it is at the center of the accountability maelstrom.

## *Conflicting Visions of the Moral Self*

Embedded in movements to rationalize schools is a deeper set of assumptions about individual psychology, organizational sociology, and human nature. Interestingly, assumptions diverge in how they conceive of students and of teachers: the very reforms that have an optimistic vision of students' potentialities take a much more pessimistic view of teachers' abilities to foster them. What are these assumptions, and why do they diverge for these two groups?

To begin with students, the modern view of what students can do has been heavily shaped by the civil rights movement and its insistence that all children can achieve to high levels. In contrast to the Progressive Era reform movement, which was explicitly designed to sort students by their measured abilities, post-1960s reform movements have sought to raise the performance of all students. The shift from norm-referenced to criterion-referenced tests was a psychometric way of reflecting these priorities: the purpose of testing was no longer simply to measure where students fell on the bell curve but rather to push all students to achieve toward a fixed standard. Efforts to limit tracking and increase the number of students taking honors or college placement classes are other manifestations of the post–civil rights movement commitment to help all children achieve to their potential. One of the central rationales for the standards movement has been the need to change teachers' views of what is possible for students, particularly high-poverty and minority students; one of the main challenges for those who would reform schools serving these students is to convince teachers that their students can learn much more than was previously expected. Implicit in these approaches is the idea that through quality teaching and student effort, students' abilities can increase and grow.[6]

No such assumptions are made about the adults teaching these students. Under No Child Left Behind, in particular, a variety of observers have noted that teachers are seen as people who need to be motivated by external incentives and sanctions. The underlying psychology here contains several key assumptions. One is its underlying behaviorism: the view here, originated by John B. Watson, popularized by B. F. Skinner, and shared by economists and rational choice theorists, is that people respond primarily to external stimuli. Therefore the way to shape their behavior is to alter the incentive structure. A contrasting view, held by a more humanistic branch of psychology,[7] is that people are motivated by a desire to find meaning and worth in their lives and work, and they will respond to opportunities that enable them to achieve that growth. While both views can be true, the rationalizing reformers have emphasized the former at the expense of the latter. In their view the key problem is not upgrading what people know how to do (that would require cognitive growth and learning); rather, it is increasing their effort (that can be done by clarifying their incentives). Finally, there is distrust of those doing the work built into this view; because they are distrusted, their efforts need to be carefully monitored, assessed, and evaluated by those (presumably more trustworthy) actors higher in the system.[8]

Why such different views of students and teachers? Part of the answer is cultural and part historical. Culturally, we simply have different views of children and adults. Theories of development have long emphasized the ways children progress through different stages as they move from infancy to adulthood.[9] These views have been bolstered by recent findings that emphasize the importance of early periods in shaping brain growth[10] and the greater facility of children than adults in picking up skills in particular domains, such as language. Children are also seen as morally innocent actors—to see students as having fixed capacities seems morally offensive and, post–civil rights, to reek of eugenics and other morally discredited theories. Adults, on the other hand, are seen as unchangeable products—they are what they are, for better or worse. Only fairly recently has a field of adult development challenged this view, suggesting that adults continue to grow and learn and that reaching the highest stages of development is something that comes only in adulthood.[11] Seeing adults as unfinished can also be seen as morally problematic, particularly in a society that prizes rugged individualism. Adults must be responsible for their actions, and to see them not as fully developed creatures but as people who are still learning, growing, and changing seems to reduce their agency and responsibility. For reasons both scientific and moral, we tend to see children as malleable bundles of potential and adults as finished products who get what they deserve.

More specific historical reasons explain why teaching as a field has acquired particularly negative valences. First, as discussed above, the institutionalization of teaching into a bureaucratically administered hierarchy placed teachers in a position equivalent to factory workers, people at the bottom of an implementation chain subject to Taylorist visions of rationalization. Despite all the talk in recent decades of empowering teachers, this structural arrangement has remained fundamentally unchanged. Second, the poor performance of schools, particularly in inner-city areas, has bred distrust among reformers. Teachers' efforts to gain trust and autonomy have frequently been thwarted by the devastating failings of the schools they work in; that is, the schools' failings undermine the teachers' credibility. Third, the choices of union leaders in recent decades have further weakened the legitimacy of the teaching profession. As described in more detail in Chapter Six, unions have, with a few exceptions, chosen to largely reify the lines between labor and management. Bargaining mainly over bread-and-butter issues, they refuse to take responsibility for running schools, seeing that as abridging the proper function of labor. The result has been the declining moral standing of the teaching profession, as teachers' collective representatives are widely seen as more dedicated to the self-interest of their members than the good of the field.

The result has been a downward spiral. The failings of schools have led to increasing regulation, which has made it more difficult to draw good people to schools, which in turn has led to yet tighter regulation. Albert Shanker, presciently identifying these dynamics as early as 1985, argued that teachers should take greater control of the quality of their profession in order to break this downward spiral. A better approach would explicitly seek to generate its opposite, an upward spiral, in which better practice in schools would bring decreasing external regulation, which would lead to greater trust and more ability to recruit talented people into those schools. Such an approach would also bring into alignment our views of adults and children; it would see adults, too, as people who can be worthy of trust and respect, people whose talents must be tapped if the goal is to improve the institutions in which they work.

## An Attack on the Profession or a Route to Professionalization?

Ironically, the seeds of such a better movement are already present in one strand of today's reform movement. One of the least appreciated features of the modern standards movement is that it is actually two movements in one: the one with many of the unattractive Taylorist features described above, and the other with the promise to finally turn teaching into a high-quality profession.

As discussed in more detail in Chapter Eight, the first view, which we might call *lay accountability*, sees current teachers as the problem and external accountability as the solution. In this view, the "educational establishment" is a huge "blob" that simply devours taxpayer money and provides little in the way of results. This view has spawned a number of reform efforts, including those that seek to inject greater choice and competition into the sector. (Some of these efforts are promising, particularly certain of the charter networks; I discuss them in the next chapter.) But the most corrosive aspects of these reforms are those that seek simply to increase pressure on teachers and schools to meet unrealistically high targets without providing any mechanism by which those doing the work could create the needed improvement in practice. This is external accountability under No Child Left Behind: a higher power asks a lower power to do something that neither the higher nor the lower power knows how to do and then proceeds to publicly embarrass the lower power for failing to achieve it. The result has been predictable levels of demoralization in schools, particularly those serving high-poverty kids, with little of the hoped-for widespread improvement.

A second view, which we might call *professional accountability*, emphasizes the responsibility that schools and the systems that support them have for creating *internal accountability* to one another to improve practice. This view seeks to combat the long-standing individualism of teaching by generating within schools a common language and culture centered on the creation of better teaching practice. A mechanism such as rounds, where teachers and administrators circulate using structured protocols to examine and reexamine existing practice, is one way in which teaching can take the kind of collective responsibility for outcomes that is common in other professions. Data become tools used by those inside schools for improvement rather than those outside for accountability. This kind of work is necessarily slow; it must happen at each and every school and thus seems to the rationalizing reformers frustratingly piecemeal. But it also goes much deeper in seeking to examine and change practice. The assumptions behind proponents of internal accountability also differ from those of the rationalizing reformers in important ways: the key problem is not lack of effort but lack of skill; the people in the schools are the solution, not the problem. The hope is that greater internal coherence will lead to improved performance and thus lessen the demands for invasive external accountability.

Of course, some of the more constructive members of the standards movement hoped that external accountability would promote greater internal accountability. Unfortunately, the *form* of external accountability chosen under No Child Left Behind seems to largely preclude this possibility. Specifically, the form chosen under NCLB emphasizes simplistic multiple-choice tests as the only measure of performance, rapidly escalating consequences with little accompanying support for improved practice, and utopian expectations about the pace of improvement. Designed by those who favored a vision of lay accountability over professional accountability, it has not surprisingly increased the levels of mistrust between policymakers and practitioners and turned the vast majority of teachers against the law. The most sophisticated studies of the consequences of these reforms suggest that we reap what we sow: at the worst schools, teachers and principals are spending more time teaching academic material; incentives work, if the problem is effort and focus.[12] The problem is that these gains have been initial and limited; greater improvement will require an upgrading of the skills and know-how of those doing the work. International examples, discussed further in the next chapter, suggest that there are ways to make external and internal accountability complement one another, without the pernicious distrust that has characterized rationalizing reform in the United States.

## *Implications for Equity: Progress or Retrenchment?*

Both before it was enacted and in the years since, No Child Left Behind has divided those who support greater equity in the school system. Longtime civil rights advocates, many of whom had worked together for 30 years or more, found themselves on opposite sides of this critical issue.[13] And the split was not a partisan one. Many of the people on both sides have been Democrats—this was less a party divide than a declaration of the emergence of conflicting visions of justice among people who counted themselves part of the left. Was this progress or retrenchment? It all depends on your point of view.

On one side was a group of academics and social activists who saw in No Child Left Behind retrenchment from the ideals of integrated schools and a more equal society. From this perspective, to "hold schools accountable" was to willfully ignore the difficulty of improving high-poverty schools. Coalescing in June 2008 in a statement titled the "Broader Bolder Approach to Education Reform," the group argued that given the long-standing correlation between students' social class origins and academic outcomes, any reform strategy limited to schools is destined to fail. "Despite the impressive academic gains registered by some schools serving disadvantaged students," these activists wrote in a joint statement, "there is no evidence that school improvement strategies by *themselves* can close these gaps in a substantial, consistent, manner."[14] No Child Left Behind, in turn, has been "undermined...by its acceptance of the popular assumption that bad schools are the major reason for low achievements, and that an academic program revolving around standards, testing, teacher training, and accountability can, in and of itself, offset the full impact of low socioeconomic status on achievement."[15] Instead, the authors argued, educational reform should be situated within a broader strategy for social reform that centers on investments in high-quality preschools, health services for students, and after-school programs.

To do anything less, argued Jonathan Kozol, one of the most prominent members of this camp, betrays the promise of *Brown* and represents severe retrenchment from the hopes that motivated civil rights activists only a generation ago. "The goal," Kozol writes, "was not to figure out a way to run a more severe and strictly regimented school for segregated children.... The goal was to unlock the chains that held these children within caste-and-color sequestration and divorced them from mainstream society."[16] In Kozol's visits to inner city schools, he writes, he "cannot discern the slightest hint that any vestige of the legal victory embodied in *Brown v. Board of Education* or the moral mandate that a generation of unselfish activists and young idealists lived and sometimes died for has survived within these schools and neighborhoods. I simply never see white children."[17] To fail to confront or even talk about these levels of segregation under the guise of "high standards for all" is to seek to evade critical issues of injustice: "If we have agreed to live with this reality [highly segregated schools] essentially unaltered for another generation or for several generations yet to come, I think we need at least to have the honesty to say so. I also think we need to recognize that our acceptance of a dual education system will have consequences that may be no less destructive than we have seen in the past century."[18]

In contrast, from the point of view of supporters of NCLB, holding schools accountable is not only the needed policy; it is the morally right policy. Precisely because of the long-standing relationship between family background and school outcomes, it is necessary to hold schools and adults responsible for breaking this cycle and closing achievement gaps. Creating employment strategies, providing after-school care, and seeking to integrate schools are worthy goals in theory, but in practice, in a real political environment, such recommendations serve at best to distract us from, at worst to make excuses for, the lack of progress in improving the schools that we have. The success of some high-poverty schools (charter and public) reveal that success is possible; what is needed at a system level is the injection of the same kind of urgency for results that characterized these currently exceptional schools. The particulars of NCLB might need to be revised, to be sure, but the basic principle of using federal power to push for equity was in accord with the spirit of *Brown*. Groups like the Education Trust and longtime civil rights advocates like Christopher Edley supported standards and accountability as the continuation of the civil rights struggle rather than the abandonment of it.

The reality is more complex than either side of the equity debate acknowledges. School accountability policies represent both progress and retrenchment—or more precisely, progress *within* retrenchment. It is true that, viewed from a longer time horizon, what we have seen is retrenchment. Up until the *Milliken v. Bradley* decision in 1974, it appeared possible that schools would become integrated by race and by class. This would have had two major effects: 1) putting parents of all races and classes in the same boat when it came to improving the schools, instead of creating parallel systems; 2) making school reform much easier and more likely to succeed; socioeconomically integrated schools are much more likely to achieve high results than concentrated poverty schools.[19] Couple political and judicial backlash against desegregation with the deindustrialization of cities in the second half of the 20th century, and it is easy to see why school reform in urban areas has had such a miserable record. At the same time, proponents of school accountability are right to emphasize that incremental progress can be made within an increasingly segregated landscape and that one critical part of such progress is for adults to forcibly assert that they are collectively responsible for improving student outcomes. Research on effective schools, Catholic schools, and most recently, high-performing charter schools has clearly demonstrated that high expectations are one critical ingredient in improving schools. International evidence also supports the view that a thoughtful school-centered strategy can lead to improved performance. For these reasons, proponents of school accountability can make a claim towards progress, even within an overall environment of retrenchment.

At the same time, the lack of greater improvement over the past decade under NCLB has led some in the second group to suggest that while the *principle* is right (schools *can* close the gap), the *strategy* (federal regulation) is at best necessary but not sufficient, at worst flawed in its underlying assumptions. The Obama administration's repeated claims that NCLB is "too prescriptive" and that it designed Race to the Top to use "more carrots and fewer sticks" are clear signs of recognition within the center-left that a top-down regulatory strategy does not have the power to create the systemwide change they seek. Teach for America founder Wendy Kopp, a signal member of the second group, said at a Harvard forum that NCLB is flawed in its assumption that the federal government can micromanage its way to better schools.[20] Instead, a more robust strategy would focus on a wider variety of dimensions (attracting more talented people, developing more relevant knowledge, creating internal accountability within schools), as opposed to relying primarily on the coercive power of external accountability. In the next chapter, I discuss how such a system might build off the best of existing practice.

One might also imagine that there may be a way in the future to create détente between the two groups of reformers. In principle, there is no reason why a school improvement strategy and an external-to-school strategy could not be complementary rather than mutually exclusive. At the moment, this debate is needlessly polarized around the accusation that to emphasize social and familial factors is to make "excuses" for failing schools; a better stance, recognizing that both schools and external factors matter, would generate a web of accountability wherein people working on different issues (social workers, housing officials, etc.) are responsible to one another for taking care of their piece of the overall problem. Geoffrey Canada's Harlem Children's Zone, which provides a range of social services around a high-performing charter school, is a good example of this kind of hybridization. Creating this kind of linkage is a necessity, not a luxury, if we want to succeed at scale. As political scientist Jeff Henig and Massachusetts Secretary of Education Paul Reville have argued: "We believe that our aspirational school reform goals cannot be achieved without attention to the impediments that undermine student attendance and motivation. Our effectiveness in addressing these factors won't depend on sudden prosperity and deep public sector pockets or a broad shift in public values. Rather, it will grow out of the same hard-nosed, pragmatic, evidence-based orientation that for the moment is supporting the narrow claim that schools can do it alone."[21]

## *The Iron Cage Revisited: Claiming an Educational Identity*

Finally, the movement to rationalize schools has had consequences for the educational field as a whole. While most discussion in education policy circles has focused on the effects of these reforms on test scores and most sociological discussion has focused on whether they have increased or decreased educational inequality, almost entirely missing from these appraisals is an account of what these reforms have done to the overall character of the educational enterprise.

The foremost consequence has been the subjugation of an *academic* vision of schooling to an *organizational* one. As we have seen, the sources of reform have varied, but they have largely come from actors external to schools who see schools as a vehicle for other important values. Civil rights advocates, the business community, political officials, and others have sought to ensure that schools respond to their concerns, and they have done so by creating a system of external measurement and accountability that they hope will ensure the needed results. But in practice what this means is that schools are seen less as educational institutions than as organizations in need of reform, a stance that has led actors of a variety of stripes towards the commensurating logic of testing and accountability.

The consequences of the elevation of this organizational vision for actual educational practice have been devastating, particularly in high-poverty schools. While there is no reason to think that these schools were producing high-quality education before the advent of test-based accountability (they weren't), research suggests that testing has not generated the kind of education that anyone would want to defend. Ethnographic work on the consequences of test-based accountability consistently paints a dismal picture of schools engaged in endless and highly formulaic test preparation. Linda Perlstein's book *Tested* describes this regimen at a Maryland elementary school, one that has been widely praised because of its high passing rate on the state exam, the Maryland State Assessment (MSA).[22] Perlstein finds that the school, Tyler Heights, spends virtually every minute of its time, from the first day of school to the day of the test in March, trying to boost test scores. It postpones field trips, class projects, labs, and anything else—including a celebration of Dr.

Seuss's birthday—that could detract from test prep. MSA tips are posted on lockers. Students sing songs about their readiness for the MSAs at assemblies. Immediately before taking the tests, students go through a bizarre relaxation ritual of caressing their earlobes, rubbing their belly and collarbones, drinking water, chanting, and eating a Pep-O-Mint, a practice supposedly grounded in research. By the time the students take the exam, they have written thousands of BCRs, brief constructed responses similar to those on the test, following a specific formula devised by the teachers (borrow from the question, answer the question, find support from the text, and so on). The MSA asks what makes something a poem, so students spend hours writing such passages as "I know 'Smart' is a poem because it has stanzas and rhyme. I know the text has stanzas and not paragraphs because they didn't indent." The test asks what features would make it easy for third graders to read, so they learn to write, "The text features that make it easy for third graders to read are font size, bold print, and numbering."[23]

Missing from the current reform discussion is any sense of what it would mean for schools to be successful educational institutions or what it would mean for students to receive a good education. Entirely absent is a discussion of the qualities of a rigorous education: exposure to high-quality texts and curriculum, a chance to grapple with important ideas past and present, and authentic tasks that are meaningful both to the students and to the outside world. Not coincidentally, these are qualities intrinsic to the educational field. Unlike equity and values like it—essentially social values that are to be achieved *through* education—these are virtues that are justified primarily on the grounds that we think being educated is a virtue in and of itself. And these are the virtues that, not coincidentally, have largely been sacrificed at the altar of an administrative vision of school reform.

In a sense, the problem lies not only in the external reformers but in the weakness of the K–12 educational field in responding. Here higher education provides a good contrast. It, too, has been subject to logics of consumerism and vocationalism—the number of majors in the humanities has dropped precipitously over the past four decades—but there has been real pushback against these trends. Professors and other intellectuals have repeatedly asserted the value of a liberal arts education both to the students who receive it and to society as a whole. Universities do not exist, these critics argue, primarily to bolster the bottom lines of the businesses to which their graduates emigrate; they exist because we think it is worthwhile for people to learn about the world in which they live, to begin to know themselves, to grapple with external questions, to read essential books. While universities, particularly public universities, do need to accommodate themselves in part to external economic and social pressures, they do not collapse in the face of these pressures. Good universities are hybrid institutions, responding both to their liberal arts missions and to external demands.

The problem with K–12 education is that there is no similar counter-vailing pressure. Schools have become administrative organs seeking to improve test scores, with no competing sense of educational values being lost in the process. As the number of actors seeking to make claims over schools has proliferated, educators have not been able to mount a credi-ble defense of distinctive educational virtues that must be preserved in any reform effort. In part, this is due to the fact that their collective representa-tives, the unions, have primarily advocated for better wages and working conditions rather than protecting core educational values.[24] If education is to escape the destructive cycles of rationalizing reform, it will need a group of educators who can speak clearly and credibly on behalf of central educa-tional values.

## Conclusion: From Rationalizing Schools to Beyond Rationalization

The quest to rationalize schools has taken us as far as it can take us. Repeatedly attractive to policymakers, the technology of standards, assessments, and accountability brings with it certain predictable virtues: it allows the state to track the performance of students and schools; it exerts pressure and focuses attention towards collective goals; it can bring attention to the ways in which schools are not achieving what we hope. But it is a limited technology: it has no mechanism to increase the skill of teachers and schools; consequently, it has made very limited progress in closing achievement gaps or improving America's educational standing in the world. It also has proved a technology with significant drawbacks: widespread demoralization is created among practitioners when policymakers ask schools to produce results that neither knows how to reach; its emphasis on control from the top is often alienat-ing to talented people on the ground; and it can trivialize the educational endeavor by pushing schools to focus on the measurable to the exclusion of the academically meaningful.

A better way would reverse this picture (see Table 9.1). We would recog-nize, most fundamentally, that it is teachers and principals, not policymakers, who create good schools; thus our best bet is to build a system that attracts talented people, equips them with relevant knowledge, and gives them the

**Table 9.1 From rationalizing schools to beyond rationalization**

|  | Rationalizing schools | Beyond rationalization |
|---|---|---|
| View of the problem/approach to the solution | Taylorist: A loosely coupled system in need of tighter coupling | Empowering: Improved school practice leads to lessening need for external regulation |
| Relationship to the teaching profession | Distrusting: people to be monitored and controlled | Earned trust: partners in reform |
| Psychology | Behaviorist/extrinsic | Humanist/intrinsic |
| Use of data | Control/evaluation/summative | Inquiring/learning/formative |
| Accountability | External accountability | Internal accountability |
| Relationship between school reform and social reform | Schools solely accountable for student outcomes | Schools and social agencies jointly accountable for student outcomes |
| Relationship between educational and economic fields | Education subjugated to economic and organizational concerns | Educational concerns balanced with economic and organizational concerns |

freedom to develop good schools. The role of higher actors in the system would be to support this work on the ground. Such a system, while a departure from much of our rationalizing past, would both draw on what we know about how good schools are created in the United States and be consistent with the approach of leading PISA nations. We turn to this next.

# Beyond Rationalization: Inverting the Pyramid, Remaking the Educational Sector

OVER AND OVER again across the 20th century and a decade into the 21st, Americans have sought to rationalize their schools, with limited results. Is there a better way?

In the pages that follow, I argue that there is. At base, you could say that the entire American educational sector was put together backwards. Beginning early in the 20th century, teaching became institutionalized as a highly feminized, low-status field; universities, unwilling to associate with training low-status teachers, trained instead a set of male administrators to control and direct those teachers; failures of schools prompted additional levels of control and regulation from afar, further diminishing autonomy and making the field less attractive to talented people.

Successful systems from abroad essentially do the reverse. They choose their teachers from among their most talented students; they train them extensively; they provide opportunities for them to collaborate within and across schools to improve their practice, they provide the needed external supports for them to do this work well; and they support this educational work within stronger welfare states. This is true of East Asian countries like Korea and Japan, but it is also true of non-Confucian countries like Canada and Finland. While it is not yet clear how much of this success are due to which of these factors, it is clear that many of the world's leading countries take a fundamentally different approach than the one favored in the United States. As a recent Organization for Economic Cooperation and Development (OECD) volume sums up what it sees as the lessons from nations that lead the Programme for International Student Assessment (PISA) rankings: "The education development progression is characterized by a movement from relatively low teacher quality to relatively high teacher quality; from a focus on low-level basic skills to a focus on high-level skills and creativity; from Tayloristic forms of work organization to professional forms of work organization; from primary accountability to superiors to primary accountability to one's professional colleagues, parents and the public; and from a belief that only some students can and need to achieve high learning standards to a conviction that all students need to meet such high standards."[1]* In all these respects, the American system is struggling to make this transition.

Central to this transformation is a different vision of the complexity of the work, as well as a different vision of those doing the work. Brian Rowan distinguishes between "control" and "commitment" strategies or between "mechanical" and "organic" views of management; others have talked about this as the difference between "compliance" and "learning" organizations. As the name implies, a control-oriented strategy "involves the development of an elaborate system of input, behavior, and output controls designed to regulate classroom teaching and standardize student opportunities for learning.... The commitment strategy, by contrast, rejects bureaucratic controls as a mode of school improvement and instead seeks to develop innovative working arrangements that support teachers' decision-making and increase teachers' engagement in the tasks of teaching."[2]

Stepping back from the educational sphere, we might say that control-oriented strategies can be appropriate when work is highly routinized and standardizable, but when work is complex and requires significant skill and discretion, a more professional structure is the better organizational form. In professional organizations across a variety of sectors, the emphasis is less on control and regulation than on creating structures in which talented, frontline practitioners can learn from one another and develop and spread new ideas. The core of the educational problem is that *we have been trying to solve a problem of professional practice by bureaucratic means.*[3]

---

* This research is still in its early stages. The existing research is more descriptive than causal; it describes clearly what leading PISA nations do, but does not yet systematically compare those strategies, either qualitatively or quantitatively, with lower performing nations. Relatedly, it also does not yet parse out the degree to which factors like differing rates of poverty across nations could affect overall PISA results. It is suggestive, however, the degree to which the leading countries tend to share the elements described above, many of which are also similar to the characteristics of stronger professions which more consistently produce quality work. As I will argue later in the chapter, much of the approach to selecting teachers, developing practical knowledge, and creating systems through which that knowledge are used in schools is also similar to the approach taken by some of the most successful charter networks of schools within the United States. Thus while much more research needs to be done, there is preliminary evidence from a variety of different angles that would support the importance of these elements in creating quality schooling.

More specifically, consider that any field has the following four components: 1) knowledge: developing the knowledge that will be used in the field; 2) human capital: attracting, selecting, training, and retaining the people who will work in the field; 3) organizational processes at the site of delivery: developing effective processes that govern the work where it is going to be carried out; and 4) overall performance management and accountability.[4] All fields have to make some choices about these four elements; ideally, they form an effective process in which the components are linked to produce good practice.

Given the way that the educational field has developed, it has, in recent years, become very strong on the last element (accountability) but has continued to be weak on the first three. By contrast, in stronger professions, such as medicine, there is considerable attention to the first three—extensive basic and applied science; high selectivity in determining who can enter the field, plus extensive clinical training; strong quality-control processes at the site of delivery—but relatively little with respect to back-end accountability (there is no No Patient Left Behind program). No Child Left Behind, in contrast, is strong on back-end accountability but weaker on the first three, an imbalance that partially explains why it has not been able to achieve its ends.

In the pages that follow, I consider what each of these elements would look like in an education system that empowered the people doing the work rather than see them as people who need to be monitored and controlled. I consider what good practice would look like within the elements, as well as the balance among them. My goal is not to offer a comprehensive blueprint but rather to draw on a range of successful examples to illustrate what a system based on these premises might look like and why I think it is more promising than the rationalization approach.

It is important to note that my argument is *not* that simply shifting power from central administrators to teachers and schools today will bring about the needed improvement. It is rather that we need to design a new type of system, indeed to remake the sector as a whole, into one in which developing consistent expertise among frontline practitioners is at its core. This would entail developing a much larger stock of practical knowledge about how to teach, creating effective training regimens to inculcate that knowledge, and building ongoing organizational processes to ensure that knowledge is consistently applied. If we did those things, we could be assured of a baseline level of quality across thousands of schools and districts and create space for experienced teachers in schools to develop new knowledge and practices that are above the baseline, knowledge that would then feed back into the professionalizing process. By reorganizing education into a full-fledged profession, we could escape the limits of rationalization and provide a way to generate needed consistency in outcomes across the education sector.

## Knowledge: Reversing Direction; Growing from Practice Outwards

One unfortunate decision made early in the 20th century undergirds rationalization: separating the functions of teaching and research. As previously discussed, universities, fearing that the training of teachers would contaminate their elite status, preferred instead to train administrators in methods of scientific management. Universities would develop specialized knowledge, policymakers and administrators would mandate its use, and teachers would implement. As it happens, virtually no link in this chain has worked out well: university research has been better at developing disciplinary knowledge than at addressing issues of practice, administrative structures have proliferated and become ever further removed from the needs of the classroom, and teachers have been highly resistant to "implementing" knowledge developed elsewhere.[5] Such a model is, however, consistent with the overall hierarchical administrative structure that governs schools and with the relative status accorded to universities (high) and schools (low). Thus it has proven durably attractive, if essentially ineffective.

A beyond-rationalization vision would reverse this equation. The needs of practice would drive creation of knowledge. There are some signs that the broader world is beginning to move in this direction. Donald Stokes's 1997 book, *Pasteur's Quadrant*, emphasized the need for more relevant and useful educational knowledge, and the attention the book has drawn suggests that parts of the field are receptive to this message.[6] The creation of the Institute for Educational Sciences (IES) was one nod toward the idea that federally sponsored research should be driven by the needs of practice. At the district level, groups like the Chicago Consortium on School Research and the Strategic Education Research Project are beginning to provide examples of more integrated models of research and practice.

How would a model that prioritized the needs of practice differ from the rationalizing vision? It would differ in a) *what motivates* the creation of knowledge, b) the *type* of knowledge created, and potentially c) *who* is generating the knowledge and d) what *standards* that knowledge is judged by.

In terms of motivation, university researchers, even at professional schools, are largely motivated to develop knowledge that expands theory in their field.

Their primary audience is other researchers; work is judged by technical quality and by its ability to advance debates within the field. It may or may not be useful in practice, but it is not fundamentally being judged on that criterion.

In an alternative world, a significant portion of research would be developed and judged primarily by how useful it is in practice. If it "works," it's useful; if it doesn't, it's not. Its purpose would be less to advance theory and more to solve practical problems. The model here is more one of a lab in an industrial setting than one of conventional academic research.

The type of knowledge developed if practice were prioritized would also likely be different. It would focus more on *actionable levers* than on *broad patterns*. While presumably there would still be research at a variety of levels (classrooms, schools, districts, and beyond), more of this research might focus on issues at a *level of granularity that is more specific and micro* than is generally rewarded in academic research. For example, rather than try to understand the pros and cons of "teacher-centered versus student-centered learning," this research might focus on why some teacher-centered classrooms achieve better results than others or what exactly makes for a successful discussion-centered class. Topics might be as prosaic as what moves to make if a student challenges a teacher's authority or as creative as how best to get students interested in the periodic table. These micro issues are often not general enough for academic communities, which prioritize broad knowledge claims, but they are the kind of specifics that are of great use to practitioners.[7]

For this shift in research to happen, much more of the knowledge needs to be created by those closer to the site of practice. At the district level, the Chicago consortium provides an example of how a practitioner community can generate knowledge of particular use to its district. The analysis of dropout patterns in Chicago schools, for example, led to improvements in policy and practice.[8] Similarly, the Center for Education Policy Research Strategic Data Project, sponsored by the Gates Foundation, embedded researchers in a number of districts to investigate questions about teacher retention and distribution. This internal research led to improvements in those districts' policies.[9] Finally, the Strategic Education Research Partnership (SERP) in Boston, San Francisco, and other districts has directly taken on the challenge by placing researchers alongside practitioners to develop knowledge that is useful for practice.[10]

Ultimately, much more of this knowledge should be created by or at least in collaboration with teachers and schools. They are the ones who know what kind of knowledge would be useful. If this happened, one consequence is that it would fundamentally change the way we think about the relationship of teachers to knowledge—from passive agents who implement ideas developed by others to people who actively create and develop knowledge.[11]

A couple of examples show what could be possible. The Park School of Baltimore (my alma mater), a private school, has a program whereby faculty members identify problems of practice during the year, apply competitively for summer funding, and then use summer time both to analyze their own internal data around the problem and acquire external expertise about steps to address it. One such project focused on gender disparities in mathematics performance. After first reviewing the most significant national and international studies on girls' achievement in mathematics, the group focused on collecting and analyzing extensive internal data (grades, teacher comments, and test scores tracked from elementary school through high school; enrollment in advanced high school mathematics courses; and comparative gender performance data in other disciplines). This is *particular* knowledge about the patterns at the school site. The summer's accumulated information and thinking were then formulated into an implementation plan presented to the administration. Such a plan, required for each Park project, is implemented at the departmental level with administrative support to provide necessary resources.[12]

Brookline High School (a public school in Brookline, MA) does something similar. There teachers apply to a "21st Century Fund" for pilot funding to develop programs that they think fill a niche at the school. Money is again doled out competitively; these programs run for a year or two, and those shown to be successful then go to the district for broader funding. In both of these cases, the pyramid is inverted: entrepreneurial teachers are identifying problems and developing solutions, and higher powers are supporting them through provision of pilot funding.[13]

The next step, one that hasn't happened yet at Brookline or Park, would be to publish or disseminate the results broadly by other means. Practitioner knowledge is too often local and invisible—a huge loss of potentially important knowledge for the field. Some journals publish peer-reviewed practitioner research, but it is not clear that, with the growth of technology, the scientific standard of knowledge is the right one. We might prefer a *use-value* test of knowledge, whereby teachers post what they have developed and other teachers rank the knowledge based on how useful it is to them. We already see this in some teacher resource-sharing websites; over time a much expanded version of this idea could significantly enrich the available knowledge.

In this world, schools would also be far more networked than they are now. Schools would present the outcomes of professional development work to one another, sharing the lessons they've learned rather than relying on experts on high. Charter networks have already taken the lead on this. In the "No Excuses" charters and Expeditionary Learning networks, leaders constantly visit one another for ideas and hold annual conferences where schools present their practices to one another. Regular public schools rarely do this kind of visiting and sharing, but there is no reason why they couldn't.

An even more ambitious version of this idea comes from Anthony Bryk and Louis Gomez's proposal to create "networked improvement communities." Here the idea is to bring together local practitioners, researchers, and commercial designers around a set of shared objectives and across a number of networked schools. Rather than stage the process in the usual way (first research, then policy, then implementation), researchers, practitioners, and designers work together in real time to develop, adapt, and revise knowledge to solve a problem of practice across a variety of institutions. Learning takes place at three levels: the classroom, the school, and across the network. This model is particularly promising because it expands upon the more familiar idea of individual "learning organizations" and provides a process by which we could capture and adapt knowledge across a diverse network of schools.[14]

The final link in this chain would be for schools to set up their own research institutes. We're starting to see this step at High Tech High in San Diego (pedagogically progressive) and the Match School in Boston (pedagogically traditional). High Tech High and Match have each created their own education schools. School-created education schools would train future practitioners (more on that in the next section); to do that, they would seek to develop practitioner-relevant knowledge.[15] These schools would have aligned incentives: their goal for research would be, not to publish in peer-reviewed journals, but to produce knowledge that would help the instructors better train their practitioners and thus enable them to improve their schools. If this training does not produce effective practitioners or if the schools don't achieve results, these institutions go out of business. Thus in the long run, these school-created training institutes might be better positioned than traditional university departments or education schools to produce practice-relevant research.

To be sure, we would still want some more traditional research done by scholars. Basic scientific research on learning processes could inform more applied work down the road. And large-scale evaluations of particular policy measures are well suited to be conducted by universities or research evaluation firms with the appropriate methodological training. Scholars could also collaborate with practitioners on more practice-focused research, bringing their methodological expertise to the equation. The Gates district researchers, the Chicago consortium, and the SERP collaborations all show what is possible. But it is important to acknowledge that such innovations require university researchers to step out of their primary roles. In the longer run, to achieve these kinds of collaborations at scale will require the creation of new hybrid institutions whose primary purpose is to create practice-relevant knowledge.

## Human Capital: Developing Communities of Talented, Committed, and Growing Faculty

If teachers are going to be knowledge workers, then we need a talented and committed teaching force. The single most striking finding of comparative international education research is that top performing systems draw their teachers from the top third of the college distribution and countries lower in the rankings do not. Leading PISA countries like Singapore, Korea, Finland, and Canada differ widely in a number of respects, but they are similar in drawing their teaching force from their ablest young people.[16] In contrast, the United States draws most of its teachers, according to a recent McKinsey report, "from the bottom two-thirds of college classes, and, for many schools in poor neighborhoods, from the bottom third."[17] The expansion of other career opportunities for women since the 1960s has only exacerbated this challenge.

How might we build a stronger teaching force? As has been frequently noted, the United States has never had a human capital "strategy"; who is drawn to and remains in teaching is a product of many decisions and non-decisions made at different levels of the system.[18] A more intentional strategy might think about human capital as a pipeline, where the key stages are *attracting*, *training*, *evaluating*, and finally *retaining* high-quality teachers.[19]

The first stage in the pipeline is attracting bright, interested, and highly academically able people into teaching. Finland, South Korea, and Singapore, which are much more selective in choosing teachers than the United States, are able to be so because many more people want to become teachers. In Finland, teaching is *the* most highly preferred career of 15-year-olds, a priority which allows the country to accept only 1 in 10 into its teacher training programs. In Singapore, 1 in 8 are accepted to teacher training programs. In South Korea, teaching is also the leading career choice for young people; students must be in the top 5 percent of their high school class to be eligible to become primary school teachers.[20] The higher status of teaching in these nations is attributable to a mixture of comparatively better pay and higher levels of cultural respect for teaching and teachers. In South Korea and Singapore, teachers on average are paid more than lawyers and engineers.[21] Overall, the U.S. ranks 20th of 29 industrialized nations with respect to initial teacher salaries. A recent McKinsey study estimated that for a state to change the pay scale so that initial teachers in high-needs schools started at $65,000, with a maximum compensation of $150,000, it would cost the average state $630 million. For that sum, it could boost the number of teachers coming from the top third of the college distribution into high-needs schools from 14 to 68 percent.[22] While the expenditure would be significant (drawn from new or, more likely, repurposed funds), given the large amounts of money already being spent on education with lackluster results, it is likely to be a good investment. We also might hope that in the long run, if teachers were better paid, the degree of respect given to the field might also grow, increasing the population of people who wanted to become teachers and creating a positive, self-reinforcing cycle.

The second stage in the pipeline is the initial training and entry point for people to become teachers. Approaches to this stage have become increasingly pluralistic since the mid-1980s. Conventional university-based teacher preparation programs have been joined by various versions of alternative certification (most famously Teach for America but also the New Teacher Project and others) and, more recently, by the creation of teacher residency programs. The research on these programs broadly suggests two things. First, the differences *within* them are greater than the differences *among* them.[23] There are high-quality and low-quality programs of each type; a lot depends on details of implementation. Second, all of these models are shifting toward in-service as opposed to preservice training.[24] Accreditation guidelines for regular teacher preparation institutions have recently been revised to stress greater in-service preparation; alternative certification providers like TFA are providing regular, ongoing feedback on practice during the year in addition to their short summer institutes; and teacher residencies offer a yearlong internship with chances to reflect, be coached, and improve.[25]

The most recent entrants to this market are schools, described briefly above, that run their own education schools and teacher training programs: High Tech High in San Diego and the Match School in Boston; also, Teacher U in New York. This idea is particularly promising; it would be the final step in teachers taking full control over their profession. While new for teaching, having new entrants trained and certified by existing practitioners is not a radical notion. Consider examples as varied as MFA programs, the second half of medical school, clinical programs at law schools, architecture programs, and the Iowa Writers Workshop.[26] There is no reason why teaching could not follow suit.

Overall, given that three of these approaches are still in their relative infancy and that there is no dispositive evidence on what works best, policymakers should continue to embrace pluralism and examine not only which approach works well but what *dimensions* of a program contribute to its success. Initial research confirms what we might expect—successful programs draw people who majored as undergraduates in the subjects they want to teach, focus on extensive clinical practice rather than classroom theory, are selective in choosing applicants rather than simply treat students as a revenue stream, and use data about how their students fare as teachers to assess and revise their practice. It is worth noting that achieving this at scale will be challenging; conventional teacher preparation institutions still train more than 90 percent of teachers, and they are the group that, as a whole, is farthest from the elements of effective practice described above.

The third stage of the pipeline is selecting who will, out of this larger pool, become practicing teachers. A recent Aspen Institute–sponsored volume suggested coupling extensive support and mentoring in the first few years with a much stricter bar for appointment as a lifelong teacher.[27] If tenure is to be retained, it should be pushed back to at least the end of the third year, potentially as late as the fifth year for those who do not immediately demonstrate high-quality teaching skills. As with tenure at a university or partnership at a law firm, it should not be awarded to everyone but instead reserved for those who have shown themselves worthy of a lifelong teaching position. The details of how such evaluations would be conducted are beyond the scope of this chapter, but presumably they would include a mixture of qualitative and quantitative measures and, over time, these measures would be refined based on their ability to predict who will become an effective teacher.

Schools would have a major role in the teacher selection process. Central to the inverted pyramid vision is the idea that schools are coherent communities of like-minded people who are working together to achieve a mutually agreed-upon set of goals. To support this vision, hiring should happen at the school level. Districts can screen résumés, much as search firms do for private schools, but the final decisions need to be made at the school level. Schools would also have the right to fire teachers at the tenure stage—either because they do not meet the tenure standard or because they do not seem like a good fit with the goals or mission of the school community. Taking these steps would allow regular public schools to become more like successful Catholic or charter schools—intentional communities of like-minded people.

The most common argument against this view is that it would give principals too much power and create the possibility of capriciousness and favoritism. But in secure schools, power would be distributed,[28] and the school's faculty would have a substantial say in who was hired, how he or she was mentored and developed, and, ultimately, who was let go.[29] In terms of hiring, teacher candidates should have on-site interviews and teach sample lessons. Departments (for middle and high schools) and grade-level teams (for elementary schools) should have significant say about candidate selection, particularly on issues of pedagogical or subject matter expertise. While unusual in most large public districts, these practices have long been standard in private schools and good charter schools (as well as universities and successful organizations in other fields), all of which long since recognized that it is very difficult to create and sustain high-quality institutions unless new entrants are chosen and respected by their colleagues.

Empowering schools to create coherent communities would also have positive benefits for the fourth and final stage of the pipeline, retaining effective teachers. While prospective teachers value pay, existing teachers value pay *and* working conditions. Research on teacher retention suggests that being part of an effective school community is a critically important factor in whether teachers decide to stay at a school or in the field.[30]

The other important component of retaining effective teachers is giving them opportunities to grow and develop. There is no shortage of writing or examples on the possibilities presented by career ladders, differentiated roles, master teachers, or other frameworks that recognize that those with greater skill or inclination should have opportunities to exercise broader leadership within schools or the profession.[31] I fully support these initiatives but suggest that these individual opportunities should be systematically coupled with chances for teachers to work with other teachers in their school to collectively deepen their practice.

## *Organizational Processes: The School as a Center of Inquiry*

If the first two parts of this revamped system would be developing practice-relevant knowledge and recruiting talented practitioners, the third part would be creating the kind of school where this knowledge is incorporated and where teachers can develop and deepen their instructional strategies. This is a school as a "center of inquiry," a notion as old as Dewey and as recent as data-informed instruction. Creating schools of inquiry would be a significant shift from the compliance mentality that characterizes top-down reforms. It asks teachers not to be implementers of ideas drawn up by others but rather be active participants, working together to develop teaching ideas and solve problems of practice.

The first step in this process is to break down the isolation of teaching. As I have emphasized throughout, the egg-crate model of teaching is not well suited to collaboration and improvement. That teaching requires complex skill and discretion does not mean that it demands untrammeled autonomy; rather, to be part of a profession means to work within a community of practitioners who are trying to collectively develop improved techniques and skills. The popularity of professional learning communities (PLCs) in recent years attests to the belated recognition that teachers can work with one another to improve their practice.

Collaboration is necessary but not sufficient. For genuine improvement to occur, a second step has to take hold, one in which teachers collectively commit to examining whether their practice is producing improvements in students' skills and performance.[32] This evaluation is something that good teachers have done forever but today goes by data-driven instruction. We see it now in a range of schools, particularly in high-performing charter networks. Many in schools are averse to external testing—they think it perverts the goals of learning (a position to which I have been sympathetic in this book)—but gathering internal, evaluative information (potentially including but certainly not limited to test scores) is essential to improving practice.

Scholars of the professions and of expertise have identified skilled work as a combination of *diagnosis* and *inference*: diagnosis is about identifying patterns amidst chaos; inference is about matching those patterns to the appropriate prescription or intervention. Essential to both parts of this process are data. Data are important to discern the nature of the problem as well as to know whether the chosen intervention is working. Ironically, using data well actually demands *more* judgment and skill, not less, because it involves selecting which bits of data are important to solve a problem of practice and determining how to interpret them.

It is important to recognize that data are not limited to test scores. Data can emerge from a review of students' writing samples to assess progress and difficulties in various aspects of composition. They can arise from reviewing student work and interviewing students after an American studies course to determine how effectively the interdisciplinary approach has translated into student understanding. They can be the product of something as simple as handing out feedback cards at the end of a class to see what has gone well and what needs to be changed. As these examples suggest, data can be qualitative or quantitative and certainly should not be limited to the off-the-shelf assessments currently available. In fact, the very attempt to understand what kind of "data" would be helpful (the answer depends on a school's mission, values, and goals) is a key element in assessment with which teachers and schools need to grapple.

Of course, analyzing data is not useful unless it leads to action. The final step in the process is using data to revise teaching practice. Business scholars of continuous improvement have emphasized a "plan-do-study-revise" cycle, which recently has been adapted to efforts to improve educational practice.[33] In a more humanistic vein, Dewey said that the good teacher is always inquiring, trying to figure out why one lesson has gone well and another has not. Thus, in a sense, these ideas are at least a century old.[34]

This kind of inquiry need not be reserved for independent or charter schools. In New York City, inquiry teams have become a staple of the school reform strategy. The program grew out of a local administrator-credential program, which combined leadership development with school inquiry; it was piloted in 300 empowerment zone schools in 2006/07 and became a systemwide requirement in 2007/08. Early results suggest substantial changes for the better in schools that engaged in this program the longest: greater use of formative and summative data, increased shared accountability, the development of a culture of examining evidence about practice to seek improvement, and a statistically significant increase in the number of students on track for graduation. It will be interesting to see whether the success of these early adopters is replicated on a districtwide basis.[35]

A number of schools have adopted this approach in recent years. One of the healthiest responses we have seen to the external standards movement is the decision by schools to utilize external pressure to develop internal cycles of improvement.[36] For the most part, schools are not places which could be characterized as centers of inquiry or places with cycles of continuous improvement. Scholars of teaching have described it as a profession that is heavy on "presentism, individualism, and conservatism"—meaning that teachers generally are trying to figure out what they need to do to get to the next day and are disinclined to invest in processes that yield longer-term improvement.[37] Thus, to achieve better practice would require a change in culture but also some changes in structure, changes that would give teachers a manageable student load and free up time to make improvement (rather than survival) a serious priority.[38] Time could be created through a variety of mechanisms: projects over the summer, sabbaticals, a daily schedule that would open up time for common reflection and problem solving.[39]

One key element of an inquiry-centered vision is to give teachers a way to expand and improve their repertoires without leaving the classroom. One frequently heard critique is that teachers do not have a career ladder; the job is essentially the same, the argument goes, from the day they enter the classroom at 22 to the day they leave at 65. But this critique is partially misdirected. In a number of fields, the activities of the job are the same on the first and last day—think of professors and doctors. But the key difference in such professions is that the level of skill in the job, within the same role, deepens or expands over time. In Singapore, this kind of deepening within one's field is formally recognized with greater pay and responsibility, on a par with moving into an administrative role.[40] We should treat teaching similarly. Recasting schools as places where inquiry is constant would allow teachers to improve their craft, nurture their souls, and avoid burnout.

This model of what it means to teach in schools would complement the knowledge and human capital strategies outlined previously. It would both demand and reward talented people who are eager to learn and improve their practice. Robert Schaefer wrote in 1967, in a passage that is unfortunately still true today, "Under present circumstances, vigorous, alive, intelligent and socially committed young people often find the schools lonely and intellectually barren places."[41] In contrast, he argued, schools that create structures for inquiry and collaboration would both be more attractive to people who want to develop and reflect upon their practice and would reward those activities rather than suppress them.

For this model to reach its potential, schools need autonomy and internal coherence, but they also need to be networked. Networks allow what is happening internally (highly relevant but potentially parochial) to be complemented with what is being learned externally (potentially less relevant but more likely to be new and different) to create and stimulate change over time. We now turn to how to organize these external support structures.

## *External Support and Accountability: Creating the Right Infrastructure to Support Good Schools*

So what should be the relationship between a school and actors external to it? While much of the debate on external agency has focused on the issue of *control*, I follow Paul Hill's suggestion that we think about this more as a question of *comparative advantage*: Who is best positioned to do what? Hill invokes the principle of subsidiarity, a notion from the Roman Catholic Church that suggests that what can be done closest to the people and the local community should be done there and only what cannot should be the responsibility of external agents.[42] The vision outlined here is similar: the school is the most important unit; it serves as the central physical and psychic home for both the students and the faculty; good teaching and learning either happens there or it does not. Consequently, most important decisions should be made there; the role of the broader system should be to support the school. Hence the image of an inverted pyramid: rather than at the bottom of an implementation chain, schools should be at the top, and the role of other actors should be to support them (with one important caveat, which I will come to).

In the United States, there is a set of emerging examples fitting this description that are known as "portfolio districts." In a portfolio district the role of the central agency is not to mandate programs and assure compliance and fidelity but to act as a portfolio manager, whose job it is to invest in schools and networks of schools that are working and to close schools that are not. The tagline for this movement is a "system of schools," as opposed to a "school system." The animating idea is that the central office, rather than seek to create uniformity across its schools, gives them autonomy to run their affairs, supports them in reaching their goals, and closes failing schools. Portfolio districts exist today in New Orleans, New York, Philadelphia, and Mapleton (CO) and in less developed forms in a number of other cities.[43]

The portfolio idea simultaneously responds to the failures of traditional implementation strategies and builds upon what has been learned about successful schools from the literature on effective schools, Catholic schools, and more recently, high-performing charter schools. As Institute of Education Sciences director John Easton notes, the traditional model is of failing schools besieged by programs that promise to fix their troubles.[44] These programs come into schools like stovepipes but are rarely successful, because their efforts to achieve programmatic change are overwhelmed by the dysfunctional culture of failing schools. Charles Payne calls this the "so much reform, so little change" pattern of school reform.[45] Conversely, the literature on effective, Catholic, and high-performing charter schools suggests that individual schools succeed by developing a coherent culture and instructional strategy that pervades everything they do.[46] A school with the ability to hire its own staff can create a community of like-minded people committed to its goals and mission. By shifting from the traditional to the portfolio model, the district avoids micromanaging from afar and gives schools the opportunity to develop the structures, norms, and culture they need to succeed.

The portfolio idea also productively channels the diversity of views and values that we have for our schools. In a nation as diverse as ours, there is bound to be legitimate disagreement about many aspects of schooling. Rather than try to reach a single compromise for all schools in a district, the portfolio model embraces a pluralistic vision of good schooling. Schools can range from the highly traditional, with students in jacket and tie sitting in rows and taking conventional examinations, to the unabashedly progressive, where students sit in circles working on projects. A school of either type can be good if it makes significant demands on students to engage and think. The portfolio district in Mapleton, Colorado, actively takes advantage of this diversity by creating a range of themed alternatives within its district schools.

These themes allow teachers, parents, and students to choose the type of school that best suits them—more structure for students who need it, more freedom for students who thrive in such an environment. Students can also follow their passions, and that increases student motivation—some students in arts high schools, others in science academies. For teachers, the portfolio model allows them, within a regular public school structure, to become part of a community they have chosen. In turn, teachers' exercise of choice allows for greater buy-in and enables the creation of a more cohesive culture. The district supplies information to parents about the different options and remains as the central authorizer of schools. It can, for example, deny charters to schools whose notions of community range so far afield as not to be academically serious (e.g., proposals not to teach evolutionary science). Thus while the district and state assure the base degree of uniformity appropriate for a public system, a portfolio model respects the legitimate diversity of values and visions held by parents, teachers, and students by creating different communities across the system.

Giving schools greater autonomy and responsibility is not to say that external support cannot be critically important for improvement at scale. But in an inverted pyramid vision, the external support would have to demonstrate its worthiness to the schools instead of schools serving as creatures of the district. The New York City case demonstrates how this would work. Schools are given money to choose from a variety of school support organizations (SSOs), outsider agencies that seek to provide expertise to schools. The SSOs are then accountable to the schools: SSOs that are useful gain market share, whereas those that are not lose it. The hope, which has not always been realized, is that by making SSOs more directly accountable to schools, they will be more responsive to the needs of practice.[47]

External agents can also perform a variety of tasks that individual schools are not as well equipped to handle. Three big functions come to mind: 1) business-related, nonacademic tasks (payroll, accounting, facilities searches);

2) certain academic program needs, including curriculum development; and 3) workable tools to aid teaching and learning. With regard to the first function, if schools are to be intellectually alive places, it makes sense to limit the number of nonacademic tasks they are expected to carry out. New Schools for New Orleans (NSNO) is a good example of an effective intermediary that helps schools focus on the academic part of their work. NSNO helps in finding facilities and space and recruits human capital to New Orleans, two sets of tasks that enable the work of local school leaders.

Intermediaries could also help in developing curriculum and materials. Right now, thousands of teachers across the country are putting together their own lessons on the periodic table of elements. That is a lot of reinventing the wheel. We don't want "teacher proof" curricula, but there is no reason there could not be a basic infrastructure of materials for teachers to draw on as they put together their lessons for the next day. There is currently energy in building this kind of knowledge sharing in a variety of quarters: for-profits and nonprofits are working to expand and refine models for lesson sharing among teachers, charter networks are developing their own platforms for shared curricula, and most recently, a broad assessment consortium of states has announced plans to develop a large online database of instructional materials pegged to the new common core standards.[48]

There is also a huge missed opportunity for investment in useful R&D— research and development, particularly the "development" part. In medicine and engineering, 5 to 15 percent of the total budget goes to R&D, with about 20 percent of it devoted to basic research and 80 percent to design and development. In contrast, in education, less than a quarter of 1 percent of total spending goes into R&D, and of that the largest part goes to research.[49] As a result, there is almost no public spending on the development of actual materials that would help people learn or help teachers teach. Rare examples— like Wireless Generation, which makes handheld devices that provide instant teacher-friendly analyses of formative assessment data—show glimmers of what might be possible if practice-driven R&D were a higher priority.

Finally, while the bulk of the external role is support, there remains an accountability function for the state, but the key is to limit the role to accountability and not allow it to move into micromanagement of schools' internal affairs. Its primary purpose is to see whether schools are meeting the goals that have been defined (in part by the schools themselves) and then offer support or decide on closure. Various models could be used, models that are much broader than the test-score metrics of today. They include the English inspectorate system, the New York quality review system, and the accreditation systems used by colleges and private schools. These generally consist of a multiday visit, review of a variety of documents (often including an institution's comprehensive self-study), student data, classroom observations, and interviews with administrators, faculty, and students. The evaluation team then creates a detailed report about what the school is doing well and how it needs to improve.[50] With this report also comes a decision on whether the school has passed, is on probation and in need of improvement in specific areas, or should be shut down.

The key elements of this kind of review system are these: a) it is multidimensional; b) it is guided, at least in part, by the school's sense of what it is trying to achieve; c) it has the potential to inform practice by offering an experienced external eye; d) it leaves the actual process of revision to the school rather than impose a micromanaged process controlled from the outside; and e) it has the power to close the school if the aforementioned strategies do not work.

Overall, in good systems the outside partner is viewed more as a resource than an enemy. There should be a sense of reciprocal accountability, not simply top-down accountability. Experience in Ontario, Canada, and Victoria, Australia, suggests ways in which outside expertise can be *welcomed* because it is respectful of the knowledge of practitioners and demonstrates its relevance to solving ongoing problems of practice.[51] The key question is less whether control resides at the top or the bottom than how top and bottom interact. Do they, as is often the case in the United States, work in cycles of mistrust and enmity, or do they work more as partners, as frequently happens in Ontario and Victoria?

## Integrating the Elements: Earned Trust and Upward Spirals

All four pieces of the puzzle (practice-relevant knowledge, strong human capital, school-level processes of improvement, external support and accountability) need to be present and integrated in order to generate quality practice. Devolving power to schools, for example, is likely to yield at best inconsistent results unless there are other processes in place to supply good people and knowledge to the schools. Similarly, developing practice-relevant knowledge is unlikely to matter if there are no school-level processes to incorporate this knowledge. If the stool is missing one of its legs, it tends to topple over, even if the other legs are strong.

Teach for America is an example of an organization whose teacher-focused strategy is delimited by the fact that it only partially controls the four levers of the process.[52] TFA came up with an ingenious way to get more smart college students to teach (human capital), and they have closely studied the most successful of their teachers to see what practices they should teach their new recruits (knowledge). They have also tried to give their graduates real-time feedback about their teaching and lesson planning over the course of a year, in an effort to break down the isolation of the profession and move toward collective standards (organizational processes). However, they are sending their young teachers into highly troubled schools that lack their own effective collective organizational processes and whose notions about teaching may be at cross-purposes with TFA. Because TFA has not been able to control all the levers needed to create a fully functioning system, its recruitment success has, in many cases, been overwhelmed by the dysfunctions of the system that its teachers are entering.[53]

Some charter schools and particularly effective CMOs have had considerably more success because they do control the various levers of the process. (Not coincidentally, many TFA alumni head these CMOs, in part because of a desire to create better conditions than those they experienced as teachers.)[54] These CMOs recruit mission-aligned teachers, develop knowledge consistent with their pedagogical beliefs, and have clear school norms and cultures consistent with their mission. Many of these networks, among them KIPP, shut down or eliminate schools that do not perform to their standards (back-end accountability). These processes are common across schools with widely varying pedagogical beliefs—project-based schools like Expeditionary Learning as well as more traditional ones like KIPP and Achievement First. Three of these CMOs, Kipp, Achievement First, and Uncommon Schools, started their own "Teacher U," in part because they wanted even greater alignment across the chain. They wanted to be able to train teachers in the pedagogical approach employed in their schools.

At a national level, Finland, one of the strongest countries on the PISA results, is a good example of a highly successful school system that integrates elements in the inverted pyramid model outlined above. In moving away from centralized control, Finland has vastly limited the role of centralized assessments and accountability. Foreign visitors often ask about the nature of the testing and accountability system and are surprised to hear that there are no centralized assessments, consequences for failing schools, or any of the other hallmarks of American efforts to rationalize schools. Instead, Finland selects its teachers carefully, invests heavily in training, and creates time and opportunity for them to collaborate. The role of central authority is limited to setting some general standards outlining what students are expected to achieve at different grade levels. The pieces all fit; the delimited role of back-end accountability works because of the strength of the up-front investment in selection and training of teachers.

In essence, the Finns have put their entire educational sector together in a different way: up-front investment in teachers and training, combined with lower child poverty rates, greater social support, and more equitable funding, leads to the creation of quality schools, which in turn engenders greater trust and respect for educators, which makes more people want to become teachers, which enables a high degree of selectivity and feeds an upward spiral of improvement and mutual respect between policymakers and practitioners. The rationalizing vision tends toward the opposite pattern: weak professionalization and high poverty rates lead to low levels of school performance, particularly in urban areas; policymakers seek to rationalize and control; while only partially achieving desired ends, this makes teaching less attractive and, in turn, creates a downward spiral of mutual distrust between policymakers and practitioners. The inverted pyramid model described above suggests how, within an American context, we can move away from the downward spiral that has characterized the past century of school reform and onto the kind of upward spiral that we can hope will characterize the next one.

## From Hard and Soft to Thick and Thin

The vision of school reform outlined above does not sit squarely in any of the existing camps because it defines the problem in different terms.

A common way of pitching the problem is as "hard" versus "soft." In this telling, valor is awarded to those willing to make hard decisions: these people support merit pay, firing bad teachers, holding schools accountable, and closing failing schools. On the other side, from this point of view, are those who are soft: people opposed to measuring outcomes, who in theory want to empower teachers but in practice support a failing status quo. Alternative certification and charter providers are good; traditional preparation and traditional public schools are bad.

Conversely, critics, among them Diane Ravitch, take precisely the opposite view. In their view, the villains are those who want to "privatize" the system through expanded charters, increased merit pay, vouchers, union busting, and other market-oriented schemes that challenge the fundamental nature of public education.[55] Ironically, despite taking this stance, Ravitch casts the debate in much the same way as do her opponents: market-oriented reformers on one side and democratic traditionalists on the other.

The view I outline cuts the problem differently. Very broadly, I see the key difference as between "thin" and "thick" theories of change. Policies like top-down accountability, No Child Left Behind–style, are "hard," but they have a "thin" theory of change. The thin theory in NCLB is that more pressure will yield more results, but it pays little attention to knowledge creation, human capital, or organizational processes. In contrast, charter networks, also generally seen as on the hard, or reformer, side of the divide, have a thick theory of change: they attend to all of elements of the system, working from the needs of practice outwards.[56]

The changes outlined above are not clearly classifiable as hard or soft. My overall stance assumes that teachers need to be capable people, people worthy of trust, who will take advantage of opportunities to learn and grow their skills (soft); at the same time, I think it is perfectly sensible for schools to fire people who are not up to snuff or for schools to be closed down if they are failing (hard). The Finland example is probably most frequently seen as soft, whereas the charter networks are hard. I laud both because they have effective, thick theories of change.

In its practice-centered focus, my argument also cuts across divides between "market"- and "profession"-oriented reformers. My vision seeks to radically strengthen or even transform the teaching profession, but it is open to people entering through alternative pathways (a view seen as challenging the jurisdictional control of the profession). Devolving hiring, firing, and budgetary powers to schools is consistent with a market approach, but I advocate this, not out of love for Milton Friedman, but because decades of experience have shown that these choices are essential for creating the kind of intentional coherent communities that work.

## *Joint and Bounded Accountability: School and Social Reform*

The above suggests a way to reorient school reform toward the needs of practice and to transform the profession of teaching. But it still limits itself to questions of school reform and leaves out the role of social reform. Pedro Noguera points this out about a Michael Fullan piece on school reform that has much of the same orientation as what I described above:

> Interestingly, Fullan makes several references to context in his paper. In fact he writes, "...if context is everything, we must directly focus on how it can be changed for the better." However, beyond making a

call for a change in context Fullan fails to elaborate and says nothing about what schools should do to address the challenges faced by poor children, their families and the schools they rely upon. In communities like Detroit, Miami, Los Angeles and Buffalo where jobs, social services and affordable housing are in short supply, what should schools do to meet the needs of the children they serve? Employment, housing and health care may not be regarded as educational issues, but in urban areas where poverty is concentrated and the poor are isolated, such issues invariably affect schools and learning. Fullan's failure to speak to schools in these kinds of areas perpetuates a form of de-contextualized analysis and benign neglect in scholarship and policy making that has rendered much of the educational research in the U.S. useless to the schools that need the most help.[57]

As we have seen, this view has been resisted by advocates of school accountability; they worry that displacing responsibility onto the problems of neighborhoods will give schools "excuses" for failure; they will no longer take responsibility for improving academic outcomes.

However, there is no reason why the debate has to be dichotomized in this fashion. We could assemble teams that link schools, communities, and social agencies, where each partner takes explicit responsibility for the portion of the problem most under its control. Charter "contracts" with parents and students are one form of this kind of joint accountability, based on the recognition that success will come only if each party plays its role. Social scientists often try to apportion responsibility to one cause rather than another, but many phenomena in the world are products of joint responsibility, in which multiple people need to hold up their end of the bargain. "Joint" doesn't mean that no one is responsible; rather, each is responsible for its part.

An example from the policing context shows how this could work. In Boston, a youth violence and homicide problem was plaguing the city in the early 1990s. A team composed of law enforcement, local ministers, youth workers, and a variety of social agencies was assembled to tackle the problem. Each actor had a different role to play: the law enforcement personnel provided the threat of sanctions for continued bad behavior; the social agencies promised support of various kinds for youth who desisted from violent behavior; the ministers provided cover and legitimacy for police crackdowns on the most violent offenders but also created some protection and second chances for less violent offenders; and the youth workers served as trusted go-betweens for the youth and the adults. The program has been credited with the considerable reduction in Boston violence in the mid-1990s. There were three keys to this work: 1) a specific problem that the groups were brought together to work on; 2) complementary roles and zones of responsibility in which each was a needed partner of the others; 3) the building of trust, established over time, that kept the parties from blaming one another in tough times.[58]

In the educational arena, community schools seek to play a similar role. Community schools are usually operated jointly between schools and other social agencies. They are open long past regular school hours and provide after-school care, health, dental, and mental health services, and a range of other supports. Community schools date to Jane Addams and Hull House at the turn of the century but have gained momentum over the past three decades, as advocates have seen in them a way to break through the often siloed and fragmented nature of social services available to children and families. Florida, a particular pioneer on this issue, has championed full-service schools as a way to push social agencies to locate their services within schools. There are now more than a thousand community schools nationwide. As with other social programs, results have varied with the quality of the program and the care in implementing it, but indications are that good community schools can increase attendance, reduce suspensions and substance abuse, increase parental involvement, and ultimately boost achievement.[59]

Research on the operation of community schools has suggested lessons that are consistent with the Boston policing example sketched above. Community schools do *not* ask school personnel to take on extraschool services; rather, they are clear that there is a division of responsibility between the schools, which are responsible for the students' academic performance, and the social agencies, which are responsible for everything else. The challenge is to create real collaboration between the two (or more) parties, as inevitably there are issues that can become trying. For example, teachers may be resentful of after-school providers if their classrooms are not as they left them when they return in the morning. Again, developing trust is critical, so that these kinds of issues do not derail the overall effort at collaboration.[60]

At the time of writing, a recently released analysis of the Harlem Children's Zone has cast doubt on the importance of the school-society nexus. HCZ provides a blanket of services for students within its 40-block Harlem radius. The evaluation suggests that much of the academic success of the program has been due to the impact of its charter school and that the associated social services have been ancillary.[61] This finding has led many policy analysts to question whether this kind of social reform is necessary to boost academic achievement.[62]

My argument here is that such a view is shortsighted. It ignores the mountains of evidence that family and community disadvantage is highly correlated with lower rates of student achievement.[63] The record of the range of community schools described above suggests that more broadly directed interventions can and do make a difference. If more of these efforts are governed by the kinds of principles we see in good schools—careful selection of staff, efforts to develop practice-relevant knowledge about what works, internal processes of data gathering aimed at continuous improvement—they could be an essential partner to school reform.

## From Here to There: Will This Time Be Different?

This is not the first time around the block for many of the above ideas. As we have seen, Dewey argued at the beginning of the 20th century for a view of teaching that integrated practice and research. That notion was defeated by an administrative imperative to create a hierarchical school system and a university imperative to separate the functions of research from teaching. Half a century later, in 1967, Robert Schaefer, the Dean of Teachers College at Columbia, wrote *The School as a Center of Inquiry*. He derided what he saw as the emerging definition of the "teacher as technician" and argued instead that schools should be collaborative, intellectually alive places where teachers seek to deepen their practice, that universities should work in tandem with schools, and that states and other external actors should support rather than regulate this work.[64] Twenty years after that, in 1990, Henrik Gideonse, former dean of the College of Education at the University of Cincinnati, in a book on the mid-1980s restructuring movement, penned a chapter titled "Organizing Schools to Encourage Teacher Inquiry"; it argued that schools could be structured and time allotted to permit teachers to work with one another to reflect upon their practice.[65] Here we are, 20 years later, and again there is a call to make inquiry-driven schools the foundation for school improvement. Is there any reason to think that this time will be different?

The safe bet is no. Existing institutions were born out of, thus reinforce, the paradigm of bureaucratically organized control of schools. To make the changes outlined above would ask states and districts to release power, authority, and control; it would ask unions to move away from industrial-style bargaining and toward a professional-style reform unionism; it would ask practitioners, commercial designers, and university researchers to assume new roles and work in different forms of collaboration. All of these changes run against the grain of the institutions in which these people work; even if individuals are on board with the ideas outlined above, the orientation of the institutions in which they are housed is not.

The restructuring movement of the 1980s provides the most recent cautionary tale. As was discussed at greater length in Chapter Six, there was a brief moment after *A Nation at Risk* when a group spurred by Carnegie proposed a second wave of school reform that would be less top-down and more organized around teachers working with one another to develop and share good practice. In reviewing this movement in 1990, Richard Elmore outlined three possibilities for its future: transformation (radical change); adaptive realignment (partial change); and co-optation (little to no real change).[66] As was discussed earlier, the third scenario came to pass, as policymakers were frustrated by the unevenness of school-by-school change and instead sought to use more sweeping mandates, culminating in No Child Left Behind. History does not suggest we should be optimistic about the fundamental changes called for here, precisely because they seek to dismantle many of the institutional pillars on which the modern school system was built.

Yet history is not destiny, and there are reasons to think that change might be afoot. A scorecard view of the four dimensions explored above suggests that there has been some progress on each. With respect to practice-relevant knowledge, there have been glimmers of potential, including many of the examples described above. Perhaps the most heartening development in this sphere is the work of CMOs to study and learn from their own practice. With respect to human capital, there is now a clear research consensus on the importance of a child's teacher, there are ever proliferating ways to enter the field, and there is now a cottage industry of people trying to rethink different aspects of the human capital pipeline. With respect to creating internal processes of improvement within schools, there is again a research consensus to build upon, this time from the effective schools literature, and there are a number of efforts both to train principals as instructional leaders and to use data to improve school performance. With respect to changing the role of external agencies from enforcing compliance to enabling schools, this has been the area of slowest and least widespread change, but at least there are now some real exemplars in the portfolio districts.

Zooming out, if the arguments above suggest why institutions in general tend toward stasis over change, there are also reasons to think that, in this particular moment, we may be in the middle of a period of serious institutional change in American public education. For many of the reasons discussed in this book, the "one best system" erected in the Progressive Era has come under attack. The result has been, not a transformation or abandoning of traditional institutions, but the creation of *parallel* institutions that seek to re-create anew many of the same functions as traditional ones. Hence we see charter schools alongside regular public schools, alternative methods of entering teaching alongside traditionally certified routes, new methods of training teachers (residencies and school-run teacher training) alongside traditional teacher training at education schools, new organizations to support school turnarounds alongside similar efforts by districts and states. Newer does not necessarily mean better, but what this pluralism provides are more opportunities for people to try different ways to create good schools and the infrastructure that supports those schools. These newcomer institutions will fail at least as often as they succeed, but they do have the advantage of not being the product of layers of history. They can develop their organizational structures and routines to directly target the problems they are trying to solve. In particular, we might expect these new organizations to be more directly responsive to the needs of practice, consistent with much of what has been advocated above.

Over the longer run, the real question is whether what works well in this diversity of institutional forms, practices, and structures will translate to the sector as a whole. There are at least three possibilities for how this might happen. The first is the sharing of ideas. We are already beginning to see some passing back and forth of intellectual property, as ideas about, for example, how to improve the hiring process have gradually migrated from leading independent and charter schools to cutting-edge regular public districts. The second is interpenetration of the old and new. We also are starting to see some blended or hybrid forms—leading districts like New York City have moved to a portfolio model that allows them to bring in high-performing charter operators to run their schools. And of course, the third and most radical is that newer institutions will gradually eclipse and replace existing ones.

Whether any of these scenarios come to pass remains to be seen, but what is clear is that the breaking up of the long-standing monopoly of the one best system has opened the door for a variety of new institutions to try new approaches and for old institutions to reform themselves to address new realities. We can only hope that they have learned from the lessons of the past and seek not to control but to empower, creating the infrastructure upon which talented practitioners can create the good schools of the future.

# A Note on Methods

The methodological approach employed in this work is a mixture of Mill's methods, process tracing, and some carefully selected comparative analysis. In terms of Mill's methods, I look at three cases of the same phenomenon (accountability movements across the 20th century) and isolate common factors or patterns across the cases. I also draw on James Mahoney's point that it is not only whether the absence or presence of an explanatory factor is correlated with the absence or presence of an outcome that is important but also that differences in degree of an explanatory factor should be related to differences in degree of the outcome.[1] In this research, I find that in the second of the three cases, the 1960s and 1970s accountability movement, one of the explanatory factors (political actors mobilizing behind logic) was only partially realized, and as a result, the outcome was also only partially realized (many laws were proposed, but they were sometimes not passed or, when passed, were not fully implemented).

Mill's methods have come under criticism from some scholars, who argue that with a small number of cases, identifying similar factors is not enough to show that those factors are important for explaining the outcomes.[2] For this reason, I draw on a qualitative logic of process tracing, seeking to show in considerable detail not simply *whether* a factor mattered in determining the outcome but also *how* it mattered. By looking in detail at case studies and analyzing this connective tissue, it is possible to ascribe with greater certainty the impact of hypothesized factors. Close examination also allows differentiation among competing explanations—evaluation of whether interest groups, institutions, ideas, or other factors are most applicable to explaining the outcomes.

I also pay close attention to counterfactuals—alternative courses of action that were advocated but failed at each of these critical junctures. Comparing these failed alternatives with their more successful rivals allows for assessment of which groups and underlying assumptions were consistently influential and which were less so. Investigating counterfactuals also addresses questions about the second and third faces of power, explaining why over time entire sets of possibilities for schooling become marginalized or excluded from the debate.[3]

One central argument in the book is that the underdevelopment of the K–12 education profession has affected how the sector has been treated by external actors. I investigate this hypothesis by comparing K–12 education with other fields that differ in their degree of professional power. In Chapter Six, I compare the impact of *A Nation at Risk* with that of a similar report on higher education released by the Department of Education the following year. By examining two fields (higher education and secondary/primary education) that are similar in some of their core functions and that have both faced demands for improved quality, it is possible to see whether (and how) the differing level of professional power across fields has affected movements for reform.[4]

The modern movement presents both challenges and opportunities for research because it encompassed 50 states and then the federal government. While tracing the federal politics of reform is a familiar strategy to explain the modern school reform movement, this work differs in offering a detailed examination of state politics as well. I agree with Paul Manna's argument that without the state-level consensus surrounding standards-based reform—42 states had adopted parts of it before the federal government began to require it in 1994—it would have been impossible to expand federal capacity into an area historically reserved to the states. But Manna does not use state-level evidence to specifically address why so many states came to support a similar approach. Given the diversity among states—in terms of partisan composition, union strength, political culture, and previous educational policies—a key question that has been largely unexplored is why such a heterogeneous collection of polities adopted such similar school reform strategies *before* they were required to by the federal government?[5]

Since my aim is to explain convergence, I selected states that vary along the several dimensions that previous scholarship has pinpointed as likely to affect the politics of education. I chose Michigan, Maryland, and Utah as case-study states. I chose these states for two reasons. First, since I was trying to understand how so many states came to adopt the same policy, I wanted to choose states that were very different on a number of dimensions that would presumably affect their education policy choices. These three states differ in the following dimensions: region, partisanship, timing of adoption of standards-based reform, minority population, initial test scores, level of local control, political culture, and per-pupil spending (see Table 11.1). Second, there has been a lot of work done on a few well-known standard leading states, particularly Kentucky, Texas, North Carolina, and California. But if the goal is to understand how 49 states came to adopt standards-based reform before No Child Left Behind, understanding the politics of lower-profile states is also important. Maryland was an early adopter of standards; thus I have one from the lead states, but also two that came later to standards. In addition, by researching less studied states, what I learn about them can be pooled with others' research on the better-known states to create a fuller understanding of the standards movement. [6]

**Table 11.1. Variation among case-study states***

| State | Utah | Michigan | Maryland |
|---|---|---|---|
| Initial test scores | High | Moderate | High |
| Initial per-pupil spending | Low (lowest in the nation) | Moderate | High |
| Minority population | Low | High | High |
| Political context | Republican | Mixed | Democratic |
| Level of local control | Moderate | High | Low |
| Finance equity cases" | No | Yes | Yes |
| Political culture† | Moralistic | Moralistic | Individualistic |
| Initial state educational capacity | Low | High | High |

* All data not specifically identified otherwise comes from the *State Politics Quarterly* database: www.unl.edu/SPPQ/datasets.html. Test scores, minority population, and measures of local control and state capacity are as of 1988, before the reforms I am interested in began. Political context is for the 1990s, the period when the reforms took place.

" Data from Reed (2001).

† Classifications based on Elazar (1984).

The data for this work come from a wide range of sources. The Progressive Era work relies primarily on secondary sources; analysis of the two more recent movements relies on a mix of interviews, archival documents, and secondary materials. I traveled to the three case study states and to Washington, DC, spending 3 to 8 weeks at each of the sites. I conducted 80 interviews with participants involved in the state and federal reforms. Interviews ranged in length from 30 minutes to 3 hours each, with an average of an hour; almost all were conducted in person. Interviews were taped and transcribed. Interviewees included state legislators, a former governor (John Engler of Michigan), federal legislative aides, policy experts, journalists, interest group representatives, federal and state department of education officials, and scholars. Some interviewees gave me access to their personal or organizational files, sources that allowed for a more complete record of what actors were thinking at times of key decision making. I also examined several thousand pages of documents from state libraries and archives in Maryland, Utah, and Michigan, as well as from Brown University[7] and the Library of Congress. I observed in person some of the deliberations around No Child Left Behind, including the Utah legislative debate over whether the state should withdraw from the federal program. I supplemented these primary materials with a newspaper review and an examination of published and unpublished dissertations, state and federal legislative records, and a variety of secondary sources. I also consulted a number of important primary documents that have affected the reform movement.

This range of material allows for triangulation to compensate for the weaknesses of individual data sources.[8] For instance, the interviews reveal information that is not in other records, while the archival and media sources provide a check against selective memory or the construing of the past in light of the present.

# Author's Note and Acknowledgments

This book has its origin in two intellectual homes. Much of its theoretical apparatus comes from my training in the Harvard Department of Sociology. The arguments about the professions, the ways that states "see," and the notions of interpenetrating logics, I owe to participating in a thriving sociological community that is interested in the cultural underpinnings of modern life. At the same time, much of the substantive punch of the book comes from my time at the Harvard Graduate School of Education (HGSE). Now at a professional school, I see more clearly the consequences of these underlying logics for actual students, teachers, and schools. The book's argument—that failed professionalization breeds external rationalization, with unfortunate consequences for policy and practice—emerged gradually as I began to put these two worlds together, the first providing the tools for explaining what I was seeing in the second.

From my time in Arts and Sciences, I thank the sociology department and its Inequality program for providing me a stimulating and rigorous home in which to think about social problems and how they can be addressed. Specifically, Christopher Winship, Jennifer Hochschild, and Theda Skocpol sparked my interest in the topics pursued in this book and provided models for how to draw on the social sciences to explore broad public questions. Particular thanks go to William Julius Wilson (my undergraduate advisor), Katherine Newman (my first graduate school advisor), and Christopher "Sandy" Jencks (my dissertation advisor), all of whom show in their own work what publicly engaged scholarship can look like and all of whom were extremely generous in their support of me and my work. Bill Wilson was my inspiration for going to graduate school in the first place because he fused a commitment to generating knowledge with a profound sense of social responsibility. Katherine Newman took me under her wing and showed me how to write for a public audience, an experience I have drawn on again and again as I worked on what became this book.

I cannot offer enough thanks to Sandy Jencks. He has been central to me as both an advisor and a mentor. When I was in graduate school, he offered line-by-line comments on my work, and since I became a professor he has continued to provide invaluable counsel and advice. In his commitment to rigorous scholarship, in his mentoring of students, in his writing for a general audience, and in his influence on policy, Sandy models how the scholarly life can and should be lived. I can only hope to pay forward to my own students what he has done for me.

In the broader sociological world, I have been lucky to find people who were willing to embrace and encourage this work. In particular, I thank Michele Lamont, Rakesh Khurana, Pamela Walters, Amy Binder, Mitchell Stevens, Scott Davies, Steven Brint, Michael Olneck, and Elizabeth Armstrong, all of whom have helped to legitimate the nexus of professions, institutions, schooling, culture, and politics that is central to this book.

The move to the Harvard Graduate School of Education has been fitting in ways that I couldn't initially have anticipated. Professional schools are hybrid institutions, with one eye toward their arts and sciences brethren and the other toward the fields they serve. For me, that has been a generative combination because it creates opportunities to bring together the worlds of scholarship and social change, knowledge and action, uniting domains that are too often falsely divided. Working in a field rather than a discipline is also liberating, because it opens up wide-ranging possibilities for intellectual inquiry. I have been fortunate to learn from my colleagues at HGSE and beyond; their work embodies how field-driven inquiry can lead to broad and enduring insights about education and social life.

Specifically, I thank Robert Kegan, Richard Elmore, Mark Moore, David Perkins, Howard Gardner, Sara Lawrence-Lightfoot, Susan Moore Johnson, Steve Seidel, Daniel Koretz, Richard Murnane, John Willett, Joe Blatt, Rick Weissbourd, Julie Reuben, Hiro Yoshikawa, Meira Levinson, Karen Mapp, Mark Warren, John Diamond, Monica Higgins, Elizabeth City, and many of my other colleagues at HGSE for encouraging me to pursue big questions and for modeling this ambition themselves. Particular thanks to Mark Moore for our many conversations about how institutions can make social change; I have always learned from them and look forward to more in the years to come. My gratitude also to our dean, Kathleen McCartney, who has made HGSE a place where it matters to do work that matters for policy and practice.

Many of my intellectual debts for the more substantive part of this work are owed to Richard Elmore. Of all the places I could have landed after graduate school, the office next to his was the best place for the development of my work. His deep knowledge of schooling, from the classroom up through the system, was a fount of information; it has informed my work at every level. In essence, he helped me to "see" the school system—what it is, why it is, what it could be—and for that gift I will always be in his debt.

Later in my trajectory I had the opportunity to learn from David Cohen, who was once Richard's teacher and who also possesses seemingly unlimited insight into the dynamics of schooling. He expertly draws on strands from history, sociology, politics, and pedagogy to fashion the kind of interdisciplinary understanding of education that serves as a model for the kind of work I aim to do. He also has been generous with his time, serving as a sounding board for nascent ideas, sharpening my thinking as he challenges it.

A different kind of thanks goes to Robert Schwartz, who has been my mentor since I joined HGSE. He is remarkable for the depth of his policy knowledge and for his ability to think about how we might feasibly move whole systems from here to there. Coteaching with Bob, with him as the "top-down" guy and me as the "bottom-up" guy, was particularly helpful in developing my thinking about what policy can and cannot achieve. More personally, Bob has been an extraordinarily supportive and generous friend and colleague.

My connection to Bob yielded two other opportunities that furthered the thinking in this book. One was the chance to work with the OECD on a cross-comparative study of PISA leaders; this work helped me to see schooling in terms of how whole educational sectors are put together. I thank Richard Hopper and, in particular, Marc Tucker for the opportunity to work on the study and for stimulating this important vein of research.

The other was the project that Robert Schwartz, Frederick Hess, and I put together on *The Futures of School Reform* (Cambridge: Harvard Education Press, 2012). Many thanks go to this group of eminent scholars, policymakers, and practitioners, who met over three years to hash out what is wrong with the current system and what the possibilities might be for significant improvement. The chance to engage with such a diverse and knowledgeable group was a boon in helping me think broadly about the challenges to the sector and what pathways forward might look like. Jim Spillane, Tony Bryk, Louis Gomez, Paul Hill, Mike Goldstein, and Greg Gunn deserve particular mention as members of this group who shaped my thinking. Rick Hess and Ben Levin, who sit at ideologically opposite poles, were, each in his own way, particularly encouraging and supportive; I hope to find occasions to work with each of them again.

The book was finished with the help of two treasured friends and colleagues, Meira Levinson and Julie Reuben, who formed a powerhouse writing group in the manuscript's later stages. Meira Levinson and I met once a week for several years, each time hashing out ideas and possibilities for our respective projects and trying to figure out ways to marry our social justice commitments to our academic and professional ones. That has been one of the most generative experiences of my professional life; I am really lucky to have Meira as a friend and colleague. Julie Reuben provided remarkably wise counsel in trying to see what I had in the book, where the arguments held up and where they needed more support, and how to frame the study in a way that would be of broad public interest.

The deeper roots of the book lie in my experiences in two distinctive institutions that shaped much of how I see the world. The first was my K–12 school, the Park School of Baltimore, which showed me what education at its best could be. The second was the Harvard Department of Social Studies, which is a special place in the contemporary academic world because of its resistance to specialization and its emphasis on helping students grapple with large questions about the nature of modernity and the social order. Both of those influences are likely clear in what I've written here.

Dave McBride at Oxford University Press is the model of what an editor should be. He saw potential in the book at an early stage, ushered it through the peer review process with skill and aplomb, and helped me shape the manuscript for a public as well as a scholarly audience. To Dave and his team at OUP I offer my sincere thanks. I also express my appreciation to the two anonymous reviewers whose critiques significantly strengthened my argument. I also thank Helen Malone, for her help on the notes for the final chapter, David Luljak, for ably preparing the index, and my assistant and friend Matt Tallon, for his tireless work in preparing the manuscript as a whole.

I also thank all of my respondents, who took time out of their busy lives not only to answer my questions but to open up to me windows into their own worlds. Many of them are mentioned in the text, but I offer special thanks to Andrew Rotherham (federal politics), Mike Bowler (Maryland), and Ed Roeber (Michigan), each of whom was critical to shaping my perspectives at important points in the research.

For primary financial support, I owe thanks to the National Science Foundation's Graduate Research Fellowship, the NSF IGERT Fellowship, a dissertation fellowship from the Center for American Political Studies at Harvard, and a Harvard doctoral dissertation completion fellowship. These granting organizations allowed me time to research and write, and for that I owe them sincere gratitude. For research support, I am indebted to two iterations of the Justice Welfare and Economics program and the NSF Doctoral Dissertation Improvement Grant. Without these research fellowships, the travel and prolonged stays at my research sites would not have been possible. The Warren Center for American History also provided a term of leave, which was helpful in finishing the revisions for the book.

A few more personal thanks. Writing is a difficult and often lonely enterprise, and at least for me, it goes best when it is complemented by warm companionship from family and friends. To that end, I thank Silloo Mehta, Kathleen McCarthy, Stephen McCarthy, Gillian McCarthy, Shern, Bob, and Sonya Mollinger, Laurie Gray, Ben Shiller, Steve, Nancy, Laura, and Carrie Young, Jason Wong, Geoff Upton, Adam Leroy, Peggy Chen, Chana Schoenberger, Nienke Grossman, Audrey Lee, Lisa Mahle, Ethan Thurow, Andrew Karch, Will Bohlen, Seth Hannah, Bikila Ochoa, David Harding, Elisabeth Jacobs, Cybelle Fox, Ethan Gray, Kate Levine, Matt Tallon, and Sarah Fine for their unflagging support and friendship during the development and writing of this book.

A few close friends were particularly important in bringing the book to fruition. Will Reckler has been my best friend since college; his advice to trust myself and be bolder in what I argued was a tremendous help. Jeff Israel and I have been close friends since second grade; it was on a walk in Hyde Park more than 20 years later that we hit upon the connection between educational accountability and Weberian rationalization that is so central to this analysis. To them, to Andrew, Zoe, and Soren Clarkwest, and to Susannah Tobin, treasured friends all, I extend my thanks for your unfailing companionship and support during the writing of this book.

The book has also profited immensely from a number of classes I taught on these subjects over the years. Students in A100, A114, S570, and L103 will recognize ideas in this book that we discussed at different points. I have learned more from them than they learned from me, and I am looking forward to watching all of them create the kind of future that our children deserve in the years to come.

A special thanks to my father- and mother-in-law, Donald and Shirley Gray, whose family I feel lucky to have married into; they have been a tremendous help with our son, Alex. Without Shirley, in particular, there would be no book—Alex is lucky to have such a loving grandma, and we are lucky to have her taking such close care of our son.

A word to my parents, Xerxes and Louise Mehta, who have in fundamental ways shaped how I think and what I value—their influence is felt on every page. No thanks I offer them could be commensurate to all they have done for me.

And finally, a brief word to Cheryl and Alex. Alex brings us more joy every day than we could possibly have hoped for and constantly reminds me of the rich life that lies beyond the printed page. As for Cheryl, I could not have found a better life partner, one whose quiet faith in me sustained the work in days in which it seemed most difficult. With the book done, I'm looking forward to many more loving days spent with both of you, doing everything and nothing at all.

# Notes

CHAPTER 1

1. National Public Radio, "Margaret Spellings: 'No Child Left Behind' is a 'Toxic Brand,'" *Morning Edition*, March 17, 2010. www.npr.org/templates/story/story.php?storyId=124758597.
2. OECD. "Strong Performers and Successful Reformers in Education: Lessons from PISA for the United States." OECD Publishing (2010), accessed June 17, 2012, www.oecd.org/dataoecd/32/50/46623978.pdf.

CHAPTER 2

1. The desire of business for a better-trained workforce produced one of the critical early voices of support for the most recent round of reforms, with business groups well represented on federal and state education commissions (Rick Ginsberg and Robert K. Wimpelberg, "Educational Change by Commission: Attempting 'Trickle Down' Reform," *Educational Evaluation and Policy Analysis* 9, no. 4 [1987], 344–360). Business groups supported the first President Bush's decision to push the issue, they were a critical voice at the second governors' summit in 1996 that reaffirmed commitment to reforms, and they remain an important proponent of standards (Milton Goldberg et al., "Why Business Backs Education Standards," in *Brookings Papers on Education Policy*, ed. Diane Ravitch [Washington, DC: Brookings Institution, 2001], 75–129). There are several problems, however, with a business-driven explanation of the standards and accountability movement. At the very least, this explanation is incomplete because it does not explain why business groups came to see their interests as lying with educational reform in the first place. With few exceptions, big business in the past had largely limited its involvement in school politics to opposing school finance measures in an effort to keep its tax burden down (Tim L. Mazzoni, "State Policy-Making and School Reform: Influences and Influentials," in *The Study of Educational Politics: The 1994 Commemorative Yearbook of the Politics of Education Association (1969–1994)*,

eds. Jay D. Scribner and Donald H. Layton [Washington, DC: Falmer, 1995], 53–73). Any business-driven explanation would also have to explain why business reassessed its interests to prioritize school reform over lower taxes. A more fundamental problem with a business-driven explanation of the reform movement is that it underemphasizes the role that political actors (and the public that elects them) played in the process of educational reform. By all accounts, governors were the leading actors in advocating the state reforms in the 1980s, and Congress and Presidents Clinton and Bush played an important role in more recent years. On the role of governors in the 1980s reforms, see Joseph T. Murphy, ed., *The Educational Reform Movement of the 1980s: Perspectives and Cases* (Berkeley, CA: McCutchan, 1990). When political interests and business interests clashed, such as over national testing, business was the loser (John F. Jennings, *Why National Standards and Tests? Politics and the Quest for Better Schools* [Thousand Oaks, CA: Sage, 1998]). Furthermore, since education is such a visible area of policy, business groups could not create the kind of cozy "iron triangles" (Emmette Redford, *Democracy in the Administrative State* [New York: Oxford University Press, 1969]) that they (and other groups) used to gain favorable policy treatment in other areas. Rather, business groups were influential only to the degree that they could convince political actors and the public to view their favored reforms as broadly desirable. For all of these reasons, a power approach to these reforms would at a minimum need to be supplemented with a more idea-centered analysis that explains why what business groups were supporting had such broad resonance.

2. Clive S. Thomas and Ronald J. Herbenar, "Nationalizing of Interest Groups and Lobbying in the States," in *Interest Group Politics*, eds. Allan J. Cigler, Burdett A. Loomis, and Congressional Quarterly, 3rd ed. (Washington, DC: CQ Press, 1991), 63–80.

3. David C. Berliner and Bruce J. Biddle, *The Manufactured Crisis: Myths, Fraud, and the Attack on America's Public Schools* (Reading, MA: Addison-Wesley, 1995).

4. David B. Tyack and Larry Cuban, *Tinkering toward Utopia: A Century of Public School Reform* (Cambridge, MA: Harvard University Press, 1995).

5. Obviously, there were minority elements within both parties that resisted accountability movements. In the current round, the most notable critics within the parties have been states' rights conservatives (who see in accountability unwarranted expansion of state and federal power), libertarian conservatives (who see it as unwanted bureaucracy), and some liberals (who see it as overly focused on testing to the neglect of resources or other supports that would improve the lives of high-poverty students). These viewpoints are discussed further in the pages to come.

6. Paul Pierson, "Big, Slow-Moving, and…Invisible: Macro-Social Processes in the Study of Comparative Politics," in *Comparative Historical Analysis in the Social Sciences*, eds. James Mahoney and Dietrich Rueschemeyer (New York: Cambridge University Press, 2003), 177–198.

7. Kathleen Ann Thelen and Sven Steinmo, "Historical Institutionalism in Comparative Politics," in *Structuring Politics: Historical Institutionalism in Comparative Analysis*,

eds. Sven Steinmo, Kathleen Ann Thelen, and Frank Longstreth (New York: Cambridge University Press, 1992), 1–32; Karen Orren and Stephen Skowronek, *The Search for American Political Development* (New York: Cambridge University Press, 2004).

8. The paradigmatic case here is health care, where the failure to establish universal care early in the 20th century strengthened private sector forces that for many years were successful at opposing efforts to create universal public health insurance. However, the Obama-led expansion of health care shows that history is not as determining as "path dependence" would predict.

9. On paradigms, see Peter A. Hall, "Policy Paradigms, Social Learning, and the State," *Comparative Politics* 25, no. 3 (1993), 275–297; Peter A. Hall, "The Role of Interests, Ideas and Institutions in the Comparative Political Economy of the Industrialized Nations," in *Comparative Politics: Rationality, Culture, and Structure*, eds. Mark Irving Lichbach and Alan S. Zuckerman (New York: Cambridge University Press, 1997), 174–207; on worldviews, see Judith Goldstein et al., eds., *Ideas and Foreign Policy: Beliefs, Institutions, and Political Change* (Ithaca, NY: Cornell University Press, 1993); on ideas, see Sheri Berman, *The Social Democratic Moment: Ideas and Politics in the Making of Interwar Europe* (Cambridge, MA: Harvard University Press, 1998).

10. Kathryn Sikkink, "The Power of Principled Ideas: Human Rights Policies in the United States and Western Europe," in *Ideas and Foreign Policy: Beliefs, Institutions, and Political Change*, eds. Judith Goldstein et al. (Ithaca, NY: Cornell University Press, 1993), 139–170; Martha Derthick and Paul J. Quirk, *The Politics of Deregulation* (Washington, DC: Brookings Institution, 1985); Frank Dobbin, *Forging Industrial Policy: The United States, Britain, and France in the Railway Age* (New York: Cambridge University Press, 1994); Berman, *The Social Democratic Moment*, 308.

11. Derthick and Quirk, *The Politics of Deregulation*. Comparative work has similarly worked to dislodge materialist explanations, using Mill's methods of agreement and difference. Berman, *The Social Democratic Moment*, for example, shows that countries similar on all but the ideational variable had different welfare state outcomes; see also Margaret R. Somers and Fred Block, "From Poverty to Perversity: Ideas, Markets, and Institutions over 200 Years of Welfare Debate," *American Sociological Review* 70, no. 2 (2005), 260–287.

12. For example, compare Theda Skocpol, *States and Social Revolutions: A Comparative Analysis of France, Russia, and China* (New York: Cambridge University Press, 1979) with Dietrich Rueschemeyer and Theda Skocpol, *States, Social Knowledge, and the Origins of Modern Social Policies* (Princeton, NJ: Princeton University Press, 1996).

13. Jal Mehta, "The Varied Roles of Ideas in Politics: From 'Whether' to 'How'," in *Ideas and Politics in Social Science Research*, eds. Daniel Béland and Robert Henry Cox (New York: Oxford University Press, 2011), 23–46.

14. John W. Kingdon, *Agendas, Alternatives, and Public Policies* (Boston: Little, Brown, 1984); Frank R. Baumgartner and Bryan D. Jones, *Agendas and Instability in American Politics* (Chicago: University of Chicago Press, 1993); Berman, *The Social Democratic Moment*; Brian Steensland, "Cultural Categories and the American Welfare State: The Case of Guaranteed Income Policy," *American Journal of Sociology* 111, no. 5 (2006), 1273–1326; Daniel Béland, "Ideas and Social Policy: An Institutionalist Perspective," *Social Policy & Administration* 39, no. 1 (2005), 1–18; Mark Blyth, *Great Transformations: Economic Ideas and Institutional Change in the Twentieth Century* (New York: Cambridge University Press, 2002).

15. On the necessity of integrating the normative and the empirical, see Hilary Putnam, *The Collapse of the Fact-Value Dichotomy and Other Essays* (Cambridge, MA: Harvard University Press, 2002).

16. Hall, "Policy Paradigms, Social Learning, and the State."

17. See also E. E. Schattschneider, *The Semisovereign People: A Realist's View of Democracy in America* (New York: Holt, 1960); Baumgartner and Jones, *Agendas and Instability in American Politics*, 298.

18. Paul Pierson, "When Effect Becomes Cause," *World Politics* 45, no. 4 (1993), 595, makes a similar distinction between interpretive and incentive effects in his discussion of policy feedback, although he does not discuss the intersubjective role of policies.

19. Colin Hay, "Ideas and the Construction of Interests," in *Ideas and Politics in Social Science Research*, eds. Daniel Béland and Robert Cox (New York: Oxford University Press, 2011), 65–82.

20. Pierson, "When Effect Becomes Cause"; Andrea Louise Campbell, *How Policies Make Citizens: Senior Political Activism and the American Welfare State* (Princeton, NJ: Princeton University Press, 2003); Eric M. Patashnik, *Reforms at Risk: What Happens after Major Policy Changes Are Enacted* (Princeton, NJ: Princeton University Press, 2008).

21. Some of these alternative providers, including Teach for America, provide what can be strong ongoing coaching and professional development for teachers once they are in the classroom. It is an open question who should be in charge of recruiting and preparing teachers to enter the profession. See the more detailed discussion of traditional, alternative, and residency models in Chapter Ten.

22. Dan C. Lortie, *Schoolteacher: A Sociological Study* (Chicago: University of Chicago Press, 1975).

23. William J. Goode, "The Theoretical Limits of Professionalization," in *The Semi-Professions and Their Organization: Teachers, Nurses, Social Workers*, ed. Amitai Etzioni (New York: Free Press, 1969).

24. Michael Huberman, "The Model of the Independent Artisan in Teachers Professional Relations," in *Teachers' Work: Individuals, Colleagues, and Contexts*, eds. Judith Warren Little and Milbrey W. McLaughlin (New York: Teachers College Press, 1993), 11–50.

25. David Cohen provides an excellent discussion of these challenges in David K. Cohen, *Teaching and Its Predicaments* (Cambridge, MA: Harvard University Press, 2011). I thank an anonymous reviewer for pushing me to respond to this point.

26. Linda Darling-Hammond and John Bransford, *Preparing Teachers for a Changing World: What Teachers Should Learn and Be Able to Do* (San Francisco: Jossey-Bass, 2005).

27. Philip W. Jackson, *Life in Classrooms* (New York: Holt, Rinehart and Winston, 1968).

28. Michelene T. H. Chi, Robert Glaser, and Marshall J. Farr, *The Nature of Expertise* (Hillsdale, NJ: Erlbaum, 1988); James Cimino, "Development of Expertise in Medical Practice," in *Tacit Knowledge in Professional Practice: Researcher and Practitioner Perspectives*, eds. Robert J. Sternberg and Joseph A. Horvath (Mahwah, NJ: Erlbaum, 1999), 101–119; Carol Livingston and Hilda Borko, "Expert-Novice Differences in Teaching: A Cognitive Analysis and Implications for Teacher Education," *Journal of Teacher Education* 40 (1989), 36–42.

29. Lortie, *Schoolteacher*, 58–59. See also James Hiebert, Ronald Gallimore, and James W. Stigler, "A Knowledge Base for the Teaching Profession: What Would It Look like and How Can We Get One?" *Educational Researcher* 31, no. 5 (2002), 3–15.

30. Cohen, *Teaching and Its Predicaments*.

31. See Pamela B. Walters, "The Politics of Science: Battles for Scientific Authority in the Field of Education Research," in *Education Research on Trial: Policy Reform and the Call for Scientific Rigor*, eds. Pamela B. Walters, Annette Lareau, and Sheri H. Ranis (New York: Routledge, 2009), 17–50; and Ellen Condliffe Lagemann, *An Elusive Science: The Troubling History of Education Research* (Chicago: University of Chicago Press, 2000).

32. Elliott A. Krause, *Death of the Guilds: Professions, States, and the Advance of Capitalism, 1930 to the Present* (New Haven, CT: Yale University Press, 1996).

33. See Donald Light, "Countervailing Powers: A Framework for Professions in Transition," in *Health Professions and the State in Europe*, eds. Terry Johnson, Gerald Larkin, and Mike Saks (New York: Routledge, 1995), 25–41.

34. There is an extensive debate in the medical sociology literature about the degree to which the growing influence of state reimbursements and HMOs has abridged doctors' control over their work. Part of this debate hinges on whether you consider technical control over clinical decision making the essence of professional control or view changes in the external circumstances in which doctors work (i.e., more patients in less time) as the issue. See Terry Johnson, "Governmentality and the Institutionalization of Expertise," in *Health Professions and the State in Europe*, eds. Terry Johnson, Gerald Larkin, and Mike Saks (New York: Routledge, 1995), 7–24.

35. See also Joshua Glazer, "Educational Professionalism: An Inside-out View," *American Journal of Education* 114 (2008): 169–189. Some similar sentiments are also expressed in Lortie, *Schoolteacher*, ch. 9, and Eliot Freidson, "Professions and the Occupational Principle," in *The Professions and their Prospects*, ed. Eliot Freidson (Beverly Hills, CA: Sage, 1973), 19–38.

36. On deprofessionalization of work, see Linda M. McNeil, *Contradictions of School Reform: Educational Costs of Standardized Testing* (New York: Routledge, 2000), and Richard M. Ingersoll, *Who Controls Teachers' Work? Power and Accountability in America's Schools* (Cambridge, MA: Harvard University Press, 2003).

37. On the costs of medical professionalization, see Light, "Countervailing Powers."

38. Pierre Bourdieu and Loïc J. D. Wacquant, *An Invitation to Reflexive Sociology* (Chicago: University of Chicago Press, 1992).

39. Andrew Abbott, *The System of Professions: An Essay on the Division of Expert Labor* (Chicago: University of Chicago Press, 1988).

40. See Roger Friedland and Robert R. Alford, "Bringing Society Back in: Symbols, Practices, and Institutional Contradictions," in *The New Institutionalism in Organizational Analysis*, eds. Walter W. Powell and Paul DiMaggio (Chicago: University of Chicago Press, 1991), 232–266, for the classic statement on institutional logics.

41. Across the 20th century, the interpenetration of outside logics has been more a consistent presence than a true jurisdictional challenge in which outsiders seek to replace traditional actors. However, over the past 20 years, we have begun to see the latter kind of intrusion, as a variety of alternative actors have sought to replace many of the more traditional actors. I explore these dynamics in Jal Mehta and Steven Teles, "Jurisdictional Politics: A New Federal Role in Education," in *Carrots, Sticks, and the Bully Pulpit: Lessons from a Half-Century of Federal Efforts to Improve America's Schools*, eds. Frederick M. Hess and Andrew P. Kelly (Cambridge, MA: Harvard Education Press, 2011), 197–215.

42. Alasdair C. MacIntyre, *After Virtue: A Study in Moral Theory* (Notre Dame, IN: University of Notre Dame Press, 1984).

43. Peter B. Evans et al., eds. *Bringing the State Back In* (New York: Cambridge University Press, 1985).

44 This is not to say that those within schools may not have blind spots or that being urged to measure things may not help them see patterns they otherwise would not have identified. But the point remains that they have access to much information about the institution that is not available from afar.

45. James C. Scott, *Seeing like a State: How Certain Schemes to Improve the Human Condition Have Failed* (New Haven, CT: Yale University Press, 1998).

46. Commensuration translates qualities into quantities; money is the paradigmatic example. The consequence is similar to that Scott describes: the varied context of the particular is translated into a measurable metric that is exchangeable and viewable from afar. The process of measurement itself becomes a social force, since people begin to attend to what is measured rather than to a more diffuse range of qualities. Much of the work on commensuration focuses on the impact of rankings, particularly the way the *U.S. News and World Report* rankings have shaped universities. This work finds that universities are tightly attuned to what will affect their rankings, with many goods that they are seeking to realize subordinated to indicators that will affect the rankings.

47. Kevin R. Kosar, *Failing Grades: The Federal Politics of Education Standards* (Boulder, CO: Lynne Rienner, 2005).

48. Of course, there have always been differences of institutional perspective between teachers and legislators, but these were overshadowed politically by differences between the political left and right over funding, busing, vouchers and other issues. As legislative elites have moved to embrace a centrist model of accountability, these left-right cleavages have receded, while simultaneously the demands for accountability have exacerbated the cleavages between teachers and legislators.

49. Lisa Stampnitzky, *Disciplining Terror: How Experts and Others Invented Terrorism*, forthcoming manuscript.

50. Pierre Bourdieu, "The Political Field, the Social Science Field, and the Journalist Field," in *Bourdieu and the Journalistic Field*, eds. Rodney Dean Benson and Erik Neveu (Cambridge, MA: Polity, 2005), 39.

51. Jal Mehta and Christopher Winship, "Moral Power," in *Handbook of the Sociology of Morality*, eds. Steven Hitlin and Stephen Vaisey (New York: Springer, 2010).

52. More specifically, David K. Cohen and Susan L. Moffitt, *The Ordeal of Equality: Did Federal Regulation Fix the Schools?* (Cambridge, MA: Harvard University Press, 2009), argue that federal and state efforts to establish standards and tests without providing high-quality curriculum or teacher training create a disjuncture between expectations and the means to fulfill those expectations. These arguments are developed in more detail in Chapter Ten.

CHAPTER 3

1. David B. Tyack, *The One Best System: A History of American Urban Education* (Cambridge, MA: Harvard University Press, 1974).

2. For the purposes of this book, I'm particularly interested in the aspects of rationalization that tie to standards, tests, accountability, and the efforts to use those tools to monitor and assess schools and teaching. Of course, the Progressive Era rationalization of schooling is much broader than that in what it encompasses.

3. David Cohen (personal correspondence) has argued that this system of control was in practice weak in directing the actual work of teachers. I don't disagree; part of the argument here is that standards, testing, and accountability offers a "thin theory" of how to actually improve practice, which is consistent with Cohen's view. But I do think that the emphasis on improving schools through methods of top-down control (and building a structure that assumes such methods) has gotten in the way of building a different kind of infrastructure that would be much thicker and attuned to the needs of practice. See Chapter Ten for more details.

4. Readers who know the literature on Progressives and schooling will notice that I emphasize the Progressives' efforts to create social control and to rationalize the school system, which to some will seem like a bleak view of a multifaceted movement seeking to enact progressive change (for details on the debates in historiography, see

Julia Wrigley, *Class Politics and Public Schools: Chicago, 1900–1950* [New Brunswick, NJ: Rutgers University Press, 1982]; Herbert M. Kliebard, *The Struggle for the American Curriculum, 1893–1958* [New York: Routledge, 1995]). My perspective draws on the work of Michael B. Katz, *The Irony of Early School Reform: Educational Innovation in Mid-Nineteenth Century Massachusetts* (Cambridge, MA: Harvard University Press, 1968), and others who challenged the previously prevailing views of educational history that uncritically saw the development of education as a triumphal story of American democracy gradually expanding equal opportunity to all (e.g., Ellwood Patterson Cubberley, *Public School Administration: A Statement of the Fundamental Principles Underlying the Organization and Administration of Public Education* [New York: Houghton Mifflin, 1916]). Katz challenged the myth of apolitical education and exposed the fault lines of power and class that affect this issue as every other. At the same time, I do not adopt a simple Marxist view and draw instead on the ideas and politics literature (John L. Campbell, "Ideas, Politics, and Public Policy," *Annual Review of Sociology* 28, no. 1 [2002], 21–38) to argue that political debate is generally many sided, with the actors' views representing a complicated mixture of public and self (including class) interest. In the case of the Progressives, the emphasis on their social control views seems particularly appropriate when the subject is school testing and accountability, which is my focus here. A broader assessment of the Progressives would need to consider these tendencies in light of their broader efforts, particularly their challenging of traditional pedagogy and their efforts to use schools as social service centers for newly arrived immigrants. For the canonical view of the Progressives as well-meaning reformers, see Lawrence Arthur Cremin, *The Transformation of the School: Progressivism in American Education, 1876–1957* (New York: Knopf, 1961).

5. There is considerable debate over the use of the term *progressive* to depict the reformers of this era. Leaving aside the broader debate about turn-of-the-century Progressivism, in education at least two kinds of progressives need to be differentiated. The first is what I call, following educational historian David Tyack, the *administrative* progressives, who were reformers from either outside education or in its top administrative layers seeking control and greater scientific management and efficiency. The second are the *pedagogical* progressives, who were educators associated with child-centered models of learning, a stance that put them in conflict with the dominant administrative progressives. See Kliebard, *The Struggle for the American Curriculum*, for an excellent discussion of these issues.

6. Tyack, *The One Best System*, 127.

7. Diane Ravitch, *Left Back: A Century of Battles over School Reforms* (New York: Simon & Schuster, 2001).

8. David B. Tyack and Elisabeth Hansot, *Managers of Virtue: Public School Leadership in America, 1820–1980* (New York: Basic Books, 1982), 165.

9. Raymond E. Callahan, *Education and the Cult of Efficiency: A Study of the Social Forces That Have Shaped the Administration of the Public Schools* (Chicago: University of

Chicago Press, 1962), 43. See Theodore M. Porter, *Trust in Numbers: The Pursuit of Objectivity in Science and Public Life* (Princeton, NJ: Princeton University Press, 1995), for examples of how cost-benefit thinking has been applied across a variety of (noneconomic) dimensions.

10. Callahan, *Education and the Cult of Efficiency*, 159. Although later scholars have heavily scrutinized Callahan's arguments on the connections between business methods and school administration, his basic conclusions have emerged largely unscathed. See William Edward Eaton, *Shaping the Superintendency: A Reexamination of Callahan and the Cult of Efficiency* (New York: Teachers College Press, 1990).

11. Quoted in Callahan, *Education and the Cult of Efficiency*, 162.

12. Ibid., 113.

13. Ibid. on the 1916 data; for the 1934 data, see Daniel P. Resnick, "Minimum Competency Testing Historically Considered," *Review of Research in Education* 8 (1980), 3–29.

14. Callahan, *Education and the Cult of Efficiency*, 182.

15. Ibid., 14.

16. Leonard Porter Ayres, *Laggards in Our Schools: A Study of Retardation and Elimination in City School Systems* (New York: Charities Publication Committee, 1909).

17. Christopher Mazzeo, "Frameworks of State: Assessment Policy in Historical Perspective," *Teachers College Record* 103, no. 3 (2001), 367–397.

18. Kliebard, *The Struggle for the American Curriculum*, 92–93.

19. Ravitch, *Left Back: A Century of Battles over School Reforms*, 130–163.

20. Kliebard, *The Struggle for the American Curriculum*, 97.

21. Ravitch, *Left Back: A Century of Battles over School Reforms*, 124.

22. Whether this more progressive policy framework actually improves things for disadvantaged students in schools that are still highly segregated and tracked is another question.

23. Obviously, this kind of overview cannot do justice to the complexity of the factors that affected the coalition partners in individual cities. For examples that do, see Wrigley, *Class Politics and Public School*, 337; Ira Katznelson and Margaret Weir, *Schooling for All: Class, Race, and the Decline of the Democratic Ideal* (New York: Basic Books, 1985); David John Hogan, *Class and Reform: School and Society in Chicago, 1880–1930* (Philadelphia: University of Pennsylvania Press, 1985); Paul E. Peterson, *The Politics of School Reform, 1870–1940* (Chicago: University of Chicago Press, 1985).

24. Tyack, *The One Best System*, 155–156.

25. Ibid., 147–167.

26. Callahan, *Education and the Cult of Efficiency*, 121.

27. The *New Republic* ran a series of six articles by Lippmann between October 25 and November 29, 1922, excoriating the growth of intelligence testing and the assumptions underlying the social sorting model. The quote is from Lippmann, "The Reliability of Intelligence Tests," *New Republic*, November 8, 1922, 277.

28. Kliebard, *The Struggle for the American Curriculum*, 105.

29. Tyack, *The One Best System*, 127.

30. Ibid., 185.

31. Wayne J. Urban and Jennings L. Wagoner Jr., *American Education: A History* (New York: McGraw-Hill, 1996), 214.

32. Alfie Kohn, *The Schools Our Children Deserve: Moving beyond Traditional Classrooms and "Tougher Standards"* (Boston: Houghton Mifflin, 1999), 7.

33. Tyack, *The One Best System*, 148.

34. Ibid., 156.

35. Emmette S. Redford, *Democracy in the Administrative State* (New York: Oxford University Press, 1969).

36. See James G. March and Johan P. Olsen, *Rediscovering Institutions: The Organizational Basis of Politics* (New York: Free Press, 1989), on norms of appropriateness.

37. Callahan, *Education and the Cult of Efficiency*, 3.

38. Richard Hofstadter, *The Age of Reform: From Bryan to F.D.R.* (New York: Knopf, 1955), 185.

39. Tyack, *The One Best System*, 128.

40. Ibid., 133.

41. Ibid., 151.

42. Gerard Giordano, *How Testing Came to Dominate American Schools: The History of Educational Assessment* (New York: Lang, 2005), 55.

43. Tyack, *The One Best System*, 133, writes that in New York, "the reformers enjoyed nearly total control of news and editorials in the major newspapers of that city as well as inside track to such periodicals as *Harper's Weekly*, *The Outlook* and *The Critic*. Thereby they could define the nature of the problem in such a way that their remedies seemed self-evident and opposition to reform selfish and misguided."

44. Callahan has been challenged on this point—namely, that superintendents were not so much vulnerable to outside pressures but rather themselves embraced the surveys and other business methods as a matter of good practice (see essays in Eaton, *Shaping the Superintendency*; Barbara Berman, "Business Efficiency, American Schooling, and the Public School Superintendency: A Reconsideration of the Callahan Thesis," *History of Education Quarterly* 23, no. 3 [1983], 297–321). I do not see these possibilities as mutually exclusive; as Callahan notes and as I discuss later in the chapter, the training of superintendents in these methods at leading institutions is an important part of this story. But that is not to say that external pressures for accountability were not also significant.

45. Callahan, *Education and the Cult of Efficiency*, 111.

46. Following Tyack, Kliebard, and most recent historians, I have emphasized the differences between administrative and pedagogical progressives; an alternative approach stresses the congruity inherent in the progressive critique of the academic curriculum. See Ravitch, *Left Back: A Century of Battles over School Reforms*; Cremin, *The Transformation of the School*.

47. Kliebard, *The Struggle for the American Curriculum, 1893–1958*, 129.

48. The psychological "science" that this drew upon was not as well regarded as the harder sciences of biology, chemistry, and physics, but it did have the legitimacy of mass use by the army and emerging scientific respectability.

49. See also Katznelson and Weir, *Schooling for All: Class, Race, and the Decline of the Democratic Ideal*.

50. Peter A. Hall, "Policy Paradigms, Social Learning, and the State," *Comparative Politics* 25, no. 3 (1993), 275–297.

51. John Dewey, *Schools of To-Morrow* (New York: Dutton, 1915),

52. Callahan, *Education and the Cult of Efficiency*, 128.

53. Kliebard, *The Struggle for the American Curriculum*, 77.

54. George S. Counts, *Dare the School Build a New Social Order?* (New York: John Day, 1932).

55. See David B. Tyack and Larry Cuban, *Tinkering toward Utopia: A Century of Public School Reform* (Cambridge, MA: Harvard University Press, 1995).

56. Peter B. Evans et al., eds., *Bringing the State Back In* (New York: Cambridge University Press, 1985); John D. Skrentny, *The Ironies of Affirmative Action: Politics, Culture, and Justice in America* (Chicago: University of Chicago Press, 1996).

57. Ellen Condliffe Lagemann, *An Elusive Science: The Troubling History of Education Research* (Chicago: University of Chicago Press, 2000), 63.

58. Ibid., 64.

59. Geraldine Jonçich Clifford and James W. Guthrie, *Ed School: A Brief for Professional Education* (Chicago: University of Chicago Press, 1988), 78.

60. Ibid., 67. By the early 1930s, Chicago had closed its college of education that prepared teachers.

61. Lagemann, *An Elusive Science*, 66–70.

62. Callahan, *Education and the Cult of Efficiency*, 198.

63. Ibid., 214.

64. Ibid., 202.

65. Cubberley, *Public School Administration*, 130.

66. As Clifford and Guthrie, *Ed School: A Brief for Professional Education*, 100, aptly sum it up: "Male teachers who stayed too long in the classroom—in the regular company of women and children—might even raise doubt about their manliness and, therefore, their suitability for dealing with the local power brokers on school boards and in chambers of commerce. Were these the men to save school administration and educational research careers from the threats of feminization, the men able to deal with businessmen and civic leaders in the hurly-burly world of *realpolitik*? Clearly not. Instead, graduate students in education must be drawn early from their classrooms or recruited from among the graduating seniors of high-status colleges."

67. Thorndike as quoted in Lagemann, *An Elusive Science*, 60.

68. Thorndike, quoted in ibid., 59.

69. Dewey, quoted in ibid., 50.

70. Ibid., 51.


CHAPTER 4

1. Barbara J. Kiavat, "The Social Side of Schooling," *Johns Hopkins Magazine*, April 2001.

2. James S. Coleman, "The Evaluation of Equality of Educational Opportunity," in *On Equality of Educational Opportunity*, eds. Frederick Mosteller, Daniel P. Moynihan, and Harvard University (New York: Random House, 1972), 149–150.

3. Kennedy is quoted from the transcript of the hearing on ESEA, Senate Education Subcommittee, 89th Congress; quotation is accessed http://www.nycsa.org/blog/2006/01/rfk-on-mind.html.

4. Gerald Grant, "The Politics of the Coleman Report" (PhD diss., Harvard University, 1972), 110–111.

5. On the growth of the social and behavioral sciences, see David L. Featherman and Maris Vinovskis, "Growth and Use of Behavioral Science in the Federal Government since World War II," in *Social Science and Policy-Making: A Search for Relevance in the Twentieth Century*, eds. David L. Featherman and Maris Vinovskis (Ann Arbor: University of Michigan Press, 2001), 40–82.

6. See Thomas Parke Hughes, *Rescuing Prometheus* (New York: Pantheon Books, 1998).

7. Bhavya Lal, "Knowledge Domains in Engineering Systems: Systems Analysis" (unpublished paper, MIT, Fall 2001), 1.

8. Charles J. Hitch and Roland N. McKean, *The Economics of Defense in the Nuclear Age* (Cambridge, MA: Harvard University Press, 1960).

9. David Raymond Jardini, "Out of the Blue Yonder: The RAND Corporation's Diversification into Social Welfare Research, 1946–1968" (PhD diss., Carnegie Mellon University, 1996), 210. Much of the discussion that follows about the connection between McNamara and Rand draws on David Jardini's excellent work; also see Alex Abella, *Soldiers of Reason: The Rand Corporation and the Rise of the American Empire* (Orlando, FL: Harcourt, 2008).

10. Jardini, "Out of the Blue Yonder," 208–209.

11. Jennifer S. Light, *From Warfare to Welfare: Defense Intellectuals and Urban Problems in Cold War America* (Baltimore: Johns Hopkins University Press, 2003), 41.

12. Jardini, "Out of the Blue Yonder," 221.

13. A similar debate has recently broken out over the publication of Michael Lewis, *Moneyball: The Art of Winning an Unfair Game* (New York: Norton, 2003), which pits those who value statistical analysis as a way of rating baseball players against those who believe that the judgment of scouts is critical.

14. See David Halberstam, *The Best and the Brightest* (New York: Random House, 1972). In *Fog of War*, one of McNamara's eleven lessons learned is "that rationality

will not save us." McNamara's written views on lessons learned from Vietnam can be found in Robert S. McNamara, *In Retrospect: The Tragedy and Lessons of Vietnam* (New York: Vintage Books, 1996).

15. The Moynihan and Wood quotes come from Light, *From Warfare to Welfare*, 52. A study by Edwin L. Harper, Fred A. Kramer, and Andrew M. Rouse, "Implementation and Use of PPB in Sixteen Federal Agencies," *Public Administration Review* 29, no. 6 (1969), 623, on the implementation of PPBS found that it had not had penetration as deep as initially intended and that only 3 of the 16 agencies had significantly changed their methods to incorporate PPBS.

16. Aaron Wildavsky, "Rescuing Policy Analysis from PPBS," *Public Administration Review* 29, no. 2 (1969), 195.

17. Ibid., 192.

18. Arthur E. Wise, *Legislated Learning: The Bureaucratization of the American Classroom* (Berkeley: University of California Press, 1979), 12. Wise also provides definitions of these various terms.

19. Harry J. Hartley and Ohio State Department of Education, "PPBS: A Systems Approach to Educational Accountability" (paper presented at the Supervision of Instruction Symposium 3: Accountability and the Supervisor, April 13, 1972), 3.

20. Lesley H. Browder and Cooperative Accountability Project, *Who's Afraid of Educational Accountability? A Representative Review of the Literature* (Denver: Cooperative Accountability Project, 1975), 1.

21. Thomas F. Koerner, *PPBS and the School: New System Promotes Efficiency, Accountability* (Washington, DC: National School Public Relations Association, 1972).

22. Leon M. Lessinger, *Every Kid a Winner: Accountability in Education* (New York: Simon & Schuster, 1970), 10.

23. Ibid., 11.

24. H. Thomas James, *The New Cult of Efficiency and Education* (Pittsburgh: University of Pittsburgh Press, 1969).

25. All of these titles are essays in Lesley H. Browder, *Emerging Patterns of Administrative Accountability* (Berkeley, CA: McCutchan, 1971).

26. Gene I. Maeroff, "Accountability Plan Angers Teachers, with Many Foreseeing Threat to Jobs," *New York Times*, July 6, 1974, 20.

27. C. A. Bowers, "Accountability from a Humanist Point of View," in *Accountability in American Education*, eds. Frank J. Sciara and Richard K. Jantz (Boston: Allyn and Bacon, 1972), 29.

28. Quoted in Sharryl Hawke, Social Science Education Consortium and ERIC Clearinghouse for Social Studies, *State Accountability Activities and the Social Studies: A Nationwide Survey, A Proposed General Accountability Model, and some Guidelines*. SSEC Publication no. 175 (1975), 6.

29. Wise, *Legislated Learning: The Bureaucratization of the American Classroom*, xi.

30. See ERIC Clearinghouse on Tests, Measurement, and Evaluation and Educational Testing Service. Office of Field Surveys, *State Testing Programs, 1973 Revision*

(Princeton, NJ: Educational Testing Service, 1973); Phyllis Hawthorne, *Legislation by the States: Accountability and Assessment in Education*. Report no. 2. Rev. (Denver: Cooperative Accountability Project, 1974); Hawke, *State Accountability Activities and the Social Studies*.

31. ERIC Clearinghouse on Tests, Measurement, and Evaluation and Educational Testing Service. Office of Field Surveys, *State Testing Programs, 1973 Revision*.

32. Hawke, *State Accountability Activities and the Social Studies*, 27.

33. An overview of the Michigan case can be found in Jerome T. Murphy and David K. Cohen, "Accountability in Education: The Michigan Experience," *Public Interest* 36 (1974), 53–82. I supplemented this with archival research from the files of the Michigan Department of Education.

34. E. E. Schattschneider, *The Semisovereign People: A Realist's View of Democracy in America* (New York: Holt, 1960).

CHAPTER 5

1. William L. Boyd and Charles T. Kerchner, eds., *The Politics of Excellence and Choice in Education: 1987 Yearbook of the Politics of Education Association* (New York: Falmer Press, 1988); Joseph T. Murphy, ed., *The Educational Reform Movement of the 1980s: Perspectives and Cases* (Berkeley, CA: McCutchan, 1990); Paul Manna, "Federalism, Agenda Setting, and the Development of Federal Education Policy, 1965–2001" (PhD diss., University of Wisconsin–Madison, 2003); James W. Guthrie and Matthew G. Springer, "*A Nation at Risk* Revisited: Did 'Wrong' Reasoning Result in 'Right' Results? At What Cost?" *Peabody Journal of Education* 79, no. 1 (2004), 7–35; Patricia Albjerg Graham and David T. Gordon, *A Nation Reformed? American Education 20 Years after "A Nation at Risk"* (Cambridge, MA: Harvard Education Press, 2003).

2. Boyd and Kerchner, *The Politics of Excellence and Choice in Education*, 364.

3. Martin Rein and Donald A. Schon, "Problem-Setting in Policy Research," in *Using Social Research in Public Policy Making*, ed. Carol H. Weiss (Lexington, MA: Lexington Books, 1977), 235–251. See also Jal Mehta, "The Varied Roles of Ideas in Politics: From 'Whether' to 'How'," in *Ideas and Politics in Social Science Research*, eds. Daniel Béland and Robert Henry Cox (New York: Oxford University Press, 2011).

4. E. E. Schattschneider, *The Semisovereign People: A Realist's View of Democracy in America* (New York: Holt, 1960); Roger W. Cobb and Charles D. Elder, *Participation in American Politics: The Dynamics of Agenda-Building* (Boston: Allyn and Bacon, 1972); William H. Riker, *The Art of Political Manipulation* (New Haven, CT: Yale University Press, 1986); Malcolm Spector and John I. Kitsuse, *Constructing Social Problems* (New York: Aldine de Gruyter, 1977); Deborah A. Stone, *Policy Paradox: The Art of Political Decision Making* (New York: Norton, 1997).

5. On policy feedback, see Hugh Heclo, *Modern Social Politics in Britain and Sweden: From Relief to Income Maintenance* (New Haven, CT: Yale University Press, 1974);

Paul Pierson, "When Effect Becomes Cause," *World Politics* 45, no. 4 (1993), 595–628; Peter A. Hall, "Policy Paradigms, Social Learning, and the State," *Comparative Politics* 25, no. 3 (1993), 275–297; on sociology of science, see Thomas S. Kuhn, *The Structure of Scientific Revolutions* (Chicago: University of Chicago Press, 1962); for an application of Kuhn-type analysis in political science, see Jeffrey W. Legro, "The Transformation of Policy Ideas," *American Journal of Political Science* 44, no. 3 (2000), 419–432.

6. Frank R. Baumgartner and Bryan D. Jones, *Agendas and Instability in American Politics* (Chicago: University of Chicago Press, 1993).

7. Frederick M. Wirt and Michael W. Kirst, *Schools in Conflict: The Politics of Education* (Berkeley, CA: McCutchan, 1982).

8. Edward Fiske, "Commission on Education Warns 'Tide of Mediocrity' Imperils U.S." *New York Times*, April 27, 1983, A1.

9. Guthrie and Springer, "*A Nation at Risk* Revisited," 12.

10. Ibid., 14.

11. David C. Berliner and Bruce J. Biddle, *The Manufactured Crisis: Myths, Fraud, and the Attack on America's Public Schools* (Reading, MA: Addison-Wesley, 1995).

12. Terrel H. Bell, *The Thirteenth Man: A Reagan Cabinet Memoir* (New York: Free Press; London: Collier Macmillan, 1988).

13. The other two were Charles A. Foster, who was the immediate past president of the Foundation for Teaching Economics, and Annette Y. Kirk, wife of conservative intellectual Russell Kirk, whose affiliation at the time was given as Kirk Associates.

14. "Commission Member Suggests Education in U.S. Still at Risk," *Education Week*, April 23, 2003.

15. Bell, *The Thirteenth Man*, provides the most detailed account of the interplay between the commission and President Reagan's office.

16. Lynn Olson, "Inside 'A Nation at Risk,'" *Education Week*, April 27, 1988.

17. Ibid.

18. Margot Slate and Wayne Biddle, "Reagan Gets a Scathing Report on Education," *New York Times*, May 1, 1983, E7.

19. With the benefit of hindsight, some critics have noted that the most fundamental assertion of the report, that the nation's economic future was tied to its educational future, has been called into question; see Guthrie and Springer, "*A Nation at Risk* Revisited."

20. Much has been written attacking and defending the commission's analysis; it is outside the scope of this study to sufficiently resolve those debates. See Lawrence C. Stedman and Marshall S. Smith, "Recent Reform Proposals for American Education," *Contemporary Education Review* 2, no. 2 (1983), 85–104; Paul E. Peterson, "Did the Education Commissions Say Anything?" *Brookings Review* 2, no. 2 (1983), 3–11; and Berliner and Biddle, *The Manufactured Crisis*. The 1977 study by the College Board presents a comprehensive and balanced analysis of the decline in SAT scores. College Entrance Examination Board. Advisory Panel on

the Scholastic Aptitude Test Score Decline, *On Further Examination: Report of the Advisory Panel on the Scholastic Aptitude Test Score Decline* (New York: College Entrance Examination Board, 1977). The College Board study finds that SAT scores did decline from 1963 to 1980; the early part of the decline (up until about 1972) was in part explained by a rising number of test takers, but the number of test takers held steady after 1972, and so other factors would have to explain the later decline. SATs were actually increasing in the years directly leading up to *A Nation at Risk*. The claim of the tie between the nation's educational performance and the economic future was clearly overstated in *A Nation at Risk*; the American economy has rebounded, the Japanese one has faltered, with relatively little change in the school performance of the two nations. Economists continue to debate whether there is a correlation between economic growth and educational performance more generally; clearly other factors—the nature of regulations and the quality of higher education, among others—also play a role in explaining economic growth. At the same time, there is a relationship between *state* educational performance and state business performance, because states compete for businesses in large part on the basis of their educational systems. To the degree that states adopted the economy-education link on the basis of *A Nation at Risk*, the analysis served them well, even if it turns out not to be true on an international basis.

21. Ibid., 12.

22. College Entrance Examination Board, *On Further Examination*, 75.

23. Institutional theorists have argued that timing is often an important factor in explaining the success or failure of public policy initiatives. See Paul Pierson, *Politics in Time: History, Institutions, and Social Analysis* (Princeton, NJ: Princeton University Press, 2004).

24. Education Commission of the States, Task Force on Education for Economic Growth, *Action for Excellence: A Comprehensive Plan to Improve our Nation's Schools* (Denver: Education Commission of the States, 1983); Twentieth Century Fund, Task Force on Federal Elementary and Secondary Education Policy, *Making the Grade* (New York: Twentieth Century Fund, 1983); Ernest L. Boyer and Carnegie Foundation for the Advancement of Teaching, *High School: A Report on Secondary Education in America* (New York: Harper & Row, 1983); John I. Goodlad, *A Place Called School: Prospects for the Future* (New York: McGraw-Hill, 1984); Theodore R. Sizer, *Horace's Compromise: The Dilemma of the American High School* (Boston: Houghton Mifflin, 1984).

25. Robert D. Putnam, *Bowling Alone: The Collapse and Revival of American Community* (New York: Simon & Schuster, 2000).

26. Stone, *Policy Paradox*, 109.

27. Given that Americans consistently give their own schools higher ratings than they give schools in general, there is considerable evidence that the public privileges these kinds of policy narratives over their own more direct knowledge of schooling. On the disjuncture between people's assessments of their own lives and their

understanding of national trends, see David Whitman, *The Optimism Gap: The I'm OK–They're Not Syndrome and the Myth of American Decline* (New York: Walker, 1998).

28. Jennifer L. Hochschild, "Rethinking Accountability Politics," in *No Child Left Behind? The Politics and Practice of School Accountability*, eds. Paul E. Peterson and Martin R. West (Washington, DC: Brookings Institution Press, 2003), 107–123. Hochschild argues that poor school performance is not a compelling explanation for the reform movement, pointing to significant evidence that some key indicators (including NAEP scores) have in fact improved over the past 30 years. Leaving aside the fact that some of this improvement has happened since *A Nation at Risk*, the analysis presented in my account suggests that what matters is less the objective indicator of the problem and more how effectively an indicator is tied to a convincing narrative. The importance of narrative to political debate is becoming more widely recognized in recent years; for example, the failures of Democrats in national politics have been ascribed in part to their inability to tell convincing stories in favor of their policy positions. See Stone, *Policy Paradox*, 394. For an in-depth account of this process on one issue (the estate, or "death," tax), see Michael J. Graetz and Ian Shapiro, *Death by a Thousand Cuts: The Fight over Taxing Inherited Wealth* (Princeton, NJ: Princeton University Press, 2005).

29. Hochschild, "Rethinking Accountability Politics," 11–12.

30. George W. Bush effectively used this trope in 2000 in his message of "compassionate conservatism," which centered, not surprisingly, on the importance of accountability in education. This issue will be explored in more depth in later chapters.

31. David B. Tyack, "School Governance in the United States: Historical Puzzles and Anomalies," in *Decentralization and School Improvement: Can We Fulfill The Promise?* eds. Jane Hannaway and Martin Carnoy (San Francisco: Jossey-Bass, CA, 1993), 1–32. Tyack quoting Michael W. Kirst, "Recent State Education Reform in the United States: Looking Backward and Forward," *Educational Administration Quarterly* 24, no. 3 (1988), 319–328.

32. Meg Greenfield, "Creating a Learning Society," *Washington Post*, May 11, 1983, A25.

33. Larry Cuban, *How Teachers Taught: Constancy and Change in American Classrooms, 1890–1990* (New York: Teachers College Press, 1993).

34. William A. Firestone, "Continuity and Incrementalism after All: State Responses to the Excellence Movement," in *The Educational Reform Movement of the 1980s: Perspectives and Cases*, ed. Joseph Murphy (Berkeley, CA: McCutchan, 1990), 145.

35. Policy analysts have argued in recent years that changes in course taking were accomplished more by schools relabeling existing courses than by changing the content of these courses. Susan Fuhrman, *From the Capitol to the Classroom: Standards-Based Reform in the States* (Chicago: National Society for the Study of Education, 2001; distributed by the University of Chicago Press). This finding was one impetus for the push for assessments of student learning after initial reforms did not yield gains on NAEP tests.

36. Diane Ravitch, "Student Performance Today: Policy Brief #23," Brookings Institution, www.brookings.edu/research/papers/1997/09/education-ravitch (accessed June 17, 2012); Caroline M. Hoxby, "Reforms for Whom?" *Education Next* 3, no. 2 (2003), 47–51.

37. Ibid.

38. Firestone, "Continuity and Incrementalism after All: State Responses to the Excellence Movement," 163.

39. Ibid., 147.

40. Ibid., 144. Firestone suggests that this continuity helps to explain why these reforms were institutionalized and pursued over a longer period in the 1980s than would be predicted if they were drawn up in reaction to a crisis.

41. Frederick M. Hess and Patrick J. McGuinn, "Seeking the Mantle of 'Opportunity': Presidential Politics and the Educational Metaphor, 1964–2000," *Educational Policy* 16, no. 1 (2002), 72–95.

42. William Milliken, State of the State Address (1982), 54.

43. John Engler, State of the State Address (1999), 1.

44. One might think that the need for upgrading the quality of the education system would be greater in states that did not have a large manufacturing sector to provide decent jobs for less-educated workers. However, my interviews with state officials in Michigan suggested that this analysis seemed well tailored to its problems (a declining manufacturing sector), whereas the Maryland officials did not indicate that the report had a similar resonance. Maryland state of the state addresses in the 1980s were also given by liberal Democratic governors who had a long laundry list of tasks that government should accomplish, and as a result no one topic constituted a very large share of the addresses.

45. Parris Glendening, State of the State Address (1999), 120.

46. On the postindustrial economy, see Daniel Bell, *The Coming of Post-industrial Society: A Venture in Social Forecasting* (New York: Basic Books, 1973).

47. Scott Matheson, State of the State Address (1983), 66.

48. Norman Bangerter, State of the State Address (1989), 71.

49. Michael Leavitt, State of the State Address (2003), 127.

50. Education Commission of the States. Task Force on Education for Economic Growth, *Action for Excellence: A Comprehensive Plan to Improve Our Nation's Schools*, 50; Twentieth Century Fund, Task Force on Federal Elementary and Secondary Education Policy, *Making the Grade*, 174. These reports were released, however, after *A Nation at Risk*, and their language, particularly in relation to excellence, clearly reflects *A Nation at Risk*.

51. State Board of Education, "Action Goals of Utah State Board of Education," (1984), 1.

52. See Guthrie and Springer, "*A Nation at Risk* Revisited"; Douglas N. Harris, Michael J. Handel, and Lawrence Mishel, "Education and the Economy Revisited: How Schools Matter," *Peabody Journal of Education* 79, no. 1 (2004), 36–63; Eric

A. Hanushek and Dennis D. Kimko, "Schooling, Labor-Force Quality, and the Growth of Nations," *American Economic Review* 90, no. 5 (2000), 1184–1208, for three perspectives on the education-economy debate.

53. Thomas L. Friedman, *The World Is Flat: A Brief History of the Twenty-First Century* (New York: Farrar, Straus and Giroux, 2005).

54. Denis P. Doyle and Terry W. Hartle, *Excellence in Education: The States Take Charge* (Washington, DC: American Enterprise Institute for Public Policy Research, 1985).

55. Robert B. Reich, *The Work of Nations: Preparing Ourselves for 21st-Century Capitalism* (New York: Knopf, 1991). Reich argued that international economic success would be built on educational success, with greater investment in schooling, training, and retraining as the central policy strategies. Bill Clinton adopted much of this rhetoric in his 1992 platform, "Putting People First," and subsequently appointed Reich as his first Secretary of Labor. Bill Clinton and Albert Gore, *Putting People First: How We Can All Change America* (New York: Times Books, 1992).

56. Frederick M. Hess and Andrew Kelly, "Education and the 2004 Presidential Contest," *Politics of Education Association Bulletin* 29, no. 1 (Fall 2004), 1–6. Hess and Kelly quote poll numbers that show that voters favored Bill Clinton over George H. W. Bush in 1992 by 47 to 24 percent on the issue of improving education, whereas George W. Bush and Al Gore were roughly even in 2000 on the issue of who would improve education, with 46 percent for Bush and 47 percent for Gore.

57. Mitchell L. Stevens, *Kingdom of Children: Culture and Controversy in the Homeschooling Movement* (Princeton, NJ: Princeton University Press, 2001). The case is stronger for the progressive left, whose heroes reject the bureaucratic view of schooling that is encapsulated within reforms emphasizing standards and accountability.

58. Jennifer Washburn, *University, Inc.: The Corporate Corruption of American Higher Education* (New York: Basic Books, 2006).

59. Joseph Van Harken, "Budgets Cut Student Experience," CNN.com, www.cnn.com/2003/EDUCATION/08/13/sprj.sch.cuts/index.html?iref=allsearch (accessed June 25, 2012).

60. Diane Ravitch, *The Troubled Crusade: American Education, 1945–1980* (New York: Basic Books, 1983); Gerald Grant, *The World We Created at Hamilton High* (Cambridge, MA: Harvard University Press, 1988).

61. See College Entrance Examination Board, *On Further Examination*, 26, and Thomas Toch, *In the Name of Excellence: The Struggle to Reform the Nation's Schools, Why It's Failing, and What Should Be Done* (New York: Oxford University Press, 1991).

62. Arthur G. Powell et al., *The Shopping Mall High School: Winners and Losers in the Educational Marketplace* (Boston: Houghton Mifflin, 1985). In the words of *A Nation at Risk*'s authors, "That we have compromised this commitment is, upon

reflection, hardly surprising, given the multitude of often conflicting demands we have placed on our Nation's schools and colleges. They are routinely called on to provide solutions to personal, social, and political problems that the home and other institutions either will not or cannot resolve. We must understand that these demands on our schools and colleges often exact an educational cost as well as a financial one." National Commission on Excellence in Education, *A Nation at Risk: The Imperative for Educational Reform: A Report to the Nation and the Secretary of Education, United States Department of Education* (Washington, DC: National Commission on Excellence in Education, 1983).

63. On boundary drawing, see Michèle Lamont and Virág Molnár, "The Study of Boundaries in the Social Sciences," *Annual Review of Sociology* 28, no. 1 (2002), 167–195.

64. Board of Inquiry Project and National Coalition of Advocates for Students, *Barriers to Excellence: Our Children at Risk* (Boston: National Coalition of Advocates for Students, 1985).

65. All quotes in this paragraph are from Toch, *In the Name of Excellence*, 59–61

66. Frederick M. Hess, *I Say "Refining," You Say "Retreating": The Politics of High-Stakes Accountability* (Cambridge, MA: Harvard University Program on Educational Policy and Governance, 2002).

67. National Commission on Excellence in Education, *A Nation at Risk*.

68. College Entrance Examination Board, *On Further Examination*, 49.

69. Ibid., 47.

70. Berliner and Biddle, *The Manufactured Crisis*.

71. On effective schools, see Ronald Edmonds, "Effective Schools for the Urban Poor," *Educational Leadership* 37, no. 1 (1979), 15. The quotation is from Doyle and Hartle, *Excellence in Education*, 13.

72. Sara Lawrence-Lightfoot, *The Good High School: Portraits of Character and Culture* (New York: Basic Books, 1983).

73. Jonathan Rieder, *Canarsie: The Jews and Italians of Brooklyn against Liberalism* (Cambridge, MA: Harvard University Press, 1985).

74. Ira Katznelson and Margaret Weir, *Schooling for all: Class, Race, and the Decline of the Democratic Ideal* (New York: Basic Books, 1985).

75. William Julius Wilson, *The Truly Disadvantaged: The Inner City, the Underclass, and Public Policy* (Chicago: University of Chicago Press, 1987).

76. Jonathan Kozol, *Savage Inequalities: Children in America's Schools* (New York: Crown, 1991); Alex Kotlowitz, *There Are No Children Here: The Story of Two Boys Growing Up in the Other America* (New York: Doubleday, 1991).

77. Scattered efforts at desegregation by race and class do continue to exist—for example in Cambridge, Raleigh, and San Francisco—but they are the exceptions to the rule. See Gary Orfield, John T. Yun, and Civil Rights Project, *Resegregation in American Schools* (Cambridge, MA: Harvard University Civil Rights Project, 1999).

78. The most frequently mentioned of the successful charter schools are the KIPP academies. See Jay Mathews, "A Miracle in the Making? KIPP Turns Its Attention to Elementary Schools," *Washington Post*, April 2, 2006.

79. This was the position of Democrats Edward Kennedy and George Miller on No Child Left Behind, and it continues to be upheld institutionally by some civil rights groups, such as the Citizens' Commission on Civil Rights.

80. Guthrie and Springer, "*A Nation at Risk* Revisited."

81. Jonathan Kozol, *Death at an Early Age: The Destruction of the Hearts and Minds of Negro Children in the Boston Public Schools* (Boston: Houghton Mifflin, 1967).

82. Maurice R. Berube and Marilyn Gittell, *Confrontation at Ocean Hill–Brownsville: The New York School Strikes of 1968* (New York: Praeger, 1969).

83. The quotation is from Toch, *In the Name of Excellence*, 9.

84. Susan H. Fuhrman, "Education Policy: A New Context for Governance," *Publius* 17, no. 3 (1987), 133.

85. Toch, *In the Name of Excellence*, 9.

86. Wirt and Kirst, *Schools in Conflict*, 11.

87. Doyle and Hartle, *Excellence in Education*, 9.

88. Ibid., 9.

89. Toch, *In the Name of Excellence*, 50.

90. Ibid., 135.

91. Fuhrman, "Education Policy: A New Context for Governance," 131–143.

92. This same instinct is present in the desire to increase teacher testing. By 1987, tests to ensure competence of beginning teachers had been adopted in two-thirds of the nation's states. Ibid.

93. Deborah Meier, *In Schools We Trust: Creating Communities of Learning in an Era of Testing and Standardization* (Boston: Beacon Press, 2002), 2. Meier is a longtime critic of the standards movement; in quoting her here I do not necessarily endorse her policy views, but as a matter of analysis, she is clearly right to identify distrust as an important attitude that affects debates over schooling.

94. Wendy Espeland and Mitchell Stevens, "Commensuration as a Social Process," *Annual Review of Sociology*, 24 (1998): 313–343.

95. If one key question is why some events become successful "focusing events" and others do not (e.g., Hurricane Katrina has thus far failed as a focusing event for antipoverty policymakers), this analysis suggests that one important differentiating factor is whether a groundwork has previously been laid in support of the new analysis. Creating a fire requires not only a match and logs but also kindling, and, in the Katrina case, liberal advocates were disadvantaged by not having previously established a structural view of poverty they could draw upon.

96. Richard Hofstadter, *Anti-Intellectualism in American Life* (New York: Knopf, 1963), 5.

CHAPTER 6

1. Eliot Freidson, *Professionalism: The Third Logic* (Cambridge, UK: Polity Press, 2001).

2. Paul Manna, "Federalism, Agenda Setting, and the Development of Federal Education Policy, 1965–2001" (PhD diss., University of Wisconsin–Madison, 2003); Patrick J. McGuinn, "Nationalizing Schools: The Politics of Federal Education Policy" (PhD diss., University of Virginia, 2003); John F. Jennings, *Why National Standards and Tests? Politics and the Quest for Better Schools* (Thousand Oaks, CA: Sage, 1998); Elizabeth H. Debray, *Politics, Ideology & Education: Federal Policy during the Clinton and Bush Administrations* (New York: Teachers College Press, 2006); Andrew Rudalevige, "Forging a Congressional Compromise," in *No Child Left Behind? The Politics and Practice of School Accountability*, eds. Paul E. Peterson and Martin R. West (Washington, DC: Brookings Institution Press, 2003), 23–54; Paul E. Peterson and Martin R. West, *No Child Left Behind? The Politics and Practice of School Accountability* (Washington, DC: Brookings Institution Press, 2003).

3. Amitai Etzioni, *The Semi-Professions and Their Organization: Teachers, Nurses, Social Workers* (New York: Free Press, 1969).

4. Linda M. McNeil, *Contradictions of Control: School Structure and School Knowledge* (New York: Routledge, 1986); Linda M. McNeil, *Contradictions of School Reform: Educational Costs of Standardized Testing* (New York: Routledge, 2000); Richard M. Ingersoll, *Who Controls Teachers' Work? Power and Accountability in America's Schools* (Cambridge, MA: Harvard University Press, 2003).

5. The one important exception to this generalization about neglect of this topic is the work by Gerald Grant and Christine E. Murray, *Teaching in America: The Slow Revolution* (Cambridge, MA: Harvard University Press, 1999). In long historical perspective, they argue, teaching is gradually becoming more professionalized compared with its status at the beginning of the 20th century.

6. Seymour Martin Lipset and William Schneider, *The Confidence Gap: Business, Labor, and Government in the Public Mind* (New York: Free Press, 1987).

7. Ibid., 17.

8. Ibid.

9. There is an extensive literature on what differentiates professionals from other workers. This literature is reviewed in Steven G. Brint, *In an Age of Experts: The Changing Role of Professionals in Politics and Public Life* (Princeton, NJ: Princeton University Press, 1994). The traits I list above are not intended to be an exhaustive or definitive list of what differentiates professionals but are frequently identified characteristics of professionals that have been under attack in recent years. Writing in more recent years has moved away from the "trait approach" and toward a more dynamic understanding of how professions negotiate their professional privileges (Andrew Abbott, *The System of Professions: An Essay on the Division of Expert Labor* [Chicago: University of Chicago Press, 1988]). While I employ the trait approach as a useful organizing device at the beginning of the chapter, the bulk of

the chapter is devoted to tracing how teachers have sought to enlarge their sphere of expertise, and the reasons that larger political forces have resisted these efforts.

10. Marie Haug, "Deprofessionalization: An Alternate Hypothesis for the Future," *Sociological Review Monograph* 20 (1973), 195–211.

11. Eliot Freidson, "The Changing Nature of Professional Control," *Annual Review of Sociology* 10 (1984), 1–20.

12. Lizabeth Cohen, *A Consumers' Republic: The Politics of Mass Consumption in Postwar America* (New York: Knopf, 2003).

13. Freidson, *Professionalism: The Third Logic*.

14. Magali Sarfatti Larson, *The Rise of Professionalism: A Sociological Analysis* (Berkeley: University of California Press, 1977).

15. Freidson, "The Changing Nature of Professional Control," 3.

16. Irving Kristol, *Neoconservatism: The Autobiography of an Idea* (New York: Free Press, 1995).

17. Freidson, *Professionalism: The Third Logic*.

18. John E. Chubb and Terry M. Moe, *Politics, Markets, and America's Schools* (Washington, DC: Brookings Institution, 1990).

19. Brint, *In an Age of Experts*.

20. Freidson, *Professionalism: The Third Logic*.

21. Etzioni, *The Semi-Professions and Their Organization*.

22. Christopher Jencks and David Riesman, *The Academic Revolution* (Garden City, NY: Doubleday, 1968).

23. National Institute of Education Study Group on the Conditions of Excellence in American Higher Education and National Institute of Education, *Involvement in Learning: Realizing the Potential of American Higher Education—Final Report of the Study Group on the Conditions of Excellence in American Higher Education* (Washington, DC: National Institute of Education, US Department of Education, 1984), 8.

24. Ibid., 13.

25. Ibid., 15.

26. Ibid., 15–16.

27. Ibid., 16.

28. Ibid., 58.

29. Of course, teachers are often among those included in creating test items, but legislators (and school boards) retain control over the goals of the standards on which the assessments are based and over the consequences to teachers and schools for failing to meet performance standards.

30. Ibid., 10.

31. Ibid., 43.

32. Alasdair C. MacIntyre, *After Virtue: A Study in Moral Theory* (Notre Dame, IN: University of Notre Dame Press, 1984), 181–203.

33. National Institute Education Study Group, *Involvement in Learning*, 77.

34. Ibid., 68.

35. Ibid., 69.

36. Thomas J. Kane and Peter R. Orszag, "Higher Education Spending: The Role of Medicaid and the Business Cycle," Brookings Institution, www.brookings.edu/~/media/research/files/papers/2003/9/useconomics%20kane/pb124.pdf (accessed June 17, 2012).

37. Some scholars of the professions have noted that stratification is also increasing within the professoriate, with tenured professors gaining job security, time for research, and a degree of institutional (or at least departmental) influence, while a growing secondary group of adjuncts and nontenured professors increasingly do the teaching with little pay, job security, or power. See Grant and Murray, *Teaching in America*, 230.

38. See Katherine Hutt Scott, "Feds Try to Push Colleges for More Accountability," *Lansing State Journal*, June 5, 2003, www.lsj.com/news/local/p_030605_college_1a-9a.html. For a more recent attempt to impose accountability on higher education, see http://insidehighered.com/news/2005/12/09/commission.

39. Turning education into a true profession had been a recurring idea among educators, particularly for the NEA in the years before it shifted its energies and tactics toward collective bargaining. See David Angus, *Professionalism and the Public Good: A Brief History of Teacher Certification*, Fordham Foundation, www.edexcellencemedia.net/publications/2001/200101_professionalismandpublicgood/angus.pdf, 35.

40. Thomas Toch, *In the Name of Excellence: The Struggle to Reform the Nation's Schools, Why It's Failing, and What Should Be Done* (New York: Oxford University Press, 1991), 141.

41. Ibid., 139–140.

42. This formulation, while true, neatly elides the fact that teachers' unions have bargained like representatives of assembly-line workers; therefore, it is not surprising that teachers have been treated as such.

43. Carnegie Corporation Forum on Education and the Economy, *A Nation Prepared: Teachers for the 21st Century—The Report of the Task Force on Teaching as a Profession* (Washington: Forum, 1986), 36.

44. Ibid., 39.

45. Ibid., 41.

46. Ibid., 42.

47. Ibid., 90.

48. Ibid., 42.

49. Joseph T. Murphy, ed., *The Educational Reform Movement of the 1980s: Perspectives and Cases* (Berkeley, CA: McCutchan, 1990); William Lowe Boyd, "Balancing Control and Autonomy in School Reform: The Politics of Perestroika," in *The Educational Reform Movement of the 1980s: Perspectives and Cases*, ed. Joseph Murphy (Berkeley, CA: McCutchan, 1990), 85–96.

50. Carnegie Corporation, *A Nation Prepared*, 58.

51. Ibid., 69.

52. Ibid., 65.

53. Ibid., 95.

54. National Commission on Teaching and America's Future, *What Matters Most: Teaching for America's Future—Report of the National Commission on Teaching & America's Future* (New York: National Commission on Teaching & America's Future, 1996).

55. David Osborne and Ted Gaebler, *Reinventing Government: How the Entrepreneurial Spirit Is Transforming the Public Sector* (Reading, MA: Addison-Wesley, 1992).

56. Ibid.

57. Carnegie Corporation, *A Nation Prepared*, 89.

58. National Governors Association, *Time for Results: The Governors' 1991 Report on Education* (Washington, DC: National Governors Association, 1986), 3.

59. Ibid, 4.

60. Archon Fung, *Empowered Participation: Reinventing Urban Democracy* (Princeton, NJ: Princeton University Press, 2004).

61. Joel H. Spring, *Political Agendas for Education: From the Religious Right to the Green Party* (Mahwah, NJ: Erlbaum, 2002).

62. The reasons for school choice and charter schools are more complicated than this short summary can suggest. The roots behind choice are deep and ideologically diverse. For an early view of choice from the left, see Christopher Jencks, *Giving Parents Money to Pay for Schooling: Education Vouchers: A Report on Financing Elementary Education through Grants to Parents* (Cambridge, MA: Center for Educational Policy Research, Harvard Graduate School of Education, 1970). Charter schools have rich antecedents, dating to alternative schools and magnet schools coming out of the 1960s. The contemporary politics are also interesting, as poor and minority parents have increasingly come out in favor of choice, arguing that better-off parents can make school choices through their housing decisions and that fairness demands similar choice be extended to poorer parents. For perspectives on the politics of choice, see Kevin J. Dougherty and Lizabeth Sostre, "Minerva and the Market: The Sources of the Movement for School Choice," in *The Choice Controversy*, ed. Peter W. Cookson (Newbury Park, CA: Corwin Press, 1992), 24–41; also see Spring, *Political Agendas for Education: From the Religious Right to the Green Party*.

63. Chester Finn, "Why We Need Choice," in *Choice in Education: Potential and Problems*, eds. William L. Boyd and Herbert J. Walberg (Berkeley, CA: McCutchan, 1990), 9.

64. Dougherty and Sostre, "Minerva and the Market: The Sources of the Movement for School Choice," 37.

65. Spring, *Political Agendas for Education: From the Religious Right to the Green Party*, 73.

66. James Cibulka, "The NEA and School Choice," in *Conflicting Missions? Teachers Unions and Educational Reform*, ed. Tom Loveless (Washington, DC: Brookings Institution Press, 2000), 150–173.

67. Theodore R. Sizer, *The Red Pencil: Convictions from Experience in Education* (New Haven, CT: Yale University Press, 2004).

68. National Commission on Teaching and America's Future, *What Matters Most*, 151.

69. In North Carolina, the state that has most aggressively supported this agenda by paying for the full cost of certification, almost 20,000 teachers are board certified—more than 20 percent of the state's teachers. See "N.C. Leads Nation in Board Certified Teachers," *News Observer*, January 8, 2013, www.newsobserver. com/2013/01/08/2591330/nc-leads-nation-in-board-certified.html. See also Anne Grosso de Leon, "After 20 Years of Educational Reform, Progress, but Plenty of Unfinished Business," *Carnegie Results: Quarterly Newsletter by Carnegie Corporation of New York* 1, no. 3 (Fall, 2003).

70. Andrew J. Rotherham and Sara Mead, "Back to the Future: The History and Politics of State Teacher Licensure and Certification," in *A Qualified Teacher in Every Classroom? Appraising Old Answers and New Ideas*, eds. Frederick M. Hess, Andrew J. Rotherham, and Kate Burke Walsh (Cambridge, MA: Harvard Education Press, 2004), 11–47. Rotherham and Mead find that as of 2004, 21 states provided additional compensation for NBPTS-certified teachers.

71. INTASC standards are also used in many individual teacher preparation programs; Danielle Dunne Wilcox, "The National Board for Professional Teaching Standards: Can It Live Up to Its Promise?" in *Better Teachers, Better Schools*, eds. Marci Kanstoroom et al. (Washington, DC: Thomas B. Fordham Foundation, 1999), 191.

72. Sandra Vergari and Frederick Hess, "The Accreditation Game," *Education Next*, nos. 2, 3 (2002): 48–57.

73. Rotherham and Mead, "Back to the Future," 40.

74. Marilyn Cochran-Smith and Mary Kim Fries, "Sticks, Stones, and Ideology: The Discourse of Reform in Teacher Education," *Educational Researcher* 30, no. 8 (2001), 3–15. Regional and state initiatives in Ohio, New York City, and California have sought to trace the impact of teacher preparation on educational outcomes. Another effort is the Teachers for a New Era project, sponsored largely by the Carnegie Corporation, which provides funding for individual institutions to study the impact of their preparation programs on teachers' knowledge growth, student learning, and teacher retention. There are also state-level initiatives that have sought to evaluate the impact on achievement gains of teachers educated in different preparatory institutions.

75. Rotherham and Mead, "Back to the Future," 31.

76. Thomas B. Fordham Foundation, "The Teachers We Need and How to Get More of Them: A Manifesto," in *Better Teachers, Better Schools*, eds. Marci Kanstoroom et al. (Washington, DC: Thomas B. Fordham Foundation, 1999), 1–18.

77. US Department of Education, Office of Postsecondary Education, Office of Policy Planning and Innovation, "Meeting the Highly Qualified Teachers Challenge: The Secretary's Annual Report on Teacher Quality," US Department of Education, http://www2.ed.gov/about/reports/annual/teachprep/2002title-ii-report.pdf (accessed June 17, 2012).

78. National Center for Alternative Certification, "Alternative Teacher Certification: A State by State Analysis," www.teach-now.org/intro.cfm (accessed January 12, 2013).

79. Frederick M. Hess, "The Predictable, but Unpredictably Personal, Politics of Teacher Licensure," *Journal of Teacher Education* 56, no. 3 (2005), 192–198.

80. Ibid, 193.

81. Cochran-Smith and Fries, "Sticks, Stones, and Ideology."

82. Linda Darling-Hammond et al., "Does Teacher Preparation Matter? Evidence about Teacher Certification, Teach for America, and Teacher Effectiveness," *Education Policy Analysis Archives* 13, no. 42 (October 12, 2005).

83. This discussion draws on Cochran-Smith and Fries, "Sticks, Stones, and Ideology."

84. Linda Darling-Hammond, "Reforming Teacher Preparation and Licensing: Debating the Evidence," *Teachers College Record* 102, no. 1 (2000), 28–56.

85. The two sides have also debated which professions are analogous to teaching, with professionalizers seeking to model teaching after law and medicine, while alternative certification proponents have argued that the apprenticeship models of journalism or business are more appropriate. See also Rotherham and Mead, "Back to the Future."

86. Richard Riley, "New Challenges, A New Resolve: Moving American Education into the 21st Century," February 16, 1999, www.ed.gov/Speeches/02-1999/990216.html.

87. Rotherham and Mead, "Back to the Future," 41.

88. Marilyn Cochran-Smith, "Reforming Teacher Education," *Journal of Teacher Education* 52, no. 4 (2001), 263–265.

89. Angus, *Professionalism and the Public Good*, 35.

90. Cochran-Smith, "Reforming Teacher Education," 264.

91. Richard M. Ingersoll, "The Problem of Underqualified Teachers in American Secondary Schools," *Educational Researcher* 28, no. 2 (1999), 26–37.

92. Penelope M. Earley, "Finding the Culprit: Federal Policy and Teacher Education," *Educational Policy* 14, no. 1 (2000), 25–39.

93. Penelope M. Earley, "Meanings, Silos, and High-Stakes Advocacy," *Journal of Teacher Education* 56, no. 3 (2005), 214.

94. Marilyn Cochran-Smith, "Teacher Education and the Outcomes Trap," *Journal of Teacher Education* 56, no. 5 (2005), 411–417.

95. Bob Chase, "The New NEA: Reinventing Teacher Unions for a New ERA," remarks before the National Press Club, February 5, 1997.

96. Shanker said of the Tennessee plan that rewarding performance with pay "might work with encyclopedia salesmen, but it won't fly with teachers." Toch, *In the Name of Excellence*, 148.

97. All of the information about Shanker and the AFT in this paragraph, including the reference to *Sleeper*, comes from ibid., 148.

98. Robert Worth, "Reforming the Teachers' Unions," *Washington Monthly* 30, no. 5 (May 1998).

99. Bob Chase, "Teacher Unionism: Bob Chase Defends His Views," *Rethinking Schools* 11, no. 4 (1997).

100. Adam Urbanski, "Reform or Be Reformed," *Education Next* 1, no. 3 (2001), 51–54.

101. Charles T. Kerchner, Julia Koppich, and Joseph G. Weeres, *United Mind Workers: Unions and Teaching in the Knowledge Society* (San Francisco: Jossey-Bass, 1997).

102. Vaishali Honawar, "Union Agitators," *Education Week*, February 1, 2006.

103. Jay Mathews, "New Ideas from Weingarten," January 10, 2010, http://voices. washingtonpost.com/class-struggle/2010/01/teacher_union_leader_for_tomor. html

104. Julia Koppich, "The As-Yet-Unfulfilled Promise of Reform Bargaining," in *Collective Bargaining in Education: Negotiating Change in Today's Schools*, eds. Jane Hannaway and Andrew J. Rotherham (Cambridge, MA: Harvard Education Press, 2006), 203–227; Julia E. Koppich, "A Tale of Two Approaches—the AFT, the NEA, and NCLB," *Peabody Journal of Education* 80, no. 2 (2005), 137–155.

105. Jeff Archer, "President Leaves Mixed Record on Pledge to 'Reinvent' NEA," *Education Week*, June 19, 2002.

106. Koppich, "The As-Yet-Unfulfilled Promise of Reform Bargaining," 231.

107. Chubb and Moe, *Politics, Markets, and America's Schools*. A transcript of a Brookings Institution forum, whose participants included both Urbanski and Moe, nicely illustrates the differences in their views of the possibility that teachers' unions could promote the public good (www.brookings.edu/comm/transcripts/20000411a.htm).

108. Frederick M. Hess and Martin R. West, "A Better Bargain: Overhauling Teacher Collective Bargaining for the 21st Century," Harvard University Program on Education Policy and Governance, www.hks.harvard.edu/pepg/PDF/Papers/BetterBargain.pdf, 6 (accessed June 17, 2012).

109. This discussion draws on Charles T. Kerchner and Julia Koppich, "Organizing around Quality: The Frontiers of Teacher Unionism," in *Conflicting Missions? Teachers Unions and Educational Reform*, ed. Tom Loveless (Washington, DC: Brookings Institution Press, 2000), 281–315. See also Grant and Murray, *Teaching in America: The Slow Revolution*.

110. Bruce S. Cooper and Marie-Elena Liotta, "Urban Teachers Unions Face their Future," *Education and Urban Society* 34, no. 1 (2001), 101–118.

111. Kerchner and Koppich, "Organizing around Quality: The Frontiers of Teacher Unionism."

112. Peter A. Hall and Rosemary C. R. Taylor, "Political Science and the Three New Institutionalisms," *Political Studies* 44, no. 5 (1996), 936–957.

113. Kerchner and Koppich, "Organizing around Quality: The Frontiers of Teacher Unionism," 299.

114. Grant and Murray, *Teaching in America: The Slow Revolution*.

115. Letter to Bob Chase, "Teacher Unionism: Bob Chase Is Attacked," *Rethinking Schools* 11, no. 4 (1997), www.rethinkingschools.org/restrict. asp?path=archive/11_04/unltr.shtml.

116. Jeff Archer, "NEA Delegates Take Hard Line against Pay for Performance," *Education Week*, July 12, 2000.

117. Angus, *Professionalism and the Public Good*, 35.

118. Thomas M. Smith and Kristie J. Rowley, "Enhancing Commitment or Tightening Control: The Function of Teacher Professional Development in an Era of Accountability," *Educational Policy* 19, no. 1 (2005), 127.

CHAPTER 7

1. I provide more details on case selection in the Note on Methods at the end of the book..

2. Given that the purpose of the study is to understand the political development of standards-based reform, I do not carry the state-level study through to the present. The relationship between the states and the federal government under NCLB is its own topic; see Paul Manna, *Collision Course: Federal Education Policy Meets State and Local Realities* (Washington, DC: Congressional Quarterly Press, 2011).

3. Interview with David Hornbeck, January 2005.

4. Memorandum from David W. Hornbeck to David Falk and Laslo Boyd, "Improving Maryland Education through Greater Accountability," May 22, 1987.

5. It is also worth noting that the representatives of business were appointed as individuals, not as representatives of a business coalition seeking to improve educational performance. The Maryland Business Roundtable was very supportive of the performance system put into place by the commission, but the state BRT was formed only after the release of the report.

6. Kathy Lally, "Balancing Standards and Performance," *Baltimore Sun*, September 10, 1989, 5K.

7. This point was recognized by Maryland State Teachers Association President Jane Stern, who drew a direct line from the governor's charge to the report's recommendations: "He asked them to come up with a method to assess school performance, and that's what they did. They came up with a system of measurement and regulation." Kathy Lally, "Teachers Take Different Views of Schools' Needs," *Baltimore Sun*, October 5, 1989, 5E.

8. Lally, "Balancing Standards and Performance," 1K.

9. Governor's Commission on School Performance, "The Report of the Governor's Commission on School Performance," 4.

10. To be fair, the authors were concerned by the possibility of producing a system that was overly heavy on testing or that emphasized economic purposes of schooling

over other values. In a reflection of the humanistic concerns of some of the report's authors, the committee cautioned against exclusive reliance on tests for accountability and instead urged the use of multiple quantitative measures of success, with the ultimate evaluation made by visiting accreditation teams that could better evaluate the range of characteristics that defined successful schools.

11. Michael Cohen, "Memorandum to Lois Martin, re: Draft Commission Report," (June 19, 1989), 3.

12. Amy Goldstein, "Maryland Teachers Have Their Own Ideas about How to Help Schools," *Washington Post*, October 4, 1989, C1; Lally, "Teachers Take Different Views of Schools' Needs," 5E.

13. Jay Merwin, "Cut Talk, Boost Funds, Teachers Says," *Baltimore Evening Sun*, January 4, 1989.

14. Kathy Lally, "M[arylan]d Task Force Proposes Public School Rating System," *Baltimore Sun*, August 23, 1989, 16A.

15. Letter from Walter Sondheim Jr. to Robert C. Embry Jr., October 9, 1989, made available to me by Sondheim.

16. This is not to say that Sondheim did not believe in the report's recommendations; clearly he did. It is only to say that on the specific point of funding, he felt that advocating for funding without accountability was no longer politically feasible.

17. "Quality Control in Education," *Baltimore Sun*, August 23, 1989, 18A; "Accountable Schools," *Evening Sun*, August 24, 1989, A20; "A New Way to Judge Schools," *Washington Post*, August 26, 1989, A20.

18. Paul Manna, *School's In: Federalism and the National Education Agenda* (Washington, DC: Georgetown University Press, 2006).

19. Minutes of the Maryland State Board of Education, December 13, 1989, 2.

20. Interview January 2005.

21. Interview with Thomas Rhoades, January 2005.

22. Description of MSPAP comes from Nancy Grasmick, "Improving Learning For All Children, Education Reform in Maryland 1977–1996" (Baltimore: Maryland State Department of Education, 1996).

23. MSPAP had trial runs in 1991 and 1992 before it was implemented for its first official use in 1993.

24. Monica Norton, "Latest Tests Are Useless, Teachers Say; State Officials Defend Them, Picture of Nude Bar and All," *Baltimore Sun*, May 22, 1992, 1E.

25. Jane Stern, "Making Schools Succeed: Our Schools after 10 Years of Reform," *Baltimore Sun*, May 5, 1993, 19A.

26. Ibid.

27. Tim Baker, "Candidates Agree: School Reforms Are Here to Stay," *Baltimore Sun*, October 3, 1994, 7A.

28. Ibid.

29. Tim Baker, "A Test That Gives Teachers the Fantods," *Baltimore Sun*, April 25, 1994, 7A.

30. Molly Rath, "See Nancy Work," *Baltimore*, September 1994, 86.

31. Jean Thompson, "Parents Join Forces against MSPAP Tests," *Baltimore Sun*, May 4, 1997, 1B.

32. Mary Maushard, "Week of State Tests Becomes Rite of Spring," *Baltimore Sun*, May 8, 1994, 1B.

33. Ibid.

34. Maryland State Teachers Association, "Report by the Maryland State Teachers Association–NEA on the Maryland School Performance Assessment Program," January 27, 1999.

35. Howard Libit, "After Six Years of Gains, Pupils Hit Wall on Tests," *Baltimore Sun*, December 2, 1999, 1A. The fact that it took the decline in scores in 1999 to create serious doubts about the program is itself a testament to the power of the program's backers and the problem definition that supported it. It should have been clear in 1998 that the program would not make its intended 2000 target since only 44 percent of the state's students passed the tests, up from 32 percent in the program's initial administration in 1993. The news coverage in the years before 1998 also emphasized progress over time (even when progress was miniscule by absolute standards), a perspective that helped to preserve the positive image of the program. For statistics in 1998, see Mary Maushard, "State Short of Its Goals, but Still Proud of Its Schools," *Baltimore Sun*, December 9, 1998, 6A.

36. Howard Libit, "State Tests Still in Favor," *Baltimore Sun*, December 3, 1999, 1A.

37. Ibid.

38. Howard Libit, "MSPAP Up, but Goals Still Distant," *Baltimore Sun*, November 30, 1999.

39. Mike Bowler, "Criticism of MSPAP Irks Officials," *Baltimore Sun*, August 3, 2000, 1B.

40. Ibid.

41. Interview with Jerry Weast, January 2005.

42. Stephanie Desmon, "Test Scores Stump Officials," *Baltimore Sun*, January 30, 2002, 1B.

43. Ibid.

44. Michigan School Finance Commission, 4.

45. Ibid.

46. Interview, October 2004.

47. Public Act 25 passed by 26–8 in the Senate and 99–4 in the House.

48. The discussion of the 1993 legislation, including many of the quotes, is largely drawn from a fine dissertation by Sandra M. Vergari, "Policy Crises and Policy Change: Toward a Theory of Crisis Policy-Making" (PhD diss., Michigan State University, 1996). Vergari, who was in Lansing at Michigan State at the time, interviewed 50 key players, including many of the legislators involved in the 1993 reforms.

49. Ibid., 213.

50. Ibid., 215.

51. Ibid., 217.

52. Ibid., 213.

53. While academics and the business community are often in tension, particularly over educational issues, in this case the collaboration proved fruitful as the academics said that they gained an entrée to the policy process, as well as needed prestige for the education departments at the two schools. (One said he agreed to participate because he was so directed by the president of his university.) Furthermore, the academics said that they believed strongly in the goals of standards-based reform and that collaboration with the business community provided an outlet for their views.

54. Aide to Governor John Engler, interview with author, October 2004.

55. It would be more accurate to say that Republican legislators and particularly the governor brought in business in order to provide public support for their positions than to say that the business community had an agenda that they persuaded political actors to adopt. Several legislative aides to the governor described the relationship this way to me, citing, for example, the way that the business community had been persuaded to pick up part of the cost to pay a firm to compile and publish school test scores.

56. Ibid., 162.

57. Ibid., 169; emphasis added.

58. Ibid., 171–172.

59. William Lowe Boyd, David N. Plank, and Gary Sykes, "Teachers Unions in Hard Times," in *Conflicting Missions? Teachers Unions and Educational Reform*, ed. Tom Loveless (Washington, DC: Brookings Institution Press, 2000), 174–210.

60. Vergari, "Policy Crises and Policy Change," 173.

61. Gongwer News Service, "Near Midnight, School Code Measure Passes in House," *Michigan Report*, sec. 34, December 12, 1995.

62. "Engler Needs to Stand Up to School Board Radicals," *Detroit Free Press*, August 6, 1995, 2F.

63. Curtis Hertel, "Core Curriculum Shouldn't Be Cut," *Detroit Free Press*, August 30, 1995, 4E.

64. Ibid.

65. Summary accreditation indicated that in addition to the schools having fulfilled other requirements, students scored at 66 percent or better on 8 of 12 state tests. Interim accreditation indicated that students scored better than 50 percent on at least one of the state tests in any of the last three years. No accreditation indicated that students had scored 50 percent or below on all state tests over the last 3 years. See Liz Arasim, *School Accreditation: An Overview* (Lansing, MI: Senate Fiscal Agency, 2000).

66. Said one education department official at the time, "Only a handful of schools are unaccredited. But I can assure you there are numerous schools that are failing our children." At the same time, there was also significant concern about the vast

middle—the bottom was seen as too low and the top too far out of reach to spur significant improvement. Said Republican State Board Member Dorothy Beardmore, "You could be buried in that [middle accreditation status] and nobody would know whether you were almost summary accredited, just barely in the interim category, or just in between." Quotations from ibid.

67. According to the new requirements, to achieve summary accreditation, schools needed to meet the following standards: 75 percent or more of students performing in the top category on the MEAP tests; no evidence of an achievement gap; 95 percent of enrolled students tested; and evidence of improvement. To be unaccredited but improving now meant that fewer than 25 percent of students scored in the top category, but otherwise the schools were in compliance in terms of lack of disparities, enrolled students taking the tests, and yearly improvement. See ibid.

68. See "So All Succeed: Delivering the Promise of Michigan Public Schools" and "Creating a Culture of Accountability: Final Report of the Michigan Accountability Task Force," both available from the Michigan Association of School Boards.

69. Katherine Kapos, "Study Calls for School-Test Overhaul," *Salt Lake Tribune,* September 8, 1997.

70. Appendix A: An Analysis of National "Indicators of Risk" (Salt Lake City: Utah State Office of Education, 1984), 46.

71. Jeffrey P. Haney, "Setting School Standards—Utahns Looking at Ways to Hold Teachers, Students Accountable," *Deseret News,* May 31, 1999.

72. Kapos, "Study Calls for School-Test Overhaul."

73. The other obvious explanation for Utah's laggard status on standards-based reform is its distance from a set of reforms that had most of its early proponents in the Southeast. This explanation is plausible but awaits a test through an event-history analysis.

74. Haney, "Setting School Standards."

75. Jennifer Toomer-Cook, "Utah Schools Do Poorly in Accountability Study," *Deseret News,* January 7, 1999.

76. Haney, "Setting School Standards."

77. Jennifer Toomer-Cook, "Education Group Talks Roles, Goals," *Deseret News,* May 11, 1999.

78. Jennifer Toomer-Cook, "Schools Must Do Better—or Else?" *Deseret News,* September 7, 1999.

79. Jeffrey P. Haney, "Setting School Standards—Utahns Looking at Ways to Hold Teachers, Students Accountable."

80. Katherine Kapos, "Testing Plan Irks Teachers," *Salt Lake Tribune,* October 21, 1999.

81. Ibid.

82. Jennifer Toomer-Cook, "Educators Flay Standardized Tests," *Deseret News,* October 21, 1999.

83. Representative Karen Morgan, "Testing Schools a Bad Idea," *Deseret News,* September 21, 2000.

84. Representative Tammy Rowan, "Task Force's Goal Is to Aid Utah Students," *Deseret News*, December 3, 1999.

85. A proposal to issue letter grades to the schools was not supported, weakening the accountability thrust of the legislation.

86. See also Margaret Dayton's comments at the Sutherland Institute's Web site: www. sutherlandinstitute.org/answers.php?question=nochildbody.htm.

87. Sam Dillon, "Utah Vote Rejects Part of Education Law," *New York Times*, April 20, 2005, A14.

88. Sam Dillon, "Education Law Finds Few Fans in Utah," *New York Times*, March 6, 2005.

89. Jennifer Toomer-Cook, "Feds Coming to Sell Ed Law," *Deseret News*, February 13, 2005. The UEA did not favor the bill that would have opted Utah out of NCLB because of concerns about the resources that would be lost.

90. Sam Dillon, "Utah Vote Rejects Part of Education Law."

91. Ronnie Lynn, "Legislator Plans to Challenge Feds' No Child Left Behind Rules," *Salt Lake Tribune*, November 11, 2004.

92. To confirm this point would require detailed case studies of the other states.

CHAPTER 8

1. Patrick J. McGuinn, "Nationalizing Schools: The Politics of Federal Education Policy" (PhD diss., University of Virginia), 98.

2. Ibid, 99.

3. Patrick J. McGuinn, *No Child Left Behind and the Transformation of Federal Education Policy, 1965–2005* (Lawrence: University Press of Kansas, 2006), 52.

4. McGuinn, "Nationalizing Schools: The Politics of Federal Education Policy," 99.

5. On this point, compare Thomas Toch, *In the Name of Excellence: The Struggle to Reform the Nation's Schools, Why It's Failing, and What Should Be Done* (New York: Oxford University Press, 1991), 325, to Paul Manna, *School's In: Federalism and the National Education Agenda* (Washington, DC: Georgetown University Press, 2006), 209.

6. Maris A. Vinovskis, "The Road to Charlottesville: The 1989 Education Summit" (1999), http://govinfo.library.unt.edu/negp/reports/negp30.pdf (accessed June 15, 2012).

7. The evidence on this point comes from Paul Manna, "Federalism, Agenda Setting, and the Development of Federal Education Policy, 1965–2001" (PhD diss., University of Wisconsin–Madison), 158, who quotes several who were present at the time, including Bush administration official Milton Goldberg, as saying that the idea came from the governors. Goldberg is quoted as saying, "Given the ideological polarization in the country at the time I couldn't see it [the development of national education goals] happening....I thought it was a crazy idea." Maris Vinovskis, who has offered the most detailed history of the period leading up to

Charlottesville, says only that the subject of setting long-range education goals "was broached" at the December 1988 meeting, but does not say by whom it was broached (see Vinovskis, "The Road to Charlottesville").

8. While a general agreement to create goals was created in Charlottesville in September 1989, a longer process of negotiation was needed to agree upon specific goals.

9. The SREB did not set national goals because it was a regional group.

10. Vinovskis, "The Road to Charlottesville," 38.

11. Ibid.

12. Ibid.

13. Richard F. Elmore, "The National Education Goals Panel: Purposes, Progress, and Prospects" (1998), http://govinfo.library.unt.edu/negp/reports/elmoref. htm; John F. Jennings, *Why National Standards and Tests? Politics and the Quest for Better Schools* (Thousand Oaks, CA: Sage, 1998), 204; Christopher T. Cross, *Political Education: National Policy Comes of Age* (New York: Teachers College Press, 2004), 194.

14. All quotations in this paragraph are from US Department of Education, *America 2000: An Education Strategy* (Washington, DC: US Department of Education, 1991).

15. See the National Center on Education and the Economy, Commission on the Skills of the American Workforce, *America's Choice: High Skills or Low Wages! The Report* (Rochester, NY: National Center on Education and the Economy, 1990), 147.

16. John W. Kingdon, *Agendas, Alternatives, and Public Policies* (Boston: Little, Brown, 1984), 240.

17. This hearing, on the topic of national testing generally, provides considerably more information on the debates over national standards and testing than do the hearings for America 2000 itself, because those hearings necessarily covered much more ground (choice, "break the mold schools," etc.) and thus covered standards and assessments only briefly. The limited debate on that topic in America 2000 raised the same objections and rebuttals as were voiced in these hearings.

18. US Congress, Committee on Education and Labor, Subcommittee on Elementary, Secondary, and Vocational Education, "Oversight Hearings on Educational Assessment: Hearings before the Subcommittee on Elementary, Secondary, and Vocational Education of the Committee on Education and Labor, House of Representatives, 102nd Congress, 1st Session, Hearings Held in Washington, DC, March 13–14, 1991," 138.

19. Ibid, 174.

20. NAACP had challenged minimum competency tests when they began to emerge in the mid to late 1970s as a form of "blaming the victim."

21. Richard Jaeger, quoted in Robert Rothman, "Researchers Say Emphasis on Testing Too Narrow, Could Set Back Reforms," *Education Week*, June 12, 1991.

22. Their views also reflected a fundamentally trusting approach to educators, who were seen as allies in the process of educational reform, not as agents who needed to be externally monitored and motivated.

23. Julie Miller, "House's Bill Would Authorize Standards, but Not Assessment," *Education Week*, May 27, 1992.

24. Jennings, *Why National Standards and Tests?*, 204; McGuinn, *No Child Left Behind and the Transformation of Federal Education Policy*, 260.

25. "A Look Ahead: Education and the New Decade," *Education Week*, January 10, 1990). In this article, *Education Week* asked 150 leading education thinkers to assess what the next decade would hold. Responses varied from greater fragmentation (Ted Sizer) to standards (David Hornbeck) to more funding (Augustus Hawkins, chair, House Education and Labor Committee) to a move away from public schooling (John Coons, professor of law, University of California–Berkeley).

26. Marshall S. Smith and Jennifer A. O'Day, "Systemic School Reform," in *The Politics of Curriculum and Testing: The 1990 Yearbook of the Politics of Education Association*, eds. Susan Fuhrman and Betty Malen (New York: Falmer Press, 1991), 233–267.

27. Hugh Heclo, *Modern Social Politics in Britain and Sweden: From Relief to Income Maintenance* (New Haven, CT: Yale University Press, 1974), 349.

28. For example, Mike Smith wrote the background paper that guided the group, and David Hornbeck had successfully advocated for a similar framework in the 1990 Kentucky reforms.

29. Interview with Bob Schwartz, June 2006.

30. Interview with Bob Schwartz, June 2006.

31. Interview with Marc Tucker, June 2006.

32. National Center on Education and the Economy. Commission on the Skills of the American Workforce, *America's Choice: High Skills or Low Wages!*, 147.

33. Interview with Marc Tucker, June 2006.

34. Lester M. Salamon, "Overview: Why Human Capital? Why Now?," in *Human Capital and America's Future: An Economic Strategy for the '90s*, eds. David W. Hornbeck and Lester M. Salamon (Baltimore: Johns Hopkins University Press, 1991), 1.

35. David Hornbeck, "New Paradigms for Action," in *Human Capital and America's Future: An Economic Strategy for the '90s*, eds. David Hornbeck and Lester M. Salamon (Baltimore: Johns Hopkins University Press, 1991), 371.

36. Smith and O'Day, "Systemic School Reform."

37. Chester E. Finn, *We Must Take Charge: Our Schools and Our Future* (New York: Maxwell Macmillan, 1991), 147–149.

38. Ibid., 150.

39. Ibid., 144.

40. Ibid., 125.

41. Interview with Mike Cohen, May 2006.

42. Smith and O'Day, "Systemic School Reform," 237.

43. Ibid, 257.

44. To see the difference in institutional vantage point between the systemic reformers and teachers, consider this interchange between Ernest Boyer, a prominent

reformer, and some of the teachers in the schools he studied, as described by Finn, *We Must Take Charge*, 133, who is clearly sympathetic to Boyer: "In an important 1983 study of secondary education, Boyer reported his conclusion that high schools lack a 'clear and vital mission.'... Nor did those whom Boyer interviewed seem perturbed by the stream of banalities. When asked about their schools' goals, he wrote, the 'response frequently was one of uncertainty, amusement, or surprise.' One teacher suggested that goals and objectives were something 'to be learned in teacher education courses and then forgotten.' Another said, even more cynically, 'If we had goals, we wouldn't follow them anyway....' Boyer was duly alarmed.... He urged, sensibly enough, that every school adopt 'clearly stated goals and purposes that are understood and supported' by teachers, students, parents and administrators." From the perspective of Boyer (and Finn), the lack of clarity over goals is a serious problem that suggests institutional drift that must be remedied. For the teachers he interviewed, however, goals are something that sit on a shelf, far from influencing the daily life of the school. There may or may not be problems in the school, the teachers seemed to be saying, but you won't learn much one way or another from looking at the goals statements.

45. Lynn Olson and Robert Rothman, "Roadmap to Reform," *Education Week*, April 21, 1993.
46. Smith and O'Day, "Systemic School Reform," 234.
47. Ibid, 239.
48. Ibid, 254.
49. Ibid, 253.
50. Jennifer A. O'Day and Marshall S. Smith, "Systemic School Reform and Educational Opportunity," in *Designing Coherent Education Policy: Improving the System*, ed. Susan Fuhrman (San Francisco: Jossey-Bass, 1993), 252.
51. Clinton himself was a "policy expert" on state standards-based reform, given his experience in Arkansas and in the NGA. Mike Cohen said that he was almost duplicative as Clinton's education policy advisor during the campaign, given that Clinton knew education as well as he did. However, Clinton's familiarity with the state approach to standards-based reform was itself largely informed by activities of these policy entrepreneurs in the NGA and in promoting standards-based reform in the states. Interview with Mike Cohen, May 2006.
52. McGuinn, "Nationalizing Schools: The Politics of Federal Education Policy," 164.
53. Richard W. Riley, "Reflections on Goals 2000," *Teachers College Record* 96, no. 3 (1995), 382.
54. For a detailed history of the legislative maneuvering around Goals 2000, see Jennings, *Why National Standards and Tests?*
55. Quoted in Robert B. Schwartz and Marian A. Robinson, "Goals 2000 and the Standards Movement," in *Brookings Papers on Education Policy*, ed. Diane Ravitch (Washington, DC: Brookings Institution, 2001), 195.
56. Quoted in Jennings, *Why National Standards and Tests?*, 57.

57. This position was expressed by Al Shanker, who strongly supported Goals 2000 and opposed the fight over the opportunity to learn standards: "It's totally wrong to hold the development of content and performance standards and stakes hostage until you solve all of the equity issues, or most of the equity issues, or even some of the equity issues." Quoted in ibid., 58.

58. Representative Bill Goodling, quoted in Cross, *Political Education: National Policy Comes of Age*, 106.

59. Jennings, *Why National Standards and Tests?*, 59.

60. Cross, *Political Education: National Policy Comes of Age*, 110.

61. Elizabeth H. Debray, *Politics, Ideology & Education: Federal Policy during the Clinton and Bush Administrations* (New York: Teachers College Press, 2006), 31; Andrew Rudalevige, "Forging a Congressional Compromise," in *No Child Left Behind? The Politics and Practice of School Accountability*, eds. Paul E. Peterson and Martin R. West (Washington, DC: Brookings Institution Press, 2003), 30.

62. The administration had expected the opposite. They had introduced Goals 2000 first, in the hopes of gaining an easy victory that would provide a "prism" through which they could carry their vision into what they expected would be a more controversial set of debates over the ESEA. But the debate over Goals 2000 stretched through 1993 and into 1994, overlapping with the introduction of the ESEA. The lengthy debate over Goals created a kind of "standards fatigue" that ironically made it easier to get the ESEA passed. Jennings, *Why National Standards and Tests?*, 204.

63. These were not unreasonable concerns. An earlier history of states, districts, and schools shifting federal money away from intended targets and toward other needs had stiffened federal resolve on this point. Marshall S. Smith, Brent W. Scoll, and Valena White Plisko, "The Improving America's Schools Act: A New Partnership," in *National Issues in Education: Elementary and Secondary Education Act*, eds. John F. Jennings, Phi Delta Kappa, and Institute for Educational Leadership (Bloomington, IN: Phi Delta Kappa International, 1995), 4.

64. Debray, *Politics, Ideology & Education*, 31.

65. US Department of Education, "Reinventing Chapter 1: The Current Chapter 1 Program and New Directions. Final Report of the National Assessment of the Chapter 1 Program" (Washington, DC: Office of Policy Planning, 1993).

66. Kati Haycock and David W. Hornbeck, "Making Schools Work for Children in Poverty," in *National Issues in Education: Elementary and Secondary Education Act*, eds. John F. Jennings and Institute for Educational Leadership (Washington, DC: Phi Delta Kappa International, 1995), 84. Both Hornbeck and Phyllis McClure, the chair of the independent review panel, testified on ESEA, and Haycock and Hornbeck report they were in close touch with Congress during the development of the bill. Two members of the Commission on Chapter One, Mike Smith and Sharon Robinson, were appointed undersecretary and assistant secretary of education.

67. Mark Pitsch, "E.D. Officials Begin Task of Marketing Their Proposals to Reinvent ESEA," *Education Week*, September 29, 1993.

68. Debray, *Politics, Ideology & Education*, 31.

69. Cross, *Political Education: National Policy Comes of Age*, 112.

70. Lorraine M. McDonnell, "No Child Left Behind and the Federal Role in Education: Evolution or Revolution?" *Peabody Journal of Education* 80, no. 2 (2005), 19–38.

71. Rudalevige, "Forging a Congressional Compromise," 50, n. 28.

72. McGuinn, *No Child Left Behind and the Transformation of Federal Education Policy*, 138–147, argues that the GOP was changing its stance on education between 1996 and 2000, although a number of respondents in his study and others argue that Bush was critical in bringing the Republican Congress to its new stance.

73. Ibid., 170.

74. Quoted in Kevin R. Kosar, *Failing Grades: The Federal Politics of Education Standards* (Boulder, CO: Lynne Rienner, 2005), 189.

75. The transcript for the debate can be found at www.debates.org/pages/trans2000a. html. The above-referenced exchange is in response to moderator Jim Lehrer's question on education.

76. Cross, *Political Education: National Policy Comes of Age*, 131.

77. Rudalevige, "Forging a Congressional Compromise," 38.

78. Quoted in Kosar, *Failing Grades: The Federal Politics of Education Standards*, 189.

79. McGuinn, *No Child Left Behind and the Transformation of Federal Education Policy*, provides evidence for both points. Democrats, being in the minority, were willing to compromise in order to gain some role on the bill, and in this sense it is the broader political shift that explains their participation. But at the same time, McGuinn notes, the mounting evidence that previous reforms were not having the intended effect was also an important influence on their thinking.

80. Citizens' Commission on Civil Rights, Corrinne M. Yu, and William L. Taylor, *Title I in Midstream: The Fight to Improve Schools for Poor Kids* (Washington, DC: Citizens' Commission on Civil Rights, 1999).

81. Clinton officials argued that with a Republican Congress that was pledging to eliminate the Department of Education, moderation in implementation was necessary to preserve the program.

82. Paul Manna, "Leaving No Child Behind," in *Political Education: National Policy Comes of Age*, ed. Christopher T. Cross (New York: Teachers College Press, 2004), 127.

83. Interview with David Shreve, May 2006.

84. Quoted in Kosar, *Failing Grades: The Federal Politics of Education Standards*, 189.

85. Rudalevige, "Forging a Congressional Compromise," 40.

86. Republican Representative Peter Hoekstra of Michigan, quoted in Cross, *Political Education: National Policy Comes of Age*, 129.

87. Interview with David Shreve, May 2006.

88. Initially, Bush had courted the New Democrats, whose proposals were substantively very similar to his own, even going so far as to set up a separate track of

evening negotiations to try to craft a package that would please Republicans and New Democrats. However, Kennedy found out about the negotiations and, not wanting to be left out of a major piece of legislation in his area and already in agreement with the bill's major emphasis on accountability and testing, dealt himself into the process.

89. Interview with Andrew Rotherham, May 2006.

90. Rudalevige, "Forging a Congressional Compromise," 36.

91. Christine Wolfe, director of policy for the undersecretary of the Department of Education in the George W. Bush administration, quoted in McGuinn, *No Child Left Behind and the Transformation of Federal Education Policy*, 142.

92. All quotations in this paragraph are from Richard F. Elmore, *School Reform from the Inside Out: Policy, Practice, and Performance* (Cambridge, MA: Harvard Education Press, 2004), 203.

93. Manna, *School's In*, 209.

94. Frank R. Baumgartner and Bryan D. Jones, *Agendas and Instability in American Politics* (Chicago: University of Chicago Press, 1993), 298.

CHAPTER 9

1. David K. Cohen and Susan L. Moffitt, *The Ordeal of Equality: Did Federal Regulation Fix the Schools?* (Cambridge, MA: Harvard University Press, 2009). More specifically, Cohen and Moffitt argue that federal and state efforts to establish standards and tests without providing high-quality curriculum or teacher training create a disjuncture between the expectations and the means to fulfill those expectations. I return to these arguments in more detail in Chapter Ten.

2. James C. Scott, *Seeing like a State: How Certain Schemes to Improve the Human Condition Have Failed* (New Haven, CT: Yale University Press, 1998).

3. Michael Power, *The Audit Explosion* (London: Demos, 1994). See also Michael Power, "Evaluating the Audit Explosion," *Law & Policy* 25, no. 3 (2003), 185–202; Cris Shore and Susan Wright, "Audit Culture and Anthropology: Neo-Liberalism in British Higher Education," *Journal of the Royal Anthropological Institute* 5, no. 4 (1999), 557–575.

4. Stewart Ranson, "Public Accountability in the Age of Neo-Liberal Governance," *Journal of Education Policy* 18, no. 5 (2003), 459–480.

5. Patricia J. Gumport, "Universities and Knowledge: Restructuring the City of Intellect," in *The Future of the City of Intellect: The Changing American University*, ed. Steven Brint (Stanford, CA: Stanford University Press, 2002), 47–81.

6. Carol S. Dweck, *Mindset: The New Psychology of Success* (New York: Random House, 2006).

7. Abraham H. Maslow, *Motivation and Personality* (New York: Harper, 1954); Carl R. Rogers, *Client-Centered Therapy: Its Current Practice, Implications, and Theory* (Boston: Houghton Mifflin, 1951).

8. We can see this in the use of "principal agent" metaphors, which stem from economics and are consistent with the behaviorist assumptions above.

9. Jean Piaget and Bärbel Inhelder, *The Psychology of the Child* (New York: Basic Books, 1972); Erik H. Erikson, *Childhood and Society* (New York: Norton, 1950).

10. Jack P. Shonkoff et al., *From Neurons to Neighborhoods: The Science of Early Child Development* (Washington, DC: National Academy Press, 2000).

11. Robert Kegan, *The Evolving Self: Problem and Process in Human Development* (Cambridge, MA: Harvard University Press, 1982); Robert Kegan, *In over Our Heads: The Mental Demands of Modern Life* (Cambridge, MA: Harvard University Press, 1994).

12. As Jonathan Supovitz, "Can High Stakes Testing Leverage Educational Improvement? Prospects from the Last Decade of Testing and Accountability Reform," *Journal of Educational Change* 10, nos. 2–3 (2009), 211, puts it in his careful review of a decade's worth of efforts to use high stakes tests to improve system performance: "Research on these trends indicates that high stakes testing does motivate teachers and administrators to change their practices, yet the changes they motivate tend to be more superficial adjustments in content coverage and test preparation activities rather than promoting deeper improvements in instructional practice."

13. Samuel Freedman, "Parting Liberal Waters over No Child Left Behind," *New York Times*, January 4, 2006.

14. See Economic Policy Institute, "A Broader, Bolder Approach to Education," www.epi.org/files/2011/bold_approach_full_statement-3.pdf (accessed June 17, 2012).

15. Ibid.

16. Jonathan Kozol, *The Shame of the Nation: The Restoration of Apartheid Schooling in America* (New York: Crown, 2005).

17. Ibid.

18. Ibid.

19. Douglas N. Harris, "High-Flying Schools, Student Disadvantage, and the Logic of NCLB," *American Journal of Education* 113, no. 3 (2007), 367–394.

20. Wendy Kopp, speaking at the Askwith Forum, Harvard Graduate School of Education, November 3, 2008.

21. Jeffrey R. Henig and Paul Reville, "Addressing Non-School Factors in the Framing and Practice of Education Reform" (unpublished paper, "The Futures of School Reform Initiative," Harvard Graduate School of Education, February 2011).

22. Linda Perlstein, *Tested: One American School Struggles to Make the Grade* (New York: Holt, 2007).

23. See my discussion of Perlstein's book in Jal Mehta, "Standard Error," *American Prospect* 18, no. 11 (October 22, 2007).

24. AFT leader Albert Shanker and Ted Sizer are perhaps the only people with national prominence who sought to make such a case; unfortunately, their voices have not been heeded in recent years.

CHAPTER 10

1. OECD, "Strong Performers and Successful Reformers in Education: Lessons from PISA for the United States," OECD Publishing (2010), www.oecd.org/dataoecd/32/50/46623978.pdf (accessed June 17, 2012).

2. Brian Rowan, "Chapter 7: Commitment and Control: Alternative Strategies for the Organizational Design of Schools," *Review of Research in Education* 16, no. 1 (1990), 354.

3. On the difference between bureaucratic and professional modes of organization, I draw largely on Henry Mintzberg, *Structure in Fives: Designing Effective Organizations* (Englewood Cliffs, NJ: Prentice Hall, 1993), ch. 10. There is also a literature on what it means to be expert in a field; it informs my discussion here. See Michelene Chi, Robert Glaser, and M. J. Farr, eds., *The Nature of Expertise* (Hillsdale, NJ: Erlbaum, 1988); James Cimino, "Development of Expertise in Medical Practice," in *Tacit Knowledge in Professional Practice*, eds. Robert Sternberg and Joseph Horvath (Mahwah, NJ: Erlbaum, 1999) 101–119, Carol Livingston and Hilda Borko, "Expert-Novice Differences in Teaching: A Cognitive Analysis and Implications for Teacher Education," *Journal of Teacher Education* 40 (1989): 36–42.

4. The idea of dividing work up into these four components emerged out of discussions in "The Futures of School Reform," a national group of leading scholars, policymakers, and practitioners convened by the Harvard Graduate School of Education between 2009 and 2012. See Jal Mehta, Robert Schwartz, and Frederick Hess, eds., *The Futures of School Reform* (Cambridge, MA: Harvard Education Press, 2012).

5. On university-developed knowledge being only orthogonally relevant to practice, see Sheri H. Ranis, "Blending Quality and Utility: Lessons Learned from the Education Research Debates," in *Education Research on Trial: Policy Reform and the Call for Scientific Rigor*, eds. Pamela B. Walters, Annette Lareau, and Sheri H. Ranis (New York: Routledge, 2009), 125–142; Anthony S. Bryk and Louis M. Gomez, "Reinventing a Research and Development Capacity," in *The Future of Educational Entrepreneurship: Possibilities for School Reform*, ed. Frederick M. Hess (Cambridge, MA: Harvard Education Press, 2008), 181–206; on the problems with implementation logic, see Jeffrey L. Pressman, Aaron B. Wildavsky and Oakland Project, *Implementation: How Great Expectations in Washington Are Dashed in Oakland; or, Why It's Amazing That Federal Programs Work at All, This Being a Saga of the Economic Development Administration As Told by Two Sympathetic Observers Who Seek to Build Morals on a Foundation of Ruined Hopes* (Berkeley: University of California Press, 1973), and more recently, Richard F. Elmore, *School Reform from the Inside Out: Policy, Practice, and Performance* (Cambridge, MA: Harvard Education Press, 2004). Note that the critique here is more fundamental than the idea that research is not properly "translated" into language usable by practitioners; instead, it argues that the knowledge itself is often not well suited to purposes of practice.

6. Donald E. Stokes, *Pasteur's Quadrant: Basic Science and Technological Innovation* (Washington, DC: Brookings Institution Press, 1997).

7. James Hiebert, Ronald Gallimore, and James W. Stigler, "A Knowledge Base for the Teaching Profession: What Would It Look like and How Can We Get One?" *Educational Researcher* 31, no. 5 (2002), 3–15. They have suggested that in the long run it might be possible to have knowledge at the level of specificity of the lesson. They argue that knowledge about "how best to teach Billy Goats Gruff" is much more useful to a teacher than is more general research knowledge about teaching stories. This level of detail would almost certainly be more likely to be developed by practitioners than researchers.

8. CCSR has since 1992 worked to develop a body of research that directly serves the school reform community, improving the capacity of districts to "use data, build effective strategies, and evaluate progress" (Melissa Roderick, John Q. Easton, and Penny Bender Sebring, "The Consortium on Chicago School Research: A New Model for the Role of Research in Supporting Urban School Reform," University of Chicago Urban Education Institute, http://ccsr.uchicago.edu/sites/default/files/publications/CCSR%20Model%20Report-final.pdf [accessed June 17, 2012]). For example, in 2005, CCSR began work with the Chicago Public Schools (CPS) around high school dropouts and retention. CCSR data on the patterns of which students dropped out and when helped principals design targeted intervention and credit-recovery programs for struggling students. The idea behind the CCSR work is to use data to encourage practitioner-driven solutions.

9. The Center for Education Policy Research Strategic Data Project embeds analytic experts for two years in school districts, state education agencies, and charter networks. These analysts seek to use data to help districts and schools make better decisions with respect to policies affecting student achievement, identification of quality teachers, and resource allocation. There is more information at www.gse.harvard.edu/~pfpie/index.php/sdp/.

10. For more information, see www.serpinstitute.org.

11. There is already a movement afoot in this direction—witness the spread of professional learning communities: Milbrey W. McLaughlin and Joan E. Talbert, *Building School-Based Teacher Learning Communities: Professional Strategies to Improve Student Achievement* (New York: Teachers College Press, 2006); Richard DuFour, "Professional Learning Communities: A Bandwagon, an Idea Worth Considering, or Our Best Hope for High Levels of Learning?," *Middle School Journal* 39, no. 1 (2007), 4–8. But even this does not go far enough—these groups are still often about discussing knowledge developed by others. The goal here should be for teachers to *identify* problems of practice (diagnostic skills being an essential characteristic of professions) and *develop* knowledge that would allow them to address these problems.

12. The Park program, called FACA (The F. Parvin Sharpless Faculty and Curricular Advancement Program), an endowed program established in 1989, is designed to

address issues of practice and to provide professional development opportunities for teachers. Approximately 40 percent of faculty participate annually in summer projects selected through a comprehensive review process. Contrary to most professional development models, FACA is a bottom-up, voluntary program, with all projects proposed and chaired by teachers. For more information, see www.parkschool.net/about/index.cfm?type=list&objectid=224.

13. The Brookline High School 21st Century Fund, formed in 1998, is used to support teacher-developed ideas for improvement. The fund has invested $3 million to support the development of 14 initiatives designed both to support the school's improvement and to serve as a model for other public high schools. Current programs include Academy of Global Leadership, African American Scholars Program, Arts Infusion, BHS Writers, and the Ithaka Project. Six programs developed through the fund have been integrated within the school, and some have been utilized elsewhere as well. There is more information at www.bhs21stcenturyfund. org.

14. Anthony S. Bryk, Louis M. Gomez, and Alicia Grunow, "Getting Ideas into Action: Building Networked Improvement Communities in Education," Carnegie Foundation for the Advancement of Teaching, www.carnegiefoundation.org/sites/ default/files/bryk-gomez_building-nics-education.pdf (accessed June 15, 2012).

15. High Tech High (HTH), founded in 2000, is a network of 11 public charter schools in the San Diego area serving 3,500 students. In 2007 it opened the HTH Graduate School of Education, which offers master's degrees with concentrations in School Leadership and Teacher Leadership. There is more information at www.hightechhigh.org.

16. Michael Barber and Mona Mourshed, "How the World's Best-Performing School Systems Come Out on Top," McKinsey & Company, http://mckinseyonsociety. com/downloads/reports/Education/Worlds_School_Systems_Final.pdf (accessed June 15, 2012).

17. Byron Auguste, Paul Kihn, and Matt Miller, "Closing the Talent Gap: Attracting and Retaining Top Third Graduates to a Career in Teaching," http://mckinseyonsociety.com/downloads/reports/Education/Closing_the_talent_gap.pdf (accessed June 15, 2012). See also Frederick M. Hess, *Common Sense School Reform* (New York: Palgrave Macmillan, 2004), 103; New Commission on the Skills of the American Workforce, *Tough Choices or Tough Times: The Report of the New Commission on the Skills of the American Workforce—Executive Summary*, 1st ed. (San Francisco: Wiley, 2007), 9.

18. Andrew Rotherham, private communication, March 2011.

19. For the most systematic take on the human capital question, see Rachel E. Curtis and Judy Wurtzel, *Teaching Talent: A Visionary Framework for Human Capital in Education* (Cambridge, MA: Harvard Education Press, 2010); the issue is also explored in interesting ways in Daniel Goldhaber and Jane Hannaway, *Creating a New Teaching Profession* (Washington, DC: Urban Institute Press, 2009).

20. Auguste, Kihn, and Miller, *Closing the Talent Gap*.

21. Nicolas Kristof, "Pay Teachers More," *New York Times*, March 12, 2011.

22. Auguste, Kihn, and Miller, *Closing the Talent Gap*, 38. Of course, this assumes that it is feasible politically to pay teachers in high-needs schools more than elsewhere in the state.

23. Pamela L. Grossman and Susanna Loeb, *Alternative Routes to Teaching: Mapping the New Landscape of Teacher Education* (Cambridge, MA: Harvard Education Press, 2008), 242; Robert Gordon, Thomas J. Kane, and Douglas O. Staiger, "Identifying Effective Teachers Using Performance on the Job: Discussion Paper 2006–01," www.brookings.edu/research/papers/2006/04/~/media/Research/Files/Papers/2006/4/education%20gordon/200604hamilton_1.PDF (accessed June 17, 2012).

24. While many alternative programs offer preservice workshops, summer institutes or certificates, the in-service training and support hours far exceed the preservice requirements. For more information, see Donald Boyd et al., "How Changes in Entry Requirements Alter the Teacher Workforce and Affect Student Achievement," www.teacherpolicyresearch.org/portals/1/pdfs/how_changes_in_entry_requirements_alter_the_teacher_workforce.pdf (accessed June 15, 2012); C. Emily Feistritzer, *The Making of a Teacher: A Report on Teacher Preparation in the U.S.* (Washington, DC: Center for Education Information, 1999), 94; Goldhaber and Hannaway, *Creating a New Teaching Profession*; Daniel C. Humphrey and Marjorie E. Wechsler, "Insights into Alternative Certification: Initial Findings from a National Study," *Teachers College Record* 109, no. 3 (2007), 483–530.

25. On revised standards for teacher preparation programs, see NCATE Blue Ribbon Panel on Clinical Preparation and Partnerships for Improved Student Learning, "Transforming Teacher Education through Clinical Practice: A National Strategy to Prepare Effective Teachers," NCATE, www.ncate.org/LinkClick.aspx?filetick et=zzeiB1OoqPk%3D&tabid=715 (accessed June 17, 2012). On feedback within TFA, see Donna Foote, *Relentless Pursuit: A Year in the Trenches with Teach for America* (New York: Knopf, 2008), 338. On teacher residencies, see Jesse Solomon, "The Boston Teacher Residency: District-Based Teacher Education," *Journal of Teacher Education* 60, no. 5 (2009), 478–488.

26. The Iowa Writing Project offers summer institutes and programs for K–College participating teachers. The workshops are taught by field practitioners, district staff, and education area experts. There is more information at www.uni.edu/continuinged/iwp/.

27. Robert Schwartz, Mindy Hernandez and Jane Ngo, "Attracting and Retaining Strong Teachers," in *Teaching Talent: A Visionary Framework for Human Capital in Education*, eds. Rachel E. Curtis and Judy Wurtzel (Cambridge, MA: Harvard Education Press, 2010).

28. John B. Diamond and James P. Spillane, *Distributed Leadership in Practice* (New York: Teachers College, Columbia University, 2007), 193. For additional research

on distributed leadership, see Northwestern University's Distributed Leadership Study, www.distributedleadership.org.

29. One example of how to do this is through the Peer Assistance and Review (PAR) program. Originally developed thirty years ago in Toledo, Ohio, PAR is an intervention through which teachers both support and assess their colleagues' performance. PAR programs generally include a mentoring component, whereby consulting (veteran) teachers assist novice teachers, as well as an intervention program that can lead to dismissal for underperforming teachers (John P. Papay et al., "Beyond Dollars and Cents: The Costs and Benefits of Teacher Peer Assistance and Review," Project on the Next Generation of Teachers, www.gse.harvard.edu/~ngt/new_papers/JPP_AERA_2009.pdf [accessed June 17, 2012]; Daniel Weisberg et al., *The Widget Effect: Our National Failure to Acknowledge and Act on Differences in Teacher Effectiveness* [New Teacher Project, 2009], http://widgeteffect.org/downloads/TheWidgetEffect.pdf).

30. The freedom to exchange ideas on instructional practice, offer peer feedback, and build strong professional relationships has been found to be important to teacher retention (Thomas R. Guskey, "Professional Development and Teacher Change," *Teachers and Teaching* 8, no. 3 [2002], 381–391; Susan Moore Johnson, *Teachers at Work: Achieving Success in our Schools* [New York: Basic Books, 1990]; Edgar H. Schein, *Organizational Culture and Leadership* [San Francisco: Jossey-Bass, 1985]).

31. See Judith A. Luce, "Career Ladders: Modifying Teachers' Work to Sustain Motivation," *Education* 119, no. 1 (1998).

32. Elizabeth A. City et al., *Instructional Rounds in Education: A Network Approach to Improving Teaching and Learning* (Cambridge, MA: Harvard Education Press, 2009).

33. The seven-step Data Wise cycle of "prepare-inquire-act," is one example of this vision applied to education (Kathryn Parker Boudett, Elizabeth A. City, and Richard J. Murnane, *Data Wise: A Step-by-Step Guide to Using Assessment Results to Improve Teaching and Learning* [Cambridge, MA: Harvard Education Press, 2005]).

34. John Dewey, *How We Think: A Restatement of the Relation of Reflective Thinking to the Educative Process* (Boston: Heath, 1933).

35. Joan Talbert, "Collaborative Inquiry to Expand Student Success in New York City Schools," in *Education Reform in New York City: Ambitious Change in the Nation's Most Complex School System*, eds. Jennifer A. O'Day, Catherine S. Bitter, and Louis M. Gomez (Cambridge, MA: Harvard Education Press, 2011), 131–155.

36. See Boudett, City and Murnane, *Data Wise*, for examples.

37. Andy Hargreaves, *Changing Teachers, Changing Times: Teachers' Work and Culture in the Postmodern Age* (New York: Teachers College Press, 1994), writing about Dan C. Lortie, *Schoolteacher: A Sociological Study* (Chicago: University of Chicago Press, 1975). See also Susan J. Rosenholtz, *Teachers' Workplace: The Social Organization of Schools* (White Plains, NY: Longman, 1989).

38. Theodore R. Sizer, *Horace's Compromise: The Dilemma of the American High School* (Boston: Houghton Mifflin, 1984).

39. The Sherman Oak Community Charter School in San Jose, California, for example, offers 90 minutes of daily professional development, which teachers can use to analyze student work, review or revise lesson plans, or discuss curriculum. In addition to access to cross-disciplinary teams and common planning time, teachers have space for reflective practices and are also encouraged to attend conferences and external training. Extended-learning-time schools frequently use the extra time not only to increase students' learning time but also to provide teachers more common and personal planning time (David A. Farbman, "Tracking an Emerging Movement: A Report on Expanded-Time Schools in America," *Education Digest: Essential Readings Condensed for Quick Review* 75, no. 6 [2010], 17–19; Melissa Lazarin and Isabel Owen, "Union and District Partnerships to Expand Learning Time: Three Schools' Experiences," Center for American Progress, www.americanprogress.org/issues/2009/11/pdf/elt_union_districts.pdf [accessed June 17, 2012]).

40. Robert B. Schwartz, Ben Levin, and Adam Gamoran, "Lessons from Abroad," *Education Week*, April 6, 2011.

41. Robert Joseph Schaefer, *The School as a Center of Inquiry* (New York: Harper & Row, 1967), 64.

42. Paul Hill, "Recovering from an Accident: Repairing Governance with Comparative Advantage," in *Who's in Charge Here? The Tangled Web of School Governance and Policy*, ed. Noel Epstein (Washington, DC: Brookings Institution Press, 2004), 75–103.

43. As with any other set of reforms, portfolio districts have had their challenges as well as their successes. For a balanced recent appraisal, see Katrina E. Bulkley, Jeffrey R. Henig, and Henry M. Levin, *Between Public and Private: Politics, Governance, and the New Portfolio Models for Urban School Reform* (Cambridge, MA: Harvard Education Press, 2010).

44. John Easton, "Five Big Ideas for IES: Speech at the American Association of Colleges for Teacher Education (AACTE)," http://ies.ed.gov/director/pdf/easton022010.pdf (accessed June 17, 2012).

45. Charles M. Payne, *So Much Reform, So Little Change: The Persistence of Failure in Urban Schools* (Cambridge, MA: Harvard Education Press, 2008).

46. On effective schools, see Stewart C. Purkey and Marshall S. Smith, "Effective Schools: A Review," *Elementary School Journal* 83 (1983), 426–452; on Catholic schools, see Anthony S. Bryk, Valerie E. Lee, and Peter Blakeley Holland, *Catholic Schools and the Common Good* (Cambridge, MA: Harvard University Press, 1993); on high-performing charter schools, see David Whitman, *Sweating the Small Stuff: Inner-City Schools and the New Paternalism* (Washington, DC: Thomas B. Fordham Institute, 2008).

47. Jennifer A. O'Day and Catherine S. Bitter, "Improving Instruction in New York City: An Evolving Approach," in *Education Reform in New York City: Ambitious*

*Change in the Nation's Most Complex School System*, eds. Jennifer A. O'Day, Catherine S. Bitter, and Louis M. Gomez (Cambridge, MA: Harvard Education Press, 2011), 109–130.

48. Catherine Gewertz, "Common-Assessment Consortia Expand Plans: Extra Federal Funds Will Go toward Curricula, Teacher Training," *Education Week*, February 23, 2011.

49. Bryk and Gomez, "Reinventing a Research and Development Capacity."

50. See Richard Rothstein, Rebecca Jacobsen, and Tamara Wilder, *Grading Education: Getting Accountability Right* (Washington, DC: Economic Policy Institute; New York: Teachers College Press, 2008). The US higher education accreditation system also illustrates this point (see www.chea.org).

51. Two examples of this kind of relationship are Ontario, Canada, and Victoria, Australia. On Ontario, see Benjamin Levin, *How to Change 5000 Schools: A Practical and Positive Approach for Leading Change at Every Level* (Cambridge, MA: Harvard Education Press, 2008), and on Victoria, see Peter Matthews, Hunter Moorman and Deborah Nusche, "School Leadership Development Strategies: Building Leadership Capacity in Victoria, Australia," OECD Directorate for Education, www.oecd.org/dataoecd/27/22/39883476.pdf (accessed June 17, 2012).

52. The teaching part of the TFA mission faces these constraints. The second part of the TFA mission, to create alumni who will become leaders in the sector, has been remarkably successful and influential, in part because its leaders have sought to take control of the various parts of the school reform puzzle. I discuss this in the pages to come.

53. Foote, *Relentless Pursuit*.

54. Monica Higgins et al., "Creating a Corps of Change Agents: What Explains the Success of Teach for America?" *Education Next* 11, no. 3 (2011), 18–25.

55. Diane Ravitch, *The Death and Life of the Great American School System: How Testing and Choice Are Undermining Education* (New York: Basic Books, 2010).

56. See Donald J. Peurach, "Designing and Managing Comprehensive School Reform: The Case of Success for all" (PhD diss., University of Michigan) for an excellent discussion of the complexity of managing these processes in comprehensive school reform networks.

57. Pedro A. Noguera, "A Critical Response to Michael Fullan's 'The Future of Educational Change: System Thinkers in Action,'" *Journal of Educational Change* 7, no. 3 (2006), 130.

58. Anthony Braga and Christopher Winship, "Partnership, Accountability and Innovation: Clarifying Boston's Experience with Pulling Levers," in *Police Innovation: Contrasting Perspectives*, eds. David Weisburd and Anthony Allan Braga (New York: Cambridge University Press, 2006).

59. Joy Dryfoos, "Full-Service Community Schools: Creating New Institutions," *Phi Delta Kappan* 83, no. 5 (2002), 393. One example of community schools is the Children's Aid Society (CAS), which exemplifies a model of shared accountability.

The CAS community schools have partnerships between principals and teachers, the education coordinator who manages out-of-school time services on the school premises, and the supplemental providers who bring academic and enrichment programs, social and health services, and family support into the schools. While each staff person plays a specialized role (e.g., teacher, nurse, dentist, family coordinator, homework tutor), school day and out-of-school time supports are aligned to meet the schools' goals and the district's academic standards. The collaboration has been linked to positive student outcomes, including higher student achievement, increased parental involvement, higher school attendance, improved school climate, and positive mental and physical health outcomes.

60. Ibid.

61. Will Dobbie and Roland G. Fryer Jr., "Are High-Quality Schools Enough to Close the Achievement Gap? Evidence from a Bold Social Experiment in Harlem," www.economics.harvard.edu/faculty/fryer/files/hcz%204.15.2009.pdf (accessed June 17, 2012).

62. Grover J. Whitehurst, Michelle Croft, and Brookings Institution, *The Harlem Children's Zone, Promise Neighborhoods, and the Broader, Bolder Approach to Education* (Washington, DC: Brookings Institution, 2010).

63. Richard Rothstein, *Class and Schools: Using Social, Economic, and Educational Reform to Close the Black-White Achievement Gap* (Washington, DC: Economic Policy Institute, 2004).

64. Schaefer, *The School as a Center of Inquiry.*

65. Hendrik Gideonse, "Organizing Schools to Encourage Teacher Inquiry," in *Restructuring Schools: The Next Generation of Educational Reform*, eds. Richard F. Elmore and Center for Policy Research in Education (San Francisco: Jossey-Bass, 1990), 97–124.

66. Richard F. Elmore, "Conclusion: Towards a Transformation of Public Schooling," in *Restructuring Schools: The Next Generation of Educational Reform*, eds. Richard F. Elmore and Center for Policy Research in Education (San Francisco: Jossey-Bass, 1990), 289–297.

### A NOTE ON METHODS

1. James Mahoney, "Nominal, Ordinal, and Narrative Appraisal in Macrocausal Analysis," *American Journal of Sociology* 104, no. 4 (1999), 1154–1196.

2. Stanley Lieberson, "Small N's and Big Conclusions: An Examination of the Reasoning in Comparative Studies Based on a Small Number of Cases," *Social Forces* 70, no. 2 (1991), 307–320.

3. On the second face of power, see Peter Bachrach and Morton S. Baratz, "Two Faces of Power," *American Political Science Review* 56, no. 4 (1962), 947–952; on the third face of power, see Steven Lukes, *Power: A Radical View* (London: Macmillan, 1974).

4. The other obvious difference between the fields is that higher education has market accountability through choice, while primary and secondary education does not. I use process tracing to examine the reasons why movements toward accountability in higher education have been weaker and find that reformers' discussion of higher education is more deferential to the professional power of its practitioners. This disparity indicates that it is professional power and not greater choice that has been the key factor in warding off claims of external accountability in higher education.

5. One obvious response to this question is simply to argue that a diffusion process is at work. I argue that this explanation is insufficient. Diffusion may explain why standards-based reform is on the agenda in different states, but it does little to explain why it was passed by the legislatures. See Andrew Karch, "Democratic Laboratories: The Politics of Innovation in the American States" (PhD diss., Harvard University, 2003), for an excellent discussion of the various stages in the diffusion process.

6. While the caveats about generalization from a limited number of cases apply, I have done my best to maximize the variation in the cases that could potentially influence the outcomes. Future research might examine the model that I derive from the study of these states using a Boolean analysis (Charles C. Ragin, *Fuzzy-Set Social Science* [Chicago: University of Chicago Press, 2000]) to evaluate whether the alternative pathways I identify are broadly representative of the nation as a whole.

7. Brown University holds the papers for *A Nation at Risk* because the lead staffer on the project, Clifford Adelman, is a Brown graduate and donated the papers to the university. Unpublished drafts of *A Nation at Risk* are not currently available to researchers, although I draw on a partial summary published in *Education Week*. Brown does have the early drafts of another report, *Involvement in Learning*, which sought to apply the thinking behind *A Nation at Risk* to higher education; I draw on this report extensively in Chapter Six.

8. Robert K. Yin, *Case Study Research: Design and Methods* (Thousand Oaks, CA: Sage, 1994); Wendy D. Roth and Jal D. Mehta, "The Rashomon Effect: Combining Positivist and Interpretivist Approaches in the Analysis of Contested Events," *Sociological Methods & Research* 31, no. 2 (2002), 131–173.

# Bibliography

Abbott, Andrew. *The System of Professions: An Essay on the Division of Expert Labor.* Chicago: University of Chicago Press, 1988.

Abella, Alex. *Soldiers of Reason: The Rand Corporation and the Rise of the American Empire.* Orlando, FL: Harcourt, 2008.

Angus, David. "Professionalism and the Public Good: A Brief History of Teacher Certification." Thomas Fordham Foundation, 2001. www.edexcellencemedia.net/publications/2001/200101_professionalismandpublicgood/angus.pdf.

Arasim, Liz. *School Accreditation: An Overview.* Lansing, MI: Senate Fiscal Agency, 2000.

Auguste, Byron, Paul Kihn, and Matt Miller. "Closing the Talent Gap: Attracting and Retaining Top Third Graduates to a Career in Teaching." Accessed June 15, 2012, http://mckinseyonsociety.com/downloads/reports/Education/Closing_the_talent_gap.pdf.

Ayres, Leonard. *Laggards in Our Schools: A Study of Retardation and Elimination in City School Systems.* Russell Sage Foundation. New York: Charities Publication Committee, 1909.

Bachrach, Peter, and Morton S. Baratz. "Two Faces of Power." *American Political Science Review* 56, no. 4 (1962): 947–952.

Barber, Michael, and Mona Mourshed. "How the World's Best-Performing School Systems Come Out on Top." McKinsey, accessed June 15, 2012, http://mckinseyonsociety.com/downloads/reports/Education/Worlds_School_Systems_Final.pdf.

Baumgartner, Frank R., and Bryan D. Jones. *Agendas and Instability in American Politics.* American Politics and Political Economy Series. Chicago: University of Chicago Press, 1993.

Béland, Daniel. "Ideas and Social Policy: An Institutionalist Perspective." *Social Policy & Administration* 39, no. 1 (2005): 1–18.

Béland, Daniel, and Robert Henry Cox. *Ideas and Politics in Social Science Research.* New York: Oxford University Press, 2011.

Bell, Daniel. *The Coming of Post-industrial Society: A Venture in Social Forecasting.* New York: Basic Books, 1973.

Bell, Terrel. *The Thirteenth Man: A Reagan Cabinet Memoir.* New York: Free Press; London: Collier Macmillan, 1988.

Berliner, David C., and Bruce J. Biddle. *The Manufactured Crisis: Myths, Fraud, and the Attack on America's Public Schools.* Reading, MA: Addison-Wesley, 1995.

Berman, Barbara. "Business Efficiency, American Schooling, and the Public School Superintendency: A Reconsideration of the Callahan Thesis." *History of Education Quarterly* 23, no. 3 (1983): 297–321.

Berman, Sheri. *The Social Democratic Moment: Ideas and Politics in the Making of Interwar Europe.* Cambridge, MA: Harvard University Press, 1998.

Berube, Maurice R., and Marilyn Gittell. *Confrontation at Ocean Hill–Brownsville: The New York School Strikes of 1968.* New York: Praeger, 1969.

Blyth, Mark. *Great Transformations: Economic Ideas and Institutional Change in the Twentieth Century.* New York: Cambridge University Press, 2002.

Board of Inquiry Project and National Coalition of Advocates for Students. *Barriers to Excellence: Our Children at Risk.* Boston: National Coalition of Advocates for Students, 1985.

Boudett, Kathryn Parker, Elizabeth A. City, and Richard J. Murnane. *Data Wise: A Step-by-Step Guide to Using Assessment Results to Improve Teaching and Learning.* Cambridge, MA: Harvard Education Press, 2005.

Bourdieu, Pierre. "The Political Field, the Social Science Field, and the Journalist Field." In *Bourdieu and the Journalistic Field*, edited by Rodney Dean Benson and Erik Neveu. Cambridge, MA: Polity, 2005.

Bourdieu, Pierre, and Loïc J. D. Wacquant. *An Invitation to Reflexive Sociology.* Chicago: University of Chicago Press, 1992.

Bowers, C. A. "Accountability from a Humanist Point of View." In *Accountability in American Education*, edited by Frank J. Sciara and Richard K. Jantz, 25–32. Boston: Allyn and Bacon, 1972.

Boyd, Donald, Pamela Grossman, Hamilton Lankford, Susanna Loeb, and James Wyckoff. "How Changes in Entry Requirements Alter the Teacher Workforce and Affect Student Achievement." *Education Finance and Policy* 1, no. 2 (2006): 176–216.

Boyd, William. "Balancing Control and Autonomy in School Reform: The Politics of Perestroika." In *The Educational Reform Movement of the 1980s: Perspectives and Cases*, edited by Joseph Murphy, 85–96. Berkeley, CA: McCutchan, 1990.

Boyd, William, and Charles Kerchner, eds. *The Politics of Excellence and Choice in Education: 1987 Yearbook of the Politics of Education Association.* New York: Falmer Press, 1988.

Boyd, William, David Plank, and Gary Sykes. "Teachers Unions in Hard Times." In *Conflicting Missions? Teachers Unions and Educational Reform*, edited by Tom Loveless, 174–210. Washington, DC: Brookings Institution Press, 2000.

Boyer, Ernest L., and Carnegie Foundation for the Advancement of Teaching. *High School: A Report on Secondary Education in America*. New York: Harper & Row, 1983.

Braga, Anthony, and Christopher Winship. "Partnership, Accountability and Innovation: Clarifying Boston's Experience with Pulling Levers." In *Police Innovation: Contrasting Perspectives*, edited by David Weisburd and Anthony Allan Braga. New York: Cambridge University Press, 2006.

Brint, Steven. *In an Age of Experts: The Changing Role of Professionals in Politics and Public Life*. Princeton, NJ: Princeton University Press, 1994.

Browder, Lesley. *Emerging Patterns of Administrative Accountability*. Berkeley, CA: McCutchan, 1971.

Browder, Lesley, and Cooperative Accountability Project. *Who's Afraid of Educational Accountability? A Representative Review of the Literature*. Denver: Cooperative Accountability Project, 1975.

Bryk, Anthony S., and Louis M. Gomez. "Reinventing a Research and Development Capacity." In *The Future of Educational Entrepreneurship: Possibilities for School Reform*, edited by Frederick M Hess, 181–206. Cambridge, MA: Harvard Education Press, 2008.

Bryk, Anthony S., Louis M. Gomez, and Alicia Grunow. "Getting Ideas into Action: Building Networked Improvement Communities in Education." Carnegie Foundation for the Advancement of Teaching, 2011. Accessed June 15, 2012, www. carnegiefoundation.org/sites/default/files/bryk-gomez_building-nics-education. pdf.

Bryk, Anthony S., Valerie E. Lee, and Peter Blakeley Holland. *Catholic Schools and the Common Good*. Cambridge, MA: Harvard University Press, 1993.

Bulkley, Katrina, Jeffrey Henig, and Henry Levin. *Between Public and Private: Politics, Governance, and the New Portfolio Models for Urban School Reform*. Cambridge, MA: Harvard Education Press, 2010.

Callahan, Raymond. *Education and the Cult of Efficiency: A Study of the Social Forces That Have Shaped the Administration of the Public Schools*. Chicago: University of Chicago Press, 1962.

Campbell, Andrea. *How Policies Make Citizens: Senior Political Activism and the American Welfare State*. Princeton, NJ: Princeton University Press, 2003.

Campbell, John. "Ideas, Politics, and Public Policy." *Annual Review of Sociology* 28, no. 1 (2002): 21–38.

Carnegie Forum on Education and the Economy. Task Force on Teaching as a Profession. *A Nation Prepared: Teachers for the 21st Century: The Report of the Task Force on Teaching as a Profession*. Washington, DC: The Forum, 1986.

Chase, Bob. "Teacher Unionism: Bob Chase Defends His Views." *Rethinking Schools* 11, no. 4 (1997), www.rethinkingschools.org/special_reports/union/chasltr.shtml.

Chi, Micheline T. H., Robert Glaser, and Marshall J. Farr, eds. *The Nature of Expertise*. Hillsdale, NJ: Erlbaum, 1988.

Chubb, John E., and Terry M. Moe. *Politics, Markets, and America's Schools*. Washington, DC: Brookings Institution, 1990.

Cibulka, James. "The NEA and School Choice." In *Conflicting Missions? Teachers Unions and Educational Reform*, edited by Tom Loveless, 150–173. Washington, DC: Brookings Institution Press, 2000.

Cimino, James. "Development of Expertise in Medical Practice." In *Tacit Knowledge in Professional Practice: Researcher and Practitioner Perspectives*, edited by Robert J. Sternberg and Joseph A. Horvath, 101–119. Mahwah, NJ: Erlbaum, 1999.

Citizens' Commission on Civil Rights. *Title I in Midstream: The Fight to Improve Schools for Poor Kids*. Washington, DC: Citizens' Commission on Civil Rights, 1999.

City, Elizabeth, Richard Elmore, Sarah Fiarman, and Lee Teitel. *Instructional Rounds in Education: A Network Approach to Improving Teaching and Learning*. Cambridge, MA: Harvard Education Press, 2009.

Clifford, Geraldine Jonçich, and James W. Guthrie. *Ed School: A Brief for Professional Education*. Chicago: University of Chicago Press, 1988.

Clinton, Bill, and Albert Gore. *Putting People First: How We Can All Change America*. New York: Times Books, 1992.

Cobb, Roger, and Charles Elder. *Participation in American Politics: The Dynamics of Agenda-Building*. Boston: Allyn and Bacon, 1972.

Cochran-Smith, Marilyn. "Reforming Teacher Education." *Journal of Teacher Education* 52, no. 4 (2001): 263–265.

———. "Teacher Education and the Outcomes Trap." *Journal of Teacher Education* 56, no. 5 (2005): 411–417.

Cochran-Smith, Marilyn, and Mary Kim Fries. "Sticks, Stones, and Ideology: The Discourse of Reform in Teacher Education." *Educational Researcher* 30, no. 8 (2001): 3–15.

Cohen, David K. *Teaching and Its Predicaments*. Cambridge, MA: Harvard University Press, 2011.

Cohen, David K., and Susan L. Moffitt. *The Ordeal of Equality: Did Federal Regulation Fix the Schools?* Cambridge, MA: Harvard University Press, 2009.

Cohen, Lizabeth. *A Consumers' Republic: The Politics of Mass Consumption in Postwar America*. New York: Knopf, 2003.

Coleman, James S. "The Evaluation of Equality of Educational Opportunity." In *On Equality of Educational Opportunity*, edited by Frederick Mosteller and Daniel P. Moynihan. New York: Random House, 1972.

College Entrance Examination Board. Advisory Panel on the Scholastic Aptitude Test Score Decline. *On Further Examination: Report of the Advisory Panel on the Scholastic Aptitude Test Score Decline*. New York: College Entrance Examination Board, 1977.

Cooper, Bruce, and Marie-Elena Liotta. "Urban Teachers Unions Face Their Future." *Education and Urban Society* 34, no. 1 (2001): 101–118.

Counts, George. *Dare the School Build a New Social Order?* John Day Pamphlets, vol. 11. New York: John Day, 1932.

Cremin, Lawrence. *The Transformation of the School: Progressivism in American Education, 1876–1957*. New York: Knopf, 1961.

Cross, Christopher. *Political Education: National Policy Comes of Age*. New York: Teachers College Press, 2004.

Cuban, Lawrence. *How Teachers Taught: Constancy and Change in American Classrooms, 1890–1990*. New York: Teachers College Press, 1993.

Cubberley, Ellwood. *Public School Administration: A Statement of the Fundamental Principles Underlying the Organization and Administration of Public Education*. New York: Houghton Mifflin, 1916.

Curtis, Rachel, and Judy Wurtzel. *Teaching Talent: A Visionary Framework for Human Capital in Education*. Cambridge, MA: Harvard Education Press, 2010.

Darling-Hammond, Linda. "Reforming Teacher Preparation and Licensing: Debating the Evidence." *Teachers College Record* 102, no. 1 (2000): 28–56.

Darling-Hammond, Linda, and John Bransford. *Preparing Teachers for a Changing World: What Teachers Should Learn and Be Able to Do*. San Francisco: Jossey-Bass, 2005.

Darling-Hammond, Linda, Deborah J. Holtzman, Su Jin Gatlin, and Julian Vasquez Heilig. "Does Teacher Preparation Matter? Evidence about Teacher Certification, Teach for America, and Teacher Effectiveness." *Education Policy Analysis Archives* 13, no. 42 (October 12, 2005): 1–48.

Debray, Elizabeth. *Politics, Ideology & Education: Federal Policy during the Clinton and Bush Administrations*. New York: Teachers College Press, 2006.

De Leon, Anne Grosso. "After 20 Years of Educational Reform, Progress, but Plenty of Unfinished Business." *Carnegie Results: Quarterly Newsletter by Carnegie Corporation of New York* 1, no. 3 (Fall 2003), http://carnegie.org/fileadmin/Media/Publications/fall_03educationalreform_01.pdf.

Derthick, Martha, and Paul Quirk. *The Politics of Deregulation*. Washington, DC: Brookings Institution, 1985.

Dewey, John. *How We Think: A Restatement of the Relation of Reflective Thinking to the Educative Process*. Boston: Heath, 1933.

——. *Schools of To-morrow*. New York: Dutton, 1915.

Diamond, John, and James Spillane. *Distributed Leadership in Practice*. New York: Teachers College Press, 2007.

Dobbie, Will, and Roland G. Fryer Jr. "Are High-Quality Schools Enough to Close the Achievement Gap? Evidence from a Bold Social Experiment in Harlem." 2009. Accessed June 17, 2012, www.economics.harvard.edu/faculty/fryer/files/hcz%20 4.15.2009.pdf.

Dobbin, Frank. *Forging Industrial Policy: The United States, Britain, and France in the Railway Age*. New York: Cambridge University Press, 1994.

Dougherty, Kevin, and Lizabeth Sostre. "Minerva and the Market: The Sources of the Movement for School Choice." In *The Choice Controversy*, edited by Peter W. Cookson, 24–41. Newbury Park, CA: Corwin Press, 1992.

Doyle, Denis, and Terry Hartle. *Excellence in Education: The States Take Charge.* Washington, DC: American Enterprise Institute, 1985.

Dryfoos, Joy. "Full-Service Community Schools: Creating New Institutions." *Phi Delta Kappan* 83, no. 5 (2002): 393–399.

DuFour, Richard. "Professional Learning Communities: A Bandwagon, an Idea Worth Considering, or Our Best Hope for High Levels of Learning?" *Middle School Journal* 39, no. 1 (2007): 4–8.

Dweck, Carol. *Mindset: The New Psychology of Success.* New York: Random House, 2006.

Earley, Penelope. "Finding the Culprit: Federal Policy and Teacher Education." *Educational Policy* 14, no. 1 (2000): 25–39.

———. "Meanings, Silos, and High-Stakes Advocacy." *Journal of Teacher Education* 56, no. 3 (2005): 214–220.

Easton, John. "Five Big Ideas for IES: Speech at the American Association of Colleges for Teacher Education (AACTE)." Accessed June 17, 2012, http://ies.ed.gov/director/pdf/easton022010.pdf.

Eaton, William. *Shaping the Superintendency: A Reexamination of Callahan and the Cult of Efficiency.* New York: Teachers College Press, 1990.

Economic Policy Institute. "A Broader, Bolder Approach to Education." Accessed June 17, 2012, www.epi.org/files/2011/bold_approach_full_statement-3.pdf.

Edmonds, Ronald. "Effective Schools for the Urban Poor." *Educational Leadership* 37, no. 1 (1979): 15.

Education Commission of the States. Task Force on Education for Economic Growth. *Action for Excellence: A Comprehensive Plan to Improve Our Nation's Schools.* Denver: Education Commission of the States, 1983.

Elazar, Daniel. 1984. *American Federalism: A View from the States.* New York: Harper & Row.

Elmore, Richard F. "Conclusion: Towards a Transformation of Public Schooling." In *Restructuring Schools: The Next Generation of Educational Reform*, edited by Richard F. Elmore, 289–297. San Francisco: Jossey-Bass, 1990.

———. *School Reform from the Inside Out: Policy, Practice, and Performance.* Cambridge, MA: Harvard Education Press, 2004.

ERIC Clearinghouse on Tests, Measurement, and Evaluation and Educational Testing Service. Office of Field Surveys. *State Testing Programs, 1973* Revision. Princeton, NJ: Educational Testing Service, 1973.

Erikson, Erik. *Childhood and Society.* New York: Norton, 1950.

Espeland, Wendy, and Mitchell Stevens, "Commensuration as a Social Process," *Annual Review of Sociology*, 24 (1998): 313–343.

Etzioni, Amitai, ed. *The Semi-Professions and Their Organization: Teachers, Nurses, Social Workers.* New York: Free Press, 1969.

Evans, Peter, Dietrich Rueschemeyer, and Theda Skocpol. *Bringing the State Back In.* New York: Cambridge University Press, 1985.

Farbman, David. "Tracking an Emerging Movement: A Report on Expanded-Time Schools in America." *Education Digest: Essential Readings Condensed for Quick Review* 75, no. 6 (2010): 17–19.

Featherman, David, and Maris Vinovskis. "Growth and Use of Behavioral Science in the Federal Government since World War II." In *Social Science and Policy-Making: A Search for Relevance in the Twentieth Century*, edited by David Featherman and Maris Vinovskis, 40–82. Ann Arbor: University of Michigan Press, 2001.

Feistritzer, C. Emily. *The Making of a Teacher: A Report on Teacher Preparation in the U.S.* Washington, DC: Center for Education Information, 1999.

Finn, Chester. *We Must Take Charge: Our Schools and Our Future*. New York: Maxwell Macmillan, 1991.

———. "Why We Need Choice." In *Choice in Education: Potential and Problems*, edited by William L. Boyd and Herbert J. Walberg, 3–18. Berkeley, CA: McCutchan, 1990.

Firestone, William. "Continuity and Incrementalism after All: State Responses to the Excellence Movement." In *The Educational Reform Movement of the 1980s: Perspectives and Cases*, edited by Joseph Murphy, 143–166. Berkeley, CA: McCutchan, 1990.

Foote, Donna. *Relentless Pursuit: A Year in the Trenches with Teach for America*. New York: Knopf, 2008.

Freidson, Eliot. "The Changing Nature of Professional Control." *Annual Review of Sociology* 10, (1984): 1–20.

———. *Professionalism: The Third Logic*. Cambridge, UK: Polity Press, 2001.

———. "Professions and the Occupational Principle." In *The Professions and Their Prospects*, edited by Eliot Freidson, 19–38. Beverly Hills, CA: Sage, 1973.

Friedland, Roger, and Robert Alford. "Bringing Society Back in: Symbols, Practices, and Institutional Contradictions." In *The New Institutionalism in Organizational Analysis*, edited by Walter Powell and Paul DiMaggio, 232–266. Chicago: University of Chicago Press, 1991.

Friedman, Thomas L. *The World Is Flat: A Brief History of the Twenty-First Century*. New York: Farrar, Straus and Giroux, 2005.

Fuhrman, Susan H. "Education Policy: A New Context for Governance." *Publius* 17, no. 3 (1987): 131–143.

———. *From the Capitol to the Classroom: Standards-Based Reform in the States*. Chicago: National Society for the Study of Education, 2001. Distributed by the University of Chicago Press.

Fung, Archon. *Empowered Participation: Reinventing Urban Democracy*. Princeton, NJ: Princeton University Press, 2004.

Gideonse, Hendrik. "Organizing Schools to Encourage Teacher Inquiry." In *Restructuring Schools: The Next Generation of Educational Reform*, edited by Richard F. Elmore, 97–124. San Francisco: Jossey-Bass, 1990.

Ginsberg, Rick, and Robert K. Wimpelberg. "Educational Change by Commission: Attempting 'Trickle Down' Reform." *Educational Evaluation and Policy Analysis* 9, no. 4 (1987): 344–360.

Giordano, Gerard. *How Testing Came to Dominate American Schools: The History of Educational Assessment.* New York: Lang, 2005.

Goldberg, Milton, Susan Traiman, Alex Molnar, and John Stevens. "Why Business Backs Education Standards." In *Brookings Papers on Education Policy*, edited by Diane Ravitch, 75–129. Washington, DC: Brookings Institution, 2001.

Goldhaber, Daniel, and Jane Hannaway. *Creating a New Teaching Profession.* Washington, DC: Urban Institute Press, 2009.

Goldstein, Judith, and Robert O. Keohane. *Ideas and Foreign Policy: Beliefs, Institutions, and Political Change.* Ithaca, NY: Cornell University Press, 1993.

Goode, William. "The Theoretical Limits of Professionalization." In *The Semi-Professions and Their Organization: Teachers, Nurses, Social Workers*, edited by Amitai Etzioni. New York: Free Press, 1969.

Goodlad, John I. *A Place Called School.* New York: McGraw-Hill, 1984.

Gordon, Robert, Thomas Kane, and Douglas Staiger. "Identifying Effective Teachers Using Performance on the Job." Discussion Paper 2006–01. Accessed June 17, 2012, www.brookings.edu/research/papers/2006/04/~/media/Research/Files/Papers/2006/4/education%20gordon/200604hamilton_1.PDF.

Graetz, Michael, and Ian Shapiro. *Death by a Thousand Cuts: The Fight over Taxing Inherited Wealth.* Princeton, NJ: Princeton University Press, 2005.

Graham, Patricia, and David Gordon. *A Nation Reformed? American Education 20 Years after "A Nation at Risk".* Cambridge, MA: Harvard Education Press, 2003.

Grant, Gerald. "The Politics of the Coleman Report." PhD diss., Harvard University, 1972.

———. *The World We Created at Hamilton High.* Cambridge, MA: Harvard University Press, 1988.

Grant, Gerald, and Christine Murray. *Teaching in America: The Slow Revolution.* Cambridge, MA: Harvard University Press, 1999.

Grossman, Pamela, and Susanna Loeb. *Alternative Routes to Teaching: Mapping the New Landscape of Teacher Education.* Cambridge, MA: Harvard Education Press, 2008.

Gumport, Patricia. "Universities and Knowledge: Restructuring the City of Intellect," in *The Future of the City of Intellect: The Changing American University*, edited by Steven Brint, 47–81. Stanford, CA: Stanford University Press, 2002.

Guskey, Thomas R. "Professional Development and Teacher Change." *Teachers and Teaching* 8, no. 3 (2002): 381–391.

Guthrie, James, and Matthew Springer. "*A Nation at Risk* Revisited: Did 'Wrong' Reasoning Result in 'Right' Results? At What Cost?" *Peabody Journal of Education* 79, no. 1 (2004): 7–35.

Halberstam, David. *The Best and the Brightest.* New York: Random House, 1972.

Hall, Peter A. "Policy Paradigms, Social Learning, and the State." *Comparative Politics* 25, no. 3 (1993): 275–297.

———. "The Role of Interests, Ideas and Institutions in the Comparative Political Economy of the Industrialized Nations." In *Comparative Politics: Rationality,*

*Culture, and Structure*, edited by Mark Lichbach and Alan Zuckerman, 174–207. New York: Cambridge University Press, 1997.

Hall, Peter A., and Rosemary Taylor. "Political Science and the Three New Institutionalisms." *Political Studies* 44, no. 5 (1996): 936–957.

Hanushek, Eric, and Dennis Kimko. "Schooling, Labor-Force Quality, and the Growth of Nations." *American Economic Review* 90, no. 5 (2000): 1184–1208.

Hargreaves, Andy. *Changing Teachers, Changing Times: Teachers' Work and Culture in the Postmodern Age*. New York: Teachers College Press, 1994.

Harper, Edwin, Fred Kramer, and Andrew Rouse. "Implementation and Use of PPB in Sixteen Federal Agencies." *Public Administration Review* 29, no. 6 (1969): 623.

Harris, Douglas, Michael Handel, and Lawrence Mishel. "Education and the Economy Revisited: How Schools Matter." *Peabody Journal of Education* 79, no. 1 (2004): 36–63.

Hartley, Harry. "PPBS: A Systems Approach to Educational Accountability." Paper presented at Supervision of Instruction Symposium 3: Accountability and the Supervisor, April 13, 1972.

Haug, Marie. "Deprofessionalization: An Alternate Hypothesis for the Future." *Sociological Review Monograph* 20, (1973): 195–211.

Hawke, Sharryl. *State Accountability Activities and the Social Studies: A Nationwide Survey, A Proposed General Accountability Model, and Some Guidelines*. SSEC Publication no. 175, 1975.

Hawthorne, Phyllis. *Legislation by the States: Accountability and Assessment in Education*. Report no. 2. Rev. Denver: Cooperative Accountability Project, 1974.

Haycock, Kati, and David W. Hornbeck. "Making Schools Work for Children in Poverty." In *National Issues in Education: Elementary and Secondary Education Act*, edited by John F. Jennings. Washington, DC: Phi Delta Kappa International, 1995.

Heclo, Hugh. *Modern Social Politics in Britain and Sweden: From Relief to Income Maintenance*. New Haven, CT: Yale University Press, 1974.

Henig, Jeffrey, and Paul Reville. "Addressing Non-School Factors in the Framing and Practice of Education Reform." Unpublished paper, Harvard Graduate School of Education, February 2011.

Hess, Frederick M. *Common Sense School Reform*. New York: Palgrave Macmillan, 2004.

———. *I Say "Refining," You Say "Retreating": The Politics of High-Stakes Accountability*. Cambridge, MA: Harvard University Program on Educational Policy and Governance, 2002.

———. "The Predictable, but Unpredictably Personal, Politics of Teacher Licensure." *Journal of Teacher Education* 56, no. 3 (2005): 192–198.

Hess, Frederick M., and Andrew Kelly. "Education and the 2004 Presidential Contest." *Politics of Education Association Bulletin* 29, no. 1 (Fall 2004): 1–6.

Hess, Frederick M., and Patrick McGuinn. "Seeking the Mantle of 'Opportunity': Presidential Politics and the Educational Metaphor, 1964–2000." *Educational Policy* 16, no. 1 (2002): 72–95.

Hess, Frederick M., and Martin West. "A Better Bargain: Overhauling Teacher Collective Bargaining for the 21st Century." Harvard University Program on Education Policy and Governance, accessed June 17, 2012, www.hks.harvard.edu/pepg/PDF/Papers/BetterBargain.pdf.

Hiebert, James, Ronald Gallimore, and James Stigler. "A Knowledge Base for the Teaching Profession: What Would It Look like and How Can We Get One?" *Educational Researcher* 31, no. 5 (2002): 3–15.

Higgins, Monica, Wendy Robison, Jennie Weiner, and Frederick Hess. "Creating a Corps of Change Agents: What Explains the Success of Teach for America?" *Education Next* 11, no. 3 (2011): 18–25.

Hill, Paul. "Recovering from an Accident: Repairing Governance with Comparative Advantage." In *Who's in Charge Here? The Tangled Web of School Governance and Policy*, edited by Noel Epstein, 75–103. Washington, DC: Brookings Institution Press, 2004.

Hitch, Charles, and Roland McKean. *The Economics of Defense in the Nuclear Age.* Cambridge, MA: Harvard University Press, 1960.

Hochschild, Jennifer. "Rethinking Accountability Politics." In *No Child Left Behind? The Politics and Practice of School Accountability*, edited by Paul E. Peterson and Martin R. West, 107–123. Washington, DC: Brookings Institution Press, 2003.

Hoecht, Andreas. "Quality Assurance in UK Higher Education: Issues of Trust, Control, Professional Autonomy and Accountability," *Higher Education* 51, no.4 (2006): 541–563.

Hofstadter, Richard. *The Age of Reform: From Bryan to F.D.R.* New York: Knopf, 1955.
———. *Anti-intellectualism in American Life.* New York: Knopf, 1963.

Hogan, David John. *Class and Reform: School and Society in Chicago, 1880–1930.* Philadelphia: University of Pennsylvania Press, 1985.

Hoxby, Caroline. "Reforms for Whom?" *Education Next* 3, no. 2 (2003): 47–51.

Huberman, Michael. "The Model of the Independent Artisan in Teachers' Professional Relations." In *Teachers' Work: Individuals, Colleagues, and Contexts*, edited by Judith Warren Little and Milbrey W. McLaughlin, 11–50. New York: Teachers College Press, 1993.

Hughes, Thomas. *Rescuing Prometheus.* New York: Pantheon Books, 1998.

Humphrey, Daniel, and Marjorie Wechsler. "Insights into Alternative Certification: Initial Findings from a National Study." *Teachers College Record* 109, no. 3 (2007): 483–530.

Ingersoll, Richard. "The Problem of Underqualified Teachers in American Secondary Schools." *Educational Researcher* 28, no. 2 (1999): 26–37.
———. *Who Controls Teachers' Work? Power and Accountability in America's Schools.* Cambridge, MA: Harvard University Press, 2003.

Jackson, Philip. *Life in Classrooms.* New York: Holt, Rinehart and Winston, 1968.

James, H. Thomas. *The New Cult of Efficiency and Education.* Pittsburgh: University of Pittsburgh Press, 1969.

Jardini, David. "Out of the Blue Yonder: The RAND Corporation's Diversification into Social Welfare Research, 1946–1968." PhD diss., Carnegie Mellon University, 1996.

Jencks, Christopher. *Giving Parents Money to Pay for Schooling: Education Vouchers—a Report on Financing Elementary Education through Grants to Parents*. Cambridge, MA: Center for Educational Policy Research, Harvard Graduate School of Education, 1970.

Jencks, Christopher, and David Riesman. *The Academic Revolution*. Garden City, NY: Doubleday, 1968.

Jennings, John F. *Why National Standards and Tests? Politics and the Quest for Better Schools*. Thousand Oaks, CA: Sage, 1998.

Johnson, Susan Moore. *Teachers at Work: Achieving Success in Our Schools*. New York: Basic Books, 1990.

Johnson, Terry. "Governmentality and the Institutionalization of Expertise." In *Health Professions and the State in Europe*, edited by Terry Johnson, Gerald Larkin, and Mike Saks, 7–24. New York: Routledge, 1995.

Kane, Thomas, and Peter Orszag. "Higher Education Spending: The Role of Medicaid and the Business Cycle." Brookings Institution, 2003. Accessed June 17, 2012, www.brookings.edu/~/media/research/files/papers/2003/9/useconomics%20kane/pb124.pdf.

Karch, Andrew. "Democratic Laboratories: The Politics of Innovation in the American States." PhD diss., Harvard University, 2003.

Katz, Michael B. *The Irony of Early School Reform: Educational Innovation in Mid-Nineteenth-Century Massachusetts*. Cambridge, MA: Harvard University Press, 1968.

Katznelson, Ira, and Margaret Weir. *Schooling for All: Class, Race, and the Decline of the Democratic Ideal*. New York: Basic Books, 1985.

Kegan, Robert. *The Evolving Self: Problem and Process in Human Development*. Cambridge, MA: Harvard University Press, 1982.

———. *In over Our Heads: The Mental Demands of Modern Life*. Cambridge, MA: Harvard University Press, 1994.

Kerchner, Charles T., and Julia Koppich. "Organizing around Quality: The Frontiers of Teacher Unionism." In *Conflicting Missions? Teachers Unions and Educational Reform*, edited by Tom Loveless, 281–315. Washington, DC: Brookings Institution Press, 2000.

Kerchner, Charles T., Julia Koppich, and Joseph Weeres. *United Mind Workers: Unions and Teaching in the Knowledge Society*. San Francisco: Jossey-Bass, 1997.

Kingdon, John. *Agendas, Alternatives, and Public Policies*. Boston: Little, Brown, 1984.

Kirst, Michael. "Recent State Education Reform in the United States: Looking Backward and Forward." *Educational Administration Quarterly* 24, no. 3 (1988): 319–328.

Kliebard, Herbert. *The Struggle for the American Curriculum, 1893–1958*. New York: Routledge, 1995.

Koerner, Thomas F. *PPBS and the School: New System Promotes Efficiency, Accountability.* Washington, DC: National School Public Relations Association, 1972.

Kohn, Alfie. *The Schools Our Children Deserve: Moving Beyond Traditional Classrooms and "Tougher Standards".* Boston: Houghton Mifflin, 1999.

Koppich, Julia. "The As-Yet-Unfulfilled Promise of Reform Bargaining." In *Collective Bargaining in Education: Negotiating Change in Today's Schools,* edited by Jane Hannaway and Andrew J. Rotherham, 203–227. Cambridge, MA: Harvard Education Press, 2006.

———. "A Tale of Two Approaches—the AFT, the NEA, and NCLB." *Peabody Journal of Education* 80, no. 2 (2005): 137–155.

Kosar, Kevin. *Failing Grades: The Federal Politics of Education Standards.* Boulder, CO: Lynne Rienner, 2005.

Kotlowitz, Alex. *There Are No Children Here: The Story of Two Boys Growing Up in the Other America.* New York: Doubleday, 1991.

Kozol, Jonathan. *Death at an Early Age: The Destruction of the Hearts and Minds of Negro Children in the Boston Public Schools.* Boston: Houghton Mifflin, 1967.

———. *Savage Inequalities: Children in America's Schools.* New York: Crown, 1991.

———. *The Shame of the Nation: The Restoration of Apartheid Schooling in America.* New York: Crown, 2005.

Krause, Elliott. *Death of the Guilds: Professions, States, and the Advance of Capitalism, 1930 to the Present.* New Haven, CT: Yale University Press, 1996.

Kristol, Irving. *Neoconservatism: The Autobiography of an Idea.* New York: Free Press, 1995.

Kuhn, Thomas S. *The Structure of Scientific Revolutions.* Chicago: University of Chicago Press, 1962.

Lagemann, Ellen Condliffe. *An Elusive Science: The Troubling History of Education Research.* Chicago: University of Chicago Press, 2000.

Lal, Bhavya. "Knowledge Domains in Engineering Systems: Systems Analysis." Unpublished paper, MIT, Fall 2001.

Lamont, Michèle, and Virág Molnár. "The Study of Boundaries in the Social Sciences." *Annual Review of Sociology* 28, no. 1 (2002): 167–195.

Larson, Magali. *The Rise of Professionalism: A Sociological Analysis.* Berkeley: University of California Press, 1977.

Lawrence-Lightfoot, Sara. *The Good High School: Portraits of Character and Culture.* New York: Basic Books, 1983.

Lazarin, Melissa, and Isabel Owen. "Union and District Partnerships to Expand Learning Time: Three Schools' Experiences." Center for American Progress, 2009. Accessed June 17, 2012, www.americanprogress.org/issues/2009/11/pdf/elt_union_districts.pdf.

Legro, Jeffrey. "The Transformation of Policy Ideas." *American Journal of Political Science* 44, no. 3 (2000): 419.

Lessinger, Leon M. *Every Kid a Winner: Accountability in Education.* New York: Simon & Schuster, 1970.

Levin, Benjamin. *How to Change 5000 Schools: A Practical and Positive Approach for Leading Change at Every Level*. Cambridge, MA: Harvard Education Press, 2008.

Lewis, Michael. *Moneyball: The Art of Winning an Unfair Game*. New York: Norton, 2003.

Lieberson, Stanley. "Small N's and Big Conclusions: An Examination of the Reasoning in Comparative Studies Based on a Small Number of Cases." *Social Forces* 70, no. 2 (1991): 307–320.

Light, Donald. "Countervailing Powers: A Framework for Professions in Transition." In *Health Professions and the State in Europe*, edited by Terry Johnson, Gerald Larkin, and Mike Saks, 25–41. New York: Routledge, 1995.

Light, Jennifer S. *From Warfare to Welfare: Defense Intellectuals and Urban Problems in Cold War America*. Baltimore: Johns Hopkins University Press, 2003.

Lipset, Seymour Martin, and William Schneider. *The Confidence Gap: Business, Labor, and Government in the Public Mind*. New York: Free Press, 1987.

Livingston, Carol, and Hilda Borko. "Expert-Novice Differences in Teaching: A Cognitive Analysis and Implications for Teacher Education." *Journal of Teacher Education* 40, (1989): 36–42.

"A Look Ahead: Education and the New Decade." *Education Week* 9, no. 16 (January 10, 1990).

Lortie, Dan C. *Schoolteacher: A Sociological Study*. Chicago: University of Chicago Press, 1975.

Luce, Judith A. "Career Ladders: Modifying Teachers' Work to Sustain Motivation." *Education* 119, no. 1 (1998).

Lukes, Steven. *Power: A Radical View*. London: Macmillan, 1974.

MacIntyre, Alasdair. *After Virtue: A Study in Moral Theory*. 2nd ed. Notre Dame, IN: University of Notre Dame Press, 1984.

Mahoney, James. "Nominal, Ordinal, and Narrative Appraisal in Macrocausal Analysis." *American Journal of Sociology* 104, no. 4 (1999): 1154–1196.

Manna, Paul. *Collision Course: Federal Education Policy Meets State and Local Realities*. Washington, DC: Congressional Quarterly Press, 2011.

———. "Federalism, Agenda Setting, and the Development of Federal Education Policy, 1965–2001." PhD diss., University of Wisconsin–Madison, 2003.

———. "Leaving No Child Behind." In *Political Education: National Policy Comes of Age*, edited by Christopher T. Cross, 126–143. New York: Teachers College Press, 2004.

———. *School's In: Federalism and the National Education Agenda*. Washington, DC: Georgetown University Press, 2006.

March, James, and Johan Olsen. *Rediscovering Institutions: The Organizational Basis of Politics*. New York: Free Press, 1989.

Maslow, Abraham. *Motivation and Personality*. New York: Harper, 1954.

Matthews, Peter, Hunter Moorman, and Deborah Nusche. "School Leadership Development Strategies: Building Leadership Capacity in Victoria, Australia."

OECD Directorate for Education, accessed June 17, 2012, www.oecd.org/dataoecd/27/22/39883476.pdf.

Mazzeo, Christopher. "Frameworks of State: Assessment Policy in Historical Perspective." *Teachers College Record* 103, no. 3 (2001): 367–397.

Mazzoni, Tim. "State Policy-Making and School Reform: Influences and Influentials." In *The Study of Educational Politics: The 1994 Commemorative Yearbook of the Politics of Education Association (1969–1994)*, edited by Jay D. Scribner and Donald H. Layton, 53–73. Washington, DC: Falmer, 1995.

McDonnell, Lorraine. "No Child Left Behind and the Federal Role in Education: Evolution or Revolution?" *Peabody Journal of Education* 80, no. 2 (2005): 19–38.

McGuinn, Patrick J. "Nationalizing Schools: The Politics of Federal Education Policy." PhD diss., University of Virginia, 2003.

———. *No Child Left Behind and the Transformation of Federal Education Policy, 1965–2005*. Lawrence: University Press of Kansas, 2006.

McLaughlin, Milbrey W., and Joan E. Talbert. *Building School-Based Teacher Learning Communities: Professional Strategies to Improve Student Achievement*. New York: Teachers College Press, 2006.

McNamara, Robert S. *In Retrospect: The Tragedy and Lessons of Vietnam*. New York: Vintage Books, 1996.

McNeil, Linda. *Contradictions of Control: School Structure and School Knowledge*. New York: Routledge, 1986.

———. *Contradictions of School Reform: Educational Costs of Standardized Testing*. New York: Routledge, 2000.

Mehta, Jal. "Standard Error." *American Prospect* 18, no. 11 (October 22, 2007).

———. "The Varied Roles of Ideas in Politics: From 'Whether' to 'How.'" In *Ideas and Politics in Social Science Research*, edited by Daniel Béland and Robert Cox. New York: Oxford University Press, 2011.

Mehta, Jal, Robert Schwartz, and Frederick Hess, eds., *The Futures of School Reform*. Cambridge, MA: Harvard Education Press, 2012.

Mehta, Jal, and Steven Teles. "Jurisdictional Politics: A New Federal Role in Education." In *Carrots, Sticks, and the Bully Pulpit: Lessons from a Half-Century of Federal Efforts to Improve America's Schools*, edited by Frederick M. Hess and Andrew P. Kelly. Cambridge, MA: Harvard Education Press, 2011.

Mehta, Jal, and Christopher Winship. "Moral Power." In *Handbook of the Sociology of Morality*, edited by Steven Hitlin and Stephen Vaisey. New York: Springer, 2010.

Meier, Deborah. *In Schools We Trust: Creating Communities of Learning in an Era of Testing and Standardization*. Boston: Beacon Press, 2002.

Murphy, Jerome T., and David K. Cohen. "Accountability in Education: The Michigan Experience." *Public Interest* 36 (1974): 53–82.

Murphy, Joseph T., ed. *The Educational Reform Movement of the 1980s: Perspectives and Cases*. Berkeley, CA: McCutchan, 1990.

National Center for Alternative Certification, "Alternative Teacher Certification: A State by State Analysis," accessed January 12, 2013, www.teach-now.org/intro.cfm.

National Center on Education and the Economy, Commission on the Skills of the American Workforce. *America's Choice: High Skills or Low Wages! The Report.* Rochester, NY: National Center on Education and the Economy, 1990.

———, New Commission on the Skills of the American Workforce. *Tough Choices or Tough Times: The Report of the New Commission on the Skills of the American Workforce—Executive Summary.* 1st ed. San Francisco: Wiley, 2007.

National Commission on Excellence in Education. *A Nation at Risk: The Imperative for Educational Reform—a Report to the Nation and the Secretary of Education, United States Department of Education.* Washington, DC: National Commission on Excellence in Education, 1983.

National Commission on Teaching and America's Future. *What Matters Most: Teaching for America's Future.* New York: National Commission on Teaching and America's Future, 1996.

National Governors Association, Center for Policy Research. Thomas H. Kean, Lamar Alexander, and Bill Clinton. *Time for Results: The Governors' 1991 Report on Education.* Washington, DC: National Governors Association, 1986.

National Institute of Education, Study Group on the Conditions of Excellence in American Higher Education. *Involvement in Learning: Realizing the Potential of American Higher Education—Final Report of the Study Group on the Conditions of Excellence in American Higher Education.* Washington, DC: National Institute of Education, US Department of Education, 1984.

NCATE Blue Ribbon Panel on Clinical Preparation and Partnerships for Improved Student Learning. "Transforming Teacher Education through Clinical Practice: A National Strategy to Prepare Effective Teachers." NCATE, accessed June 17, 2012, www.ncate.org/LinkClick.aspx?fileticket=zzeiB1OoqPk%3D&tabid=715.

Noguera, Pedro A. "A Critical Response to Michael Fullan's 'The Future of Educational Change: System Thinkers in Action.'" *Journal of Educational Change* 7, no. 3 (2006): 129–132.

O'Day, Jennifer A., and Catherine S. Bitter. "Improving Instruction in New York City: An Evolving Approach." In *Education Reform in New York City: Ambitious Change in the Nation's Most Complex School System*, edited by Jennifer O'Day, Catherine Bitter and Louis Gomez, 109–130. Cambridge, MA: Harvard Education Press, 2011.

O'Day, Jennifer A., and Marshall S. Smith. "Systemic School Reform and Educational Opportunity." In *Designing Coherent Education Policy: Improving the System*, edited by Susan Fuhrman, 250–312. San Francisco: Jossey-Bass, 1993.

OECD. "Strong Performers and Successful Reformers in Education: Lessons from PISA for the United States." OECD Publishing, accessed June 17, 2012, www.oecd.org/dataoecd/32/50/46623978.pdf.

Orfield, Gary, John T. Yun, and the Civil Rights Project. *Resegregation in American Schools.* Cambridge, MA: Harvard University Civil Rights Project, 1999.

Orren, Karen, and Stephen Skowronek. *The Search for American Political Development.* New York: Cambridge University Press, 2004.

Osborne, David, and Ted Gaebler. *Reinventing Government: How the Entrepreneurial Spirit Is Transforming the Public Sector*. Reading, MA: Addison-Wesley, 1992.

Papay, John, Susan Moore Johnson, Sarah Fiarman, Mindy Munger, and Emily Qazilbash. "Beyond Dollars and Cents: The Costs and Benefits of Teacher Peer Assistance and Review." Project on the Next Generation of Teachers, 2009. Accessed June 17, 2012, www.gse.harvard.edu/~ngt/new_papers/JPP_AERA_2009.pdf.

Patashnik, Eric. *Reforms at Risk: What Happens after Major Policy Changes Are Enacted*. Princeton, NJ: Princeton University Press, 2008.

Payne, Charles. *So Much Reform, So Little Change: The Persistence of Failure in Urban Schools*. Cambridge, MA: Harvard Education Press, 2008.

Perlstein, Linda. *Tested: One American School Struggles to Make the Grade*. New York: Holt, 2007.

Peterson, Paul. "Did the Education Commissions Say Anything?" *Brookings Review* 2, no. 2 (1983): 3–11.

———. *The Politics of School Reform, 1870–1940*. Chicago: University of Chicago Press, 1985.

Peterson, Paul E., and Martin R. West, eds. *No Child Left Behind? The Politics and Practice of School Accountability*. Washington, DC: Brookings Institution Press, 2003.

Peurach, Donald. "Designing and Managing Comprehensive School Reform: The Case of Success for All." PhD diss., University of Michigan, 2005.

Piaget, Jean, and Bärbel Inhelder. *The Psychology of the Child*. New York: Basic Books, 1972.

Pierson, Paul. "Big, Slow-Moving, and … Invisible: Macro-Social Processes in the Study of Comparative Politics." In *Comparative Historical Analysis in the Social Sciences*, edited by James Mahoney and Dietrich Rueschemeyer, 177–198. New York: Cambridge University Press, 2003.

———. *Politics in Time: History, Institutions, and Social Analysis*. Princeton, NJ: Princeton University Press, 2004.

———. "When Effect Becomes Cause." *World Politics* 45, no. 4 (1993): 595.

Porter, Theodore M. *Trust in Numbers: The Pursuit of Objectivity in Science and Public Life*. Princeton, NJ: Princeton University Press, 1995.

Powell, Arthur, Eleanor Farrar, and David K. Cohen. *The Shopping Mall High School: Winners and Losers in the Educational Marketplace*. Boston: Houghton Mifflin, 1985.

Power, Michael. *The Audit Explosion*. London: Demos, 1994.

———. "Evaluating the Audit Explosion." *Law & Policy* 25, no. 3 (2003): 185–202.

Pressman, Jeffrey L., and Aaron B. Wildavsky. *Implementation: How Great Expectations in Washington Are Dashed in Oakland*. Berkeley: University of California Press, 1973.

Purkey, Stewart C., and Marshall S. Smith. "Effective Schools: A Review." *Elementary School Journal* 83, (1983): 426–452.

Putnam, Hilary. *The Collapse of the Fact-Value Dichotomy and Other Essays*. Cambridge, MA: Harvard University Press, 2002.

Putnam, Robert D. *Bowling Alone: The Collapse and Revival of American Community*. New York: Simon & Schuster, 2000.

Ragin, Charles C. *Fuzzy-Set Social Science*. Chicago: University of Chicago Press, 2000.

Ranis, Sheri H. "Blending Quality and Utility: Lessons Learned from the Education Research Debates." In *Education Research on Trial: Policy Reform and the Call for Scientific Rigor*, edited by Pamela Walters, Annette Lareau, and Sheri Ranis, 125–142. New York: Routledge, 2009.

Ranson, Stewart. "Public Accountability in the Age of Neo-Liberal Governance." *Journal of Education Policy* 18, no. 5 (2003): 459–480.

Ravitch, Diane. *The Death and Life of the Great American School System: How Testing and Choice Are Undermining Education*. New York: Basic Books, 2010.

———. *Left Back: A Century of Battles over School Reforms*. New York: Simon & Schuster, 2001.

———. "Student Performance Today: Policy Brief #23." Brookings Institution, 1997. Accessed June 17, 2012, www.brookings.edu/research/papers/1997/09/education-ravitch.

———. *The Troubled Crusade: American Education, 1945–1980*. New York: Basic Books, 1983.

Redford, Emmette. *Democracy in the Administrative State*. New York: Oxford University Press, 1969.

Reed, Douglas. *On Equal Terms: The Constitutional Politics of Equal Opportunity*. Princeton, NJ: Princeton University Press, 2001.

Reich, Robert. *The Work of Nations: Preparing Ourselves for 21st-Century Capitalism*. New York: Knopf, 1991.

Rein, Martin, and Donald A. Schon. "Problem-Setting in Policy Research." In *Using Social Research in Public Policy Making*, edited by Carol Weiss, 235–251. Lexington, MA: Lexington Books, 1977.

Resnick, Daniel P. "Minimum Competency Testing Historically Considered." *Review of Research in Education* 8, (1980): 3–29.

Rieder, Jonathan. *Canarsie: The Jews and Italians of Brooklyn against Liberalism*. Cambridge, MA: Harvard University Press, 1985.

Riker, William H. *The Art of Political Manipulation*. New Haven, CT: Yale University Press, 1986.

Riley, Richard W. "Reflections on Goals 2000." *Teachers College Record* 96, no. 3 (1995): 380.

Roderick, Melissa, John Q. Easton, and Penny B. Sebring. "The Consortium on Chicago School Research: A New Model for the Role of Research in Supporting Urban School Reform." Urban Education Institute, 2009. Accessed June 17, 2012, http://ccsr.uchicago.edu/sites/default/files/publications/CCSR%20Model%20Report-final.pdf.

Rogers, Carl R. *Client-Centered Therapy: Its Current Practice, Implications, and Theory*. Boston: Houghton Mifflin, 1951.

Rosenholtz, Susan J. *Teachers' Workplace: The Social Organization of Schools*. White Plains, NY: Longman, 1989.

Roth, Wendy, and Jal Mehta. "The Rashomon Effect: Combining Positivist and Interpretivist Approaches in the Analysis of Contested Events." *Sociological Methods & Research* 31, no. 2 (2002): 131–173.

Rotherham, Andrew J., and Sara Mead. "Back to the Future: The History and Politics of State Teacher Licensure and Certification." In *A Qualified Teacher in Every Classroom? Appraising Old Answers and New Ideas*, edited by Frederick M Hess, Andrew J. Rotherham, and Kate B. Walsh, 11–47. Cambridge, MA: Harvard Education Press, 2004.

Rothstein, Richard. *Class and Schools: Using Social, Economic, and Educational Reform to Close the Black-White Achievement Gap*. Washington, DC: Economic Policy Institute, 2004.

Rothstein, Richard, Rebecca Jacobsen, and Tamara Wilder. *Grading Education: Getting Accountability Right*. Washington, DC; New York: Economic Policy Institute; Teachers College Press, 2008.

Rowan, Brian. "Commitment and Control: Alternative Strategies for the Organizational Design of Schools." *Review of Research in Education* 16, no. 1 (1990): 353–389.

Rudalevige, Andrew. "Forging a Congressional Compromise." In *No Child Left Behind? The Politics and Practice of School Accountability*, edited by Paul E. Peterson and Martin R. West, 23–54. Washington, DC: Brookings Institution Press, 2003.

Rueschemeyer, Dietrich, and Theda Skocpol. *States, Social Knowledge, and the Origins of Modern Social Policies*. Princeton, NJ: Princeton University Press, 1996.

Salamon, Lester M. "Overview: Why Human Capital? Why Now?" In *Human Capital and America's Future: An Economic Strategy for the '90s*, edited by David W. Hornbeck and Lester M. Salamon, 1–39. Baltimore: Johns Hopkins University Press, 1991.

Schaefer, Robert J. *The School as a Center of Inquiry*. New York: Harper & Row, 1967.

Schattschneider, E. E. *The Semisovereign People: A Realist's View of Democracy in America*. New York: Holt, 1960.

Schein, Edgar H. *Organizational Culture and Leadership*. San Francisco: Jossey-Bass, 1985.

Schwartz, Robert, Mindy Hernandez, and Jane Ngo. "Attracting and Retaining Strong Teachers." In *Teaching Talent: A Visionary Framework for Human Capital in Education*, edited by Rachel Curtis and Judy Wurtzel, 113–128. Cambridge, MA: Harvard Education Press, 2010.

Schwartz, Robert B., Ben Levin, and Adam Gamoran. "Lessons from Abroad." *Education Week*, April 6, 2011.

Schwartz, Robert B., and Marian A. Robinson. "Goals 2000 and the Standards Movement." In *Brookings Papers on Education Policy*, edited by Diane Ravitch, 173–206. Washington, DC: Brookings Institution, 2001.

Scott, James C. *Seeing like a State: How Certain Schemes to Improve the Human Condition Have Failed*. New Haven, CT: Yale University Press, 1998.

Shonkoff, Jack P., et al. *From Neurons to Neighborhoods: The Science of Early Child Development*. Washington, DC: National Academy Press, 2000.

Shore, Cris, and Susan Wright. "Audit Culture and Anthropology: Neo-Liberalism in British Higher Education." *Journal of the Royal Anthropological Institute* 5, no. 4 (1999): 557–575.

Sikkink, Kathryn. "The Power of Principled Ideas: Human Rights Policies in the United States and Western Europe." In *Ideas and Foreign Policy: Beliefs, Institutions, and Political Change*, edited by Judith Goldstein and Robert O. Keohane, 139–170. Ithaca, NY: Cornell University Press, 1993.

Sizer, Theodore R. *Horace's Compromise: The Dilemma of the American High School*. Boston: Houghton Mifflin, 1984.

———. *The Red Pencil: Convictions from Experience in Education*. New Haven, CT: Yale University Press, 2004.

Skocpol, Theda. *States and Social Revolutions: A Comparative Analysis of France, Russia, and China*. New York: Cambridge University Press, 1979.

Skrentny, John. *The Ironies of Affirmative Action: Politics, Culture, and Justice in America*. Chicago: University of Chicago Press, 1996.

Smith, Marshall S., and Jennifer A. O'Day. "Systemic School Reform." In *The Politics of Curriculum and Testing: The 1990 Yearbook of the Politics of Education Association*, edited by Susan Fuhrman and Betty Malen, 233–267. New York: Falmer Press, 1991.

Smith, Marshall S., Brent Scoll, and Valena White Plisko. "The Improving America's Schools Act: A New Partnership." In *National Issues in Education: Elementary and Secondary Education Act*, edited by John F. Jennings, 3–17. Bloomington, IN: Phi Delta Kappa International, 1995.

Smith, Thomas, and Kristie Rowley. "Enhancing Commitment or Tightening Control: The Function of Teacher Professional Development in an Era of Accountability." *Educational Policy* 19, no. 1 (2005): 126–154.

Solomon, Jesse. "The Boston Teacher Residency: District-Based Teacher Education." *Journal of Teacher Education* 60, no. 5 (2009): 478–488.

Somers, Margaret, and Fred Block. "From Poverty to Perversity: Ideas, Markets, and Institutions over 200 Years of Welfare Debate." *American Sociological Review* 70, no. 2 (2005): 260–287.

Spector, Malcolm, and John Kitsuse. *Constructing Social Problems*. New York: Aldine de Gruyter, 1977.

Spring, Joel H. *Political Agendas for Education: From the Religious Right to the Green Party*. Mahwah, NJ: Erlbaum, 2002.

Stedman, Lawrence C., and Marshall S. Smith. "Recent Reform Proposals for American Education." *Contemporary Education Review* 2, no. 2 (1983): 85–104.

Steensland, Brian. "Cultural Categories and the American Welfare State: The Case of Guaranteed Income Policy." *American Journal of Sociology* 111, no. 5 (2006): 1273–1326.

Stevens, Mitchell. *Kingdom of Children: Culture and Controversy in the Homeschooling Movement*. Princeton, NJ: Princeton University Press, 2001.

Stokes, Donald E. *Pasteur's Quadrant: Basic Science and Technological Innovation*. Washington, DC: Brookings Institution Press, 1997.

Stone, Deborah A. *Policy Paradox: The Art of Political Decision Making*. New York: Norton, 1997.

Supovitz, Jonathan. "Can High Stakes Testing Leverage Educational Improvement? Prospects from the Last Decade of Testing and Accountability Reform." *Journal of Educational Change* 10, no. 2–3 (2009): 211–227.

Talbert, Joan. "Collaborative Inquiry to Expand Student Success in New York City Schools." In *Education Reform in New York City: Ambitious Change in the Nation's Most Complex School System*, edited by Jennifer O'Day, Catherine S. Bitter, and Louis M. Gomez, 131–155. Cambridge, MA: Harvard Education Press, 2011.

Thelen, Kathleen, and Sven Steinmo. "Historical Institutionalism in Comparative Politics." In *Structuring Politics: Historical Institutionalism in Comparative Analysis*, edited by Sven Steinmo, Kathleen Thelen, and Frank Longstreth, 1–32. New York: Cambridge University Press, 1992.

Thomas, Clive S., and Ronald J. Herbenar. "Nationalizing of Interest Groups and Lobbying in the States." In *Interest Group Politics*, 3rd ed., edited by Allan Cigler and Burdett Loomis, 63–80. Washington, DC: Congressional Quarterly Press, 1991.

Thomas B. Fordham Foundation. "The Teachers We Need and How to Get More of Them: A Manifesto." In *Better Teachers, Better Schools*, edited by Marci Kanstoroom and Chester E. Finn, 1–18. Washington, DC: Thomas B. Fordham Foundation, 1999.

Toch, Thomas. *In the Name of Excellence: The Struggle to Reform the Nation's Schools, Why It's Failing, and What Should Be Done*. New York: Oxford University Press, 1991.

Twentieth Century Fund, Task Force on Federal Elementary and Secondary Education Police. *Making the Grade*. New York: Twentieth Century Fund, 1983.

Tyack, David B. *The One Best System: A History of American Urban Education*. Cambridge, MA: Harvard University Press, 1974.

———. "School Governance in the United States: Historical Puzzles and Anomalies." In *Decentralization and School Improvement: Can We Fulfill the Promise?*, edited by Jane Hannaway and Martin Carnoy, 1–32. San Francisco: Jossey-Bass, CA, 1993.

Tyack, David B., and Larry Cuban. *Tinkering toward Utopia: A Century of Public School Reform*. Cambridge, MA: Harvard University Press, 1995.

Tyack, David B., and Elisabeth Hansot. *Managers of Virtue: Public School Leadership in America, 1820–1980*. New York: Basic Books, 1982.

United States Department of Education. *America 2000: An Education Strategy*. Washington, DC: US Department of Education, 1991.

———, Office of Postsecondary Education, Office of Policy Planning and Innovation. "Meeting the Highly Qualified Teachers Challenge: The Secretary's Annual Report on Teacher Quality." U.S. Department of Education, accessed June 17, 2012, http://www2.ed.gov/about/reports/annual/teachprep/2002title-ii-report.pdf.

Urban, Wayne J., and Jennings L. Wagoner Jr. *American Education: A History*. New York: McGraw-Hill, 1996.

Urbanski, Adam. "Reform or Be Reformed." *Education Next* 1, no. 3 (2001): 51–54.

Vergari, Sandra M. "Policy Crises and Policy Change: Toward a Theory of Crisis Policy-Making." PhD diss., Michigan State University, 1996.

Vergari, Sandra and Frederick Hess. "The Accreditation Game," *Education Next*, 2, no. 3 (2002): 48–57.

Vinovskis, Maris A. "The Road to Charlottesville: The 1989 Education Summit." National Education Goals Panel, 1999. Accessed June 15, 2012, http://govinfo.library.unt.edu/negp/reports/negp30.pdf.

Walters, Pamela B. "The Politics of Science: Battles for Scientific Authority in the Field of Education Research." In *Education Research on Trial: Policy Reform and the Call for Scientific Rigor*, edited by Pamela B. Walters, Annette Lareau, and Sheri H. Ranis, 17–50. New York: Routledge, 2009.

Walzer, Michael. *Spheres of Justice: A Defense of Pluralism and Equality*. New York: Basic Books, 1983.

Washburn, Jennifer. *University, Inc.: The Corporate Corruption of American Higher Education*. New York: Basic Books, 2006.

Weisberg, Daniel, et al. *The Widget Effect: Our National Failure to Acknowledge and Act on Differences in Teacher Effectiveness*. New Teacher Project, 2009. http://widgeteffect.org/downloads/TheWidgetEffect.pdf.

Whitehurst, Grover, and Michelle Croft. *The Harlem Children's Zone, Promise Neighborhoods, and the Broader, Bolder Approach to Education*. Washington, DC: Brookings Institution, 2010.

Whitman, David. *The Optimism Gap: The I'm OK–They're Not Syndrome and the Myth of American Decline*. New York: Walker, 1998.

———. *Sweating the Small Stuff: Inner-City Schools and the New Paternalism*. Washington, DC: Thomas B. Fordham Institute, 2008.

Wilcox, Danielle Dunne. "The National Board for Professional Teaching Standards: Can It Live Up to Its Promise?" In *Better Teachers, Better Schools*, edited by Marci Kanstoroom and Chester E. Finn, 163–197. Washington, DC: Thomas B. Fordham Foundation, 1999.

Wildavsky, Aaron. "Rescuing Policy Analysis from PPBS." *Public Administration Review* 29, no. 2 (1969): 189–202.

Wilson, William J. *The Truly Disadvantaged: The Inner City, the Underclass, and Public Policy*. Chicago: University of Chicago Press, 1987.

Wirt, Frederick, and Michael Kirst. *Schools in Conflict: The Politics of Education*. Berkeley, CA: McCutchan, 1982.

Wise, Arthur E. *Legislated Learning: The Bureaucratization of the American Classroom*. Berkeley: University of California Press, 1979.

Worth, Robert. "Reforming the Teachers' Unions." *Washington Monthly* 30, no. 5 (May 1998).

Wrigley, Julia. *Class Politics and Public Schools: Chicago, 1900–1950.* New Brunswick, NJ: Rutgers University Press, 1982.

Yin, Robert K. *Case Study Research: Design and Methods.* Thousand Oaks, CA: Sage, 1994.

# Index